Borderless Business

Managing the Far-Flung Enterprise

Edited by

CLARENCE J. MANN AND KLAUS GÖTZ

*A Research Project Sponsored by
the Institute for Global Management,
University of Maryland University College,
and DaimlerChrysler, A.G.*

**Westport, Connecticut
London**

Library of Congress Cataloging-in-Publication Data

Borderless business : managing the far-flung enterprise / edited by Clarence J. Mann and Klaus Götz.

    p. cm.

    Includes bibliographical references and index.

    ISBN 0-275-99147-4 ((cloth): alk. paper)–ISBN 0-275-99217-9 ((pbk): alk. paper)

    1. International business enterprises—Management.   2. Industrial management.

3. Globalization.   I. Mann, Clarence J., 1935–   II. Götz, Klaus, 1957–

    HD62.4.B67 2006

    658'.049—dc22   2006009793

British Library Cataloguing in Publication Data is available.

Library of Congress Catalog Card Number: 2006009793
ISBN: 0-275-99147-4 (cloth)
ISBN: 0-275-99217-9 (paper)

First published in 2006

Praeger Publishers, 88 Post Road West, Westport, CT 06881
An imprint of Greenwood Publishing Group, Inc.
www.praeger.com

Printed in the United States of America

The paper used in this book complies with the Permanent Paper Standard issued by the National Information Standards Organization (Z39.48-1984).

10 9 8 7 6 5 4 3 2 1

Praise for *Borderless Business*

Borderless Business should be the book of choice for managers, potential managers, students, and the general reader seeking to understand the complexities of globalization and its effects on business firms, nations, executives, and employees. Its distinctive features include a crystal-clear writing style, a wide and all-encompassing range of topics, vivid examples, summary highlighted points of emphasis, insightful charts and figures, and deep understanding of each major topic. I strongly recommend the book.
Martin Gannon
Professor of Strategy and Global Management
California State University San Marcos
Professor Emeritus
University of Maryland College Park
author of *Understanding Global Culture*

This is a truly first rate book—one of the best I have read on the current challenges and opportunities of globalization. It is eminently readable, and addresses a set of key issues in international business from an interdisciplinary perspective. Its emphasis on the cultural and institutional imperatives of local and regional communities, and on mobilizing creativity and commitment in MNEs, is particularly germane to our contemporary globalizing economy. The editors are to be congratulated for assembling and integrating such an interesting, incisive, and relevant selection of essays. This work deserves the widest possible audience of business students, scholars, and executives of global companies.
John H. Dunning
Emeritus, Professor of International Business
Reading and Rutgers Universities

Borderless Business is essential reading for senior managers and CEOs looking beyond their domestic markets at new growth territories. The book realistically maps some of the key transition challenges that corporations often underestimate while expanding their operations overseas, and it also provides important lessons for managers who often have to tussle between short-term shareholder pressures and long-term vision. I recommend this book for all practicing managers.
Sunil K. Munjal
Chairman of Hero Corporate Service Ltd. (a Hero Group Company)
New Delhi, India

Borderless Business is remarkable for both its breadth and depth. Its discussion of the scope of globalization and its consequences for firms is matched by its detailed look at the spectrum of issues facing today's managers, such as legal, accounting, finance, supply networks, and human resources. Anyone expecting to manage in today's global environment would be wise to study this book.
William Reinsch
President
National Foreign Trade Council

Borderless Business brings a unique perspective to the managers engaged in global operations. It has great learning and insights for businesses that are seeking new markets, suppliers, finances and joint ventures internationally. Its focus on managing global enterprises—covering a wide spectrum of management skills of supply networks, markets, government relations, international finance and cultural perspectives—and blending conceptual framework with real-life examples makes it of outstanding value and a "must read" for practicing managers.
Gautam Thapar
Vice Chairman and Managing Director
Ballarpur Industries Limited

This book is dedicated to the many experienced managers from different countries who, as UMUC graduate students, challenged the authors over the years to provide global perspective and practical insight to assist them with their management tasks.

CONTENTS

FOREWORD

As globalization advances, it becomes clear that managers need to rethink their perspective on the business environment and to retool their skills. The two go hand-in-hand, for without a global mindset conventional management practices will not capture the economic, political, and cultural nuances of global business. With this in mind, a group of faculty at University of Maryland University College Graduate School of Management and Technology decided to examine their respective management disciplines by asking three questions:

- What challenges do the forces of globalization present to managers in their respective roles?
- In what respect do these challenges call for a shift in management thinking?
- What distinctive management competencies and skills does this shift in thinking entail?

After delineating the forces of globalization in the Overview, these themes are explored in the subject matter of each chapter. The fourteen chapters are clustered into four sections, each of which highlights an overarching management theme: Section I—Focusing Enterprise Operations, Section II—Leveraging the Environment, Section III—Adding Enterprise Value, and Section IV—Mobilizing Creativity and Commitment.

The Conclusions summarize this "bottom up" analysis, identifying ten touchstones of an emerging paradigm in global management thinking. These touchstones inform managers about the competencies they require and the skills they need to function effectively in the global environment. In no way, however, are they a recipe for success. The global environment of business is far too complex and volatile for formulaic management responses. Ultimately, the soundness of decision-making depends on the perspective, judgment, farsightedness, and moral character of the managers themselves.

HOW THIS BOOK ORIGINATED

For more than fifteen years, the Graduate School of Management and Technology of University of Maryland University College (UMUC) has conducted a Master of International Management (MIM) Program. The program is designed to equip experienced managers with the perspective and analytical skills needed to work effectively in an increasingly globally competitive environment. Its faculty incorporate their professional and management experience into their academic disciplines.

During the past fifteen years, it has become apparent how powerfully the forces of globalization are shaping the operating environment of enterprises everywhere as well as the role of their managers. In 2005, UMUC and the State of Maryland approved a new Global MBA (GMBA) degree program that builds on the experience of the existing master's program and expands the curriculum to encompass country and regional projects in concert with business schools in major commercial countries around the world. The GMBA program enables students to gain a global perspective, to combine online coursework with short project residencies, and through the projects to hone their intercultural management skills by working with enterprises and business students in major commercial countries around the world.

ACKNOWLEDGMENTS

The authors are deeply indebted to UMUC's Institute for Global Management and the generous contribution of DaimlerChrysler, A.G. for sponsoring their efforts. A previous volume, published in 2000 through a similar collaboration of the Institute and DaimlerChrysler and entitled *The Development of Management Theory and Practice in the United States*, was designed to familiarize readers with the distinguishing characteristics and rich legacy of U.S. management thinking. Our hope is that the new volume will provide insight to all who seek to understand the critical role managers play in guiding their enterprises through the complexities of global business. Both books sprang from suggestions by co-editor Dr. Klaus Götz, who at the time headed the Management–Konzepte office at DaimlerChrysler.

We are most grateful to our editor, Nick Philipson, Senior Editor of Business/Economics at Praeger/Greenwood Publishers and his assistant Dan Harmon. Nick was most patient and supportive over the many months we labored to pull together this multi-authored volume. We also deeply appreciate the copyediting, copy development, and coaching provided by Suzanne Harris and her colleagues at Magnificent Publications, who were determined to make the text readable. Of course, we reserve ownership to any errors of omission or commission found here.

Special thanks also to Anita Schmied and Pam Peseux, graduates of the MIM program, who assisted in reviewing chapter copy and vetting graphic ideas; to Patricia Spencer for coordinating administrative and copyediting matters; and to Nicolle Brunson for her ever-present assistance. And a very special thanks to Gary S. Medovich (The Medovich Studio) for his wonderful sense of humor in creating the graphic figures found in Figure 0.1 of the Overview and each of the four section prefaces.

Clarence J. Mann
March 2006

Forces Shaping the Global Business Environment

CLARENCE J. MANN

GLOBALIZATION PRESENTS BOTH CHALLENGES AND OPPORTUNITIES

Globalization is rapidly changing the dynamics of business as well as the tasks of management. This book considers the challenges facing managers and the mindset and competencies they must possess in order to function effectively and guide their firms amid the forces and counterforces of globalization. This Overview sets the stage by defining the globalizing environment and the tensions it creates for managers. Each subsequent chapter focuses on a particular management area or function, showing how globalization is presenting managers with both distinctive challenges and opportunities—but also how these can be grasped and successfully addressed only through a new perspective on management thinking and by having the skills required to carry it out in practice. While this is true particularly for managers of firms that have explicit global agendas, it applies as well to managers of firms with less ambitious plans but whose competitors often think in global terms.

Drawing insights from various chapters, the Conclusion sums up the shift required of management thinking and practice. It outlines in effect a management paradigm—the mindset required to function effectively in the emerging global business environment.

Throughout the book, the phenomenon called "globalization" is taken for granted. It refers to the intensification of "connectedness" and "interdependence"

Opportunities

Forces   Counterforces

Expanding Trade   Diverse Regulatory Regimes

Foreign Direct Investment   Weak Economic Infrastructure

Free Capital Movement   Varying Workforce Productivity

Technology Convergence   Distinctive Cultural Patterns

Information/IT Revolution

Intensifying Competition   Alienation and Distrust

Growing Consciousness

Challenges
Facing Enterprise Managers

FIGURE 0.1.   Management Squeeze Play among Forces of Globalization

among peoples, institutions, and nations around the world. Our task is not to critique it, but to define it in terms that help managers appreciate its consequences for their thinking and practice. The authors readily admit that globalization raises issues and challenges for society, especially for traditional social values, but on balance we believe its benefits are likely to outweigh its adverse consequences for mankind as a whole.

The situation facing managers is depicted in Figure 0.1 as a "squeeze play." Managers are caught between the forces driving globalization—for example, trade, finance, investment, technology—and counterforces emanating from a wide variety of nation-states across the world, whose socioeconomic systems, policies, cultures, infrastructures, and interest groups widely diverge and often resist the intrusion of global standards and ventures. On the one hand, globalization is generating new challenges and opportunities—in the face of intensified competition—for firms that are able to see, and that have the resources and skills to exploit them. On the other hand, it can frustrate and possibly destroy firms unprepared to move quickly enough or deal with the precise nature of the challenges. These forces and counterforces are discussed in detail in this Overview.

One casualty of this "squeeze play," for instance, was the 1990s multi-billion-dollar Iridium satellite telephone system to provide global mobile phone service. Iridium identified a lucrative underserved high-margin market and its cross-linked network of seventy-seven low-orbit satellites was highly innovative, but its system took ten years from concept to launch. This delay was its downfall. Iridium's sophisticated 1980s technology was overtaken by much more versatile and inexpensive earthbound systems of cellular telephony. It encountered stiff resistance from largely state-owned postal, telephone, and telegraph (PTT) systems, whose approval was needed to gain financing as well as global spectrum allocation from 170 countries. Many PTTs saw Iridium as a direct threat to their revenues and prerogatives. Others saw it as an imperialist move by Americans to monopolize the market for satellite communications. Although big telcos refused financial support, Iridium finally gained the spectrum approval it needed, but at a cost. Iridium had to redesign its satellite system to interface with many local PTT systems, thereby enabling investors to independently manage the interface for switching and billing purposes. This resulted in a governance nightmare—a board of twenty-eight members from seventeen countries, meeting quarterly at various locations around the world—a veritable mini–United Nations functioning via simultaneous translation in Chinese, English, Japanese, and Russian.[1] By the end of 1999, Iridium counted only 55,000 subscribers, when it needed 600,000 to break even.

Given the breadth of opportunities as well as constraints bound up with globalization, what do managers caught in this "squeeze play" need to know and what competencies should they possess in order to function effectively? In a competitive world, where continuous change is a foregone conclusion, it is not enough for managers simply to recognize and address issues and problems as they arise. "I told you so" is the cry of the evident loser. Nor is it enough that managers anticipate issues and problems, although foresight is essential. Instead, managers must be able to grasp specifically how profoundly the forces of globalization are changing their industry environments, and they must possess the individual and organizational competencies needed to reinvent their organizations in keeping with the pace of globalization.

This book is not seeking to redefine principles of management. The authors agree with Peter Drucker that management is a generic discipline, whose principles apply 90 percent in equal measure to all organizations, whether their mission is for profit or not, private or public sector, or purely domestic, international, or global.[2] Indeed, even for the remaining 10 percent, the differences in management principles that do exist may be attributable largely to industry differences and not simply to the global nature of the business. Nevertheless, while management principles in general may not differ significantly for firms operating internationally or globally, the manner in which these principles are applied to the tasks of managing global enterprises calls for perspective and understanding very different from primarily domestic contexts. This broadened management perspective and the applications it entails make all the difference.

GLOBALIZATION IS A DECADES-LONG
TRANSITIONAL PROCESS

While globalization is often discussed as a fait accompli, in fact it is only in its infancy. Indeed, skeptics like to point out that in many respects the world economy—at least among the major powers—was more globally integrated during the first decade of the twentieth century than it is today. As the discussion below indicates, however, the forces driving globalization today are far more comprehensive and penetrating than a century ago. Nevertheless, it is important to keep in mind that the process of globalization is far from complete. Presently, only about one-third of world economic activity is estimated to occur in industries that could be defined as global.[3] Even for those industries, the forces of globalization remain most visible among a dozen rich countries, commonly referred to as developed or highly industrialized countries. Despite the recent surge of foreign direct investment (FDI) into China, these developed countries still account for approximately two-thirds of all FDI inflows and 87 percent of all outflows. As a group, they also account for 50 percent of world trade.[4] Only in the last decade have concepts of free trade and open markets begun to take hold in the mammoth countries of China and India, while in Russia they are halting at best. Yet even countries lying more at the periphery of the global economy are increasingly feeling the effects of globalization.

These facts point out that **globalization is essentially a transitional process**, one that is likely to continue and accelerate over the next three to four decades. During these decades, as trade barriers fall and the dissemination of new technology undercuts proprietary positions, firms will face a globally broadening and changing array of market and supplier options, but also a diminishing range of "safe harbors" from foreign competitors. Also, during this thirty- to forty-year period, the world economy is likely to triple—and probably to quadruple in size—from its present $41 trillion, given an average growth rate of around 3.5 percent. While this rate may be high for the highly industrialized countries with one-sixth of the world's population, it is well within the range of emerging nations and, in particular, China and India which together embrace about one-third of the world's population. Concurrently, the scope of global competition is expected to expand dramatically—from its present 20 to 25 percent to as high as 80 percent of gross world product.[5] This means that the size of the *global* market during this period could well increase from its present $8 to $10 trillion to possibly $90 to $130 trillion—or ten- to fourteen-fold! Understandably, the pace of this transformation will vary widely by industry, being led by more standardized products and services with broad appeal to global market segments. Industries serving localized preferences or offering personalized services or highly perishable products will continue, but some aspects of all industries will feel the red-hot breath of external competition.

During this transition, as industries become more globally competitive, the management mindset of firms is being transformed in two major respects:

1. **Managers will need to change the way they think about their industry.** The fast pace of innovation and technology convergence is dissolving the accepted notions of industry structure. The convergence of computers, information technology, and medical devices, or of pharmaceuticals and biotechnology, for example, provide ample evidence of this. Moreover, innovation can come from any corner of the world.

2. **Managers will need to change the way they think about their firms and their management tasks.** Instead of simply internationalizing operations by extending existing domestic products and services across borders, whether through exports or similar operations, firms will be need to globalize their operations through a multilevel coordination of functions and capabilities that are integrated in varying degrees across a broad range of activities, geography, and cultures. Complexity is the order of the day.

An emerging "global" management mindset implies no standard organizational structure or management approach. Enterprise structures and management styles will be highly diverse, depending on the distinctive nature of the industry itself, the dominant forces driving industry globalization, and differing regulatory regimes, business practices, and cultures among countries, as well as the individual creativity of firms. And because firms will continue to find themselves and their industries at different stages in the process of globalization—from domestic or nationally protected to multidomestic or multinational, and from regional or bi- or multiregional to fully global or "transnational" in scope—the organizational requirements of firms will vary widely. References to firms (companies or enterprises) throughout this book, therefore, are simply to firms that have global agendas or to firms seeking to globalize their operations, whatever terms are used. This terminology is not intended to reject the organizational nomenclature developed by other authors or the view that organizational structure may need to change as firms globalize.[6] Rather, the intention of this book is to focus attention on how globalization is bringing about a shift in the mindset and competencies required of managers and organizations.

SEVEN DIVERSE FORCES OF MARKET CAPITALISM ARE DRIVING GLOBALIZATION

Beginning with the end of World War II, the world economy witnessed enormous expansion and growth. The stage was set by the repeated lowering of national trade barriers and the free flow of capital and technology, and has been reinforced through the information revolution and the collapse of Soviet-style communism. But the real agents driving this expansion and growth—and the phenomenon we call "globalization"—are the many thousands of firms and their managers and investors who pool their creativity and risk their capital to bring forth new goods and services and to develop new markets and the institutions that support them.

To appreciate the tension and complexity these firms and managers face, this section reviews seven types of forces identified in Figure 0.1. While it is tempting to prioritize these forces, in fact they tend to be mutually reinforcing, and should be viewed in this light. Nevertheless, these forces are held in check to a significant extent by five types of counterforces. These will be considered in the following section. These forces and counterforces will be revisited in the various chapters as authors analyze their impact on management thinking.

Expanding Trade Spurs Economic Growth across the World

The past fifty years have been marked, above all, by the wealth generated from expanded world trade and the division of labor it encourages. This expansion was triggered by eight successive rounds of trade negotiations within the framework of the General Agreement on Tariffs and Trade (GATT), culminating in the establishment of the World Trade Organization (WTO) in 1998. These market-opening rounds reduced U.S. tariffs, for instance, from an average high of 44 percent in 1950 to the present average of 3.6 percent, even though duties on some goods like textiles have been considerably higher. Concurrently, the introduction of containerized shipping enabled the accelerating volume of merchandise to clear potential port bottlenecks.

During the last half century, world trade in merchandise increased almost twenty-fold after adjusting for inflation. Averaging just over 6 percent annually, this growth has varied widely over the years—from a high of 12.8 percent (1960) to a low of −7.3 percent (1975)—reflecting underlying economic conditions especially among the major commercial nations.[7] Real trade growth, however, has been in manufactures, which multiplied eighty-six times over the past five decades, from $84 billion in 1953 to $7.294 trillion in 2003.[8] Trade in commercial services, though only about 20 percent of world trade, has grown rapidly over the past fifteen years—slightly exceeding average annual growth in manufactured goods. Approximately two-thirds of this trade— for example, telecommunications, financial, management, advertising, professional, and technical services—is conducted by the top fifteen commercial countries.[9]

Not surprisingly, the lion's share of growth in trade has been enjoyed by economies in Western Europe, North America, and East and Southeast Asia. They also account for most of the world's economic integration over the past twenty years. Indeed, there is a high correlation between trade and GDP growth, with trade leading growth by a substantial margin. Trade-oriented "open economies" have grown on average about 2 percent faster per year than "closed economies."[10] According to a World Bank study, a ten-percentage-point improvement in a country's trade is associated with a 0.71-point increase in its growth rate.[11] Moreover, a 10 percent reduction in a country's average tariff could bring about a welfare gain of 10 to 37 percent in its present value of consumption.[12] Countries can benefit significantly, therefore, by opening their borders to trade. Those that restrict trade are likely to lose ground. These conclusions may vary depending on other regulatory policies, such as tax and foreign direct investment.

Beyond this trade picture, a major shift in world trade is taking place (this is explored in more detail in chapter 5, "Trade and Government Relations"). Understandably, as the European and Japanese powers recovered from the destruction of World War II, and with the development of the European Union, the North American share of trade has declined as a proportion of total world trade—from 24.2 percent in 1953 to 13.7 percent in 2003. At the same time, Western Europe's share of world trade increased from 34.1 percent to 43.1 percent, while that of Asia doubled from 13.1 percent to 26.1 percent. The emergence of China as a dominant Asian economy, however, signals a major shift in the world balance of economic power. China now accounts for 6 percent of world trade and, measured by gross domestic product, is displacing Japan, which heretofore has occupied second place. While India lags well behind—with only 0.8 percent of world trade—its economy is also likely to make its world presence felt soon. As a result, the present tripolar world economy, dominated by the United States, the European Union, and Japan, appears to be moving toward a multipolar economy embracing China and ultimately India.[13]

Foreign Direct Investment and Technology Are Deepening Economic Penetration

As forces of globalization, foreign direct investment (FDI) and technology transfer have in recent years become as critical as—if not more so—than trade in goods. While the growth rates of FDI and trade generally paralleled each other during the period 1970–85, the growth of FDI surged past trade during the following fifteen years. It ballooned from a mere $50 billion to over $1.5 trillion in 2000, but receded to $648 billion by 2004.[14] As this suggests, FDI and its primary agents, transnational enterprises, have become important drivers of globalization; for these enterprises, which number 70,000 parent companies and their 690,000 affiliates, not only account for about two-thirds of world trade—about half of which is among affiliated firms—they also are the primary channel for both FDI and technology dissemination.

As FDI has grown, its makeup has also shifted. Whereas 99 percent of total world outward FDI in 1960 originated from developed countries in North America, Western Europe, and Japan, the remaining 1 percent from seven developing countries (chiefly Hong Kong) has grown to 13 percent today. Moreover, while the United States, United Kingdom, and the Benelux countries dominated outward FDI in 1960, their present combined world share has fallen to about 43 percent.[15] At the same time, the recipients of FDI largely have been developed countries. And the one-third of total world FDI absorbed by developing countries is largely concentrated among the ten more industrialized nations among them, including Argentina, Brazil, Chile, China, Hong Kong, Malaysia, Mexico, Singapore, and South Korea. China in particular is notable, as it received the most FDI in 2002 while ranking third behind the United States and the United Kingdom in 2004.

These shifts in FDI reflect a growing participation by transnational enterprises and their suppliers among a **broader range of countries**—both developed and developing—in the growth of the world economy. They account for about half of global R&D expenditures from all sources, and at least two-thirds of business R&D expenditures.[16] They also reflect a **deepening of economic integration across countries and regions**—from **adaptive R&D**, which encompasses basic production support and upgrading technologies, to **innovative R&D** involving the development of new products or processes.[17] "Deep integration" derives from the long-term commitment and the firm-specific technology, management systems, and know-how that are intertwined with all forms of FDI. As a result, over the past fifty years, international enterprises have been a main source and one of the most efficient channels for the transfer of technology and skills. Indeed, it is estimated that 70 percent of all royalty payments occur between parent firms and their foreign affiliates.[18] "In a knowledge economy," notes John Michlethwait and Adrian Wooldridge in their analysis of globalization, "multinational companies are essentially machines transferring ideas across borders."[19]

Free Movement of Capital Brings Both Liquidity and Volatility

The third force of globalization today, and one of the most widespread, is what Thomas Friedman terms "the democratization of finance."[20] By this is meant the ability of a broad array of small and large financial institutions and millions of individual investors to participate in portfolio and other short-term international movements of capital, both debt and equity. Part of this liberalization can be traced to improvements in communication—the fax machine, expanded bandwidth, reductions in phone rates, and the Internet. "Technology," observed The Economist, "has made possible a global digital financial market where, in theory, any security in any currency could be traded anywhere at any time, and where that trade could be settled instantly."[21] Equally important have been innovations in financial instruments and investment options, including mutual funds of all kinds, the securitization and retail marketing of debt of all kinds and risks (from home mortgages to World Bank issues), and, extending over the past three decades, the introduction of a wide variety of derivatives and index pricing of stocks, bonds, and commodities.

At the beginning of the twenty-first century, therefore, the world is brimming with highly liquid financial capital. Each day $1.5 to $2.0 trillion exchanges hands each day—an eightfold increase since the mid-1980s—settling international payments of all kinds for trade, tourism, short- and long-term investment, hedging, and derivatives. The result is a global flow of financial transactions amounting to more than $500 trillion annually, dwarfing $7 trillion annually in global trade and global GDP of approximately $41 trillion. This flow is based on an estimated world stock of $80 trillion in liquid financial assets, nearly seven times larger than in 1980. It consists one-fifth in money supply and two-fifths each in equities and international, government, and corporate bonds.[22] Comparing these liquid assets and their turnover to the meager holdings of reserves in central banks around the world—a little more than $2.5 trillion[23]—dramatizes the limited leverage these banks have to staunch shifts in currency exchange rates.

Because a primary function of this type of investment is liquidity, its role as a force in globalization should be distinguished sharply from FDI and technology flows. Unlike an enterprise that has overseas operations, where commitment is long term, a portfolio investor expects to be able to shift or hedge investments readily with changes in the environment and enterprise performance. The potential for volatility in this form of investment was clearly visible during the 1997–98 Asian crisis and its aftermath, when short-term borrowing was employed to fund long-term investment. This mismatch devastated the payments balance as well as the economies for a number of countries as profit opportunities shifted and short-term credit was withdrawn.[24]

As a result, a sharp difference of opinion exists among economists and policy-makers on whether capital markets should be allowed to function as freely as trade finance. On the one hand, it is argued, the three emerging market countries with the most open capital markets—Singapore, Taiwan, and Hong Kong—survived the Asian contagion of 1997 with the least damage. Among countries that suffered most, such as Indonesia, South Korea, and Russia, governmental intervention and cronyism were rife.[25] On the other side, the potential mismatch between short-term and long-term capital flows leaves smaller countries especially vulnerable to financial volatility. For them, argues George Soros (whose fortune was built on financial arbitrage), capital markets do not necessarily move like a pendulum toward equilibrium, but instead may act "more like a giant wrecking ball, knocking over one economy after the other."[26] As a result, many countries maintain controls on FDI and regulate short-term capital flows.

Technology Convergence Is Spawning an Array of New Industries

The enormous scope of technology convergence distinguishes post-industrial society from the first Industrial Revolution (powered by steam) and the second Industrial Revolution (powered by electricity). At the end of the nineteenth century, following a spectacular wave of innovation, the U.S. Commissioner of Patents proposed to shut down his office, reasoning: "Everything that can be invented has been invented."[27] A century later, technological convergence is being felt throughout society and around the world, blurring traditional lines separating industries and making it increasingly difficult for firms to gain foresight on future markets and eliminate investment risk.

Postindustrial society is being powered by at least eight different, rapidly advancing, converging fields of technology:

1. Microelectronics   5. Telecommunications
2. Biotechnology   6. Energy
3. Robotics   7. Space exploration
4. Computers   8. Man-made materials

As these basic technologies converge, new applications create the opportunity for an endless stream of new and often unforeseen products, from pharmaceuticals to weaponry. The combination of telephone and computer technologies created digital switching in the 1970s, which integrated further with fiber-optic materials technology to enable broadband Internet connectivity. Superconductivity combines materials science with electromagnetism. The computer itself integrates at least five different fields of knowledge, and microprocessors are combined in various ways with other technologies— optics, encryption, and voice recognition—to produce a host of new products and services. Whereas technologies had previously tended to originate and remain tied to an industry, it is as if they now have been freed from their moorings and set adrift, spawning new industries around the world.

The breadth, depth, and speed of this technological convergence is being driven and supported by institutionalized linkages of science and technology via industry, government, and university collaboration. Over the past five decades these linkages have taken on a life of their own. Economic leadership, remarks Lester Thurow, has "become a matter of systematic investment in R&D to deliberately invent new technologies."[28] The deliberate, systematic character of this investment combines private firms seeking to maintain their competitive edge with the demands of national policies that emphasize everything from medical research to space exploration. In the United States, 70 percent of this investment is made by industry, while the remainder comes largely from the federal government plus some from nonprofit organizations. The five largest investors in science and technology—United States, Japan, Germany, France, and the United Kingdom, in that order—each dedicate 2.3 to 2.8 percent of their respective GNPs annually to research and development.[29] Like other countries, they wear their Nobel laureates in science as badges of national achievement. At the same time, centers of technological excellence are emerging among less-advanced economies, whether they are software programming in India or appliance and electronics manufacturing in China.

Virtually all the world's innovations, including major advances in technology convergence, are generated within and among the more highly developed countries, comprising 15 percent of the world's population. By contrast, says Jeffrey Sachs, a second, larger group of countries, which makes up approximately half the world's population, are able to merely adopt these technologies in production and consumption. The starkest situation remains for the other third of the world's population, which "is technologically disconnected, neither innovating at home nor adopting foreign technologies."[30] As this implies, technological innovation plays a prominent role in the increasing disparity between winners and losers in globalization. Moreover, as Harold Malmgren puts it: "Accelerated technological change is transforming what is traded around the world, . . . the location of economic activity, . . . the fundamental institutional structures underlying global commerce and investment, . . . [and] most important, it is speeding up the structural changes that result from globalization markets."[31]

The Information Revolution Is Transforming Business and Government Practices

One particular form of technology convergence, information technology, has catapulted the information revolution to the forefront of globalization. Integrating rapid advances in computers, data processing, and global telecommunications, the information revolution is creating a global knowledge economy, transforming whole industries and requiring management to rethink the very nature of business. Communication, remarks Kevin Kelly, executive editor of *Wired* magazine, "is not just a sector of the economy. Communication is the economy." It is distinguished by its global reach, by its focus on ideas, information, and relationships, and by being intensely interlinked through a ubiquitous high-speed digital, mobile network.[32] Its connectedness is creating a web of networked societies across the globe whose centers are the participants themselves.

This fifth force driving globalization, the explosion in information technology, is transforming the workplace, organizational relationships, and government accountability. Telecom prices have fallen annually by 7 percent on average over the past twenty years.[33] In the workplace, computer-aided design and manufacturing (CAD/CAM) is reinventing the factory, while the Internet is transforming value and supply chain management and reinventing the retail industry as a whole. IT strategy has become a field of its own and is critical to the operation of globalizing firms. The result is the rapid pace of technological dissemination across industries; the incorporation of information technology into almost every part of the value chain; and shortened product and process life cycles through relaying design and development work 24/7 within and among firms and their affiliates around the world. Information technology also has spawned the shift from manufacturing to services (financial, software, health care, retailing, etc.) that is occurring in advanced industrial economies.

By dramatically reducing transaction costs, moreover, information technology is transforming the way firms relate to each other and conduct business. Organizational borders become much more porous as common operating and product standards are more easily communicated, tracked, and coordinated. As informational barriers collapse, concludes a McKinsey study, "We are moving from a world where 90% of the competitive advantage was derived from geography to a world where 90% will be non-geographic."[34] In the information society, tangible assets become much less important, human resources and expertise are absolutely critical, world-class products are vital, and collaboration with talented, well-positioned partners is necessary for survival and success. This shift also entails a new style of management, adapted to conscious networking, motivating people, flexible production, teamwork, and continuous innovation.

The information revolution also is generating demands for greater government accountability. As information borders dissolve, governments can no longer isolate or propagandize their people with impunity. On a very fundamental level, says Thomas Friedman: "We can all look into each other's windows now, [and] are less willing to accept a lower standard of living than [our] neighbors enjoy."[35] Better informed populations are less patient with ineffective or corrupt political leaders. Thus, charges of bribery and abuse of authority in recent years brought hundreds of thousands to the streets in the Philippines, Indonesia, Georgia, Ukraine, and Kyrgyzstan to demand the resignation or ouster of their presidents.[36] Activists of all kinds launch their efforts from the Internet, lead campaigns to ban land mines, organize demonstrations against globalization, and so forth. Impatient electorates are pressuring governments to make their operations more efficient and transparent—whether through online access to laws and regulations, streamlined customs clearance, or privatization. Equally important, governments are discovering they must provide increasing levels of service in order to attract foreign capital.

The Extension of Market Capitalism Is Intensifying Global Competition

A further force for globalization comes from the growing intensity of competition among firms within and across the world's major markets. In a real sense, globalization is simply the extension of market capitalism, or of the free enterprise system, across the world. These competitive forces were unleashed through rounds of trade negotiations that successively lowered trade barriers over the past five decades. They were deepened by international rules requiring GATT (General Agreement on Tariffs and Trade) member states to treat foreign firms equally with their own and to provide protection for their investments and intellectual property. Competitive forces were further reinforced as national barriers to financial markets fell among advanced economies in the 1980s and the information revolution created greater market transparency, lowered transaction costs, and generally accelerated the course of business transactions.

This fact explains the role of transnational enterprises, for they embody the self-interest lying at the heart of competition and the drive to penetrate foreign markets and internationalize operations. Self-interest, remarks Martin Wolf, "exceeds the power of charity as the Amazon exceeds a rivulet."[37] Self-interest also explains to a large extent the resistance to globalization of many organized groups, protected industries, and governmental policies. For free market competition engenders the dynamic of "creative destruction," as first conceived by Joseph Schumpeter, committing firms to ongoing innovation if they are to survive and prosper.[38] Over the next three decades, as global market forces expand to encompass 80 percent of world GDP, as previously noted, vested interests lose safe harbors and political leverage. At the same time, in a global market ten times its present size, firms with global agendas will have enormous opportunities before them.

To take advantage of globally expanding markets, firms must be prepared to engage in unrelenting competition with a highly diverse set of competitors, suppliers, and buyers. It also entails two "wild cards" that may be played at any time: shifting government regulation and ongoing innovation and technological developments. The dynamics of global competition tend to move firms along a path calling for:

- **Increased consumer choice**, including lower prices and ongoing quality improvement,
- Which calls for **ongoing innovation, coupled with scale economies, standardization**, and possibly industry consolidation,
- Which requires **ever-increasing specialization and division of labor as well as investment** to control costs and enhance quality through a worldwide supplier network,
- Which means firms need to nurture **long-term value networks** among their partners,
- Which enables firms to meet heightened consumer expectations—and continue the **virtuous cycle toward superior value**.

This cycle of global competition can be seen, for example, in the finance and electronics industries. As national barriers fell and markets expanded, scale economies took hold and new products emerged tailored to the rising expectations of consumers across the world. The downward pressure on prices led to standardization, the internationalization of production, and expanded consumer demand. A similar cycle of economic expansion and renewal can be seen on a smaller but more intense scale within the European Union over the past decade as the 1992 initiatives and the European Monetary Union have taken effect. The introduction of the euro in particular is triggering standardization, intensifying competition and consolidation across borders within the finance industry. Common standards combined with state-of-the-art communications enable firms to disaggregate their operations and disperse them across a wider array of locations in order to reduce costs and leverage comparative advantages. Member state governments may fight a rearguard action, seeking to preserve national champions, but ultimately firms that think and act regionally and then globally can preempt markets, resources, and suppliers. Firms that fail to do this ultimately will lose out. Citibank and HSBC in the finance industry, Boeing and Airbus in the aircraft industry, and Nokia, Ericsson, and Motorola in the cellphone industry are enterprises that clearly are taking this lesson to heart.

The real lesson for all firms is that size and an established industry position are no longer safeguards for sustaining a competitive advantage. High-tech skills and innovation are now spread much more widely and can occur anywhere. For all its assets and market clout, Microsoft Corporation was unable to prevent the small Linux group of Finnish programmers from turning their free access operating system into a legitimate rival to Windows. And Nokia came out of nowhere to challenge the established leadership of Motorola and later Ericsson in the telephony market for mobile phones. In the global arena, as Jeffrey Garten puts it, "the race is less against some identified competitor than for markets that don't yet exist, for consumer markets not yet ... identified [and] for young talent whose creativity has yet to blossom."[39]

Global Connectedness Is Enhancing Global Consciousness

Much less tangible than the other forces, but possibly more potent in the long run, is the growing recognition that the world functions as an integrated system of sorts. This global consciousness had been growing and became palpable throughout the twentieth century, during the first half through the world wars and a worldwide recession and during the last half as an expanding system of markets. During the 1990s, remarks Robert Heilbroner, the ascendance of market capitalism brought with it a common understanding, or ideology, of economic prosperity linked to a relentless "extraordinary propensity for self-generated change."[40] As a result, there is a growing consciousness among people everywhere—including those who oppose globalization—that their lives and destinies are interconnected, interdependent, and subject to societal lifestyles and practices in other countries and regions of the world.

Globalization has become a new point of reference in economic and cultural respects. Economically, the "deep integration" among economies resulting from international investment and technology flows (the second force discussed above) is blurring boundaries between nations and compelling firms to track their progress based on global rather than national industry standards. "World class" is a standard that firms and their customers use to measure goods and services. The economic performance, per capita incomes, and competitiveness of countries as well are measured by global comparisons, as periodic comparative reports and statistics published by the World Bank, International Monetary Fund, World Competitiveness Scoreboard, and Transparency International (corruption) attest. We now are in an era, conclude Daniel Yergin and Joseph Stanislaw in *The Commanding Heights*, "in which the ideas of competition, openness, privatization, and deregulation have captured world economic thinking." Increasingly, people talk about markets as "us"—not "them."[41]

Individuals and families are participating in this global consciousness through travel, inexpensive communication, and the Internet, and by working outside their home countries. In 2000, according to the United Nations, 175 million people lived and worked outside their home country compared to 154 million a decade earlier. These numbers are fed not only by migrant laborers in lower-paid jobs but also by high-tech workers of all types who populate, for instance, scarce programmer and health care positions. The earnings they remit annually to families and communities back home ($80 billion in 2002) anchor global consciousness in very tangible benefits. Indeed, so significant are these fund flows that the governments of such countries as India, Mexico, the Philippines, and Turkey officially encourage them, and international banks like Citibank are establishing thousands of agents and branches to facilitate their transfer.[42]

Culturally, there is growing consciousness that globalization is not the preserve of any one nation or any one group of players. To succeed, globalization must belong to all and benefit all. In this sense, globalization has unleashed a consciousness about individual self-worth that extends well beyond economic value. And once unleashed, it is almost impossible to suppress. In a cultural sense, "America" has become a global aspiration and phenomenon, disembodied from its geography and politics. It represents a lifestyle of individual freedom and choice where individuals can exchange ideas and realize their potential, unbound by unreasonable constraints imposed by governments and cultural traditions. "Today, for better or for worse," says Thomas Friedman, "globalization is a means for spreading the fantasy of America around the world. In today's global village people know there is another way to live, they know about the American lifestyle, and many of them want as big a slice of it as they can get—with all the toppings."[43]

The seven forces discussed above combine in various ways to shape the pace and scope of globalization. At times, one or another is the driving force, but there is no clear sequential cause-effect among them. Indeed, there is no set path or timeline marking globalization, and no particular outcome or set of outcomes. It is likely to evolve in fits and starts, as it has over the past century. It is simply an amorphous process that in recent years has gathered momentum in the face of political and technological developments. These developments exert increasing pressure on governments and enterprises alike. Like the Chinese written character for "crisis," they hold in store both dangers and opportunities for managers of global enterprises. While the opportunities arise from taking advantage of the globalizing environment, they can be exploited only after wrestling with a number of environmental constraints now to be addressed.

FIVE MAJOR COUNTERFORCES IMPEDE GLOBAL AGENDAS

However alluring the opportunities of globalization, their benefits do not accrue automatically, either for firms or for countries. Differing geography, history, local institutions, national cultures, and management mindsets have not been obliterated. Distance is not yet dead, even if radically altered in some respects by telecommunications. Place and space remain critical to the way markets and organizations function, but the balance is shifting. For the institutional effectiveness of societies now tends to matter more than their natural resource endowment. By the same token, regulatory policies, economic and social institutions, and business styles often are cemented in place by vested interests, long-held customs, and societal ideologies. These change only slowly, although many are unlikely to withstand the forces of globalization.

Firms, like countries, can be trapped in the legacies of existing strategies, policies, asset configurations, organizational capabilities, and management mindsets. These too must be reformulated or rebuilt to take advantage of the globalizing environment. But this takes commitment and outside-the-box thinking. Change at General Electric, says Jack Welch about his twenty-one-year reign as CEO, "was very difficult. It took us several years to transform a culture that was more based on seniority and bureaucracy to one of entrepreneurship."[44] Other firms, less successful in transforming themselves, have disappeared from the scene.

The common condition facing all firms that operate globally is a highly fragmented system of nation-states involving a multiplicity of regulatory regimes, infrastructures, and cultures. Over the past six decades, the nation-state system has changed dramatically from a group of about a dozen European and North American countries, which dominated international trade, investment, and law among themselves and their colonies, to 200 highly diverse sovereign states. For global ventures like Iridium, which needed spectrum allocation from 170 countries (as discussed earlier in this Overview), the cost, delay, and governance complexity involved in launching its innovative satellite telephone system led in large part to its downfall. In addition to nation-state regulatory systems, firms face regional and international trade regimes. Few common standards exist on many critical policies and commercial practices. While a network of international agencies, industry associations, nongovernmental organizations (NGOs), and treaties and conventions is gradually expanding to fill some of the gaps, its progress and the results are still largely at the mercy of national interests.

Reconciling multiple and sometimes conflicting national—as well as regional—requirements lies at the very heart of global business. These are a major source of management complexity as indicated by the five major categories of counterforces or constraints facing managers of transnational enterprises: diverse regulatory regimes, weak economic infrastructures, varying workforce productivity, distinctive cultural patterns, and dislocation and alienation among a highly diverse range of disaffected interest groups. These constraints affect the productivity of firms and their capacity to function effectively as global organizations.

Diverse Regulatory Regimes Buffer and Resist the Impact of Globalization

For most firms entering a new market, the regulatory framework of the targeted country commands their greatest attention. The nation-state system, under the mantle of sovereignty, accords countries great leeway in organizing and administering their internal affairs and commercial relations with other states. Despite pressure on states to adopt more common standards, international rules of law related to commerce require only that national governments respect the life and property of foreign nationals and regulate foreign firms using standards equivalent to those imposed upon their own nationals. (See chapters 5, "Trade and Government Relations," and 6, "The Fragmented Legal Environment of Global Business.") As a result, firms face policies, laws, regulations, and procedures that are distinctive for every country. These regulatory regimes in turn shape national institutions and institutional practices as well as the orderly and effective conduct of enterprise operations, including financing, banking, business negotiations, stock offerings and sales, courts, and dispute resolution. They also may affect the universality of the Internet, as governments such as China and the twenty-two-nation Arab League build website and e-mail systems using Chinese or Arabic suffixes.[45]

Beyond the more immediate concerns of commerce, governments perform a protective role for their citizens. This is reflected in policies and laws—some anchored in constitutions—governing such matters as civil rights, health care, education, labor, pensions, the environment, food and drug sales, securities transactions, and advertising. Taken together, these laws and practices comprise a "social compact" between a citizenry and its government, embodying their mutual expectations. These compacts reflect deep-seated values and guiding ideologies that change only slowly over time. (See chapter 7,

"Managing Country Risk.") They may seek to address market failures, for example, as reflected in environment pollution, the weak bargaining position of labor, or collusive or monopolistic practices. Social compacts affect the costs of doing business, whether in the form of employee benefits, restrictions on labor practices (e.g., workweek limits, minimum wages, termination of employment), environmental protection equipment, corporate governance (e.g., Germany's codetermination law), or resistance to offshoring production activities.

However justified, the varying nature of regulatory regimes can significantly influence the global operations of firms. Indeed, A. T. Kearney's 2003 Foreign Direct Investment Confidence Index ranks government regulation first among fifteen country risk factors affecting foreign investment decisions—somewhat higher than financial, currency, and sociopolitical disturbance risks, but far above risks from theft of intellectual property, terrorist attacks, and security threats to employees and assets.[46] And the World Bank's *World Development Report, 2005*, based on surveys of more than twenty-six thousand firms in fifty-three developing countries, lists policy uncertainty along with macro instability and tax rates as the leading "investment climate constraints."[47] Uncertainty is due largely to the unpredictable manner in which government agencies—laboring under information constraints, rigidly framed policies, and intense lobbying by vested interests—interpret and enforce regulations. "Almost 95% of firms [surveyed]," notes the Bank, "report a gap between formal policies and their implementation."[48] These policies may protect certain types and sizes of firms or restrict investments in certain sectors or impose ineffective or costly administrative requirements. Considering the diversity and complexity of these regulatory regimes and the costs involved in charting and addressing their requirements, firms with limited resources will find themselves at a disadvantage in expanding their international operations. Complexity also invites bribery. Ultimately, as former Citicorp chairman Walter Wriston pointed out: "Money goes where it wants and stays where it is well treated."[49]

Weak Economic Infrastructure Can Prove Costly to Business Operations

Another potential barrier to the operations of a global enterprise are weaknesses in the economic infrastructure of the business' home country, both its physical structures and its diverse range of government services and institutionalized systems and practices. Whether state or privately sponsored and managed, or some combination of these, the economic infrastructure provides the support structures and services that enable firms to function effectively. It varies widely from country to country, especially among developing economies, and often also among country regions.

A country's physical economic infrastructure includes utilities (power, water and sanitation, telecommunications lines, and cellphone towers), roads, railroads, waterways, dams, harbors, and airports as well as the ongoing oversight and maintenance required to ensure their performance. In globalizing industries, expectations run high for just-in-time production, quality products, lower production costs, and the timely delivery of orders. The interruption of electric power, for instance, can disrupt sensitive manufacturing processes, requiring firms to invest in costly backup equipment. Of thirty thousand firms surveyed by the World Bank in fifty-three developing countries, approximately 40 percent indicated that electricity outages were a moderate to severe obstacle, causing firms in some countries to lose on average 5 percent of their annual sales.[50] In the same survey, 25 percent and 22 percent of firms considered transportation and telecommunications to be concerns of equal magnitude. In Latin America, for instance, a 10 percent increase in the number of phone lines per worker or in electricity-generating capacity is estimated to increase output per worker by about 1.5 percent, while a 10 percent increase in the length of roads per worker would increase gross domestic product (GDP) per worker by nearly 2 percent.[51] Weaknesses in the physical infrastructure, therefore, can significantly affect worker productivity as well as the success of operations overall.

The institutional side of the economic infrastructure is equally critical for firms. It encompasses banking and currency systems, legal systems and courts, law enforcement, postal services, and securities exchanges, plus the myriad professional and technical services (lawyers, accountants, testing laboratories, freight forwarders, etc.) that enable courts and government agencies to function well and evenhandedly, property to be protected, and commercial transactions to be consummated. There are obviously huge variations among countries in the way banking and legal systems operate, issues to be addressed in several chapters in this book. Firms in developing countries, for instance, list "cost and access to finance" among the five top constraints to doing business, an issue of particular concern to smaller international and indigenous firms that may not have access to alternative international sources of financing.[52] The effect of institutional weaknesses on business operations can be substantial; for instance, the time it takes to start a business: a two-step procedure that takes only two days in Australia takes twelve steps and 151 days in Indonesia. Similarly, to enforce a contract varies from 27 days in Tunisia to 1,390 days in Italy. Registering property can vary from one day in Norway to 956 days in Croatia. Among developing countries, clearing goods through customs can take from 1.2 days in Latvia to 21.6 days in Algeria. Standard bankruptcy procedures can be completed in Ireland in five months, for instance, but require ten years in Brazil.[53]

These procedural differences, incidentally, do *not* always correlate with the level of a country's economic development. Advanced industrialized countries have an ample share of cumbersome and burdensome requirements. The longer any of these procedures takes, the costlier they become in professional expense and managerial time and the more they impede firm operations and their coordination worldwide. Further, as the World Bank points out, an increase in procedural steps and time-to-completion and the loss of transparency in the process generates opportunity for corrupt payments to hurry the process along.[54] For example, according to the Bank, "Costs [to a firm] associated with crime, corruption, regulation, unreliable infrastructure, and poor contract enforcement can amount to over 25 percent of sales—or more than three times what is typically paid in taxes."[55]

Workforce Productivity Varies Widely with the Quality of Human Capital

The human capital of a country shapes the productivity of its workforce. By "human capital" is meant the knowledge, skills, competencies, and other attributes embodied in individuals that are relevant to economic activity.[56] These vary widely from country to country, even among advanced economies and global firms where "knowledge workers" set the work standard. Thus, IBM located its Asian Pacific e-Business Innovation Center in Sydney, Australia, rather than in Singapore, in order to take advantage of Australia's pool of graduates and experienced professionals in technology and marketing.[57] IBM's investment, exceeding $13.5 million, has generated several hundred jobs.

The United Nations' Human Development Index (HDI) for 2004 reflects a vast difference among regions and countries, especially as between advanced economies and developing countries. The index ranks countries in terms of life expectancy, adult literacy, education, and per capita gross domestic product (GDP). Of the 177 countries, 55 are ranked in the high human development category, 86 in the medium, and 36 in the low.[58] Not surprisingly, those ranked high are relatively affluent industrialized countries that have been trade- and market-oriented during the past half century. Included as well are small resource-rich countries such as Kuwait, Bahrain, and the United Arab Emirates, and small, staunchly free-trade entrepots such as Hong Kong and Singapore. On the other hand, a number of resource-rich countries are rated "medium," such as Iran and Saudi Arabia, while Nigeria is rated low. Clearly, as the HDI suggests, an abundance of natural resources and wealth by itself is insufficient to ensure a capable workforce.

HDI, however, does not measure the availability of requisite skills. The World Bank's Investment Climate Survey found, for instance, that on average more than 20 percent of firms in developing countries "rate inadequate skills and education of workers a major or severe obstacle to their operations"—for example, Algeria (25%), Bangladesh (20%), Brazil (40%), China (30%), Estonia (33%), and Zambia (35%).[59] The skills shortage is exacerbated by weak, ineffective, or costly health care systems, rigidities in the labor market, and bloated bureaucracies that tend to crowd out talent from the private sector. It is particularly acute for small firms that cannot afford training programs and for firms that are seeking to innovate and expand. Expensive welfare systems, government requirements for job and wage security, and a reluctance of employees to change locales (typical, for instance, in Europe) restrict labor mobility and raise labor costs. The importance of available skills explains the decades-long investments in engineers and technicians by rapid globalizers like Ireland, Malaysia's expenditure of $3.6 billion on its Multimedia Super Corridor, and India's leading position and out-performance of China in A. T. Kearney's Offshore Location Attractiveness Index 2004. Despite low labor costs, China lags behind India in such key factors as IT, management education, and language skills. There are also concerns about China's protection of intellectual property and its business environment.[60]

Finally, two major factors complicate firms' global agendas: the impact of technology on global competition and of changing demographics on the nature of the workforce. In the face of intense competition, firms are required to upgrade continually the skills and competencies of employees. They are engaged in an ongoing trade-off between increasing the top line through **product innovation**—requiring new skills and added capacity—and improving the bottom line by reducing production costs and jobs through **process innovation**. This leads firms more and more, through the use of information and communication technologies (ICT), to outsource and offshore activities where feasible. It requires firms to think clearly and strategically about the skills they need in-house for their competitive advantage and the skills expected of their suppliers and partners. It also requires managers to grasp this difference and to adapt their production and organizational processes to a variety of cultures. "There's a shortage of management talent in many of the markets where we operate," says Motorola's director of executive development. "We realized we need to develop our next-generation managers."[61]

Equally complicating are the shifting demographics of societies and of the workforce across the globe. At their heart lies what has been termed the "Florida-ization" of the world, particularly among advanced economies in Europe, Japan, and North America. (But China, South Korea, and Taiwan are not far behind!) Not only are these aging societies having to deal with the costs associated with the longevity of their retirees, they also are facing scarcity in critical skills due to their "baby bust." The scarcity is not immediate, but will become apparent over the next ten to fifteen years, depending on the industry. At the same time as some countries are experiencing scarcity, other countries have an abundance of youth; 50 percent of the Indian population, for instance, is twenty-five years or younger. In the chemical industry it is estimated that 10 to 20 percent of senior scientists have already retired, and this figure may reach 50 percent over the next ten years.[62] By 2020, estimates the All India Management Association, the gap for talented workers will reach 17 million in the United States, 9 million in Japan, and 2 million each in France, Germany, and the United Kingdom.[63] This means, of course, that firms must begin planning now, and planning globally, how they will staff and configure their organizations geographically and technologically.

Distinctive Cultural Patterns Resist Standardization

Cultural diversity may require firms to customize or adopt their global operations to local values in three critical respects: marketing, the conduct of business, and management effectiveness, all three of which are addressed in various chapters of this book. For each aspect, the challenge lies not so much in realizing that cultural differences exist as in appreciating that culture is a mindset that permeates society. It cannot be grasped piecemeal simply as a collection of protocols. By "culture" is meant "the values, attitudes, beliefs, orientations, and underlying assumptions prevalent among people in a society" (Samuel Huntington); and, speaking metaphorically, "the collective programming of the mind which distinguishes the members of one human group from another" (Geert Hofstede).[64] Cultural issues for managers stem largely from the fact that firms' products and services as well as marketing, management, and workplace practices have deeply seated home-country orientations that often are at odds with the cultures of the countries in which they operate.

With respect to marketing, the blunders are legend. They relate to all aspects of marketing, whether to the product or service itself, or to its pricing, promotion, or distribution channels. Repeatedly, even the most sophisticated firms, known for their marketing prowess in their home countries, have stumbled badly. A well-known American designer, for instance, launched a new fragrance in Latin America emphasizing the perfume's fresh camellia scent, overlooking the fact that in most Latin American countries camellias are funeral flowers. In other cases the company name does not translate well: A private Egyptian airline, Misair, faced problems in France because its name too closely resembled "misery" for the French. In Australia, the launch of an airline was complicated by its name, EMU, an Australian bird incapable of flying. The Helmsley Palace Hotel in New York compared itself with the Taj Mahal in India, forgetting that the latter is a mausoleum. And Fiat's promotional campaign in Spain for its Cinquencento car backfired, because the anonymous "love letters" sent to attract "independent, modern, working women" came across as threatening or provoked spousal jealousy. To avoid such missteps, Volvo differentiates its promotion tactics among countries—for example, status and leisure in France, performance in Germany, and economy, durability, and safety in the United States.[65]

Another dimension of this cultural challenge arises in the conduct of business. The cultural differences here relate largely to the practices and institutions that define a country's commercial system. They may be as obvious as the severe limits that Islam's *Shari'ah* law places on the practice of charging or paying interest. They are reflected as well in the disdain with which many Europeans hold profit-maximizing American-style capitalism that readily lays off workers or closes and dismembers enterprises when performance lags. Indeed, the task- and rule-oriented, individualistic Americans, with their penchant for quick deals, may come across as arrogant and uncaring to those for whom personal relationships and group consensus are essential to any working partnership. By contrast, the latter may be viewed by the former as slow and noncommittal or indecisive. For enterprises operating in many countries, these misunderstandings too easily multiply.

Country attitudes may also differ over the ethics of favoritism, nepotism, and kickbacks in hiring or awarding of contracts. At what point do such practices corrupt the market system, undercut economic and social development, and scare off foreign investors? In its 2004 Corruption Perception Index, where 10 is highly clean and 0 is highly corrupt, Transparency International ranks only 40 out of 146 countries at 5 or above. Sixty countries are ranked below 3.[66] "Widespread and unchecked corruption," conclude Dennis Rondinelli and Jack Behrman, "seriously weakens or destroys people's trust in public policies and the operation of markets because it undermines the 'arm's length' relationship and the checks-and-balances between government and the private sector on which transactions in market systems should rely."[67]

Finally, culture also affects approaches to management and, therefore, the effectiveness of foreign management practices in that culture. It is well recognized, as Geert Hofstede points out, that management practices differ widely among country or regional cultures.[68] This fact underscores the view of Fons Trompenaars and Charles Hampden-Turner that culture is "the way in which a group of people solves problems and reconciles dilemmas."[69] The challenge for the global enterprise is ensuring productive and innovative behavior as well as operational productivity among its multicountry workforce. Given the many dimensions along which cultures differ, the enterprise's response is not simply to adopt some "best" management way or practice, for this is more yearning than reality. Tensions are a continuing presence among differing cultures—whether within or among countries. For the global enterprise, the crux of the management challenge is to reconcile potentially conflicting cultural patterns in a way that enriches the firm's operations and development as a whole. Indeed, cultural tension is often a fertile source of innovation. While the resulting management styles and emphases will vary from enterprise to enterprise, they will share a common respect for cultural diversity.

Alienation and Distrust of Globalization May Generate Resistance

Beyond cultural aspects, the advance of globalization is greeted by some with genuine reservation and distrust. These attitudes reflect differently rooted concerns, ranging from ideologically based hostility to concerns about national policies, vested interests, and societal values. As standard-bearers of free market capitalism, a primary force driving globalization, managers of transnational corporations face these attitudes in one forum or another. They confront them in the news media, negotiations with government officials, and protests of environmental activists.

Among the most dramatic expressions of concern, perhaps, are ideological charges—sometimes mixed with nationalistic sentiment—that globalization is exploitative and undermines societal values. In Germany's 2005 election campaign, the Social Democrats decried foreign capital as "locusts" descending to dismember German industry, while the French government has identified a number of sectors to protect from foreign takeovers. In essence, globalization is viewed as the expansion of predatory and monopolistic capitalism across the world economy. Multinational firms are viewed as exploiting weaker and poorer nations, playing them off against each other in order to gain concessions and cheap labor. The result, it is said, is a "race to the bottom" for environmental, wage and labor, human rights, and consumer product and safety standards.[70] While there undoubtedly are many examples of rapacious behavior on the part of enterprises—both domestic and foreign, it should be added—global trade and free market capitalism as components of globalization appear, on balance, to be clearly beneficial to the world as a whole.[71] Indeed, despite some concerns about possible negative effects on jobs, health care, and retirement savings, the 2003 Pew survey, "Visions of a Changing World," covering thirty-eight thousand persons in forty-four countries, found that "people around the world credit globalization for conditions they see as improving, but do not blame growing economic and social problems on globalization."[72]

More reasoned concerns for possible adverse effects of globalization are presented by those who point out the limits of the market mechanism and of market capitalism as functioning systems. For the most part, they grant that the market system can be the most efficient and powerful engine of economic growth when allowed to function freely and allocate a country's resources. In the real world, however, markets are only relatively efficient due to limits on information and time for decision-making and to the difficulty of monetizing many values and priorities. Equally important, the efficiency of markets depends on an environment of supporting institutions and policies. Even then, markets limit participation to the extent that consumers have disposable income. Demand is skewed in their favor.

Moreover, as John Dunning argues, if global capitalism is to be responsible, "it is not enough for [its] institutions . . . to perform efficiently. They must do so in a way which conforms to certain *moral standards*" (emphasis added). By this he means that the choices of goods to be produced, how and where to produce them, and how to distribute their benefits "critically depend on the values and priorities of the individuals and institutions participating in the system." To maximize effectiveness, therefore, markets must function not only relatively efficiently but equitably as well. While efficient markets require a relatively well-ordered and reliable environment, equitable markets require that "transacting participants must behave in an ethically responsible manner."[73] (This theme will be explored in more detail in Chapter 14, "Ethics and Corporate Social Responsibility.") It also indicates the role and leeway that government has to correct for shortfalls in the functioning of the market.

GLOBALIZATION CALLS FOR A REORIENTATION OF MANAGEMENT THINKING

As this Overview has attempted to show, managers of firms with global agendas are destined to operate on a daily basis between the forces and counterforces of globalization. On the one hand, the forces driving globalization present managers with enormous opportunities for growing and extending their operations. As the global economy grows over the next three decades, the share that is subject to global competition will expand from approximately one-fourth to over four-fifths. The result is a tenfold increase in globalized market demand—from approximately $10 trillion to $100 trillion. On the other hand, the multiplicity of jurisdictions and variations in the business environment embodied in the nation-state system pose a broad range of challenges that in many ways run counter to, or seek to contain, the forces of globalization. The choice for the manager is not whether but how to embrace both sides of this global equation.

The resulting "squeeze play" explored in the various chapters of this book introduces a heightened degree of tension and complexity into enterprise management. The complexity lies in the multiplicity of values, norms, and practices found in the environment. There is no supranational system to clarify, let alone resolve, conflicting national expectations and requirements. The tension stems from the necessity to make decisions in the midst of this ambiguity and the accelerating pace of business innovation and environmental change. Few aspects of business operations, internal or external, can be taken for granted. Globalization, note *Economist* editors John Michlethwait and Adrian Wooldridge, "is incredibly difficult to manage, and for most managers it is usually more a source of fear than of excitement."[74] The chapters that follow will seek to allay these fears and restore and validate the excitement by showing how managers can constructively address the challenges of globalization and turn them into opportunities. They also reveal that, to do this, managers need to reorient their management thinking and hone the competencies needed to carry out their global agendas.

NOTES

1. Alan MacCormack and Kerry Herman, *The Rise and Fall of Iridium* (Boston: Harvard Business School Press, November 28, 2001); Case 9-601-040.

2. Peter F. Drucker, "Management's New Paradigms," *Forbes* 162, no. 7 (October 5, 1998): 152–77.

3. L. Bryan, J. Fraser, J. Oppenheim, and W. Rall, *Race for the World: Strategies to Build a Great Global Firm* (Boston: Harvard Business School Press, 1999), 44–48.

4. UNCTAD (United Nations Conference on Trade and Development), *World Investment Report, 2005* (New York & Geneva: United Nations, 2005). Among the developed countries in 2004, the United States, United Kingdom, and Luxembourg accounted for almost half the outward FDI.

5. Estimate of current world GDP by the World Bank Group, World Development Indicators database, August 2005; World Data Profile, 2004. See the website: http://devdata.worldbank.org/data-query/. The estimates of the share of world GDP subject to global competition is based on projections presented by Bryan et al., *Race for the World*, 4.

6. Christopher Bartlett and Sumantra Ghoshal, *Managing across Borders* (Boston: Harvard Business School Press, 1998), for instance, suggest a structural topology for firms that have global agendas, which they classify as primarily "global" (ethnocentric firms, which centralize their production in a home country and export worldwide to maximize efficiencies), "multinational" (polycentric firms, which decentralize their operations among countries, that is, operate essentially multidomestically, to ensure responsiveness to local environments), "international" (firms that centralize their R&D and management, but spread by duplication their manufacturing operations around the world), and "transnational" (flexibly configured firms that combine the strengths of the previous three types through a matrix structure that assigns varying tasks and responsibilities among headquarters and affiliates as necessary to ensure efficiency of operations, responsiveness to markets, and continuous learning and innovation for the firm as a whole).

7. WTO, *International Trade Statistics, 2004* (long-term trade statistics). http://www.wto.org/english/res_e/statis_e/its2004_e/its04_toc_e.htm. During the period 1953–2003, in fact, annual world trade growth exceeded 10 percent in eleven of those years and fell into the red in only four—of which 1975 was decidedly the deepest decline.

8. WTO, 2004, *Trade Statistics*. http://www.wto.org/english/res_e/statis_e/its2004_e/its04_toc_e.htm.

9. WTO, *International Trade Statistics, 2004* (world trade in 2003, overview). http://www.wto.org/english/res_e/statis_e/its2004_e/its04_toc_e.htm.

10. Steve Radelet, J. D. Sachs, and Lee Jong-Wha, "Economic Growth in Asia" (1995), p. 14; background paper prepared for the Asian Development Bank's study: "Emerging Asia: Changes and Challenges." As the authors point out, this finding (specifically, 1.97 percent) does not differ significantly from other research on this point.

11. R. Warcziarg, "Measuring the Dynamic Gains from Trade," *Policy Research Working Paper, 2001* (Washington, DC: World Bank, 1998).

12. T. F. Rutherford and D. G. Tarr, "Trade Liberalization and Endogenous Growth in a Small Open Economy: A Quantitative Assessment," *Policy Working Paper* (Washington, DC: World Bank, September 1998).

13. Arvind Virmani, *ICRIER Working Paper No. 150* (December 2004).

14. UNCTAD, *World Investment Report*, 2005, xix.

15. Ibid.

16. Ibid., xxvi.

17. Ibid., xxvii.

18. United Nations, *World Investment Report, 1997*.

19. J. Michlethwait and A. Wooldridge, *A Future Perfect: The Challenge and Hidden Promise of Globalization* (New York: Crown Publishing, 2000), 68.

20. T. L. Friedman, *The Lexus and the Olive Tree* (New York: Farrar, Straus and Giroux, 1999).

21. *The Economist* (May 20, 2000).

22. Bryan et al., *Race for the World*, 21; based on data from the International Monetary Fund and the International Finance Corporation, as analyzed by McKinsey & Company, Inc.

23. This figure includes $2,087 trillion in currency reserves and $385 billion in gold. An additional $190 billion in currency and gold is held by such multilateral agencies as the International Monetary Fund, the Bank for International Settlements (BIS), and the European Monetary Institute. See Gold Reserves at http://www .pamp.com/gold_c/Info_site/in_glos/in_glos_goldreserves.html; and BIS at http:// www.bis.org/banking/index.htm#pgtop.

24. Robert Gilpin, *The Challenge of Global Capitalism: The World Economy in the 21st Century* (Princeton, NJ: Princeton University Press, 2000), 136–39.

25. G. Yago and D. Goldman, *Capital Access Index, Fall 1998: Emerging and Submerging Markets* (Santa Barbara, CA: Milken Institute, 1998).

26. G. Soros, *The Crisis of Global Capitalism* (New York: Public Affairs Perseus Books,1998), xxvi–xxx.

27. "Untangling e-conomics," *The Economist* (September 21, 2000).

28. L. Thurow, *Building Wealth: The New Rules for Individuals, Companies, and Nations in a Knowledge-Based Economy* (New York: HarperCollins, 1999), 18.

29. UNCTAD, 2005, p. 105. See also ibid., 107, 115.

30. "A New Map of the World," *The Economist* (June 22, 2000).

31. H. B. Malmgren, "Trade and Technology in the Single Global Marketplace," *Global Focus* 12, no. 1 (2000): 31.

32. K. Kelly, *New Rules for the New Economy* (New York: Penguin Putnam/Viking Press, 1998), 5.

33. World Bank, *World Development Report, 2005: A Better Investment Climate for Everyone* (New York: Oxford University Press), 130.

34. Bryan et al., *Race for the World*, 36.

35. Friedman, *Lexus*, 56.

36. C. Chandler, P. P. Pan, and D. Struck, "Outrage over Corruption Rattles Leaders across Asia." Washington.Com (http://www.washingtonpost.com/wp-dyn/articles).

37. M. Wolf, *Why Globalization Works* (New Haven: Yale University Press, 2004), 46.

38. Joseph Schumpeter's thesis has been updated and refined by William J. Baumol in his book *The Free-Market Innovation Machine: Analyzing the Growth Miracle of Capitalism* (Princeton, NJ: Princeton University Press, 2002).

39. J. E. Garten, "The Mind of the CEO," *Business Week* (February 5, 2001): 106.

40. R. L. Heilbroner, *Twentieth-first Century Capitalism* (New York: W. W. Norton, 1993), 41.

41. D. Yergin and J. Stanislaw, *The Commanding Heights: The Battle between Government and the Marketplace That Is Remaking the Modern World* (New York: Simon & Schuster (First Touchstone Edition), 1999), 11. See also discussion in P. Hofheinz, "Looking Ahead: What Now?" *Wall Street Journal Reports*, World Business: Ten Years

Later—The State of Capitalism a Decade after the Fall of the Wall (September 27, 1999), R25.

42. Devesh Kapur and John McHale, "Migration's New Payoff," *Foreign Policy* (November–December 2003).

43. Friedman, *Lexus*, 235.

44. Quoted by Hofheinz, "Looking Ahead," R25.

45. Christopher Rhoads, "In Threat to Internet's Clout, Some are Starting Alternatives," *Wall Street Journal* (January 19, 2006), A1.

46. A. T. Kearney Foreign Direct Investment Confidence Index 2003 (http://www.atkearney.com), p. 9. This index is based on a survey of corporate managers whose firms are said to represent 70 percent of global foreign direct investment flows.

47. World Bank, *World Development Report, 2005: A Better Investment Climate for Everyone* (New York: Oxford University Press). The bank's report evaluates how the *costs, risks, and barriers to competition* generated by government policies affect firms' investment behavior around the world.

48. Ibid., 23.

49. Walter B. Wriston, *TheTwilight of Sovereignty: How the Information Revolution Is Transforming Our World* (New York: Charles Scribner's Sons, 1992).

50. Mary Hallward-Dreimeier and David Stewart, "How Do Investment Climate Conditions Vary across Countries, Regions, and Types of Firms?" Background paper for the World Bank, *World Development Report, 2005* (revised September 2005), 4.

51. World Bank, *World Development Report, 2005*, selected indicators, pp. 40–43, 246–49; also see pp. 129, 132, 135.

52. Ibid.; also see p. 5.

53. Ibid., 104.

54. Ibid., selected indicators, pp. 40–43, 246–49.

55. Ibid., 22.

56. The definition is used by the Centre for Educational Research & Innovation, in *Human Capital Investment: An International Comparison*. Organisation for Economic Co-Operation and Development (OECD), 1998. http://213.253.13429/oecd/pdfs/browseit/968021E.PDF.

57. C. M. Yee, "The Global Battle: Let's Make a Deal," *Wall Street Journal* (September 25, 2000), R10.

58. *United Nations Human Development Index, 2004* (statistics are for the year 2002). http://hdr.undp.org/reports/global/2004/pdf/hdr04_HDI.pdf.

59. Ibid., 136 and 139.

60. A. T. Kearney, 2004 Offshore Location Attractiveness Index: "Making Offshore Decisions," figure 1. www.atkearney.com/shared_res/pdf/Making_Offshore_S.pdf.

61. D. Woodruff, "Career Journal: Distractions Make Local Managers a Difficult Role." *Wall Street Journal* (Eastern edition, November 21, 2000), B1.

62. Patricia Van Arnum and Pamela Sauer, "The Changing Workforce of the Chemical Industry," *Chemical Market Reporter* (June 3, 2002).

63. "Bank on Workforce for Growth" (panel), *Times of India* (April 18, 2003).

64. See Samuel Huntington in *Culture Matters* (2000), xv, and see also Geert Hofstede, *Culture's Consequences: International Differences in Work-Related Values*, abridged ed. (Beverly Hills, CA: Sage, 1984), who speaks metaphorically of culture as "the collective programming of the mind which distinguishes the members of one

human group from another." Despite the differences in formulation, all three are quite similar. For purposes of this book, "culture" is essentially territorial and refers to groups whose values have been shaped largely by geographical proximity. Typically, this geography is subject to a common government, generally national in scope, but it can reflect subdivisions within nations where value systems differ substantially.

65. Examples from David A. Ricks, *Blunders in International Business,* 3d ed. (Malden, MA: Blackwell Publishers, 1999), 45–62.

66. Transparency International, Corruption Perceptions Index, 2004. http://www .transparency.org/cpi/2004/dnld/media_pack_en.pdf.

67. Dennis A. Rondinelli and Jack N. Behrman, "The Promises and Pains of Globalization," *Global Focus* 12, no. 1 (2000): 3–15, 71.

68. Geert Hofstede, "Cultural Constraints in Management Systems," *Academy of Management Executive* 7, no. 1: 81–94.

69. Fons Trompenaars and Charles Hampden-Turner, *Riding the Waves of Culture: Understanding Diversity in Global Business,* 2d ed. (New York: McGraw-Hill).

70. For an overview of antiglobalization ideologies, see Vincent Cable, *Globalization and Global Governance*, Chatham House Papers (London: Royal Institute of International Affairs, 1999), 121–23.

71. The "on balance" positive effects of globalization are amply supported by economists in two recent books: Jagdish Bhagwati, *In Defense of Globalization* (New York: Oxford University Press, 2004), and Wolf, *Why Globalization Works.*

72. Pew Research Center for The People & The Press, *Views of a Changing World* (June 2003), 10–11.

73. John Dunning, "The Moral Imperatives of Global Capitalism: An Overview," in John Dunning, ed., *Making Globalization Good* (New York: Oxford University Press, 2003), 13–14.

74. Michlethwait and Wooldridge, *A Future Perfect,* 120.

SECTION I

FOCUSING ENTERPRISE OPERATIONS

Globalization presents a world rife with opportunities. These lie in expanding markets and rising incomes, new and converging technologies, highly diverse and competitively priced supplier and distributor networks, and a vast and increasingly accessible labor pool. Due to continuously intense competition, however, none of these opportunities can be achieved without clearly focused enterprise operations all along a firm's value chain. The complexity, diversity, and volatility of the global environment—strewn among two hundred countries—deny firms the luxury of pursuing opportunities willy-nilly or of spreading scarce resources among multiple operations without well-defined strategic objectives and coherent performance targets. Strategy is the means for disciplining the scope, scale, and location of an enterprise's operations across the world; for defining and targeting its markets and supplier networks; and for shaping and developing its workforce.

The chapters in this section examine four management perspectives for focusing the operations of enterprises that have far-flung operations. They consider the strategic challenges firms face and the management mindset and competencies that firms need in order to succeed.

• The **Corporate Strategist** must enable the enterprise to maintain its competitive edge by continually upgrading—to the point of reinventing—its value proposition and to align its core competencies accordingly. In focusing their operations, firms necessarily engage in three-dimensional strategic trade-offs: balancing productivity with innovation, positioning assets across the world to gain access to resources, technology, and markets, and deepening critical competencies in tandem with building external value networks.

• The **Marketing Manager** faces the competing requirements of responding sensitively to local demand and culture while building an infrastructure that efficiently serves a wide variety of markets across the globe. This entails a focus within the marketing function to both encompass and add value throughout the value chain. It represents a shift from global marketing to strategic global marketing management.

• The **Supply Chain Manager**, afloat in an endless sea of possibilities, must organize a broad array of supplier firms into a cost-effective cross-border system. In doing so, the supply chain manager must capture both economies of scale and essential quality as well as ongoing technological advances by suppliers. The focus here is on building a value chain of partnerships that enhances the firm's value proposition.

• The **Human Resource Manager** needs to cultivate a collaborative and skilled workforce at every level of operations. The increasing array of knowledge workers in global firms is matched only by their cultural diversity and potential creativity. The human resource manager, therefore, must be single-mindedly committed to turning individual knowledge into intellectual capital and organizational capability.

In perusing these chapters, consider how globalization requires managers to think differently about their strategic tasks and the management competencies needed for this.

1

Strategy in a Global Context

CLARENCE J. MANN

HALLMARKS OF GLOBAL STRATEGY: CHALLENGE AND RESPONSE

In its simplest form, strategy is about getting from A to B as cost-effectively as possible. Implicit in this process are: assessing a firm's existing situation (A), both external and internal; clarifying strategic objectives (B) and the opportunities they encompass; and determining the pathway of long-term activities (strategies) that most effectively lead from A to B. The strategic pathway must reflect not only the changing environment, but also changes called for in a firm's capabilities. As such, strategy necessarily combines both internal and external aspects of a firm. When the environment is complex and at times volatile, as is true for the global economy, these two aspects are continuously in play and shaping each other.

As process, strategy-making should generate a singleness of purpose, enabling firms to both prioritize their activities and mobilize resources around the accomplishment of these activities. In a broader sense, strategy-making should enable firms to fully assess their interests, how their industries and the world work, and their underlying assumptions about their situation. This chapter examines strategy as a discipline, both as a process of renewal and as a system for formulating strategy in a global context, thus enabling firms to operate effectively in the global economy. It also highlights the management competencies necessary to exercise this discipline.

Firms with Global Agendas Need a Strategic Lodestar

In the transition to a global economy, strategy plays a particularly critical role. Like a lodestar, strategy enables enterprises to stay on course in uncharted waters. While it may be possible to run a business by the seat of one's pants in a purely domestic environment, this becomes increasingly difficult in a regional and globalizing environment because of three complicating factors:

• **The sheer number and complexity of variables at play.** However alluring the concepts of a "borderless world" or the "end of the nation state," as proposed by Kenichi Ohmae,[1] every country added to a firm's operations introduces significant competitive, regulatory, infrastructural, institutional, and cultural nuances or constraints. While financial principles in market economies provide the least common denominator for international business, political and cultural perspectives are distinctive for most countries.

• **More volatility at country and industry levels.** As more countries open their borders to commercial activity from outside, they expose themselves to winds of change—whether in the form of technological innovation, financial flows, market-driven decisions, or information and lifestyle aspirations. In the absence of mature institutions and policies, skills, and the experience to channel these forces, the financial and political fortunes of many countries will be buffeted from time to time, as happened during the 1997–98 Asian contagion.

• **Interdependence.** This is the defining challenge. Interdependence has both external and internal aspects. Geography still counts, for competitive advantage is tied largely to product acceptance at local and national levels. Further, some country environments are friendlier to business, and to foreign firms in particular. Internally, firms typically need to make choices about where to concentrate and how to coordinate business assets and functions in order to enhance productivity and sustain a competitive advantage. Such choices may be determined at least in part by how the forces of globalization affect an industry. For example, the retail trade, restaurants, residential construction, and legal and accounting services, by their very nature, are likely to be much more localized and subject to extensive coordination than trade in commodities, such as oil, industrial chemicals, and consumer electronics, in which national barriers are relatively low. The latter have become, in essence, global.

Moreover, global firms profit from the synergies they achieve by operating transnationally, reaping economies of scale and scope. Interdependence for firms, therefore, means achieving singleness of purpose among disparate worldwide operations and amid the multiplicity of external forces and interests at play. It means leveraging various aspects of a firm's worldwide resource network to compete in national markets. Out of this interdependence among country operations is emerging a new strategic paradigm. "This paradigm," says Michael Porter, "must guide a new generation of thinking about global strategy, one that integrates localization and globalization in wholly new ways."[2]

Many Paths Lead To a Global Enterprise

Firms vary considerably in the motivations and paths that guide them toward their global agendas. They begin at different points in their development, pursue different visions, and operate under different industry conditions; moreover, much of what passes for global business is, in fact, regional. As Alan Rugman argues, present world trade and investment patterns suggest that the competitive structure of industries and the location and activities of multinational enterprises today are in many respects more regional than global.[3] These facts underscore the importance of seeing globalization as a long-term, highly varied transition, not as a fait accompli.

Viewed in motivational terms, six types of drivers are at work.[4] Two are classic: the drive for **scarce or cheaper factors** of production, and for **new or expanded markets** that feed economies of scale. Spawned by intensifying global competition, there is the drive for **strategic assets**, as reflected in the acquisition by Deutsche Bank and Dresdner Bank of the prestige and know-how of London investment banks; and the drive for **efficiency** as firms seek to streamline their operations or advance their production technology through acquisitions. Finally, firms are driven to seek strategic advantages by locating in a favorable **business climate** or market, such as the United States offers (for the present at least) to pharmaceutical companies, and by **challenging competitors in their home markets**—as Kodak did with Fuji Photo and Caterpillar with Komatsu in Japan—in order to deprive the latter of a profit sanctuary.

Firms also have a broad choice of the strategic path they take to achieve their global agendas. Some firms in the medical, biotech, and computer software fields may be viewed as "born global," because their products have immediate widespread acceptance in an identifiable market niche around the world. But even then, like most firms, they must traverse one or more of three broadly different paths to globalize their operations—through growth, extension, or transformation. Scarcity of resources and management talent as well as competitive pressures tends to encourage the latter two paths.

• **Growers**. Emphasize **internal resources** to globalize operations "organically," especially during their early years. Apple Computer and Sony grew by exploiting their technological prowess in consumer electronics, while mass merchandisers Wal-Mart, IKEA, and Nike pursued their competitive advantage as mass merchants.

• **Extenders**. Establish global positions primarily by leveraging assets **externally** to expand their capabilities in one of two ways. Through **mergers and**

acquisitions, for instance, the power systems giant ABB—itself formed through a cross-border merger—acquired a worldwide network that by 1993 included more than thirteen hundred wholly owned subsidiaries. General Electric aggressively honed its multibusiness company during the 1990s through hundreds of acquisitions worldwide. Extenders also rely heavily on capital-saving **alliances and networks** that encompass a wide variety of approaches, from relatively simple distributorship, franchising (McDonald's, KFC), or subcontracting (Coca-Cola bottlers) networks to complex partnerships such as the Renault-Nissan alliance. Reversing its go-it-alone policy, IBM counted more than 20,000 alliances worldwide by 1992, including 400 with equity holdings.

• **Transformers** globalize their operations in significant respects by re-working existing widespread operations in one of two ways. They may do this by **specializing**, that is, redirecting their focus, possibly downsizing and nar-rowing it. Thus, Corning shed its consumer division in 1998 and intensified research efforts to become a world-class producer and supplier of high-tech materials, particularly fiber optics. Firms also may transform by **reconfiguring** existing operations, that is, converting a group of affiliated companies, buyers, and sources into an interactive global network. Thus, ABB, British Petroleum, General Electric, IBM, and Philips consolidated and transformed their far-flung business empires in the 1990s into integrated networks with globally coordinated agendas. Approaches varied, as did results.

While many firms pursue a combination of all three approaches, others adopt them in stages. At some point, however, all firms embracing a global agenda must come to grips with their transformation, that is, what it means for them to think and act as an integrated global enterprise.

This is no simple task. One study identifying three successive stages to achieve a global organization—rationalization, revitalization, and regeneration—suggests GE got it right.[5] Beginning in the early and mid-1980s, GE began the first stage by downsizing, delayering, and portfolio pruning, to ensure that each of GE's core businesses was defined clearly and performing well. In the next phase, revitalization, GE integrated its thirteen more sharply focused businesses to achieve scale economies and promote organizational learning by developing collaboration among units. Only when this objective was com-pleted, approximately a decade later, did Jack Welch launch his campaign to instill a regenerative "boundaryless" culture across GE, where "it's a badge of honor to learn something here no matter where it comes from." Welch himself, however, acknowledges that GE has not achieved the last stage in transfor-mation. For him the final stage entails "a state of mind: when firms become 'multicultural multinationals' [and] the nationality of the staff ceases to mat-ter."[6] While GE currently derives about half of its revenues from sales abroad and has a global attitude toward resources, it is still run by Americans from America.

STRATEGY-MAKING: A QUINTESSENTIAL
PROCESS OF RENEWAL

There are many ways to formulate strategy, whether the context is local or global. Some view the process principally as prescriptive, rational, and analytical, involving deliberate planning and possibly changes in direction. Others see it as a gradually emerging sense within a firm of its direction, as organizational learning or the sum of ad hoc innovation over time, or as the intuitive vision of the CEO or some management guru. Some say it is "visioning," others say it is "positioning" or that it is organizational capability. Still others find it rooted in power relationships and corporate culture, where outcomes are negotiated or brokered among key players. In fact, all these aspects are at work at various points in any strategy process. In particular, the emergent and deliberate approaches should complement each other, forming an interactive dialogue.

An Overlapping Three-Phased Strategy Process

This chapter adopts a three-phase process of strategy formulation and renewal, embracing those aspects most frequently discussed by writers and practitioners in the field. These phases—practical visioning, strategy formulation, and action planning and evaluation—are distributed over five steps and build upon one another, as depicted in Figure 1.1.

While the five steps suggest a discrete cycle, they in fact are interdependent and often overlapping. Moreover, they are affected constantly by shifting trends and discontinuities in the global environment. As a result, strategic thinking—especially for established companies—may actually be initiated at any point around the cycle. In formulating and executing strategy, each step should be vetted and tested periodically against the step preceding and following it. Thus, in order to understand and critique a firm's strategic posture, a strategist might begin with existing strategies and, working backward, ask what environmental constraints they are intended to address and what core competencies they are designed to build. Or, she might begin with a firm's vision and core competencies and, working forward, reality-test them against its internal and external situation. Either way, the substance of the phases and the steps must prove to be reasonably aligned with each other.

Phase I: Practical Visioning

Every business begins with a notion of value, or a value proposition, that is intended to distinguish it in the marketplace. As this notion is fleshed out into a full range of images, it becomes a practical vision of a firm's future success. A firm's "vision" should not be confused with its "mission." While the mission defines a firm's present focus—its business and place in the industry value chain—the vision is dynamic, looking to the future and conveying a sense of

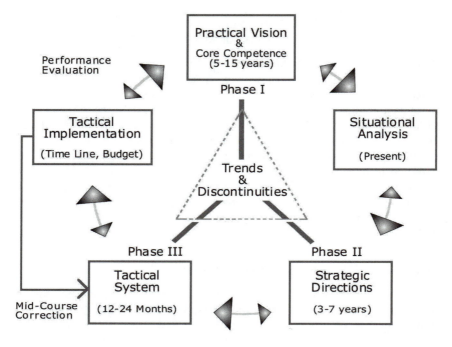

FIGURE 1.1.   The Strategy Process

direction. The two are clearly related, but for purposes of strategic thinking the vision becomes most critical. Its value proposition is just that: a proposition, or hypothesis, to be proven and shaped further in the marketplace. The value sheds light on an identifiable market, either existing or potential, but always evolving. The strategy process gives firms license to think boldly about their prospects. "For the first time in history," declares Gary Hamel, "we can work backward from our imagination rather than forward from our past."[7]

Implicit in any refined practical vision is a **business model** that generates and delivers customer value. This model consists of proprietary assets, a distinct set of activities or processes for delivering customer value, a value network providing access to resources and markets, and an enabling architecture of management systems, corporate values, and policies that weaves these together into a coherent operating concept. At the heart of every business model lies a firm's **core competence**, the bundle of skills and technologies that yields perceived customer value, differentiates a firm from its competitors, and provides a platform for future products and markets.[8] Core competence may take the form of miniaturization and mobility for Sony's Walkman; flawless logistics for Federal Express's reliable overnight delivery; and streamlined connectedness for RIM's BlackBerry. At the same time, core competencies must evolve in keeping with a firm's vision and value proposition, available technology, and how a firm intends to shape its value network. Core competencies, therefore, are not simply a firm's strengths or what it is presently good at, but what it needs to be good at if it is to deliver its value proposition.

Phase II: Strategy Formulation

Compared to Phase I, where intuition and instinct take precedence, the strategy formulation phase is highly analytical. At this point the practical vision and core competencies are reality-tested in terms of a firm's internal capability and external environment. Strategies should be designed primarily to reshape a firm's **present situation**, that is, to remove or otherwise overcome constraints that are impeding its growth and the realization of its practical vision. There are many models for conducting this analysis, such as the familiar market and competitor analyses, SWOT (strengths, weaknesses, opportunities, and threats), and STEPE (social, technological, economic, political, and ecological), and the five-forces industry and value chain models. Whatever methods or models are used, situation analysis must yield two results.

First, situation analysis must **reality-test** the initial drafts of a firm's practical vision and core competence, and it must indicate any refinements needed. Arguing that "only the paranoid survive," Intel's CEO Andrew Grove suggests that in making fundamental decisions about a firm's future, managers should "adopt an outsider's intellectual objectivity," actively looking for evidence that disproves your hypothesis "unfettered by any emotional attachment to the past."[9] Grove did just this in making Intel's historic decision to abandon memory chip manufacturing in favor of microprocessors and CISC chip architecture.* A firm must uncover and test all assumptions about the environment and a firm's capabilities. Unarticulated assumptions, for example, about a technology's viability and regulatory approvals in other countries, are a frequent trap in formulating strategy.

Second, situation analysis should identify **underlying constraints**, those conditions external to and within a firm that currently are impeding a firm's ability to realize its practical vision and generate the requisite core competencies. Constraints are not mere issues or problems that irritate and frustrate the smooth operations of an organization. Rather, they are deep-seated, substantial blocks to a firm's success and effective functioning, whether they show up as product or market misalignments, governmental restrictions, skill deficiencies, bureaucratic rigidities, competitor inroads, management infighting, poor financial systems, or obsolete technology. In some cases constraints are self-imposed, as when "big steel" chose to ignore the opportunity of mini-mill technology and the U.S. auto industry chose to ignore the high-performance products of Japanese firms. While

---

*CISC stands for complex instruction set computer or computing and refers to computers designed with a full set of computer instructions that were intended to provide needed capabilities in the most efficient way.

firms have enormous leeway to define their constraints, it is critical to define them well. Constraints should be seen as points of leverage or "doors to the future," for they enable firms to focus on developing the capabilities they need to thrive in a volatile, complex global environment.

Strategy, therefore, provides long-term direction for mobilizing the scarce resources of a particular firm in a way that builds its distinctive competencies, systems architecture, and positions in the marketplace. Benchmarking, while it can be useful to track the competition, is no substitute for strategic thinking. Moreover, these are not "cookie-cutter" or generic strategies, but must be designed to address constraints particular to each firm, its industry, its market, and its stage of development. The strategic dimensions and management competencies required in a global context are developed in detail in later sections of this chapter.

Phase III: Action Planning and Evaluation

This phase marks the payoff or bottom line of the strategic planning effort, for it positions a firm externally and internally to carry out its strategic intent. Its two components are: a) building the tactical system or action plan, and b) implementing and evaluating a firm's performance in mobilizing resources to build competencies. For the strategist, this phase also marks the beginning of a learning curve and of rethinking a firm's strategic future.

Action planning, therefore, goes hand in hand with evaluation by building a baseline for improving future performance. In this sense, tactical and strategic evaluations are akin to single-loop and double-loop learning.[10] Single-loop learning focuses on enacting existing strategies. Double-loop learning focuses on revising them. In the fast-changing global environment, firms may need to revise tactics every six months and reassess strategies on an annual or at least alternate-year basis. At this point it is meaningful to speak of measurable accomplishments, assign champions with specific accountability, and push for structural and cross-departmental efficiencies. Here is where good day-to-day administration and coordination become paramount.

Building Competitive Advantage for Global Agendas

For firms with global agendas, the strategy process described here helps build competitive advantage in three distinctive ways.

First and foremost, strategy-making compels firms to **clarify their interface** with their wide-ranging environments. As previously noted, the complexity and uncertainty emerging from the global environment far exceeds anything experienced either domestically or in more limited international operations. For this reason, the task of the strategist is to clarify the interface—not to find a proper "fit"—for the firm's vision and products or services within the interstices of an industry and the larger environment. Much the same as when

Michelangelo surveyed the ruined surfaces of the discarded duomo block from which he sculpted his David—the strategist is looking for lines of attack to transform the "stuff" (markets, resources, talent, idiosyncrasies, discontinuities) of the environment into a vehicle that freights a firm's vision. Indeed, if successful, a firm's vision is likely to reshape the industry environment. This happened for Sony when it created the Walkman, Apple with the Macintosh and then the iPod, Microsoft with Windows, Honda with the motorcycle, ConAgra with its line of Healthy Choice products, and Google with its search algorithm.

Second, strategy-making must be both **multilevel and multifunctional**. Geographically, firms working in a global context must conduct analysis and decision-making from multiple perspectives. Depending on the corporate level and business function, these perspectives need to be local, national, binational, regional, and worldwide in varying degrees. Thus, the finance function is likely to be centralized or at least coordinated globally by senior management, while marketing and government relations are likely to be guided by more local factors. The strategy process needs to integrate, and thereby become a composite of, these geographic and functional perspectives at various levels of an enterprise.

Christopher Bartlett and Sumantra Ghoshal capture these multilevel and multifunctional perspectives in the roles they depict for the emerging "transnational" company. As Table 1.1 indicates, no role is dominant, for each "is vital in contributing to one or the other of the company's multidimensional strategic capabilities." The challenge is to develop executives "with the skills, knowledge, and sophistication to operate in the specialized yet interdependent roles that each needs to play in the transnational's tightly linked and less hierarchical network."[11] As these widely varying management roles suggest, moreover, the firm's strategy process should take their disparate management perspectives into account and weave them into a global vision.

Third, strategy-making in a global context is perpetually shaped by the firm's **evolving future**. The firm's future evolves in two ways—one external, related to the impact of trends and discontinuities in the environment; the other internal, related to a firm's long-term perspective or vision. For Intel's former board chairman and CEO Andrew Grove, these two aspects intersect at a firm's "strategic inflection point" (SIP).[12] This point is reached when, due to a fundamental shift in the environment, a firm's fate hangs in the balance. For Intel and Grove, this occurred in the mid-1980s when, in the face of the production prowess and price-cutting practices of Japanese competitors, Intel decided to halt further development of its one-megabit DRAM so that it could focus on microprocessors. At the same time, Intel bet on CISC in lieu of RISC* as the dominant chip architecture for the future. Now, a decade later, Grove's

---

*RISC stands for reduced instruction set computing. It takes each of the longer, more complex instructions from a CISC design and reduces them to multiple instructions that are shorter and faster to process.

TABLE 1.1. Transnational Managers: New Roles and Tasks

Position	Roles		
Business Manager of global business or product division	*Strategist* Integrate and coordinate operations	*Architect* Allocate assets and resources efficiently	*Coordinator* Synchronize and control the flow of assets and resources
Country Manager of country (or regionally oriented) subsidiary	*Sensor* Interpret information and outcomes	*Builder* Identify, develop, and leverage local resources	*Contributor* Contribute actively to worldwide strategy
Functional Manager of specialized activity	*Repository* Develop and guard specialized resources	*Cross-Pollinator* Develop specialists with global perspectives	*Champion* Manage expertise as corporate-wide resource
Corporate Manager responsible for worldwide operations	*Visionary* Integrate vision and purpose	*Talent Scout* Identify and allocate scarce talent	*Framer* Clarify and legitimize diverse manager roles

successor Paul Otellini is reinventing Intel again, shifting the firm's focus essentially from PC/microprocessors to more consumer-oriented electronic "platforms" that power numerous applications from the living room to the emergency room.[13]

Making strategic decisions, according to Grove, is a two-step process. First, spot the SIP by scanning the environment—using a modified framework of Porter's industry "five forces"—to identify "order-of-magnitude, or '10X,' changes" in any of the forces affecting Intel's future.[14] Second, make a decision. In fact, the decision-making process in this case was quite sophisticated, reflecting in large part an accumulation of daily decisions by Intel's middle managers, which bit by bit were favoring microprocessors.[15] In effect, the functions and scope of day-to-day responsibility that Intel assigned its line managers framed much of Intel's strategic planning process.

The strategy process, therefore, enables firms to renew themselves from within. The process is not linear but cyclical, a never-ending learning process that proceeds in fits and starts as insight into the environment is gained and a firm's practical vision evolves. At the same time, this process needs to be nurtured and embrace perspectives throughout the organization. Endemic to the strategy process in every organization is the tendency toward entropy—that is, narrowing perspectives, foreshortening a firm's time horizon, and neglecting innovation. This is human enough, because rethinking strategy disrupts vested lines of authority and routine expectations. If strategic thinking is to be kept alive, therefore, the strategy process requires a deliberative framework that balances organizational continuity with the continuing need to incorporate spontaneous creativity and innovative long-term perspectives.

THREE-DIMENSIONAL STRATEGY IN A GLOBAL CONTEXT

Given the complexity of business operations in the high-velocity globalizing economy, the formulation of strategy should be guided by a mode of thinking that is at once process *and* systems oriented. The three-stage process was discussed in the previous section, while the systems logic is considered now.

The system consists of three complementary and interdependent dimensions—technological, organizational, and transactional—that should guide strategy formulation and the value trade-offs each entails (see Figure 1.2). These dimensions and their value trade-offs continuously interact to shape and reshape the content and possibly the directions of existing strategies. They are intrinsic to every strategic decision and, as will be seen, are especially critical for firms with global agendas. Their function, taken together, is to overcome or otherwise address the constraints a firm faces in developing its core competencies and thereby strengthen its long-term competitive advantage. Each dimension is defined in terms of the primary purpose it serves, the dominant condition it addresses in the global economy, and the value trade-off or choices it entails. In sum, these dimensions determine *how* a firm generates and delivers its value proposition, *where* a firm locates it operations, and *by whom* a firm's value chain activities are performed.

The Technological Dimension: Generating the Firm's Value Proposition

The first of the three dimensions—technological—refers to those aspects of a firm's core competencies focused primarily on achieving long-term productive performance. It encompasses the constellation of activities and management processes by which a firm generates, delivers, and continuously improves in the most cost-effective way its value proposition.

Primary purpose: Ensuring productive performance. "Productive performance" emphasizes not only a firm's conventional concerns for labor and capital productivity, but also the quality of its products and services and the speed at which it can bring new concepts to market and rethink and adapt them to changing markets.[16] It emphasizes ongoing innovation throughout the enterprise directed at improving and extending—to the point of reinventing— the value proposition. Innovation may show up as a new feature or extension to an existing product line, a new production platform, or possibly a wholly new business or business model or value proposition. This enlarges the concept of "productive performance" well beyond notions of "strategy implementation"[17] and "operational effectiveness."[18]

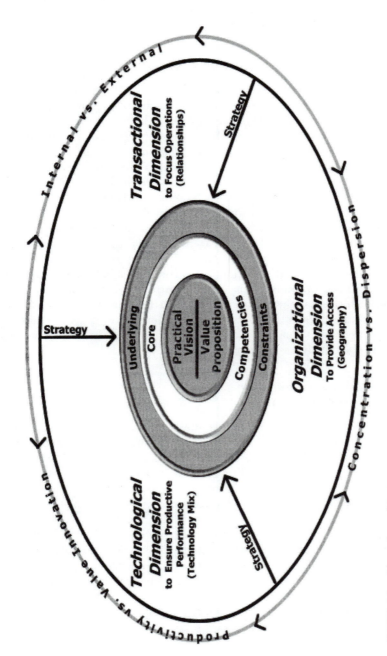

FIGURE 1.2. Dimensions of Strategy

Global conditions addressed: Unremitting technological innovation. Driven by the unremitting pace of technological development and convergence throughout the global economy, firms are forced continually to reassess and adjust their mix of technology applications in all aspects of their value propositions. Generic strategies provide little guidance, as they are largely static. Low-cost producers are overtaken by technology and innovations. Differentiated product today will soon be challenged in concept, as knockoffs inundate the market, and then will be bested on price by more efficient producers. So, like a modern-day Sisyphus, every firm in a globalizing market is condemned periodically—and sometimes in rapid succession, like Microsoft or Intel—to reformulate its product line as well as its technology mix.

Value trade-offs: Productivity versus innovation. A firm's technology mix reflects trade-offs not only in production, but also across its whole range of business functions and processes. To fully appreciate the nature and scope of these trade-offs, "technology" must be understood in the broadest and original sense: as the "science of techniques," of how to do work, or how to get things done. It is "the processes by which an organization transforms labor, capital, materials, and information into products and services of greater value."[19] Whether or not technology is proprietary, it runs through every primary and support activity in the value chain. Technology mix may shift, for example, as between labor and capital-intensive manufacturing, mass and customized production or marketing, high- and low-skilled staffing, or salaried and hourly or piecework compensation. Strategies that reflect particular technology mixes—and, therefore, trade-offs—bear such names as automation, lean production and management, direct marketing, just-in-time sourcing, and so on.

In general, a firm's technology mix plays out in two competing sets of value trade-offs. These value sets are but two sides of the same coin, intending to ensure the long-term productive performance of the firm. One set of trade-offs occurs at a firm's **"productivity frontier,"** reflecting the value delivered to the buyer and the relative cost to deliver it (Figure 1.3, left graphic). This frontier reflects a firm's operational effectiveness. Michael Porter defines it as consisting of "the sum of all existing best practices at any given time"; that is, "the maximum value that a company delivering a particular product or service can create at a given cost, using the best available technologies, skills, management techniques, and purchased inputs."[20]

A second type of trade-off (Figure 1.3, right graphic) occurs along what may be termed a firm's **"value innovation frontier."** Advances outward along the axes of this frontier are tangible expressions of two learning curves, each one represented by an axis. One learning curve (horizontal axis) is driven by new insight about existing and potential customer behavior and needs as well as by potential new market opportunities; the other (vertical axis) incorporates the "best practices" technology mix represented by Porter's productivity frontier as well as a firm's readiness to embrace the changing state-of-the-art as new and converging technology becomes available. As these two learning

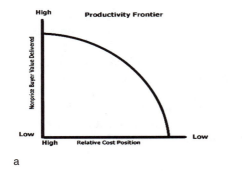
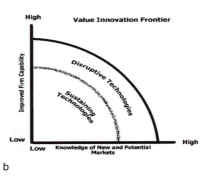

a   b

FIGURE 1.3. Technology Mix Frontiers
Sources: a) M. Porter, "What Is Strategy?" *Harvard Business Review*, November–December 1996.
b) Adapted from P. J. Williamson, "Strategy as Options on the Future," *Sloan Management Review*,
Spring 1999.

curves (axes) are integrated into a firm's operations, the value innovation
frontier moves outward. Structuring and managing a firm to incorporate new
market knowledge on an ongoing basis, therefore, is as much an investment
in its future as in improving its operational capability. See chapter 8, "Managing Knowledge in the Extended Enterprise," for further discussion of this
point.

Trade-offs for the technological dimension may be triggered by a wide
variety of circumstances—by shifting consumer values, relative changes in
production costs, and regulatory and deregulatory initiatives as well as by
technological innovations. They also may affect firms differently. A current
line of thinking, as depicted in Figure 1.3 (right side), divides these triggering
events between whether their impact on the firm and industry is sustaining or
disruptive. Sustaining technological developments, whether incremental or
breakthrough, tend to complement, improve, or extend existing product lines
in ways that cater to existing customers, while disruptive technological developments call for a redefinition of a firm's value proposition and market as
well as a significant rethinking of core competencies and their supporting
value network.[21] Intel's Grove referred to the latter as a firm's "strategic inflection point" (noted in the previous section). Thus, increasing the yield of
fault-free memory chips and introducing color TVs served to improve and
sustain the products among mainstream customers, while the technology of
PCs, mini–steel mills, and discount retailing disrupted and seriously weakened
or destroyed once-dominant industries. Similarly, deregulating the U.S. airline
industry has had disruptive effects.

The two frontiers of productivity and innovation necessarily work in
tandem. Entrepreneurship scholars term these frontiers the "creation/per-
formance" interface.[22] While firms need to remain on the edge of both,
others point out the "built-in conflict between trying to extract the greatest

**Box 1.1 How Firms Bridge the
Productivity-Innovation Interface**

- Where the technology is **sustaining** and, therefore, reinforces existing product lines and caters to mainstream customers:

    - Establish a rhythm of innovation, such as "continuous innovation," so that change can be paced, retraining can be scheduled, and employees have time to "buy in."
    - Use cross-functional task groups to assess and incorporate sustaining technologies into existing product lines.
    - Educate consumers as to the value of the improvements to meet their needs.
    - Adopt policies and practices, including a degree of slack in the organization, that encourage and reward innovative suggestions and feedback from customers and employers.

Where the technology is **disruptive** and, therefore, likely to challenge existing product lines and to require reinventing a value proposition and redefining the market:

    - House the innovative initiative in a separate unit with a budget, lines of authority, and choice of management systems that are independent of the mainstream businesses and appropriate to its mission.
    - Staff the new unit with strong entrepreneurial leadership and relevant technical expertise.
    - Provide the new unit with recognition and rewards distinctive to its mission and without penalizing failure when made in good faith.
    - Review the potential and results of the new unit from the viewpoint of a venture capitalist and not of an established business.

productivity out of existing operations and the willingness to make short-term sacrifices of efficiency to invest in innovations."[23] The conflict can be bridged, as suggested in Box 1.1, by appreciating that in an intensely competitive global economy, the only hope for sustainable competitive advantage is ongoing value innovation. Indeed, argue W. Chan Kim and Renee Mauborgne, firms should pursue value so exceptional that, as a result, comparison with competitors becomes irrelevant. Examples include CNN in news broadcasting; Wal-Mart in discount retailing; Home Depot in home improvement; SAP in business application software; IKEA in home products; Southwest Airlines in short-haul air travel; and Charles Schwab & Co. in investment and brokerage. The irony of competition, they conclude, "is it makes innovation indispensable, but an obsessive focus on the competition makes innovation difficult to attain."[24]

The Organizational Dimension: Gaining Access Worldwide

The second dimension of strategy focuses on trade-offs firms face as they build their value networks across the world. Where should they locate and how should they coordinate their assets and business functions in order to generate core competencies and build the value networks needed to deliver their value propositions? While this dimension is dominated by geopolitical, economic, and cultural considerations, it must ensure a harmonious interface for the firm's multilevel value chain. It encompasses both organizational structure and processes.

Primary purpose: Access to resources, technology, information, markets, and national endowments. The overriding purpose of the organizational dimension of strategy is to enable firms to gain specific locational advantages. These advantages parallel the motivations that have driven firms to expand overseas, noted earlier in the discussion of the various paths that lead firms to a global agenda. Forces of globalization are spurring firms to position themselves within countries and regions around the world in order to secure strategic assets and markets, heightened productivity and manufacturing efficiencies, scarce talent, attractive business climates, and industry intelligence. These are the country endowments and competitive advantages that matter among countries in the twenty-first century.

BMW and Daimler-Benz, for example, shed burdensome German labor regulations by establishing manufacturing operations in the southern United States. Deutsche Bank and Dresdner Bank gained prestige and know-how by acquiring London investment banks. Renault and Nissan built an alliance that combines their individual strengths—Renault's operational efficiencies and Nissan's auto designs—and geographical positions across four continents. Other firms have dispersed their operations in order to deprive a competitor of a country-specific market advantage, as when Caterpillar entered the Japanese market against Komatsu and Kodak did against Fuji Film. And many firms are offshoring production in China and India both to lower costs and ultimately to capture their large and growing markets. The importance of this strategic dimension is underscored by the dramatic rise in foreign direct investment (FDI) since the mid-1980s, outpacing increases both in international trade and world gross national product.

Global conditions addressed: Diversity among national regimes, their economies, institutions, and markets. For firms with global agendas, the organizational dimension is dominated by geography. The two-hundred-odd nations in the world today embody not only varying regulatory regimes and industry practices, but also have factor, operating, and market differences that can be tapped only through a firm's presence. To operate competitively with a global agenda, therefore, firms must be anchored in as well as integrated across local geography.[25]

The growth of global R&D networks provides a striking example of the transformative role of geography for firm strategy. Contrary to the accepted practice of concentrating R&D in the home country, an increasing number of firms in technologically intensive industries are locating their R&D function across a number of countries. Thus, Canon now has eight dedicated R&D facilities in five countries, Motorola has fourteen facilities in seven countries, and Bristol-Myers Squibb has twelve facilities in six countries. These decentralized networks enable firms to tap multiple sources of relevant knowledge around the world and integrate this knowledge speedily into product development and commercialization. The success of these networks depends on close cooperation among corporate and senior R&D managers.[26]

Value trade-offs: Dispersion versus coordination of assets. The trade-off for this dimension occurs as firms weigh the advantages and costs associated with dispersing or concentrating their assets, business functions and activities, decision points, and lines of authority. Coordination, it should be noted, is always a significant cost, for it requires the collection and assessment of relevant data, pooling of analysis and judgment in decision-making, and monitoring performance. It occurs within and across units and divisions as well as among affiliated enterprises and the various levels of these affiliates with headquarters. Coordination also entails making substantial investments in information technology (IT) equipment and operations as well as training, expenditures that will escalate as assets are dispersed around the globe. A 1997 McKinsey & Company study estimated that advances in IT would increase "the overall interactive capability in developed economies by a factor of two-to-five over the next five to 10 years."[27]

The complexity of this trade-off becomes immediately apparent when coupled with a firm's value chain and its array of multilevel business functions. Some functions, like marketing—or some aspects of these functions—should be localized (e.g., the Coke taste, training), while other functions (possibly finance) or their aspects (e.g., the promotion of Coca-Cola's logo) can and should be globally synchronized. Moreover, some functions can better be regionalized, for instance where consumer tastes, business practices, industry intelligence, or regulatory regimes have a common regional denominator different from the firm as a whole. This is increasingly possible in North America and Western Europe.

Whether a function is localized or regionalized, sound management requires that this be done using common standards, at least in some critical respects. Otherwise, it becomes difficult for firms to coordinate their operations or learn from country-specific results. The corollary to the global-local paradox noted by Porter, therefore, is its local-global converse: When firm assets and functions are dispersed to fit with local or regional circumstances, they must be coordinated to serve its global operating effectiveness (see Box 1.2).

**Box 1.2 How Firms Optimize Location
Advantages and Achieve Access**

1. In configuring the firm's operations across geography—

   - Clearly distinguish the activities and business functions in a firm's value chain and determine at what level (local, national, regional, global) they can be performed most cost-effectively.
   - Determine the comparative advantage to the firm of performing the various levels of each activity or function in one or more countries or regions. Consider carefully the adequacy of local institutions to support the firm's operations, for example, banking, accounting, technical, logistics, training, and so on.
   - For each possible location, assess what risks need to be hedged and the feasibility of hedging them.
   - Provide a clear and convincing design of the firm's (multilevel, geographically configured) operations, for example, HQ functions, locus of R&D, lead markets, regional production centers.

2. In coordinating a firm's operations, ensure global effectiveness through—

   - Common management systems, including common standards.
   - Clear lines of authority and reporting across the organization.
   - Common culture and mindset.
   - Effective IT and communication protocol.
   - Shared vision and story of firm destiny.
   - Common strategy and action plans.
   - Concentrating activities, as appropriate, for example, R&D, where personal interaction engenders creativity; and finance, where unified control and rapid decision-making is essential.

Finally, the strategic importance of configuring operations worldwide should be reflected in the different roles and responsibilities taken on by affiliates in a firm's overall network. Every multinational firm's asset map already reflects significant geographical diversity, including a residue of experience in certain countries or regions, an array of available resources, and hard-won insight into the changing world marketplace. Instead of treating all affiliates alike, therefore, firms can assign them complementary roles and tasks depending on their strategic location, resources, and capabilities. By way of example, Christopher Bartlett and Sumantra Ghoshal propose four different generic roles for affiliates. In countries of great strategic importance (largely because of the size of the market), affiliates with high levels of resources and capabilities should be "strategic leaders" in product development and commercialization, while those with low levels occupy a "black hole" and so can play at best a monitoring and intelligence role. In countries of low strategic importance, by contrast, affiliates can act either as "contributors" to a firm's overall R&D or manufacturing effort (given the high levels of their resources and capabilities) or simply be "implementers" given the market's limited potential and the corresponding low level of resources committed.[28]

The Transactional Dimension: Focusing Global Operations

The third dimension of strategy concerns the need for firms to focus their operations by off-loading the less critical activities. This not merely conserves capital, it also ensures that core competencies and ancillary processes are properly targeted and developed in depth. It requires firms to critically assess their full range of activities up and down the value chain—including suppliers and buyer channels, wherever they may be located—and determine which activities would best be internalized or externalized for long-term success. This may entail an overall reconfiguration of a firm's operations as well as reshaping its management tasks and style.

Primary purpose: Focus operations on core competencies. Deciding the focus of firm operations is a perennial issue for executives. The decision involves only in small part a cost-benefit analysis, that is, calculating the efficiency of performing an activity in-house or outsourcing it. Primarily, the decision is about strategy—about creating depth, extendibility, sustainability, and manageability of core competencies. These trade-offs may be far-reaching, especially as they relate directly to the other two dimensions. They require firms to be clear, in particular, about their competitive advantages—now and in the future—and the likely effects of trade-offs on the competitive structure of their industries.

On the other hand, firms may need to acquire assets or license-in technologies in order to develop or fill gaps in their core competencies. When NEC decided in the early 1970s to build its core competency around the convergence of computing and communications, for example, it entered into a myriad of discrete alliances with many other firms over many years in order to learn and absorb their know-how.[29] However extensive, firms must develop any number of "value networks" of suppliers and channel partners in order to develop and deliver their value propositions.[30] In a broader sense, says James Moore, firms should see these networks as being part of larger business "ecosystems" or mutually reinforcing industry environments, where disparate business elements are brought together "into new economic wholes from which new businesses, new rules of competition and cooperation, and new industries can emerge."[31] The competition that counts, therefore, is not firm versus firm, but business system versus business system or, as Benjamin Gomes-Casseres puts it, one alliance or network versus another.[32]

Global condition addressed: Intensifying competition. In the highly competitive, rapidly changing global environment, firms increasingly are able to most productively employ and effectively manage *only* those activities and assets most critical to their business. "Shareholder value," the battle cry of demanding investors worldwide, does not long tolerate weak-performing or stagnant operations. Due in large part to consolidation in the oil industry, for instance, the Royal Dutch/Shell Group is conducting a far-reaching global reorganization. It is purging its refineries and gasoline stations—from Japan to Portugal and Peru, and in the United States, from Delaware to California—in order to boost profitability.[33] Cost-reduction is a constant issue for most firms all along the value chain, as the worldwide outsourcing phenomenon reminds us.

But overall productive performance, not simply costs, is the heart of the issue. Seasoned managers as well as talented technical, logistical, and marketing personnel are a scarce and expensive resource with overhead costs of their own. Bureaucracies, moreover, can be costly, uncommunicative, and unresponsive, especially where turf battles exist or rewards are ambiguous. Cut off from the rigor of market discipline by internal hierarchies and obsolete routines, managers may become less sensitive to the need for responsive and innovative approaches. At the same time, falling information and communication costs, along with trade and market barriers, are reducing transaction costs and the costs of interaction among and within firms generally—costs that have hampered collaborative business relationships in the past.[34] Then, too, the rapidly changing technology landscape often preempts firms from long enjoying the exclusive benefit of their intellectual property. Externalization, therefore, is becoming attractive and even imperative in many cases.

Intense competition is forcing Sony, one of Japan's most innovative firms, to reorganize itself into a leaner and more integrated enterprise. Its consumer electronics business, accounting for two-thirds of its revenues, has faced increasingly stiff price competition, while coping internally with rivalrous and uncommunicative divisions. Further, Sony's attempt to wed proprietary content with its hardware has yet to yield a market advantage. Sony's stock price slid around 60 percent during 2000–2005, leading to the momentous decision in March 2005 to replace its CEO with Sir Howard Stringer, the Welsh-born head of its American operations. In order to increase its meager profit margins, Sony plans over the next two years to eliminate unprofitable products, close eleven of its sixty-five plants around the world, and reduce its workforce by seven percent, or approximately ten thousand jobs.[35] The intent is to realize scale economies and move Sony away from the Japanese penchant for manufacturing every part of a product to the last screw. Additionally, as part of its restructuring, Sony will abolish forty-five paid adviser positions—managers retained after retirement.[36] Perhaps most revealing, Sony has broken with its traditional "loner" approach by collaborating with other firms: with IBM to produce the "cell chip," an ultra-fast microprocessor; with Samsung Electronics to build a joint liquid-crystal display production line; with Bertelsmann in a music joint venture; and with Ericsson on a mobile aimed at business users.[37]

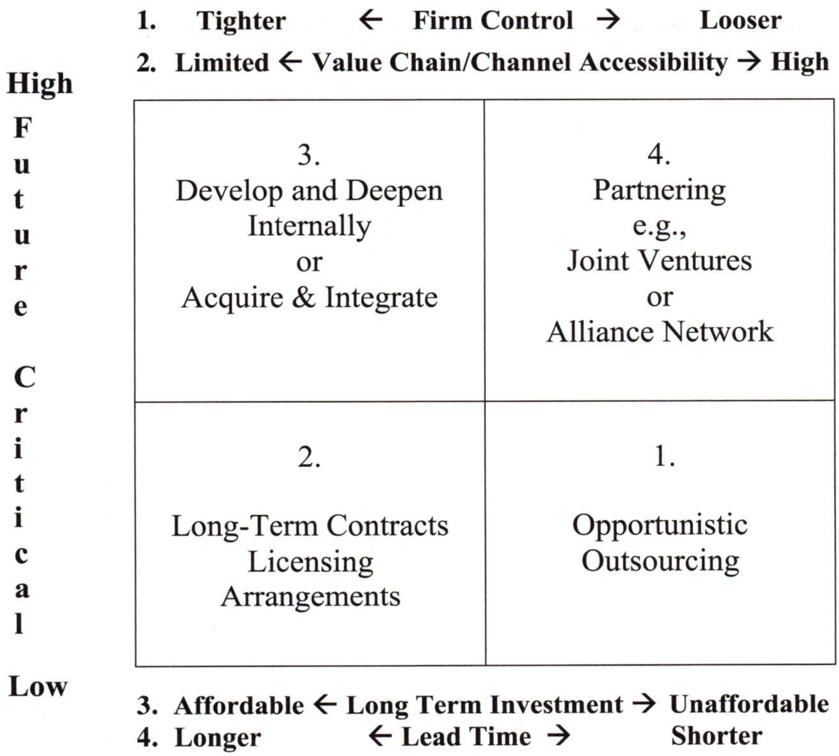

1. **Tighter** ← **Firm Control** → **Looser**
2. **Limited** ← **Value Chain/Channel Accessibility** → **High**

High	

| 3.

Develop and Deepen
Internally
or
Acquire & Integrate | 4.

Partnering
e.g.,
Joint Ventures
or
Alliance Network |
| 2.

Long-Term Contracts
Licensing
Arrangements | 1.

Opportunistic
Outsourcing |

Left vertical axis (top to bottom): High Future Critical Low

3. **Affordable** ← **Long Term Investment** → **Unaffordable**
4. **Longer** ← **Lead Time** → **Shorter**

FIGURE 1.4. Bridging Transactional Trade-Offs

Value trade-offs: Internalized operations versus external collaboration. As firms seek to focus and streamline their operations more cost-effectively, the "internal versus external" trade-offs they face can be complex as well as risky. The future is largely uncertain, yet the decisions are unavoidable. Firms will be guided by a number of competing considerations, as the conceptual framework in Figure 1.4 indicates. Chief among these, firms must determine which activities are critical and which ones are peripheral or nonessential for sustaining or developing its future competitive advantage. "Future critical" activities should be assigned "core competency" status. By contrast, a firm's existing strengths may not be essential for its future.

In general, "future critical" activities should be held closely and developed in-house to the extent feasible, while other activities are candidates for outsourcing. This determination, however, depends on a number of variables—four are identified in Figure 1.4 along the horizontal axis and discussed below. These **variables** in turn suggest a variety of options, depicted in the four quadrants. Risk as such is not included among these variables, for various types of risks are found in all options. It can be just as risky, for instance, not to invest overseas and thereby yield the market to competitors as to invest and take on the vagaries of a foreign partner and environment.

1. **Firm control over proprietary information and technology**. Tighter control is needed, for example, to counter weak intellectual property regimes, integrate new product features, or capture direct feedback from customers.

2. **Accessibility to critical supplier and buyer channels**. In a fast-changing industry, equity-based vertical integration is as likely to be a trap as a pre-emptive competitive advantage.

3. **Long-term affordability** for acquiring a competency or sustaining or developing it in-house. This assessment should be a factor, for instance, in the stage of a product's development and commercialization, the pace of techno-logical and market change, and the significance and reliability of scale economies over the long term.

4. **Lead time required** to launch new products or product generations. Could it be improved through outsourcing or collaborative arrangements?

Given these four variables, firms have **four broad options** for bridging value trade-offs in the transactional dimension, depending on the "future critical" importance of an activity to its operations. Each option, of course, must be tailored closely to the firm's distinctive situation.

- **Peripheral or nonessential activities** (quadrants 1 and 2) generally are not "future critical." They lend themselves, therefore, to outsourcing—guided by cost-effectiveness.[38] They may be managed opportunistically through the market (quadrant 1), unless they need to be closely controlled or tightly in-tegrated into core activities or access to them is likely to be limited or pre-empted by competitors. Where these exceptions rule (quadrant 2), firms will likely turn to long-term supply or buyer channel (contractual) arrangements or license-in technology in order to limit costs while stabilizing their external environment. On the other hand, where supply is readily accessible, lead time is short, and investment levels are high but transaction costs are manageable (quadrant 2), firms are likely to source their needs opportunistically. These activities are market commodities for the most part.

- **"Future critical" or core activities**, including closely related competen-cies, on the other hand, call for a longer-term perspective and investment commitment. These activities are deemed essential to a firm's long-term competitive advantage. Where the level of investment needed to develop these competencies is affordable to the firm over the long term (quadrant 3), they normally will be developed wholly in-house or added through acquisitions or licensed-in technology. This serves not only to protect a firm's intellectual property, but gives the firm the control needed to incorporate market feedback and evolving technology and to pace product upgrades. This is common practice for software firms—similar to Coca-Cola's concentrate formula—that wish to maintain strict secrecy of their source codes. As the requisite level of investment becomes less affordable or the pace of technology cuts lead times dramatically (quadrant 4), firms are forced to look outside for partners in order to pool assets or technology or build channel strengths (distributorships, franchising). With the loss of internal control comes increased risk for intellectual property, for the risks in external dealings can be offset only in part by contracts and reliable legal systems. Mutual equity investments may also be employed by the partners to reinforce working relationships, while providing them with management access and oversight of joint operations. Ultimately, however, the success of any joint venture or collaborative alliance depends largely on the enlightened self-interest of the parties in the success of the common venture.

The transactional dimension, therefore, opens up a rich array of working relationships, ranging from arm's-length to collaboration to full ownership. A clear distinction, however, must be drawn between these tactical relationships or "vehicles" and the strategic considerations that freight them. Strategy shapes the depth, scope, and future of a firm's core competencies, while tactics are concerned essentially with the best vehicle for implementing or extending these competencies—distributorships, licensing (in or out), franchising, long-term sourcing, minority investments, equity swaps, and a wide variety of joint ventures and other types of alliances. These tactical alternatives are used to structure an international expansion strategy once its objectives are clearly in mind. The various types of alliances formed by the Big Three U.S. auto companies with Japanese firms during the late 1960s and early 1970s, for instance, were undertaken not for the sake of themselves, but in order for these companies to better focus their operations through outsourcing to low-cost producers or, in some cases, to become familiar with and possibly insource Japanese management and operational practices and process technology improvements.[39] The New United Motor Manufacturing, Inc. (NUMMI) joint venture between GM and Toyota established in 1984 at Fremont, California is an example of the latter.[40]

Taken together, these three strategic dimensions constitute **a paradigm shift** for formulating strategy—not because they are new but because they must be seen and treated as inextricably interdependent for firms with global agendas. First, these three dimensions focus the firm's efforts on removing constraints to future operations, thus developing core competencies that will open doors to innovation and new opportunities. Accomplishing this requires both geographical as well as collaborative positioning. The dimensions are intended not only to obtain specific objectives, but to maintain a vigorous, robust organization. Second, each dimension necessarily incorporates facets both internal and external to a firm's operations. The ongoing debate on whether strategy is primarily market positioning or resource-based loses relevance. Finally, no strategy can be formulated without simultaneously affecting the other two dimensions. In developing a new product or service, a firm necessarily must determine not only the most productive mix of technology (productivity frontier), but also ensure its capability to continually enhance product value in light of new market potential (innovation frontier). This technology trade-off is affected in turn by the geography of markets and the optimum location of manufacturing plants (organizational dimension) as well as by an assessment of which competencies to develop in-house and which to develop through collaboration with providers of critical components (transactional dimensions). Whatever the strategy, it necessarily encompasses expressly or by implication all three dimensions.

STRATEGIC COMPETENCIES FOR GLOBAL MANAGERS

The strategy process and the three strategic dimensions provide a framework for formulating strategy in a global context. By implication, they entail new modes of management thinking and their competencies. Three of these management competencies—global perspective, aptitude for risk assessment, and open systems thinking—are discussed here in terms of the **skill sets** called for by the three strategic dimensions. These skill sets do not so much depict individual traits as the type of management style, thinking, and robust teamwork that firms will need in order to thrive in the global economy.

Skill Set I: Global Strategic Perspective

Any firm with a global agenda needs a global strategic perspective on every aspect of the strategy-making process. The CEO, of course, must lead the way, but the global perspective must be embedded throughout the organization. "Global leaders become globally civilized," remarks Howard Perlmutter, "to the degree they formulate a global vision they can communicate to a wide range of audiences around the world."[41] In point of fact, most CEOs are not educated or trained to have a global perspective. A McKinsey survey of two hundred managers in twenty large, globally oriented companies found that most managers tended to "assume away the complexity" of the global economy and "failed to see clearly" its opportunities and risks. Most managers in these firms operate "as if opportunities are bounded by geographic constraints."[42]

Above all, a global strategic perspective consists of a value framework for **understanding in real time** how the competitive, market, technological, and environmental (economic, political, and cultural) forces are shaping an industry worldwide. This is only the starting point, however, for the real issue is to understand how an industry is being restructured globally and the forces behind the restructuring. Since the 1990s and the fall of communism, the baseline for this framework in general has been the dynamics of the market system, subject to a wide variety of (sometimes conflicting) regulatory checks and balances imposed by national governments. This diversity offers perceptive managers an ever-changing kaleidoscope of opportunities.

The following three skills enable managers to employ their global perspective.

1. **Opportunity Scanning** (Technological Dimension). Global perspective enables managers to see the ongoing convergence and dissemination of technology as it impacts a firm's innovation frontier. It provides firms an "early-mover" advantage, enabling them to preempt opportunities (or threats) by repositioning their firms, where others see only overwhelming complexity. Compare the viewpoints of two mass merchants. Wal-Mart, for instance, sees opportunity in overseas operations: "We are confident," said its CEO David Glass, "that the Wal-Mart concept is 'exportable'... [through] 'global learning.'"[43] Whereas Sears CEO Arthur Martinez saw only a "degree of complexity" and an "order of difficulty [that] is geometric." With this worldview, Sears—once an international mass merchant leader—gradually exited its foreign operations.[44] In the financial sector, by contrast, Citibank saw an opportunity in Southeast Asia early on, introducing its credit card while others held back. Similarly, undeterred by the financial crisis of the late 1990s, GE Capital saw opportunity in the bargain asset prices of financial service firms in the region and aggressively entered the Asian market. In both cases, Citibank and GE were leveraging geographically the scope of an existing competitive advantage.

For global scanning to work, firms must be open to what Peter Senge terms "a shift of mind... from seeing ourselves as separate from the world to connected to the world." They must be open to test and update their vision and value proposition, "continually discovering how they create their reality. And how they can change it."[45] Thus, Ericsson became a leader in telecommunications switching in the 1980s because it was open and alert to the technological advances generated by engineers in its Australian subsidiary.[46] Motorola, however, grasped too late Nokia's challenge—coming out of nowhere from a small, distant country—to its competitive position in cellphones. Scanning, moreover, applies as much to technology as to geography. Sony demonstrated this ability by innovatively crossbreeding microprocessors with game machines for its PlayStation in the 1990s. Ten years later, Sony is seeking to shrug off ingrained internal turf habits and build the next-generation products around self-designed chips and software that cannot be easily copied.[47]

2. **Valuing Societal Differences** (Organizational Dimension). Global perspective strengthens the organizational dimension as managers appreciate the deep-seated sociological differences that distinguish societies and the way their markets and market systems function. Recognizing societal differences, for instance, led Fiat to assemble a team of engineers from Argentina, Brazil,

Poland, and Turkey—all with experience designing vehicles for poor roads—
to develop a new car for emerging markets.[48] Firms such as General Electric
and Microsoft, on the other hand, have learned the hard way that antitrust
laws, while invented in the United States, can vary significantly in their application in other jurisdictions such as the European Union.

Equally important, global perspective enables managers to better judge how
to disperse and where to concentrate assets and suppliers, which markets or
combinations of markets to target, and the type of entry positions most likely
to succeed. Markets, including product and service features as well as marketing channels, are deeply embedded in the socioeconomic environments of
countries, as chapter 2, "Marketing across the World," clearly demonstrates.
Business cultures as well differ enormously, as Microsoft has discovered when
it tried to pursue its typical confrontational approach in China for combating
software piracy (discussed more fully in chapter 7, "Managing Country Risk").
Indeed, given the globalization of the workforce for some skills[49] and the spread
of outsourcing and offshoring through informational technology, managers
need to be able to assess the distinctive capabilities of workforces around the
world.

3. **Building Value Networks** (Transactional Dimension). Successful value
networks are built around an astute assessment of the distinctive technical and
managerial capabilities that exist among network partners and of their widely
differing operating environments. A global perspective is essential, for the
choice of partners depends vitally on their ability to deliver quality product or
service in a timely and reliable way, preferably over the long term. This in turn
entails an appreciation of widely varying regulatory environments, business
cultures, managerial styles, and work ethics. Similar assessment skills are
valuable internally as well among affiliated units, as exemplified by Ericsson's
success with telecom switching (see above, "Opportunity Scanning"; see also
the discussion of value networks in chapter 3, "Managing Global Supply
Networks.")

Skill Set II: Aptitude for Risk

Part and parcel of a firm's global strategic perspective is the ambiguity,
complexity, and enormous range of choice—and thereby of risk—that accompanies any attempt to exploit opportunities. In this context, "risk" is not
simply the financial or conventional commercial risks of operating internationally, although these are an important part of the entire equation. Equally
important is the strategic risk of misreading the direction of the market;
moving too quickly or too slowly on new opportunities; investing too little or
too much too soon or too late in R&D, market research, or product development; overpromising and underdelivering product quality; and giving priority to the wrong countries and markets or allying the firm with the wrong
partners. In a fast-changing environment, doing nothing may entail more risk

than doing something, however inadequate. Sears was overtaken by competitors in its major overseas markets (Brazil, Mexico, Spain), for instance, due to its failure to invest aggressively. In a global environment, where firms are competing against the world's best, tolerance is low for faulty decision-making. Ultimately, the real risk lies in misdirecting and misusing scarce assets and valuable human resources, while the competition moves to occupy strategic high ground and preempts market space and partners.

"It is perverse," notes Gary Hamel, "that in many companies billion-dollar commitments to moribund businesses can be thought of as 'safe,' while Lilliputian experiments are viewed as risky."[50] In the end, "companies don't need more risk takers; they need people who understand how to de-risk big aspirations."[51] To a large extent, therefore, this competency consists of employing proven risk principles. First, disaggregate risks into understandable or familiar components and levels of uncertainty. For instance, determine whether the risk lies in the unproven nature of the technology, in the product design, in the uncertainty of the market, or in a firm's limited capabilities. Is the technology "sustaining" or "disruptive," how stable or turbulent is the environment,[52] and how clear or ambiguous is the future?[53] In most cases firms have a competitive advantage when dealing with familiar risks. Next, prioritize and evaluate risks in terms of a firm's future. What are the opportunity costs and benefits of an initiative if pursued? Would the initiative provide a firm with a distinct competitive advantage? Finally, design strategies that foster or extend core competencies that are critical to the firm's future.

Risk competencies concur with the three strategic dimensions.

Time-Pacing (Technology Dimension). Firms can manage risk by scheduling their deployment of technology. Time-pacing seeks to pace the introduction of new technologies and products in keeping with a predictable rhythm for a firm and its industry. This enables a firm to "counteract the natural tendency of managers to wait too long, move too slowly, and lose momentum."[54] In effect, time-pacing turns the notion of forced obsolescence into a management discipline. Instead of waiting for external events to force change—whether stemming from the market, a shift in technology, or poor financial performance—firms adopt a proactive tempo for refreshing, extending, or reinventing a product line or some aspect of their core competency. They also may populate their core competencies with technologies in various stages of development, pacing and increasing investments as the technologies prove themselves. Pacing may be used as well to highlight a firm's products, put pressure on competitors, or promote a climate of innovation and overcome resistance to change.

Location Leveraging (Organizational Dimension). In one sense, leveraging location simply means creating space for entrepreneurship to thrive. Firms do this with "skunk works" in order to insulate a potential product from the incursion and biases of established operations. In a global context, firms also can use differences in national endowments to ameliorate risk. Siemens, for instance, turned its expatriate-dominated compound in northern Beijing into an R&D center where indigenous Chinese engineers are given the freedom to redesign Siemens mobile phones for low-end markets in China as well as the Middle East and Eastern Europe.[55] Not only has this decision substantially reduced Siemens's product development costs and lead time, the cellphone design meets Siemens's high standards and is much more attuned to the targeted market segment.

Firms also may leverage geography and manage risk by applying the concept of **arbitrage**—found in financial markets—to the real economy of factors, technology, and products. In addition to exploiting price differentials among markets, arbitrage in the real economy enables firms to leverage their capabilities or advantages in one country by employing them in another. Employing its capabilities from one market in another, a firm may introduce a slightly altered product, employ its technology in an innovative way, lower manufacturing costs, or generate value chain efficiencies by partnering or combining disparate businesses. Through "callback" systems introduced in the 1990s, for example, intermediaries successfully exploited drastically lower U.S. rates to capture lucrative segments of foreign long-distance markets. Over time, however, arbitrage tends to eliminate the underlying opportunity as imitators pile on, market rigidities are eliminated (e.g., markets are deregulated), or, as occurred in Hong Kong, when the government intervenes to preempt the business opportunity.[56] For arbitrage to work successfully, firms need good intelligence networks and the capability to move into and exit opportunities rapidly at acceptable costs.

Risk-Sharing (Transactional Dimension). Risk also can be managed through sharing or off-loading approaches. Risk-sharing is typically found in joint venturing and R&D pooling arrangements, and is often factored into long-term supplier contracts, licensing, and a variety of subcontracts and alliances. In the longer term, collaborative networks can lower risk by sharing the costs of innovation, product development, and market insight. But networks bring risks of their own, including dependency and substantial demands on management. Their effectiveness requires careful attention to nurturing and monitoring relationships, communication and coordination among the partners, and ensuring that the results and learning from partnerships are integrated into a firm's operations.

Emphasizing intangible assets also can serve to off-load risk, for it enables firms to focus capital on competencies and less on bricks and mortar. Indeed, in the knowledge economy, a strong case can be made that "intangible assets are the core of building superior value propositions" and, ultimately, of shaping any global industry.[57] Major international hotel chains, for instance, have long leveraged their marketing and management systems and know-how by mobilizing investor interest in local facilities. Coca-Cola's success as a global enterprise stems largely from the way it has built and leveraged, and continues to manage, its partner network of locally owned bottling and delivery plants around the world. In contrast to Pepsi, with 17 percent of the global soft drink market, Coke, with almost 50 percent of this global market, owns very few physical assets. As a result, Coke is able "to focus ever greater investment into its proprietary intangible assets—brands, marketing skills, global talent—to gain intangible scale economies and to generate specialization effects, particularly in marketing."[58]

Skill Set III: Open Systems Thinking

"Open systems thinking" describes the ability of managers and firms to understand and work holistically with the interplay of economic, political, and cultural forces that are shaping their environment and organization. "Systems thinking," notes Peter Senge, is "a discipline for *seeing wholes*, . . . a framework for seeing *relationships* rather than things, [and] for seeing *patterns of change* rather than static 'snapshots'" (emphasis added).[59]

Indeed, systems thinking is the cornerstone of strategic competency for the global enterprise. It provides the dynamic context and a body of knowledge and tools for recognizing the "*underlying structures and patterns of behavior* that are obscured in the fury of daily events and the incessant activity that characterizes the manager's life" (emphasis added).[60] In devising and implementing global strategy, firms need to appreciate that their initiatives are both affected by and likely to affect other parts of their value chain, their industry, and the larger environment. This means that firms need to integrate external (environmental) and internal (firm-specific) aspects of all three strategic dimensions.

The competencies required for open systems thinking run throughout the three dimensions of strategy.

Continuous Learning (Technological Dimension). For systems thinking to result in strategic learning, it must be embedded in the habits, structure, and decision-making processes of an organization. Creating a learning organization, reasons BP's group chief executive John Browne, it is necessary "to instill the belief that competitive performance matters—that producing value is everyone's job . . . [and] that, individually and collectively, [BP's employees] could control the destiny of our businesses." The top management team, therefore, "must stimulate the organization, not control it, . . . provide strategic directives to encourage learning, and make sure there are mechanisms for transferring the lessons."[61] There also must be mechanisms for collecting and embedding this learning in the institutional memory of the organization.

To ensure a long-term perspective, moreover, firms ultimately must build in a cycle of renewal that involves every level of the organization, as incorporated in the strategy process previously discussed in this chapter. This cycle, says Henry Mintzberg, is not a substitute for the learning and innovative thinking that occurs on a day-to-day basis in an organization.[62] Rather, the strategy process provides periodically the opportunity for firms to step back from day-to-day operations, take stock of the environment, examine working assumptions, assess and consolidate breakthrough initiatives, and set markers for the future of the enterprise. Strategic planning should not be allowed to become a bureaucratic or wearisome activity or lock a firm into rigid goals. Instead, says BP's Browne, strategic planning should be "designed to keep ideas flowing and to stimulate thinking" both within and across business groups, and to "help us constantly reexamine what we are doing" relative to the world and our competitors.[63]

Holistic Analysis (Organizational Dimension). In a global organizational context, where market, governmental, and other societal differences are rapidly shifting over time, holistic analysis offers both a discipline and a source of leverage. As a discipline, it cautions managers to see—as transparently as possible—the interrelation among events, decisions, and actions and the underlying structures that are shaping the relationships. Thomas Friedman provides a lexicon of images for understanding how forces of globalization have achieved a momentum of their own that firms and countries alike cannot escape.[64] Either nations adopt or adapt to the "golden straightjacket" of free market capitalism and the institutions that channel and discipline its forces or they pay a significant economic price. The Asian crisis of 1997–98 became a proving ground for this discipline.

Holistic analysis also entails a shift of mind—from seeing parts to seeing wholes and from seeing things to seeing relationships. Learning confronts us with a dilemma, notes Senge, for "we learn best from experience but we never directly experience the consequences of many of our most important decisions."[65] Firms pay a heavy price for short-term leadership that neglects R&D and innovation in favor of this year's bottom line or heralded acquisitions that often become a successor's headache. This underscores the importance of strategic decision-making that embraces the views of more than one generation of managers. Moreover, the world pays a heavy price if business decisions ignore externalities. To overcome shortsightedness, the Forest Stewardship Council brings together activists with Home Depot, Lowe's, and other major building suppliers to replace potentially destructive environmental practices with industry-wide collaboration built around ecologically sound lumbering and timber management practices.[66]

Finally, holistic thinking provides the insight needed to discern new opportunity horizons. In the fast-paced global economy, as Moore suggests, success is not concerned so much with "what is" but with "what could be," seeing innovative value propositions within emerging "business ecosystems," where new technologies, unserved markets, and existing industries are converging.[67] In this context, new opportunity horizons arise from looking beneath traditional industry paradigms and market segments for innovations that can lead to enduring advantages. NEC saw this horizon in its C&C strategy of combining computers and communication; Microsoft in its Windows operating system; Matsushita in preempting the industry standard for its VHS video recording system; and Sony in marrying video games with microprocessors and software partners. In each case the new value proposition became the rallying point for recruiting an interdependent network of partners and "co-evolving" a new business ecosystem.

Collaborative Leadership (Transactional Dimension). The systems challenge for collaborative leaders is to ensure that all members of a network—whether wholly internal or external, or some combination of these—function in a mutually beneficial way. To do this the network leader (also termed the "flagship firm,"[68] "network orchestrator,"[69] or "global network corporation")[70] has several challenges. First, network leaders need to foster network buy-in through a shared vision. This includes an encompassing value proposition as well as quality performance standards. Independent network members, however, typically do not share their core technologies, for they seek to maintain bargaining power within the network. Network leaders and members, therefore, should be skilled in systems thinking, so they can accurately assess their network interests and the conditions required for these interests to materialize.

Further, to function effectively, networks need a common language and architecture. At a minimum, network leaders need to establish a clear understanding of members' roles and responsibilities and a common operating and information platform for their interaction. Whether or not the platform is "gated"—as is Cisco's Connection Online for customers and partners and Schwab's online system for referring customers to its six thousand independent financial advisers—it is critical that it become the shared standard for the network.[71] In this way, network members gain access to cumulating knowledge, expertise, and innovation of their partners as well as to the efficiencies derived from a customized division of labor and sharing of assets. Finally, leaders need to manage the network in a way that promotes collaboration and actively nurtures trust among members. This entails monitoring and benchmarking member performance and enlisting open-ended relationships and feedback among members to promote innovation. At times, leaders may seek to discipline errant members, a practice that may raise antitrust concerns, as the Microsoft litigation demonstrates.

Networks, of course, will be organized very differently, depending on their origin, the industry, and the purpose served. In each case network architecture and leadership will be tailored to the need at hand. British Petroleum's network emerged, for instance, from an intractable effort to find a cost-effective means for producing oil and gas from smaller fields. When in-house efforts failed to achieve results on the North Sea's Andrew field, BP turned to a group of outside contractors. Instead of its usual approach of treating contractors as adversaries, BP decided to challenge them, working as an allied group, to come up with an innovative solution by giving them a financial interest in the project's success. Not only did the group generate a breakthrough on "how to develop the undevelopable," as BP put it, it met the extremely challenging cost target and completed its task more than six months early. As a result, this "alliance approach" for developing other oil fields spread throughout BP. The Andrew field project, says BP's group chief excutive Browne, "taught us a new way of doing things by building relationships to mutual advantage with a variety of people. It was a major watershed."[72]

As BP's Andrew oil field project suggests, the skills implied in all aspects of open systems thinking—continuous learning, holistic analysis, and collaborative leadership—run throughout the three strategic dimensions. Through its leadership, BP transformed an ad hoc group of outside contractors into a team of allies searching for an innovative solution that would accommodate global market requirements for the oil industry. In the course of this transformation, BP transformed its own modus operandi. This is the essence of systems thinking, including systems that at first appear to originate external to a firm.

Finally, open systems thinking and the collaboration it engenders calls for relationship-style management—a style that is at least as horizontally as it is hierarchically oriented. Far-flung enterprises, stretching across numerous affiliates and countries as well as partners and value networks, depend as much on well-developed working relationships as on head-to-head competition. This applies as much among members of a value network as among units within enterprises themselves. Mutually beneficial working relationships open lines of communication that expand the range of value-creating ideas and business opportunities. As management hierarchies flatten, firms are recognizing as well the need to devolve more decision-making authority to the front ranks in order to respond to customer needs and to gain the time-sensitive insight needed to stay abreast of the rapidly changing industry environment. Relationship-style management, whether practiced externally or internally, should seek to generate synergies among individuals, units, divisions, and affiliates of a firm as well as its partners.

CONCLUSIONS

This chapter has focused on the role of strategy in the emerging global economy. While firms may pursue any number of different strategic pathways during the course of this transition, some common attributes of formulating strategy in a global context are becoming discernible. One is the need for **an embedded cycle of renewal**, a disciplined process for formulating strategy that updates and clarifies a firm's global environmental interface, integrates the multiple levels and the functions required for seasoned decision-making, and takes into account a firm's evolving future and vision. As the value proposition and core competencies—forming the focal point of strategy—are constantly under pressure to innovate, strategy is always subject to review and reformulation.

Second, in the broad-ranging global context, strategy necessarily encompasses **three interdependent dimensions**—technological, organizational, and transactional. Each individually and the three taken together embody value trade-offs in a firm's operations, structure, and management style. These trade-offs incorporate both external (environmental) and internal (firm-specific) aspects, which for the most part cannot be treated independently from one another. The dimensions must be viewed holistically as a triad, for they are both complementary and interdependent facets of every strategy. A shift in the trade-offs of one dimension inevitably entails shifts in the others.

Third, in order for a global enterprise to function effectively, this threefold perspective on strategy entails a number of **management competencies**. Nine are discussed here under the headings global perspective, aptitude for risk, and open systems thinking. Of these, open systems thinking forms the capstone. Like the three strategic dimensions themselves, these competencies are necessarily complementary. Management teams, taken as a whole, should embody them all in substantial depth.

NOTES

1. Kenichi Ohmae, *The Borderless World: Power and Strategy in the Interlinked Economy* (New York: HarperCollins, 1990); and K. Ohmae, *The End of the Nation State: The Rise of Regional Economies* (London: R. R. Bowker, Reed Elsevier, 1998).

2. M. E. Porter, "Competing across Locations: Enhancing Competitive Advantage through a Global Strategy. In M. E. Porter, *On Competition* (Boston: Harvard Business School Press, 1998), 23.

3. A. Rugman, "Multinational Enterprises Are Regional, Not Global," *Multinational Business Review*, 11, no. 1 (2000): 3–12.

4. Compare, for instance, the motivation typologies of Jack N. Behrman, *The Role of International Companies in Latin America: Autos and Petrochemicals* (Lexington, MA: Lexington Books, 1972); and of John H. Dunning, *Multinational Enterprises and the Global Economy* (New York: Addison-Wesley, 1993).

5. C. A. Bartlett and S. Ghoshal, *Managing across Borders: The Transnational Solution,* 2d ed. (Boston: Harvard Business School Press, 1998), 256.

6. "The House that Jack Built," *The Economist* (September 16, 1999).

7. G. Hamel, *Leading the Revolution* (Boston: Harvard Business School Press, 2000), 10.

8. C. K. Prahalad and G. Hamel, "The Core Competence of the Corporation," *Harvard Business Review* (May–June 1990): 79–91.

9. Andrew S. Grove, *Only the Paranoid Survive* (New York: Currency/Doubleday, 1996), 93.

10. C. Argyris and D. A. Schon, *Organizational Learning: A Theory of Action Perspective* (Reading, MA: Addison-Wesley, 1978).

11. Bartlett and Ghoshal, *Managing across Borders.*

12. Grove, *Only the Paranoid Survive,* 32–35.

13. Cliff Edwards, "Inside Intel," Business Week (January 9, 2006), 46–54.

14. Ibid., 27–35. Grove looks for "major changes . . . taking place in the balance of [six] forces," that is, "the power, vigor and competence" of a company's *existing competitors, potential competitors, suppliers, customers, substitutes* ("the most deadly of all," such as new techniques, new approaches, or new technologies) as well as *complementors,* providing products or services that may have your products work better (e.g., software).

15. Ibid., 96.

16. See M. L. Dertouzos, R. K. Lester, R. M. Solow, and the MIT Commission on Industrial Productivity, *Made in America: Regaining the Productive Edge* (Cambridge: MIT Press, 1989).

17. W. G. Egelhoff, "Great Strategy or Great Strategy Implementation: Two Ways of Competing in Global Markets," *Sloan Management Review* (winter 1993): 37–50.

18. M. Porter, "What Is Strategy?" *Harvard Business Review* (November–December 1996): 61–78.

19. C. M. Christensen, *The Innovator's Dilemma: When New Technologies Cause Great Firms To Fail* (New York: HarperCollins, 2000), xiii.

20. Porter, "What Is Strategy?" 62.

21. C. M. Christensen and M. R. Raynor, *The Innovator's Solution: Creating and Sustaining Successful Growth* (Boston: Harvard Business School Press, 2003).

22. M. A. Hitt, "Strategic Entrepreneurship: Integrating Entrepreneurial and Strategic Management Perspectives," in M. A. Hitt, R. D. Ireland, S. M. Camp, and D. L. Sexton, *Strategic Entrepreneurship: Creating a New Mindset* (Malden, MA: Blackwell Publishers, 2002), 3.

23. S. Ghoshal, C. A. Bartlett, and P. Moran, "The New Management Manifesto Challenges Market Forces and Creates New Value," *Executive Excellence* 17, no. 11 (November 20, 2000): 10–11.

24. W. C. Kim and R. Mauborgne, "Strategy, Value Innovation, and the Knowledge Economy," *Sloan Management Review* (spring 1999): 41–54, p. 49.

25. Porter, "What Is Strategy?"

26. W. Kuemmerle, "Building Effective R&D Capabilities Abroad," *Harvard Business Review* (March–April 1997): 61–70, p.69.

27. P. Butler, T. Hall, A. Hanna, L. Mendonca, B. Auguste, J. Manyika, and A. Sahay, "A Revolution in Interaction," *McKinsey Quarterly* 1 (1997): 4–23. (Internet source). The study finds that "interactions make up a large part of even an industrial company's activities; in one U.S. electric utility, 58% of all employee activity could be attributed to interactions." By "interactions" is meant "the searching, coordinating, and monitoring that people and firms do when they exchange goods, services, or ideas," including "management meetings, conferences, phone conversations, sales calls, problem solving, reports, memos."

28. Bartlett and Ghoshal, *Managing across Borders*.

29. Prahalad and Hamel, "Core Competence."

30. Christensen and Raynor, *Innovator's Solution*, 44.

31. James Moore, *Death of Competition: Leadership and Strategy in an Age of Business Ecosystems* (New York: HarperCollins, 1997), 12.

32. B. Gomes-Casseres, "Group Versus Group: How Alliance Networks Compete," *Harvard Business Review* 72, no. 4 (July–August 1994): 62–67.

33. M. Long, "Shell Sheds Refineries, Gas Stations," *Wall Street Journal*, August 31, 2004, B3.

34. Butler et al., "Revolution in Interaction"; and B. Anand, T. Khanna, and J. W. Rivkin, *Market Failures* (Boston: Harvard Business School Press, 2000).

35. "Stringing Along," *The Economist* (September 29, 2005); "Can Stringer Stop Sony Malfunctioning?" *The Economist* (March 8, 2005).

36. Reuters News Service, "Sony to Cut Advisers as Part of Restructuring," *Wall Street Journal*, February 23, 2006, B9.

37. P. Landers, "Silver Lining? Amid Japan's Gloom, Corporate Overhauls Offer Hints of Revival—Companies Shed Units, Grow More Nimble," *Wall Street Journal*, February 21, 2002, A1; Magnus Hansson, "Sony Ericsson Delays New Phone," *Wall Street Journal*, February 7, 2006, B6; Ethan Smith, "Sony, Bertelsmann Take Step To Mend Rift at Music Venture," *Wall Street Journal*, February 11, 2006, A4.

38. When considering cost-effectiveness, the costs of cross-border operations can be quite substantial. Simply the cost of *processing* trade documentation, for instance, is estimated to be more than 5 percent of the total annual value of world trade. See D. Furlonger, "Trade Finance Struggles To Move from Parchment To Internet," Garnter G2 Research (June 19, 2002). Add to this: the uncertainties present in the international environment—including varying exchange rates, business cultures, work ethics, and legal standards—then transactional costs for firms sourcing or selling quality-critical components across a number of countries may increase geometrically.

39. M. Y. Yoshino and U. S. Rangan, *Strategic Alliances: An Entrepreneurial Approach To Globalization* (Boston: Harvard Business School Press, 1995).

40. S. E. Weiss, M. T. Hogan, J. W. Chai, E. J. Meigher, E. F. Glynn, and D. C. Cuneo, "The General Motors–Toyota Joint Venture, 1982–1984," *International Negotiation* 1, no. 2 (1996): 277–92.

41. H. V. Perlmutter, "Becoming Globally Civilized: Managing across Culture," *Financial Times* 6, no. 12 (December 1, 1995): XII.

42. L. Bryan, J. Fraser, J. Oppenheim, and W. Raff, *Race for the World: Strategies to Build a Great Global Firm* (Boston: Harvard Business School Press, 1999), 135–36.

43. Letter to Shareholders, 1994 and 1999 Annual Reports, Wal-Mart Stores, Inc.

44. As quoted by J. L. Johnson, "Sears Questions Global Quest," *Discount Merchandiser* 35, no. 2 (February 1995), 10.

45. P. Senge, *The Fifth Discipline: The Art and Practice of the Learning Organization* (New York: Currency Doubleday, 1990), 12–13.

46. Bartlett and Ghoshal, *Managing across Borders*.

47. P. Dvorak, "Videogame Whiz Reprograms Sony after 10-Year Funk," *Wall Street Journal*, September 2, 2004, A1.

48. "Over the Rainbow: Cultural Diversity in the Workplace Is Good Business," *The Economist* (November 20, 1997).

49. See the report by members of the McKinsey Global Institute: D. Farrell, M. Laboissiere, R. Pascal, J. Rosenfeld, C. de Segundo, S. Stuerze, and F. Umezawa, *The Emerging Global Labor Market* (June 2005).

50. G. Hamel, *Leading the Revolution* (Boston: Harvard Business School Press, 2000), 266.

51. Ibid., 267.

52. R. A. D'Aveni, "Strategic Supremacy through Disruption and Dominance," *Sloan Management Review* (September 1999): 127–45.

53. K. P. Coyne and S. Subramaniam, "Bringing Discipline To Strategy," *McKinsey Quarterly* 4: 61–70; and H. Courtney, J. Kirkland, and P. Viguerie, "Strategy under Uncertainty," *Harvard Business Review* (November–December 1997): 66–79.

54. K. M. Eisenhardt and S. L. Brown, "Time Pacing: Competing in Markets That Won't Stand Still," *Harvard Business Review* (March–April, 1998): 59–69, p. 60.

55. M. Karnitschnig, "Vaunted German Engineers Face Competition from China," *Wall Street Journal*, July 15, 2004, A1.

56. G. Lynch, "Hong Kong's Bargain Basement IDD Sale," *Telecom Asia*, 10, no. 2 (February 1999): 10.

57. Bryan et al., *Race for the World*, 177–79. See also: Kim and Maubourgne, "Strategy, Value Innovation, and the Knowledge Economy," *Sloan Management Review* (spring 1999): 41–54.

58. Bryan et al., *Race for the World*, 55.

59. Senge, *Fifth Discipline*, 68.

60. Ibid., 364.

61. S. E. Prokesch, "Unleashing the Power of Learning: An Interview with British Petroleum's John Browne," *Harvard Business Review* 75, no. 5 (September–October 1997): 157–58.

62. H. Mintzberg, "Crafting Strategy," *Harvard Business Review* (July–August 1987): 66–75.

63. Prokesch, "Unleashing the Power," 168.

64. T. L. Friedman, *The Lexus and the Olive Tree* (New York: Farrar, Straus and Giroux, 1999).

65. Senge, *Fifth Discipline*, 23.

66. G. Gereffi, R. Garcia-Johnson, and E. Sasser, "The NGO-Industrial Complex," *Foreign Policy* (August 2001): 56–65.

67. Moore, *Death of Competition*.

68. A. M. Rugman and J. R. D'Cruz, *Multinationals as Flagship Firms: Regional Business Networks* (Oxford: Oxford University Press, 2000).

69. R. Häcki and J. Lighton, "The Future of the Networked Company," *McKinsey Quarterly* 3 (2001): 26–39.

70. Yoshino and Rangan, *Strategic Alliances*.

71. Häcki and Lighton, "Future."

72. Prokesch, "Unleashing the Power," 157.

2

Marketing across the World

ALFRED S. RAIDER

DESPITE GLOBALIZATION, MARKET DEMAND
REMAINS STUBBORNLY LOCAL

Marketing has become the critical success factor in this wired and wireless world where goods and services can be moved around the world cheaply and efficiently. Technology has become the means to integrate aspects of different country markets into a virtual global marketplace. This global "marketing infrastructure," however, has not eliminated the challenges to marketing across borders. Local and country-specific cultures often result in fragmented demand, requiring enterprises to customize their product, services, and marketing campaigns accordingly. The constant threat from global competitors intensifies pressure on prices and for ongoing product improvement.

Marketing managers are squeezed, therefore, between the need to globalize their marketing infrastructure while demand remains stubbornly local. This is complicated by the appearance of homogenized markets throughout the world even though substantial differences remain submerged beneath the appearance of similarity. Thus, the squeeze is between those forces demanding a standardized approach to marketing in all markets and residual forces requiring that marketing be adapted for each and every individual market. How to balance standardization with customization is the key to navigating a world where differences are less conspicuous. In addition, the shift to marketing services as well as global advertising saturation require more complex marketing strategies sensitive to both the similarities and differences between consumers in each national market.

At the outset, it is logical to define the discipline of marketing and then place it in the context of globalization. The American Marketing Association's definition of marketing, adopted in 1985, reflects the broad concept of marketing that evolved through the twentieth century. "The process of planning and executing the conception, pricing, promotion and distribution of ideas, goods, and services creates exchanges that satisfy individual and organizational objectives."[1] The essence of marketing as currently practiced, therefore, is a feedback loop between buyers and sellers of goods, services, and ideas, designed to result in an exchange of value between the buyer and seller.

Historically, marketing has evolved from a narrow focus on the promotion and distribution functions to encompassing the entire length of the value chain. As it evolved, it began to encompass much more of the exchange between buyer and seller. Now marketing is no longer lodged in a department by itself, but permeates all functions of an enterprise. All managers must understand that they are involved in the marketing process no matter what their functions. It may be argued that for some organizations, marketing and brand management have become their primary functions. For instance, Sara Lee sold over one hundred factories in order to become a "mean, lean, marketing machine."[2] Nike outsources all of its manufacturing and focuses on its marketing of the Nike brand; yet its value chain is integrated from shoe design forward through shoe production and sales.

Viewed globally, rapid trade expansion since World War II has changed the marketing climate in a number of ways. Obstacles to trade have been lowered to relatively negligible levels, presenting relatively free access to most markets. This access has made it virtually impossible to shield national producers from global competition. Regional and global companies are free to compete with indigenous producers. Global producers are likely to have an advantage in both economies of scale as well as research and development. Local producers will have to face new competitors with large marketing budgets and a great deal of marketing experience. At the same time, new market entrants must learn to match the advantage of an indigenous producer.

Pinpointing the effects of globalization on marketing is difficult simply because they are so pervasive. Two perspectives may help. The first considers the effect globalization has had on markets themselves. The second is to assess how the process of marketing itself has been affected. These perspectives are inextricably linked because the process of marketing, primarily marketing strategy, is going to be affected by where and to whom one is marketing.

The Vast Village

It is often assumed that globalization's effect on markets themselves has been a march toward uniformity on a worldwide scale. In fact, the process of marketing in the current environment is far more complicated. To dispel this simplistic picture, for example, take a website featuring silk scarves in bright, vibrant colors. The process is a familiar one. The shopper clicks on various pictures of scarves to enlarge and examine them more closely. When a scarf is chosen for purchase, the shopper clicks on the order form, entering address and credit card information. The shipping costs are added to the final price and the sale is completed. The order is transmitted to the factory where the scarf is made and the order is fulfilled. On its face, this is an ordinary purchase over the Internet that is an everyday process in the early twenty-first century.

What is extraordinary about this particular transaction is that the electronic order for the scarves is transmitted to Rovieng, a small rural village in Cambodia without electricity or telephone service. Once the order is received, women in the village hand-produce the scarves. Rovieng has Internet access and a village website thanks to funding from an American aid organization. With solar panels powering desktop computers and a satellite dish linking them to the Internet, Rovieng has joined the global economy.[3] Although the Rovieng example is an unusual one, it is illustrative of the evolution that is taking place in the marketing of goods and services throughout the world. Marketing on a global scale used to be limited to large corporations that had a physical presence in many parts of the world. Now it is possible for the women of a small rural village in a developing country to market worldwide.

But this is only half the story, for across the Asian subcontinent five hundred thousand Indian villages are rapidly being equipped with satellite TV. While rural Indian households presently earn only half the income earned by urban households, many own their homes, and education and health care is mostly free. Moreover, the $30 billion aggregate spending power of these 826 million rural Indians is growing about 25 percent annually. It is being spent on everything from shampoo and household detergents to air conditioners. Says Vikram Kaushik, chief executive of Space TV (the new Tata-Star TV joint venture), "There is a huge market waiting to be tapped. No mass-market service can afford to ignore rural India today."[4] Due to communications technologies, a potentially vast village-to-village production and marketing network is emerging across the world.

New technologies and business methods are revolutionizing the practice of marketing. Marshall McLuhan used the term "global village" before the Internet and digital TV were ever conceived. He was prescient in perceiving in the 1960s, a world that could be accessed by a true village such as Rovieng. But reality has become even larger than the musing of an academic. McLuhan's global village is in fact a *vast village network spanning continents*. The global village network has arrived and its marketplace is becoming very different than the markets of the past. It is undercutting the assumption, as C. K. Prahalad argues so forcefully, that "the poor have no purchasing power and therefore do not represent a viable market."[5]

FIGURE 2.1. Technology Enables Villagers to Access Global Markets
Source: http://www.villageleap.com/

The Rovieng example highlights how globalization is changing the nature of markets. Open markets, technology that provides access to any market, any-time, at minimum cost, are all considered both the drivers and the indicators of the global marketplace. The real lesson of Rovieng is not the globalization of marketing so much as the globalization of the marketing infrastructure. The women of Rovieng are not global marketers, but rather villagers with access to global markets. These are very different things.

Globalization of the Marketing Infrastructure

The villagers in Rovieng sold their wares by accessing a global marketing infrastructure. Marketing infrastructure refers to the elements required to make a product or service, distribute it to the point of sale, and communicate its availability to potential buyers. As discussed in other chapters, the infra-structure to design and manufacture is global. An automobile may be designed in California for a Japanese company that has a factory in Europe. The ma-terials and parts required to manufacture that automobile will be acquired through a global supply chain network.

The distribution network to move that automobile to any market in the world is also global. Shipping companies with facilities all over the world can move something as bulky as an automobile in a relatively short time at a very reasonable cost. Even overnight deliveries of small parts are available in most parts of the world. Globalization has created an infrastructure that permits distribution of products virtually anywhere in the world. The Internet has created a global distribution network for both physical products as well those moved in electronic format, such as music or software. Global communications technologies have also made it possible to deliver services from virtually anywhere to anywhere.

The financial infrastructure has made it possible for buyers and sellers to do business almost anywhere in the world. Dealing in different currencies used to be an arduous task that only large companies could undertake. Now small companies and even individual consumers can deal in multiple currencies without much trouble. For instance, credit cards, now ubiquitous, allow consumers to charge purchases over the Internet in any exchangeable currency.

The Death of Distance

Finally, channels of communication to reach buyers are also global. The Internet serves as an efficient, inexpensive way to reach buyers anywhere in the world. Although some mass media is global, such as CNN, much of it remains localized. Most television and radio content is localized in order to appeal to the local market. However, global telecommunications have made it easy to utilize media, wherever located, to communicate a message to the local market. Both McLuhan and Theodore Levitt pinpointed trends that are driving the convergence of consumer wants and preferences across the globe. The most important of these is the global reach of telecommunications, which began with the telegraph and has evolved into a wired and, indeed, wireless world where voice, data, and video travel in 1's and 0's. The significance of this change cannot be overstated, for it has permitted different markets to share aspects of their culture and be subject to common cultural influences.

This reflects in part what has been called the "death of distance."[6] Globally available mass media give individuals in different nations some familiarity with one another's culture and lifestyle. Foreigners no longer seem so foreign. Music, entertainment, fashion, and fads now move across the globe instantaneously. This is in contrast to the lengthy lag that used to exist in moving from one market to another. The death of distance has made the process of marketing a much more challenging one.

Interactive technologies are a primary driver of marketing strategies, and these include both the telephone and the Internet. Indeed, based upon current trends, there is a convergence between the two that will render the distinctions meaningless. The death of distance radically levels the playing field for businesses. Managing international operations used to require huge investments in private networks and communications infrastructure. In 1985, Citibank, a pioneer in the use of global networks, reportedly spent over $100 million on linking its global operations using satellites and creating one of the first company-owned private global networks.[7] Through the Internet, Citibank can create the same global network for a fraction of its earlier cost. Thus, small and medium-sized enterprises can market their products and services in distant markets that were once prohibitively expensive. The leveling of the playing field for small business through technology has led to what has been termed the "micro-multinational," where a small business may have two employees in the U.S., eight in Spain, and two in Italy.[8]

The global nature of the Internet, in fact, creates complexity for marketers. It is no longer possible to isolate markets from one another. Buyers can now shop across borders. This makes it much more difficult to create inconsistent product positioning in different markets. Furthermore, while the Internet extends its reach globally, it is also evolving from a primarily English-based medium to a medium of many languages. In 1996, English speakers comprised 80 percent of the total population of Internet users.[9] In 2004 that figure fell to 36.2 percent.[10]

Ease of travel and the ubiquity of both one-to-one and mass media have led many to conclude that a company can market the same product, in the same way, to the same market segment anywhere in the world. This is a common misinterpretation of the effect globalization has had on marketing. It has caused many a misstep in marketing strategies. Bangladesh's proudest achievement, of late, is the completion of a new megamall that was modeled on the Mall of America. Within its confines, one could be in any mall in any developed country in the world.[11] However, that does not mean that marketers can approach Bangladesh in the same way they approach Minneapolis. While markets may look alike, they will reflect differences in consumer tastes and preferences and price points.

Rather than causing market differences and barriers to disappear, globalization has simply made them less visible. It is somewhat like the reef that disappears under the waves during high tide. The hazards to the ship become invisible, but they must nevertheless be taken into account lest the ship go aground. McLuhan's global village has come into existence, but it is more of a vast village network, encompassing a wide range of tribes and tribal differences that call for a subtle approach to marketing. Marketing managers must become sensitive to these subtle differences, and companies must become organized in a way that permits them to detect these differences.

The Illusion of Homogeneous Markets

In 1983, Theodore Levitt recognized that the multinational approach was being rendered obsolete by the convergence of markets. He envisioned a global corporation which "operates with resolute constancy—at low relative cost—as if the entire world (or major regions of it) were a single entity; it sells the same thing in the same way everywhere"[12] To some degree, Levitt was correct. As consumer preferences converge, it should be possible to market the same product in the same way around the world. After all, businesspeople in Japan, Europe, China, and elsewhere in the world dress similarly, buy many of the same brands, and watch many of the same movies. Based upon appearances, many cities around the world do look somewhat alike.

But the world has progressed beyond the vision of a homogeneous market. Tastes have become more fragmented. Worldwide, people are increasingly spending money in ways that reflect individual values, which in turn are embedded in their respective cultures. As such, global strategies based on

Box 2.1 Wal-Mart Learns To Adapt

Wal-Mart experienced many challenges when it opened stores in foreign markets, described by Constance Hays in the *New York Times* as "trying to transplant their stores without molding them to local custom." Wal-Mart stores failed to go over in Indonesia because they were well lit, well organized, and allowed no bargaining over price. Germans, on the other hand, dislike store greeters because they are considered personally invasive. Brazilians and Argentines were put off by Wal-Mart's lack of familiarity with their preferences for particular cuts of beef.[13] It has become clear that the transformation envisioned by Levitt is unlikely to become a reality.

uniform tastes have not lived up to their early billings.[14] Indeed, there is evidence that people around the world are continuing to hang on stubbornly to their own preferences despite all of these outside influences (see Box 2.1). Vodaphone found this to be the case with their operations in Japan, which is described in Box 2.2.

Demand for mobile phones also took an unexpected turn in China. Logic dictates that in a developing country like China, the demand for mobile phones would be different from a developed country such as Japan. However, the opposite is true. Despite the fact that China's demand for mobile phones has been growing at double digit percentages, Chinese manufacturers of mobile

Box 2.2 Vodaphone Stumbles in Japan

When Vodaphone acquired J-Phone, an up-and-coming wireless phone operator ranking third in Japan, expectations for the future were high. Within two years Vodaphone was losing subscribers and market share at a surprising rate.

Vodaphone's mistake was to approach Japan much as it had other markets. The company emphasized its global service and shifted its handsets to a standardized design it sold in other markets. These were phones designed primarily for voice with few bells and whistles. Vodaphone overlooked the fact that Japanese subscribers used wireless phones differently than subscribers in other markets. Japanese customers used their phones more for e-mail, text messaging, and playing games than for voice traffic. Japanese customers were less interested in Vodaphone's global capability, because they did not travel that much. While wireless service is viewed as being fairly standardized, and capable of being marketed using a standardized strategy, the Vodaphone example illustrates that significant differences persist and require a marketing strategy adapted to particular markets.[15] "Vodaphone's woes in Japan," caution Martin Packer and Ken Belson in the *New York Times*, "are a lesson in how global corporations can stumble if a sales agenda is pushed across national markets without heeding local quirks."[16]

phones have been floundering. Their products are low-cost, have a basic design, and few bells and whistles. It would seem that these phones should do well in China, with many consumers new to the mobile market. However, the demand has been for high-end phones with many advanced features made by foreign companies such as Nokia and Motorola. The basic model simply is not selling well.[17] In the automotive industry in China, by contrast, the low-cost, basic-model strategy has worked quite well. General Motors has emerged as the dominant player in China by offering a very basic minivan that gets good gas mileage and can be used for both family and business.[18]

THE CHANGING MARKETING MINDSET

Shift To Services

There is a marked shift in emphasis from selling products to selling services. Traditionally, companies sell products and make their profit from the sale. Now it is common to find instances where the sale of products becomes an excuse for selling a service. Buy an automobile in the United States and the buyer is offered a broad array of services to go with it. The auto itself becomes a fulcrum for offering financing, service warranties, satellite radio subscriptions, and emergency service subscriptions. Buy a Dell computer and you will be offered an extended warranty, helpdesk support, and online training as well as financing. Apple's popular iPod enables the company to sell downloads of music from the iTunes website. Even an industrial company such as GE earns a substantial portion of its revenue from the sale of services.

Trade in services is also growing in importance in the global economy. This shift to services is significant to marketing managers for a number of reasons. That same global marketing infrastructure that is facilitating the sale of goods across borders is also facilitating the delivery of services across borders. The sale of services across borders, however, presents challenges that product sales do not. Many services are highly regulated by national authorities, such as financial, legal, or accounting services.

More important, the marketing and branding of services is much more difficult than it is for products. Services are intangible, the consumer can neither see nor touch them. Getting a consumer to value and prefer one brand of services over another is more difficult than for a tangible product. Because services are rendered by people, cultural issues come to the fore more often than with tangible products. This adds to the challenges managers face in marketing services.

Global Advertising Saturation

Marketing and marketing communications have grown in every nook and cranny of virtually all markets in the world. Moscow, the capital of the former communist USSR, was recently referred to by the *Wall Street Journal* as "the city of billboards."[19] Moscow is not alone in its transformation to a sea of marketing communications. From Vietnam to Hungary, former anticapitalist landscapes are sprouting forests of billboards advertising branded goods.

Ad "clutter" refers to the phenomenon where advertising is so ubiquitous that marketing communications lose their effectiveness. It is not limited to billboards. Broadcast ad clutter has made it more difficult for marketers to get their message across. Broadcast television has a greater number of commercials, and the shift to cable and satellite television has made the situation even worse. The growth of the infomercial is making it more difficult to distinguish the content of the program from the commercials themselves. In the United States, marketers have imported the European practice of showing ads at movie theaters.

On the Internet, the trend is even worse. Consumers and businesses have been so overwhelmed with unwanted e-mails that an entire new industry has arisen to filter out this unwanted spam. Pop-up ads, that initially were highly effective, have become so annoying to consumers that all Web browsers now have features to disable pop-ups.

Ad clutter makes it ever more difficult to get consumers to pay attention to advertising. It also has spawned a backlash against marketing, resulting in a culture that is anticommercial and antimarketing. Digital video recorders (DVRs), such as Tivo, have made it easy for viewers to skip the commercials in a television program. Accenture estimates that by 2009, 10 percent of all commercials in the United States will be skipped using DVRs.[20]

As a consequence, marketers have had to resort to using new tactics to reach consumers. For instance, a tactic known as "buzz marketing" has arisen in the United States. Buzz marketing uses members of the targeted demographic group to promote the product. It is an attempt to harness the power of word of mouth. These individuals, "buzz agents," are generally volunteers and may promote the product in cyberspace or in real time. Thus the person sitting at the bar offering you a new brand of cigarette and talking up its merits may be a buzz agent. The person you invited to a barbecue who brings a new brand of sausages may be a volunteer promoting the product. Someone talking up a new movie in an online chat room may be a volunteer for the studio.[21] It is unclear whether buzz marketing techniques will catch on in markets outside the United States.

Another technique that has grown in importance is "branded entertainment," where the product is woven into the show. This may be as simple as a character driving a particular brand of auto, or as complex as having many elements of the premise of the show tied into a particular advertiser. For instance, the show *Extreme Makeover: Home Edition* is built around products and services from Sears based upon an arrangement between Sears and the show's producers. All of this is only the beginning of a mad scramble to create new ways for marketers to cut through the ad clutter.

Global Marketing Management Replaces Global Marketing

As the era of mass marketing wanes, the challenge for international marketing is to capture the benefits of globalization without sacrificing local market responsiveness. David Arnold contends that global marketing management is key—not global marketing.[22] This entails a significant shift in the mindset of marketing managers, including a different way of understanding global markets and of integrating that understanding throughout the value chain.

How does an organization re-image its thinking? It requires a balancing act that demands a different way of looking at managing marketing where infrastructure is global and demand remains local. Michael Porter views this balancing act as an interaction between marketing and other activities the company performs in the value chain. He views marketing as a downstream activity because "marketing activities must inherently be performed where the buyer is."[23] He views that the most important role of international marketing strategy is affecting upstream activities such as product design and manufacturing.

Porter is correct in that global marketing management, when practiced well, unleashes global efficiencies of scale and learning by integrating experience from all the company's national markets. However, Porter's view of marketing as a discrete downstream activity reflects an outdated view of marketing's role within a company. The old approach compartmentalized marketing to a department. It was the department that handled advertising or ran the sales force. It was very much the "make and sell" mentality of marketing. That is, you make something and then the marketing people figure out how to sell it. The shift has been from "make and sell" to "sense and respond." In other words, marketing has shifted from selling what a company could make to sensing what the market wants and then producing and delivering that value.[24]

This evolution is based on ease of travel, instant and inexpensive communications, and the ubiquity of the Internet, which makes market information easily accessible. This evolution moved the focus of marketing from mass markets to segmented markets and ultimately to the market of one. Thus it became possible to customize all aspects of marketing to a particular customer. Dell pioneered the concept of a product made to order for each particular customer. While developed in the U.S. market, the made-to-order concept has been taken by Dell to Asia, Europe, and South America.

Philip Kotler, Dipak Jain and Suvit Maesincee have described the paradigm shift in marketing brought about by the advent of the Internet. Although their description is not expressly based on the forces of globalization, the Internet is so inextricably tied to globalization that what they describe as the paradigm shift is highly instructive for marketing. Their model identifies three fundamental shifts: from selling to marketing to holistic marketing.

This model envisions an evolution from mass markets to a market-of-one. Based upon the technological trends in marketing, there is some basis in fact

TABLE 2.1. The Three Stages of a New Marketing Paradigm

Name	Starting Point	Focus	Means	Ends
Selling Concept	Factory	Products	Selling and promoting	Profits through sales volume
Marketing Concept	Customers' varying needs	Appropriate offerings and marketing mixes	Market segmentation, targeting, and positioning	Profits through customer satisfaction
Holistic Marketing Concept	Individual customer requirements	Customer value, company's core competencies, and collaborative network	Database management and value chain integration linking collaborators	Profitable growth through capturing customer share, customer loyalty, and customer lifetime value

Source: Kotler, Marketing Moves, 26.

for that view. But mass marketing is still the norm. Some authors argue that mass marketing is evolving rather than disappearing.[25] One-to-one marketing has some validity when using the Internet as a medium. Some products can be made to order, such as the Dell case. More significantly, the advertising served up on the Internet is often tailored to the recipient. However, these few examples are a far cry from the dominance of one-to-one marketing on a global basis. Consumer goods will continue to be sold mostly in a mass marketing model for the foreseeable future. Although there are some attempts to turn mass media into interactive media, such as interactive television, these attempts have not met with wide success. For the foreseeable future, disposable diapers, laundry detergent, and soft drinks are going to be sold using mass marketing methods.

Although marketing management has not yet evolved primarily to a one-to-one model, it represents a shift in how to think about and approach markets. Globalization has created global market segments that can allow for some degree of standardization in marketing strategy. Two areas where this has been true for some time is the youth market as well as high-end luxury goods.

Companies have succeeded in different markets by targeting different market segments. Citibank, for instance, has adopted just such a strategy as illustrated in Box 2.3.

Another difference in the marketing paradigm is the way managers should think about market intelligence and how they should use it from one market to another. What happens in one market may have an important impact on what goes on in another. Fads move from leading markets to lagging markets and may become trends that affect demand globally. The conventional approach

Box 2.3 Citibank Shifts Focus To the Working Class

Citibank used to target the same market segment in all markets outside of the United States. It marketed to very wealthy customers, especially in developing countries, where it assumed there was no profit to be made from the middle class. This wealthiest segment, however, has not been growing fast enough to support Citibank's ambitious plans for expansion. So, Citibank is shifting its marketing efforts from the very wealthy to the working class.

In Mexico, Citibank has introduced some innovative marketing strategies to persuade working-class Mexicans to trust their money to a bank instead of using cash. Even though the average Mexican earns only $461 a month, Citibank believes it can earn sufficient profit from the segment to make it worthwhile. To pursue this market, Citibank struck agreements with small businesses such as drugstores and gas stations around Mexico to serve as bank branches. It then convinced employers to shift from paying their employees in cash to handing out preloaded debit cards. Once these caught on, Citibank had a ready-made market for their loans and credit cards. It is now turning its attention to Brazil, India, and China.[26]

Citibank used to view its markets as either within or outside the United States. The fact that there was room for customized marketing strategies for different groups of non-U.S. markets opened up new horizons of profit for Citibank.

funneled intelligence from a national market to company headquarters. That intelligence may or may not have been distributed to other country organizations. In the current environment where infrastructure is global, market intelligence should be distributed rather than centralized.

The core of the new marketing paradigm is to find both commonalities **and** differences among and between markets and to draw on these to create more effective marketing strategies. This requires flexibility and an openness to new ideas in formulating strategy. With the advent of real-time market information, the time to react to changes in the market has been severely reduced. There is much less time to contemplate changes in marketing strategies. Both managers and companies must be nimble and capable of changing direction very quickly.

MARKETING COMPETENCIES FOR A GLOBAL ENVIRONMENT

Management competency is a somewhat fuzzy term, requiring a framework to bring it into focus. It encompasses the competencies of organizations as well as individual managers. This section focuses mostly on competencies of individual managers. These competencies are defined by Christopher Bartlett and Sumantra Ghoshal as "observable and habitual behaviors that enable a person to succeed in her activity or function."[27]

TABLE 2.2. Management Competencies for Local Marketing Managers

Role/Task	Attitude/Traits	Knowledge/Experience	Skills/Abilities
Identifying and pursuing local market opportunities	Observant, intuitive, analytical	Knowledge of local market drivers	Ability to assess buyer behavior and market infrastructure in a different cultural environment
Attracting and marshaling company resources to the local market	Entrepreneurial, persuasive, competitive	Knowledge of company resources and strategic direction of company	Ability to communicate and marshal data
Sensing local market demand and adjusting local marketing strategy	Flexible, creative, fast study	Knowledge of local market conditions and local culture	Ability to understand market data in the context of a different culture and market infrastructure

For Bartlett and Ghoshal, relevant competencies vary depending on the level and function of the manager. Drawing distinctions between what they called the "myth of the generic manager" and the reality of evolving global companies, their model can be adapted for marketing.[28] It examines managerial competencies from three different perspectives: attitude and traits, knowledge and experience, and skills and abilities.

In a global environment where marketing infrastructure is global but demand is local, it makes sense to examine the roles and competencies of marketing managers on two levels. First, the marketing manager at the local level deals with the local side of the marketing equation. Second, the marketing manager at headquarters focuses on the global infrastructure and coordinates the activities of various local managers.

Local market managers are essentially the "sense and respond" organs of the organization. Their competencies enable them to sense and then create strategies that can with the subtle differences and similarities of the market. Their role enables an organization to enjoy the benefits of market responsiveness. Using the Bartlett and Ghoshal model, the charts below illustrate the different roles and competencies of both local and global managers.

Global marketing managers, by contrast, enable enterprises to capture the benefits of globalization by maximizing use of a global marketing infrastructure. Their efforts are directed up and down the value chain—toward integrating upstream with local market activities. They ensure that the similarities and differences among different markets are leveraged to the company's maximum benefit.

TABLE 2.3.   Management Competencies for Global Marketing Managers

Role/Task	Attitude/Traits	Knowledge/Experience	Skills/Abilities
Integrating intelligence from local markets	Systems thinker, analytical	Knowledge of statistical analysis	Ability to spot trends and anticipate their impact globally
Coordinating local marketing strategies with regional and global strategies	Integrator, strategist, creative coach	Understanding the interaction between cultures and divergent market conditions	Ability to motivate and create cross-cultural teams
Allocating marketing resources between local and global efforts	Decisive, diplomat, communicator	Understanding company's strategic goals and means necessary to achieve them	Ability to reconcile company objectives with those of individual managers

The ability to perceive cultural differences and similarities is one of the overlaps in the competencies between these two types of marketing managers. The fact that globalization has made different cultures appear similar on the surface makes this competency even more important to successful global marketing management. This competency comes from a mix of experience and education. Intercultural courses can be found in business programs, providing marketing managers with general frameworks and dimensions for recognizing cultural differences. All marketing managers should take such courses, but realize that the lessons require careful adaptation to the subtleties of local culture. For this reason, direct experience is critical. Nothing teaches culture better than immersion through living and traveling abroad. Those interested in global marketing management should pursue opportunities to spend time outside of their own cultures. They should cultivate friends and business colleagues with different cultural backgrounds. Much learning about different cultures happens through simple interaction.

The ability to analyze data to discern patterns, both locally and globally, is a second overlap in competency. Through the Internet and information systems, the amount of information available on buyers and specific markets has become overwhelming. Marketing managers must learn to discern relevant data patterns that separate significant from insignificant information. This requires a background in statistics and the ability to see the big picture through systems thinking. The basics can be gained through the study of statistics and logic. The ability to discern and analyze patterns can be honed through courses in music, literature, and art courses, which contribute to an appreciation of how parts contribute to the whole.

The ability to encourage and manage creativity is a third overlap. Creativity is essential to new product development, to marketing communication by discerning innovative ways to reach and gain the attention of customers, and to the formulation of marketing strategies and plans. Although creativity may be an innate characteristic in individuals, it can be encouraged and cultivated. For organizations and managers, fostering creativity entails a degree of tolerance for risk and a great deal of flexibility. This is because the most creative people are mavericks who tend to ignore the code of corporate conduct. They tend to be people who think differently and do not repress those different perspectives. Broad backgrounds are helpful, for they enable creative people to take methods and strategies that worked in one area and transplant them to another. For this reason, too, the former CEO of Disney, Michael Eisner, prefers hiring English rather than economics majors.[29]

In order to develop creativity within an organization, risk needs to be encouraged and failures rewarded as well as successes. Stigmatizing failures only makes employees risk averse, encouraging the same old way of doing things. Hiring people with varied backgrounds, who have not solved the kinds of challenges to be faced, is another way of encouraging diversity of thinking that leads to creative breakthroughs. A good example of this is Lotus before it was acquired by IBM. Lotus was started by a small group of diverse and creative people. As the business grew, professional managers were brought in to run the business. Lotus began to decline due to lack of innovation. On a hunch, one of the original founders submitted the résumés of the people who started the company under different names. None of those, including the founder Mitch Kapor, were considered for a position. The professional managers had standardized the profile of those being hired. In doing so, they screened out the eclectic backgrounds of the creative people who had formed the company.[30]

The ability to use and adapt technologies related to marketing is a final overlap in competencies between local and global marketing managers. These include Internet-based technologies, databases, and to certain extent wireless technologies. The global marketing infrastructure is based around these technologies, and marketing managers must understand them well enough to know their capabilities and limits. These should be part of any course of study leading to a degree in marketing. Marketing managers should also be willing to ask questions about any new technology from the experts, outside or internal, who work with them.

CONCLUSION

Due to intensifying competition, globalization is requiring the marketing infrastructure to become global even as demand remains stubbornly local. Indeed, despite these local market differences in demand and buyer behavior, globalization has created an illusion of uniformity among markets. This illusion makes it increasingly difficult to discern market differences. The marketing manager is squeezed between the requirement to standardize the marketing infrastructure and the need to localize marketing strategies. This has created two different roles for marketing managers. Marketing managers at head-quarters must leverage the efficiencies of the global marketing infrastructure while balancing off the differences between different local market operations. Marketing managers in the field must optimize local market effectiveness.

Despite the different roles marketing managers play in this bifurcated environment, certain competencies are needed for both; being flexibile yet responding quickly, perceiving cultural differences and similarities, analyzing data to discern patterns, encouraging and managing creativity, and using and adapting communications technologies. These are all necessary capabilities for effective global marketing management—capabilities the villagers of Rovieng do not yet possess.

NOTES

1. American Marketing Association, 1999. Definitions. Retrieved April 19, 2001, from http://www.ama.org/about/ama/markdef.asp.

2. "Sara Lee: Changing the Recipe Again," *Business Week* (September 10, 2001).

3. R. Chandrasekaran, "Cambodian Village Wired To Future; Satellite Internet Link Transforming Economy and Culture," *Washington Post*, May 13, 2001, national news section.

4. John Larkin, "Rural India Goes Digital," *Wall Street Journal,* October 3, 2005, A15.

5. C. K. Prahalad, *The Fortune at the Bottom of the Pyramid* (Upper Saddle River, NJ: Pearson Publishing, 2005), 10.

6. Frances Cairncross, "The Death of Distance," *The Economist* 336, no. 7934 (September 30, 1995): 5.

7. T. Kerver, "Citibank's Satellite Network, after Recent Expansion, Seems to Be Satisfying Corporate Needs," *Satellite Communications* (June 1985): 39–42.

8. Hal Varian, "Technology Levels the Business Playing Field," *New York Times,* August 25, 2005.

9. Global Reach, http://www.glreach.com/globstats/evol.html.

10. Global Reach, http://global-reach.biz/globstats/index.php3.

11. David Rhode, "A Lot of Cash in a Very Poor Nation: Welcome To the Mall," *New York Times*, July 19, 2005.

12. Theodore Levitt, "The Globalization of Markets," *Harvard Business Review* (May–June, 1983): 92.

13. Constance Hays, "From Bentonville, Beijing and Beyond," *New York Times,* December 6, 2004.

14. Paul A. Laudicina, *World Out of Balance: Navigating Global Risks to Seize Competitive Advantage,* McGraw-Hill (2004), 81.

15. G. Parker, "Going Global Can Hit Snags, Vodaphone Finds," *Wall Street Journal*, June 16, 2004.

16. Martin Packer and Ken Belson, "A Major Backfire in Japan Deflates Vodaphone's One-Size-Fits-All Strategy," *New York Times*, September 5, 2005.

17. Rebecca Buckman, "China Spurns Homegrown Phones," *Washington Post*, June 1, 2005.

18. Keith Bradsher, "GM Thrives in China with Small, Thrift Vans," *New York Times*, August 9, 2005.

19. Guy Chazan, "Moscow, City of Billboards; Building-Size Ads Transform Russian Capital into Version of New York's Times Square," *Wall Street Journal*, July 18, 2005, B1.

20. "1 in 10 U.S. Advertisments Could Be Skipped by '09: Study," *Dow Jones Newswire*, June 22, 2005.

21. Rob Walker, "The Hidden (in Plain Sight) Persuaders," *New York Times Magazine* (December 5, 2004): 69.

22. David Arnold, *The Mirage of Global Markets* (Upper Saddle River, NJ: Pearson Education, 2004), 3.

23. Michael Porter, "The Strategic Importance of International Marketing," *Journal of Consumer Marketing* 15, no. 2 (1986): 17, 20.

24. Philip Kotler, Dipak C. Jain, and Suvit Maesincee, *Marketing Moves: A New Approach to Profits, Growth, and Renewal* (Harvard Business School Press, 2002).

25. Paul Nunes, Brian A. Johnson, and Timothy S. Breene, "Selling To the Moneyed Masses," *Harvard Business Review* (July–August 2004).

26. Mitchell Pacelle and John Lyons, "Citigroup Courts a New Clientele: Mexican Workers," *Wall Street Journal*, June 27, 2004.

27. Pablo Cardona and Nuria Chinchilla, "Evaluating and Developing Management Competencies," technical note of the Research Department at IESE (1999): 3.

28. Christopher A. Bartlett and Sumantra Ghoshal and "The Myth of the Generic Manager: New Personal Competencies for New Management Roles," *California Management Review* 40, no. 1 (fall 1997).

29. Michael Eisner, "Managing Creativity," *Executive Excellence* 15, no. 1 (January 1998).

30. Robert I. Sutton, "The Weird Rules of Creativity," *Harvard Business Review* (September 1, 2001).

——— 3 ———

Managing Global Supply Networks

FRANK R. POWER

SUPPLY IS THE LIFEBLOOD OF THE MANUFACTURER

Like a heart attack victim felled by poor circulation, companies that suffer a sudden blockage in their flow of products to consumers face a long road to recovery, says Vinod Singhal, professor of operations management at Georgia Tech's College of Management.[1] When Motorola introduced its first camera phone in late 2003, it couldn't acquire enough lenses and chipsets to meet demand for the hot new product. In Nike's case, the crisis came in May 2001, when the company announced that sales for the preceding quarter were $100 million lower than expected because of confusion in its supply chain. This loss was soon eclipsed by Cisco's announcement that it was writing down $2.2 billion in unusable inventory due to problems in its supply chain. This was the largest inventory write-off in the history of business.

> In the 21st century, being the best at producing or selling a superior product is no longer enough. Success now depends on assembling a team of companies that can rise above the win/lose negotiations of conventional trading relationships and work together to deliver the best products at the best price. Excellence in manufacturing is just the admission fee to be a player in the larger game of supply chain competition.[2]

A supply chain is a network of facilities and supply options through which an organization procures materials, transforms them into intermediate

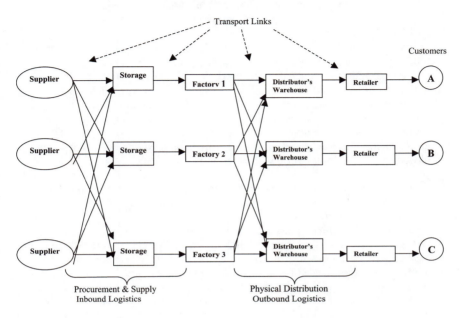

FIGURE 3.1.   Conceptual Supply Chain

and finished products, and distributes the finished products to customers. Supply chains exist in both manufacturing and service businesses, although the complexity of the chain may vary greatly from industry to industry and firm to firm.[3] A conceptual supply chain identifying the traditional components of a multifactory manufacturing company with attendant suppliers, distributors, retailers, and logistics links might be diagrammed as shown in Figure 3.1.

Some sense of the real-world complications of a global supply chain such as location of manufacturing facilities and sourcing of components can be gained from the description of Toyota's international operations in Box 3.1.

Complex Logistics Decisions Confront Managers

Distribution and logistics costs are a significant and increasing portion of the world's GDP. The basic objectives of global supply chain management can be described by two opposing goals: **effectiveness** in satisfying customer needs for quality products and service on a worldwide basis and **efficiency** in achieving the lowest possible total supply cost. Increased efficiency in designing and operating supply chains is critical for success, and revolutionary developments in information systems, communications, and transportation technologies have made such efficiency possible.

Box 3.1 Toyota's Optimized Global Manufacturing and Supply System

Toyota Motor Corporation[4] is the world's third-largest automaker, offering a full range of models, from minivehicles to large trucks. Global sales of its Toyota and Lexus brands, combined with those of Daihatsu and Hino, totaled 6.78 million units in FY2003 that came to a consolidated ¥17.29 trillion (approximately $144.24 billion). Besides its own 12 assembly plants and 11 manufacturing subsidiaries and affiliates in Japan, Toyota has 51 manufacturing companies in 26 countries/locations, a worldwide supplier organization, and more than 160 importers/distributors and numerous retail dealers. As of March 2004, Toyota employed 264,000 people worldwide and marketed vehicles in more than 140 countries.

Toyota produced its first small car in 1947. Toyota then proceeded to build a traditional "mother plant" system based in and around Toyota City and other areas of Aichi Prefecture in Japan.

Production of vehicles outside Japan began in 1959 at a small plant in Brazil, and continued with a growing network of overseas plants. Toyota believed in localizing its operations to provide customers with the localized products they needed where they needed them; this philosophy built mutually beneficial long-term relationships with local suppliers and helped the company fulfill its commitments to local labor. Toyota's overseas vehicle production posted a year-on-year increase of 18.7 percent in FY2003 and another 20 percent in FY2004.

In the summer of 2004, Toyota initiated the international multipurpose vehicle (IMV) project to create an optimized global manufacturing and supply system for pickup trucks and multipurpose vehicles to satisfy market demand in more than 140 countries worldwide. IMV calls for diesel engines to be made in Thailand, gasoline engines in Indonesia, and manual transmissions in the Philippines and India. For vehicle assembly, Toyota will use plants in Thailand, Indonesia, Argentina, and South Africa. These four main IMV production and export bases will supply Asia, Europe, Africa, Oceania, Latin America, and the Middle East with the five all-new IMV vehicles. IMV-series vehicle production including that in countries other than the four main production bases is projected to exceed 500,000 units in 2006. One of Toyota's ultimate goals in the production of IMV models is to procure nearly 100 percent of vehicle components from sources outside Japan. At the time of the initial Thai and Indonesian launches, non-Japanese sources accounted for approximately 95 percent of vehicle content. Toyota's IMV lines in Argentina and South Africa will also be aiming to maximize non-Japanese procurement.

Toyota is confident that it can maintain high quality standards because of its long manufacturing experience in all of the areas where it is establishing IMV production bases.

On a geographical and historical scale, the IMV project represents the third stage of manufacturing for Toyota. In the first stage, Toyota made vehicles only in Japan and exported the units to world markets. This was followed in the second stage by local manufacturing in key market areas. Now, supported by trade liberalization, such as CEPT (Common Effective Preferential Tariff) in the ASEAN countries, Toyota has entered the third stage by taking up the challenge of building a more efficient production and supply system on a global scale.

Future managers must be prepared to add product value and quality, reduce costs, and optimize profits by addressing complex decisions in plant location, supply sources, production methods, inventory management, transportation modes, distribution channels, and information/communication networks. There are both strategic and operational elements in each of these decisions and there is a high degree of interrelationship among them. New competencies will be required in: sourcing, production, distribution, and information management strategies in the global environment; identifying and integrating e-business opportunities within the supply chain; and increasing efficiency in designing, building, and operating global supply chains.

While they do not move large physical volumes of product, service industries have logistical needs of their own. Hospitals must have medicines and a wide range of materials and supplies ready for use. The postal service or small parcel carriers must meet their transportation needs. Often, service industries such as banks and public utilities process paper records and must set up steps to move papers that are analogous to procedures that manufacturing firms employ to move goods. Linked computers are used increasingly for many of these paperwork-integrating tasks.

GLOBAL SUPPLY CHAIN MANAGEMENT
ENTAILS A SYSTEMS APPROACH

Supply chain management is a systematic approach to managing the entire flow of information, materials, products and services from suppliers through factories, transportation modes, warehouses and distributors to the final consumer. Supply chain management (SCM) is different from supply management in that supply management emphasizes only the buyer-supplier relationship. SCM thus represents a business philosophy that stresses processes and integration across the entire value chain.[5] The goal of SCM is to improve efficiency in the ways a company buys, produces, and sells, thereby reducing the associated costs of each step. But cost is only one reason for paying attention to the supply chain; quality is another reason. The quality of a company's suppliers is often the most direct link to the quality of its finished product or service. Additionally, many companies' ability to expand into new markets, either within a country or globally, depends on their suppliers and the logistics infrastructures in those markets. Volkswagen, for example, has been considered to be the most successful automotive manufacturer in China, and the company attributes the bulk of its success to its suppliers' ability to set up operations and provide support in the Chinese marketplace.

Supply chain management also differs from simple logistics management. If all firms involved in a particular supply chain individually optimize their logistical systems independently of other firms in that chain, the flow management across the whole chain, or "pipeline," is likely to be suboptimal as, for example, when the retailer's desire for frequent restocking conflicts with the distributor's desire to optimize transportation cost. Systemic efforts to over-come this individual suboptimization have resulted in the creation of a global supply chain management (GSCM) approach.

GSCM extends the principles of logistics management over all firms in the supply chain regardless of geographical and organizational boundaries, and extending over the entire world.

Historically, organizations along the supply chain responsible for market-ing, distribution, manufacturing, and purchasing operated independently. These functional organizations had their own sometimes conflicting objectives. Marketing's desire for maximizing sales volume and achieving customer sat-isfaction through high levels of customer service conflicted with manufac-turing's goals to maximize throughput and lower costs, or with distribution's objectives to minimize inventory and transportation expenses. Purchasing contracts were often negotiated with very little information beyond historical buying patterns Often, no single, integrated supply management plan existed for the organization—there were as many plans as departments. We have only to look into Cisco Systems 2001 write-off of $2.5 billion in obsolete supplier inventories to see the results of such uncoordinated planning. Clearly a man-agement approach was needed so these different functions could be integrated. Supply chain management emerged as the approach for achieving this inte-gration.

GSCM focuses on integrating a multiplicity of suppliers, products, services, and capital from around the world into a coherent whole. Issues and problems include:

- Total cost analyses (reliability of delivery, quality, transportation costs, cycle times, etc.);
- Culture (language, customs, ethics, stability, literacy);
- Economics (labor force, economic system, tariffs, duties, import/export quotas);
- Politics (taxes, local content and employment requirements, counter trade, offsets, barter, WTO, NAFTA, EC, other regional economic trade agreements, political stability, possible military hostilities, health, safety, and human rights);
- Establishment of international purchasing offices, currency fluctuations, and countermeasures such as hedging, and staffing with expatriates and/ or natives.

Complex trading networks continue to evolve to pursue market opportunities or to exploit labor cost differentials and the availability of raw materials in particular countries. Ten years ago very few would have forecast that India would become a major supplier of software services. Development of networks has been facilitated by major regulatory and technological trends. Trade lib-eralization, particularly within trading blocs such as the EU and NAFTA, has

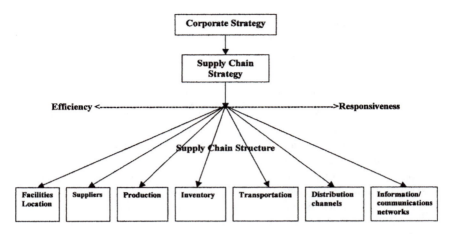

FIGURE 3.2.   Relationship of Supply Chain Structure To Corporate Strategy

removed constraints on cross-border movement and reduced related "barrier costs." Advances in communications and information technology provide the means to manage the physical movement of products over long, often circuitous, routes. Many carriers have invested heavily in "track and trace" systems that enable them to establish the location of any consignment at any time, improving the visibility of the global supply chain to shippers and their customers. These trends manifest themselves differently, depending upon the geographical scale at which companies and markets are operating.

As illustrated in Figure 3.2, the overall objective then is to plan, organize, operate, and control a global supply chain structure that integrates and optimizes the seven critical decision areas to meet forecasted demand requirements. This must be done within the framework of a global supply chain strategy that optimizes the balance between cost efficiency and responsiveness to customer needs and meets the higher-level requirements of the overall corporate strategy. The successful implementation of a global supply chain approach has usually encompassed important strategies, including reduction of order cycle time, quality management, increased asset productivity, new organizational approaches, and an emphasis upon customer satisfaction.

This global supply chain strategy, in turn, must be integrated within the comprehensive corporate strategy that encompasses such additional elements as marketing, finance, and human resource plans. In today's global economy, the historical logistics issues of facility locations, transportation modes, sourcing, and distribution are complicated by such political and economic factors as physical security, taxes, customs duties, quotas, local content requirements, and offset trade. What was already a complex analytical challenge now becomes a combinatorial problem of astronomical proportions. Deciding how best to allocate scarce resources with so many supply chain options and constraints that impact on cost and cycle time requires new magnitudes of information-processing capability.[6]

MAJOR DECISION POINTS FOR GLOBAL SUPPLY CHAIN SYSTEMS

All decisions about supply chain design and long-range planning are based on forecasts of customer demand. The firm uses forecasts developed with the involvement of the marketing and manufacturing staff and customers to assess the logistics needs of the next planning period. These needs include both delivery requirements of customers and the resultant need for manufacturing inputs and lead times. Because the marketing staff is involved with order processing, it also has early information about what customers are actually ordering. This is important intelligence for planning and scheduling production.

There are seven major decision areas in supply chain management: 1) location and size of facilities, 2) suppliers, 3) production, 4) inventory, 5) transportation, 6) distribution channels, and 7) information/communication technology (ICT). There are both strategic and operational elements in each of these decision areas, and there is a high degree of interrelationship among them (see Table 3.1).

Worldwide Options for Facilities' Location and Size

The geographic placement of production plants, stocking points, and sourcing points is the natural first step in creating a supply chain. This point is touched on in chapter 1 as the "organizational dimension" of strategy. The basic questions are: How many and what kinds of facilities do I need? Where in the world should each facility be located? How big should they be?

The specific choice of facilities involves a long-term commitment of resources. Once the type, size, number, and locations of all facilities are determined, so are the possible paths by which the product reaches the final customer. These decisions, therefore, set the company's strategy for accessing markets, and impact revenue, cost, and level of service. In making these facility decisions, firms should use an optimization program that considers factors such as production costs and limitations, economies of scale, taxes, tariffs and nontariff barriers, local content requirements, and transportation and distribution costs. Additional considerations include political climate, investment incentives, infrastructure, and free trade zones. Although location decisions are primarily strategic, they also have important operational considerations.

Economies of scale enable firms to lower the average unit cost of producing a commodity as output of the commodity rises. Scale economies may be internal to the firm, as when existing assets are used more intensively to expand production. And they may be external to the firm, as when industry

TABLE 3.1   Comparison of Key Characteristics of Traditional Systems with GSCM

Key Factor	Traditional Approach	New Global Paradigm	GSCM Approach
Facilities' location and size	Local to national market focus	Worldwide options	Optimum location Economies of scale for world market
Suppliers	Local Adversarial approach	World search for long-term high quality/low cost	Multinational strategic partners
Production	Standardized mass production for domestic market	Diverse customer requirements	Agile manufacturing
Inventory management and flows	Internally focused Interrupted	Optimize service and cost	Pipeline coordination Seamless
Transportation	Domestic surface	Multiple options: Containerization Intermodal Low-cost air freight	Optimized for supply and distribution
Distribution channels	Local to national	Worldwide channels attuned to local customers	Multinational
Information and communications technology (ICT)	Separate functional systems	Ongoing integration of constant technical advances	Integrated corporate systems and large-scale networks

development produces ancillary services of benefit to all firms. These benefits may derive, for instance, from the existence of a labor force skilled in the crafts of the industry; a components industry equipped to supply precisely the right parts; physical infrastructure such as ports, highways, and electric power; and business infrastructure such as accountants and attorneys. These benefits can at least partly explain the observed tendency for firms to cluster geographically, as can be seen in such areas as Silicon Valley near San Francisco and Route 128 near Boston in the United States; the areas around Stuttgart, Germany; Lyon, France; and Cambridge in the UK.

Some industries have been located based on proximity to raw materials and markets and minimizing transportation costs. Oil refineries were originally located in close proximity to an oil field. Now, however, they are located in consumer markets around the world because it is less expensive to transport crude oil than finished products. Also, the market-located refinery could process crude from a variety of geographic sources, thereby enhancing both economics and security.

Supplier Decisions Entail a Global Search for Quality and Price

Again, analysis begins with a series of questions: How many suppliers are best? Which suppliers should send which parts to which plants? Am I missing opportunities by sourcing one part at a time? What parts of my supply chain should I keep in-house and what parts should I outsource? The answers to these questions involve a world perspective. This point is touched on in chapter 1 as the "transactional dimension" of strategy.

Relationships between manufacturers and their suppliers have traditionally been antagonistic because of the former's desire to pay as low a price as possible for materials. In the words of one general manager: "The best approach to supply is to have as many players as possible fighting for their piece of the pie—that's when you get the best pricing."

Modern supply chain management, however, requires a more enlightened approach—recognizing, as a more progressive manufacturer did: "Our supplier's costs are in effect our costs. If we force our supplier to provide 90 days of consigned material when 30 days are sufficient, the cost of that inventory will find its way back into the supplier's price to us since it increases his cost structure." This leads to gain-sharing arrangements to reward suppliers who contribute to greater profitability. For example, the U.S. Postal Service charges lower rates to mass mailers that barcode and sort their mail by delivery area, thereby sharing the Postal Service's cost savings.

To effectively manage gain-sharing, companies must know their entire cost structure. This includes not only direct materials but also maintenance, repair, and operating supplies, plus utilities, travel, and everything else. Manufacturers can then consider how to approach suppliers—seeking short-term competitive bids, entering into long-term contracts and strategic supplier relationships, outsourcing, or integrating vertically.[7] Security of supply and alternative sourcing are necessary considerations.

A strategic buyer-supplier "partnering" alliance is a cooperative and collaborative way in which a buying firm and a few of its key suppliers interact intensively to achieve mutual "win-win" long-term results. These alliances are characterized by long-term commitments, a high degree of mutual trust, confidential information sharing, cooperative continuous improvement efforts, and the sharing of risks and rewards associated with the relationship.[8] A comparison of the historically adversarial relationship of General Motors, Ford, and now DaimlerChrysler to their parts suppliers with the more cooperative relationships of Toyota and Honda shows the positive impacts on costs, quality, and new model introduction time spans of the Japanese approach.

Outsourcing is the transfer to a third party of responsibility for activities that used to be performed internally. The degree of outsourcing pursued by an organization can vary considerably, from outsourcing the manufacture of a discrete part to outsourcing an activity or even an entire function such as final assembly of the entire product.[9] Contract manufacturing is becoming increasingly important, because it can totally eliminate the need for plant investment. Outsourcing is also passing beyond the search for low labor costs to a search for new technical skills in countries such as India and China.

Vertical integration in this context involves moving back in the supply chain to substitute a firm's own inputs for those previously supplied by a third party. This strategy may serve to lower costs and enhance security of supply, but it is usually applicable only where the firm can utilize a major portion of a supply source possessing economy of scale. It runs the risk of tying the firm to a supply source that ultimately becomes uneconomic. It is more common that by leveraging global buying power, a firm will achieve competitive materials pricing and sourcing flexibility.

Production Decisions Increasingly Are Aligned with Customer Requirements

Strategic decisions include the number of products and product variants to be produced; which plants to produce them in; what process technologies each plant should have; capacity of individual facilities; and allocation of suppliers to plants, plants to distribution channels, and distribution channels to customer markets. Like the decisions discussed above, these decisions have a major impact on the revenues, costs, and customer service levels of the firm. Operational decisions focus on detailed production scheduling, workload balancing, and quality control measures. The classic issue is product standardization (more cost efficient) versus adaptation (more responsive to individual customer preferences). The global issue is that now customers are located in many diverse cultural and geographic markets.

There is growing fragmentation of almost all markets. Customers are no longer satisfied with mass produced, standardized products; but are requiring more customized goods and demanding to be treated as individuals. Companies are responding with much wider product ranges and are introducing more new products more quickly.[10] In the 1990s many companies tried to achieve world-class quality status through total quality management methods. New manufacturing techniques were introduced, including cellular manufacturing (using work units larger than an individual machine or workstation but smaller than the usual department) and quick changeover (a series of techniques for rapid changeovers of production machinery to perform new functions). In Japan, the long-term objective has been "zero setup," in which changeovers are instantaneous and do not interfere in any way with continuous flow; kanban (a technique for "just-in-time" manufacturing); and zero inventories. Industry also moved to team-based continuous improvement and experimented with self-directed work teams. Companies studied best practices and benchmarked themselves.[11]

Now industry must build upon these improvements to develop truly agile manufacturing approaches. Lean or world-class manufacturing requires skill in managing controllable manufacturing variables. Agile manufacturing deals

---

Box 3.2 Agile Manufacturing Spells Success at Dell

Dell[13] is a tough competitor because its supply chain operations are brilliantly managed. All of Dell's plants are run on the basis of the continual monitoring of critical success factors:

- Minimizing the amount of inventory held in production. In Dell PC plants it averages seven hours.
- Maximizing the amount of time that the plant is online by avoiding machine failure or lack of supplies. The target is 97 percent, but most Dell plants run at 99 percent.
- Minimizing the ship and delivery to customer time: In the server plant in Austin, the target is five days from order to shipment. When the factory is really humming, it can get down to two days, but that's exceptional.

Plants are automated by a Manufacturing Resource Planning or Enterprise Resource Planning System, built by Dell itself from various commercial software packages with a good deal of customization. This picks off the orders to be built and sends a request for components to the inbound supplies area of the plant. The components are picked and routed to an assembler, with the more difficult assemblies going to the more experienced staff.

Once built, the computer goes to a load and test area, where the requested software is automatically loaded and the whole assembly is tested. Then it goes to packaging where it is put in boxes along with documentation and other accoutrements and is shipped. There are just four steps in all this; pick, assemble, load and test, and box. Dell describes this whole process as "high-velocity mass customization."

However, Dell is always improving its processes. Dell's manufacturing is very much a team-based activity with every member of staff involved in at least one Business Process Improvement (BPI) project. These projects run at every plant and are always targeted at squeezing out cost. In 2003, Dell claimed to have squeezed out $1 billion from costs. Mostly this came from the BPI projects.

It's not surprising then that Dell wins awards for having one of the top manufacturing plants in the United States. It is a little surprising that it has cut costs to the point where manufacturing in the United States is no more expensive for it than manufacturing in Malaysia or anywhere else. In the end it all adds up to Dell's killer advantage. It can offer lower prices. That's why it wins market share.

with the rapid response to things one cannot control, such as quickly changing consumer tastes. Agility is the key to being able to thrive and prosper in an environment of constant and unpredictable change. Agile manufacturing requires that the company already be world-class and using lean manufacturing methods.[12] This is the starting point, and the point where Dell has honed its supply chain advantage (see Box 3.2). Agile manufacturing is the ability to move from the assembly of one product to the assembly of a similar product with a minimum of change in tooling and software. Rapid changeover enables the production of small lot sizes, allowing for "just-in-time" production, or in Dell's case, for individually customized computers.

For many companies, the swift trend toward a broader line of finished products with short development and production lead times has created problems in managing more complex inventories, controlling overhead, and achieving manufacturing efficiencies. They are trying to apply traditional mass-production techniques without realizing that the whole market environment has changed. Traditional mass production does not apply to products where customers require small quantities of highly customized, designed-to-order products, and where additional attributes and value-added benefits like product upgrades and future reconfigurations are as important as the initial product. There are many telling signs that mass production must be replaced with new approaches: the proliferation of finished product models, the rapidly increasing introduction of new products, short product life cycles, and customer demand for products that specifically address their needs. All these trends are directly counter to the fundamental ideas of mass production that have served Western industry so well for decades.[14] The multiplicity of cellular telephone and personal computer models on the market provides an excellent example of this trend. Reducing and controlling demand variability through product design, designing products to facilitate procurement, and delaying product differentiation until the last possible point in the supply chain process cycle are but some of the techniques employed to control costs while still responding to customer demand for products adapted to their specific requirements.

Inventory Decisions Must Optimize Service and Cost

Inventories exist at every stage of the supply chain as raw materials, components, work-in-process, or finished goods. Inventories must be rotated, or "turned," with new units replacing old ones. Rotation is especially important in the food industry, where many items are perishable, and even packaged goods have expiration or "pull" dates because the manufacturer does not want them sold after a certain date. For products that might be traded internationally, there are additional inventory classifications: the country of origin, because import duties or charges sometimes vary by country of origin; countries where goods can be sold (e.g., some foreign automobiles cannot be sold in the United

States because of emission control requirements); and the specific languages used on the product or in packaging or in catalogs.

Since the holding cost of inventories can represent 20 to 40 percent of their value, efficient management is critical in supply chain operations. The basic issue is: What is the minimum amount of inventory necessary? The answer is strategic in the sense that top management sets goals. However, most research approaches the management of inventory from an operational perspective such as optimal levels of order quantities and reorder points and setting safety stock levels at each stocking location. These levels are critical, since they are primary determinants of customer service levels. Formulations such as overall obsolescence costs, stock-out situations, and clerical and labor costs in procurement should all see improvements as a result of GSCM adoption or enhancement.

Safety inventory helps a supply chain provide to customers a high level of product availability in spite of supply and demand variability. It is carried in case demand exceeds the amount forecasted or supply arrives later than expected. It also provides security from supply chain disruptions such as the airline shutdowns resulting from the September 11, 2001, terrorist attacks, natural disasters, or labor interruptions. Construction equipment manufacturer Caterpillar's global dealer network gives it a key competitive edge by providing comprehensive spare parts service to keep customers' equipment up and running, thereby saving days of downtime and getting them back to work faster. This requires a carefully calibrated investment in spare parts inventory.

It follows that the required level of safety inventory can be reduced and product availability improved if we can reduce demand variability, replenishment lead times, and variability of lead times. A switch from periodic monitoring to continuous monitoring can help reduce inventories. Another tool is to exploit aggregation by physically aggregating inventories, virtually aggregating inventories using information centralization, specializing inventories based on demand volumes, exploiting substitution, using component commonality, and postponing product differentiation.

The need to reduce inventory investment by reducing holding time has led away from **push** systems, which are driven by the supply of raw materials and products, to **pull** systems, in which actual demand for products triggers material flow. Just-in-time and quick-response are some of the names given to these logistics systems. New production or ordering is postponed until previously produced products are sold or consumed. The product is produced and transported in smaller quantities. Because the product demand is known with great accuracy, products bypass the traditional holding processes and are delivered directly to customers. In a pure pull system, the firm does not hold any inventory and only produces to order. When Amazon.com started, for example, its supply chain was a pure pull system—with no warehouses and no stock.

The Japanese practice of just-in-time inventory management works to eliminate inventories rather than optimize them. The inventory of raw materials and work-in-process is reduced to that needed for a single day's operations. Suppliers have to make more frequent deliveries or move close to the user plants to support this practice. This approach is widely used in automobile assembly operations. Two things made just-in-time work. Dogged attention to quality at all levels of the total system obviated the need for parts inventories to cover manufacturing defects, and a close coordination of plans with suppliers permitted them to align their schedules and shipments with the last-minute needs of the manufacturer. Elements of the just-in-time approach now have been adopted by numerous companies in the United States and Europe, although many cannot use the system to its fullest extent because their supplier networks are larger and more widely dispersed than in Japan.

Vendor managed inventory (VMI) is a means of optimizing supply chain performance in which the manufacturer is responsible for maintaining the distributor's inventory levels. The manufacturer has electronic access to the distributor's inventory data and is responsible for generating purchase orders. Under the VMI model, the manufacturer, which can be located anywhere in the world, receives data that tells it the distributor's sales and stock levels. The manufacturer can view every item that the distributor carries as well as true point of sale data. The manufacturer is responsible for creating and maintaining the inventory plan. Under VMI the manufacturer generates the order, not the distributor.[15] What we are calling VMI today has been going on for quite a long time. Frito-Lay's drivers/salespersons stock the shelves for their retail snack food customers to keep the shelves full, the product fresh, and the paperwork simple. Much fresh produce moves into convenience shops in the same way. Procter & Gamble started managing disposable diaper inventory for Wal-Mart over fifteen years ago. More recent adopters of VMI include Cisco, Flextronics, and Solectron for electronic components and publisher R. R. Donnelly for paper and ink.

Transportation Decisions Entail a Balance of Multiple Options

The importance of transportation has grown with the increasing globalization of supply chains as well as the growth of e-commerce, because both trends increase the distances products must travel. It encompasses many modes including truck, water, rail, pipeline, and air, all with varying issues, costs, and levels of service. The mode choice decisions are the more strategic ones. These are closely linked to the inventory decisions, since the best choice of mode is often found by trading off the cost of transport with the cost of inventory associated with that mode. While air shipments may be fast, reliable, and warrant lesser safety stocks, they are expensive. Shipping by sea or rail may be much cheaper, but it necessitates holding relatively large amounts of inventory in transit to buffer against delay. Customer service levels and

Box 3.3 Your Global Distributor May Be Brown

Founded in 1907 as a messenger company in the United States, UPS[16] has grown into a $30 billion corporation that is the world's largest package delivery company as well as one of the most recognized and admired brands in the world.

Over the course of its history, UPS has become an expert in global distribution. This involves managing not only the movement of goods, but also the flow of information and finance that moves with the goods. UPS customers increasingly asked to tap into this expertise, which ultimately led to the formation of UPS Supply Chain Solutions to provide logistics, global freight, financial services, mail services, and consulting to enhance customers' business performance and improve their global supply chains.

By 1993, UPS was delivering 11.5 million packages and documents a day for more than 1 million regular customers. With such a huge volume, UPS had to develop new technology to maintain efficiency, keep prices competitive, and provide new customer services. Technology at UPS spans an incredible range, from small handheld devices to specially designed package delivery vehicles, to global computer and communications systems.

The handheld Delivery Information Acquisition Device (DIAD), carried by every UPS driver, was developed to upload delivery information in real time to the UPS network. The DIAD information even includes digital pictures of a recipient's signature. This proprietary device also allows drivers to stay in constant contact with their headquarters, keeping abreast of changing pickup schedules, traffic patterns, and other important messages.

At the other end of the spectrum, UPSnet is a global electronic data communications network that provides an information processing pipeline for international package delivery. UPSnet uses more than 500,000 miles of communications lines and a dedicated satellite to link more than 1,300 UPS distribution sites in 46 countries. The system tracks 821,000 packages daily.

In 1992, UPS began tracking all ground packages. In 1994, UPS.com went live, and consumer demand for information about packages in transit soared. Today UPS.com receives millions of online tracking requests daily.

By the late 1990s, UPS was in the midst of another transition. Although the core of the business remained the distribution of goods and the information that accompanies them, the company's expertise in shipping and tracking positioned it to become an enabler of global commerce and a facilitator of the three flows that make up commerce: goods, information, and capital. In 1995, UPS formed the UPS Logistics Group to provide global supply chain management solutions and consulting services. In 1998, UPS Capital was founded with a mission to provide a comprehensive menu of integrated financial products and services that enable companies to grow their business.

geographic location play vital roles in such decisions. Since transportation may be more than 30 percent of the logistics costs, operating efficiently makes good economic sense.

The development of express package delivery services such as UPS, FedEx, and DHL have enabled e-commerce and even more traditional businesses to serve their customers without the need to provide their own delivery infrastructure.

Intermodal transportation, with the flexibility of integrating multiple modes, provides an agile response to the changing supply chain management requirements in global markets and distribution systems. Muller notes that the integrating of modes requires a process or systems approach for execution and "a higher degree of skill and broader knowledge of the transportation/supply chain processes: information, equipment, and infrastructure."[17] The trend is that freight movement increasingly will be intermodal and multimodal.

Direct shipments are most effective when large quantities have to be moved. When shipments are small, using an intermediate distribution center takes longer and is more complex, but lowers total transportation costs by aggregating the smaller shipments. Shipments may also be consolidated within a single vehicle by picking up and/or dropping off at multiple locations. Passenger airlines, package delivery, and ocean container shipping carriers make extensive use of hub-and-spoke and multiple stop strategies.

Last, the firm may decide to operate its own transportation fleet. Here, operation and control are the responsibility of the firm's traffic manager, who must become familiar with the many national and local regulations that govern the operation and safety of various types of vehicular equipment and the people operating this equipment. As in vertical integration in manufacturing, this is economical in very limited situations.

When designing transportation networks, shippers must consider the trade-offs between transportation cost, inventory cost, operating cost, and customer responsiveness. As always, the goal is to minimize total cost while providing the desired level of responsiveness to customers.

Worldwide Distribution Channels Attuned To Local Customers

Marketing-channel decisions are among the most critical decisions facing management. Deciding which type(s) of channels to use calls for analyzing customer needs, establishing channel objectives, and identifying and evaluating the major alternatives, including the types and numbers of intermediaries involved in the channel. The company must determine whether to distribute its product exclusively, selectively, or intensively, and it must clearly spell out the terms and responsibilities of each channel member. The strategic decisions include the selection of one or more distribution channels and allocation of distribution channels to customer markets. Effective channel management calls for training and motivating intermediaries to build a long-term partnership that will be profitable for all channel members. Individual members must be periodically evaluated against preestablished standards. Channel arrangements may need to be modified when market conditions change. Channel arrangements are up to the company, but there are certain legal and ethical issues to be considered with regard to practices such as exclusive dealing or territories, tying agreements, and dealers' rights.

ICT Networks Need to Continually Integrate Advances in Technology

In attempting to design any GSCM system, a threshold question is: What information/communications technology (ICT) do I need to effectively manage the system? Many chain stores, for instance, have scanners at checkout counters to provide instantaneous information as to what is being sold. Knowing this, they can restock the store and intermediate channels immediately rather than having a large inventory at that store in anticipation of what might sell.

Today, all companies with global supply chains need to build an information technology infrastructure that integrates three types of capabilities. For the short term, the system must be able to handle day-to-day transactions and electronic commerce across the entire supply chain and thus help align supply and demand by sharing information on orders and daily scheduling in real time or near real time. From an intermediate-term perspective, the system must support the procurement and shipment planning and master production scheduling needed to allocate resources efficiently. To add long-term value, the system must enable strategic planning by providing tools, such as an integrated network model, that synthesize data for use in high-level "what-if" scenario planning to help managers evaluate facilities, suppliers, distributors, inventories, and outsourcing alternatives. This optimizes control and coordination of all areas of the global supply chain in real time. Wal-Mart has been at the forefront of the application ICT and this has enabled it to become the world's largest company with $256 billion sales and 1.5 million employee "associates."

Probably the most eye-catching developments are related to the Internet. The World Wide Web, the global computer network of information databases, has experienced phenomenal growth in both the amount of information available and the total number of users. The Internet can be seen as a trading platform as well as a supply chain management concept.

When we regard the Internet as a trading platform, its features can be used for new forms of trade, usually referred to as e-commerce. E-commerce via the Internet may range from a simple advertisement on the Web to a full-fledged interactive site at which customers can shop in virtual shopping malls or bid at virtual auctions. As such, the Internet is a powerful instrument to bring together particular supply and demand at a global level. Companies can use it to get rid of excess stock, and small companies can benefit from this by obtaining

Box 3.4 Winning through Info Technology

Wal-Mart[18] has a presence in every corner of America and stores in nine foreign countries. The company turned to global sourcing as far back as the 1970s to obtain merchandise at low cost so the company could pass the savings on to consumers. Wal-Mart's successful high-stakes technological bets—including developing its own distribution network and software system—revolutionized the relationship between suppliers and retailers. Before Wal-Mart decided to take charge of its own distribution, retailers traditionally depended on wholesalers, who procured, warehoused, and distributed manufactured products. But Wal-Mart found that none of the wholesale distributors at the time were interested in giving adequate service to a geographically remote discount retailer. Wholesalers would be shut out of Wal-Mart's business model.

Wal-Mart's power started to really develop with its control over information technology. The key that Wal-Mart saw and was one of the first retailers to harness was the power of the information that is hidden in the ubiquitous bar code. The universal bar code system adopted in 1973 contains information on the product, its manufacturer, and its country of origin; a laser beam recognizes all the information as the scanner "reads" the bars by the degrees of light reflected back from the bars and spaces.

No one has used this technology more effectively than Wal-Mart, which tracks sales on specific items and specific hours of the day. Through this knowledge the company has changed its communication process with its suppliers, creating a power shift from the manufacturer to the retailer by setting price points and forcing suppliers to meet their targets. Wal-Mart is very demanding, and it has a lot of bargaining clout to back up its demands representing the consolidated buying power of 100 million customers who shop in its 3,500 stores every week. Thus, Wal-Mart used its buying power and its information about consumer buying habits to force vendors into squeezing their costs and keeping their profit margins low.

Wal-Mart's use of IT has enabled it to fine-tune its supply chain from factory floor to store shelf, insisting on just-in-time deliveries from suppliers to cut waste and downtime in warehouses.

Wal-Mart recently announced that it is taking technology a step further, drilling even deeper into sales and production tracking. It will now require its suppliers to provide microchips for radio frequency identification, or RFID, which will provide much more detailed descriptions than those in a bar code. Wal-Mart will be able to have instant information that will be even more powerful when deciding which products to purchase from its suppliers.

As a world leader in logistics, Wal-Mart has taken its logistical genius around the globe and made the most of it.

necessary products that would otherwise have been relatively expensive for them.

The Internet and e-commerce initially offered a level playing field for small and larger companies: Everyone had easier access to world markets. As such, it could have been a major competitive weapon for smaller companies. Yet, the fast pace of ICT developments makes it very difficult for smaller enterprises to follow the changes. An attractive e-commerce website requires large investments, both in terms of technology and maintenance as well as in the supporting logistics functions.

A major consequence of ICT is that it changes the **structure** of supply chains. This is caused by the fact that information and physical flows can be decoupled. As a consequence, processes become more flexible and companies can become more agile. This may lead to quick changes in the configuration of a supply chain. The increase of electronic trade in business-to-business relations will most likely lead to more global sourcing, increasing the average haulage distance. Information technology and e-business solutions allow companies to leverage their global buying power and enhance decision making with timely access to information.

MANAGING THE SUPPLY CHAIN OF THE FUTURE

The transition from traditional management approaches for supply chains to the new global paradigm embodied in the GSCM approach requires a new skill set. These new approaches and skills, however, must still be applied to the same major decision areas in supply chain management (see Table 3.2).

Focus has broadened from the individual firm to the multitude of firms that comprise the links of the entire supply chain. Since customers, distributors, and suppliers are now often global, new skills in building and maintaining international supply chain partnerships with emphasis on relationship management and "win-win" orientation are required.

The shift in focus from functions to processes as we move toward integrated management of goods and information flows requires new skills in cross-functional and network planning and implementation. The paradigm shift from focus on physical inventory to information about inventory status leads to demand-based replenishment and quick response systems, which in turn require real-time demand-forecasting capabilities like those used so effectively by Toyota and Honda. Inventory will be held only briefly for staging, such as cross-docking, and the future focus will be primarily on inventory in transit and not inventory in storage, distribution centers, or warehouses.

As we move increasingly from domestic to international markets, growing interactions with worldwide customers will require new levels of cross-cultural marketing skills. The evolution from standardized mass production primarily for domestic markets to mass customization in order to meet increasing global customer demand for greater product choice requires the

TABLE 3.2 Managing the Supply Chain of the Future

Paradigm Shift	Leading To	New Skills Required
From firm to entire supply chain	International supply chain partnerships	Relationship management and "win-win" orientation
From functions to processes	Integrated management of goods and information flows	Cross-functional and network planning and implementation
From domestic to international markets	Worldwide customers	Cross-cultural marketing skills
From inventory to information	Demand-based replenishment and quick response systems	Real-time demand forecasting
From mass production to mass customization	Greater product choice	Agile manufacturing technology
From revenue to performance	Focus on key profit drivers	Using true costs of all value chain components
From products to customers	Focus on customer requirements and creation of customer value	Defining and managing product requirements by multinational market segment

practice of agile manufacturing technology such as practiced already in consumer electronics.

As emphasis moves from revenue to overall performance, we shall see an increasing focus on key profit drivers, which necessitates knowing and using true costs of all value chain components. This will put heavy attention on the primary functions of inbound and outbound logistics, operations, and distribution as well as on procurement strategies. Here, Wal-Mart provides a benchmark.

Finally, as we shift focus from products to customer requirements and the creation of customer value, managers will need to develop new skills in defining and managing product requirements by multinational market segment.

The traditional concept of business is undergoing rapid change. Global supply chain management focuses on globalization of business and information management tools that integrate procurement, operations, and logistics from raw materials to customer satisfaction. Future managers must be prepared to add product value, increase quality, reduce costs, and increase profits by addressing major decisions in plant location and size, suppliers, production methods, inventory management, transportation modes, distribution channels, and information/communication networks. E-commerce will have a substantial future role in the supply chain process. The customer will expect highly coordinated and customized delivery with great flexibility as marketplaces shift and change, driven by increased information flows. In addition, the almost unlimited range of sourcing and distribution options will demand close focus on intermodal operational and information and communications technology. Reliability levels (i.e., the removal of variance) will be a higher requirement to permit satisfaction of customer demand while minimizing the costs of the supply chain. Customers will expect the transportation systems supporting supply chains to be focused on speed, flexibility, and variance elimination. New competencies will be required in: purchasing, production, distribution, and information management strategies in the global environment; identifying and integrating e-business opportunities within the supply chain; and increasing efficiency in designing, building, and operating global supply chains.

NOTES

1. "Broken Links in Supply Chain Cause Serious Damage"; Atlanta: Georgia Tech news release May 26, 2005.

2. David A. Taylor, "Supply Chain vs. Supply Chain: The Very Nature of Business Competition Is Changing, and IT Has a Big, Challenging Role," *Computer World* (November 10, 2003).

3. Infoscaler. http://www.infoscaler.com/pcscm.htm.

4. Toyota 2003 Annual Report, "IMV Project Shifts into Production Gear: Toyota Introduces Its Optimized Global Manufacturing and Supply System," Toyota special report, December 9, 2004.

5. Kelley Direct Online Programs, Indiana University Kelly School of Business. http://kd.iu.edu/courseinfo.aspx?CohortID=9.

6. *What is GSCM®? How does it work?* http://www.gsca.com/whathow.htm.

7. http://www.emahamillionaire.com/resources/webstrategy/eOperations/Supply%20Chain%20Management.pdf retrieved 7/04/03.

8. http://capsresearch.org/ReportPDFs/MultiStudyAll.pdf retrieved 4/23/03.

9. Ibid.

10. Brian Maskell, "The Age of Agile Manufacturing," *Supply Chain Management* 6, no. 1.

11. Ibid.

12. Ibid.

13. Robin Bloor, "Dell—Awesome Manufacturing—Says It All," *IT-Director.com* (March 12, 2003).

14. Maskell, "The Age of Agile Manufacturing."

15. *Definition of Vendor Managed Inventory* retrieved 4/23/03 from http://www.vendormanagedinventory.com/definition.htm.

16. UPS 2003 Annual Report and website.

17. G. Muller, *Intermodal Freight Transportation* (Washington: Eno Transportation Foundation, 1999).

18. PBS *Frontline*, "Is Wal-Mart Good for America?" posted November 16, 2004.

———— 4 ————

Human Resources Development Strategy

JOE MANICKAVASAGAM

G lobalization requires managers to think differently about human resources development (HRD). In a highly competitive environment
where ongoing innovation is essential for survival, HRD must focus on acquiring, developing, and utilizing intellectual capital in ways that serve an
enterprise's strategic objectives. People are a firm's key assets. Conventional
"training" concepts become subservient to these overriding purposes. Hence,
the rethinking of the HRD function flows from an appreciation of the challenges implicit in globalization. This in turn suggests three managerial competencies: communications, team learning, and introspection.

GLOBALIZATION'S CHALLENGES TO HRD

Globalization is challenging HRD managers in three distinct ways: to encourage and foster continuous innovation, to cope with diversity, and to develop leadership and management skills.

Enhancing Competitive Advantage through Continuous Innovation

Continuous innovation has become the watchword for firms whose revenues depend largely on international commerce. Innovation is introducing
improved or new things such as processes, methods, or devices. Innovatio

must be continuous, because while globalization has created opportunities, it has also created intense competition. Furthermore, new entrants such as China and India are contributing to this intensity.

Philips, the Netherlands-based electronics company, is the world's biggest in its field: At the end of 2004, Philips had more than 160,000 employees, of whom only 16 to 17 percent were in the Netherlands. Total sales for 2004 were more than $30 billion, with most of it coming from outside the Netherlands. Philips has production sites in 32 countries and sales and service centers in 150 countries, and its product divisions include medical systems, domestic appliances and personal care, consumer electronics, lighting, and semi-conductors.[1]

Rapid changes in technology, new research discoveries, and intense competition in the electronics industry make knowledge a critical issue for the company. Some years ago Philips concluded that unless it was able to find new ways of product differentiation in the consumer electronics market, its competitive edge might be jeopardized.[2] The electronics industry's trend toward digitalization decreased product differentiation through technical performance. Furthermore, developments such as desktop personal computers and the emergence of low-cost competitors (e.g., Taiwan) made product differentiation through other means more compelling. Innovation plays a key role in Philips's competitiveness in the industry. This in turn places an emphasis on knowledge, not only new knowledge such as that related to technology or processes, but also knowledge about end-users and consumer preferences.

Knowledge is a key driver of Philips's HRD strategy, as shown by the emphasis management places on it. Philips has established research centers in several countries covering Europe, the United States, and Asia. More than two thousand employees of diverse disciplines and backgrounds are involved in the research function. A key element of Philips's HRD strategy is to promote learning, both as a team and from others, with innovation as a primary goal. At the management board and in committees, innovation is a regular item on meeting agendas, with discussion of projects, research findings, and innovation-related items. These become more in-depth learning opportunities on a quarterly basis when the focus is subject specific. These learning opportunities extend to the staff level as well as to suppliers and others, such as selected users. This approach helps achieve cross-fertilization and synergy.

Harnessing Diversity

Cultural diversity is a way of life for transnational firms. It requires employees from a variety of countries and cultures to interface with each other and with an equally diverse network of suppliers on a daily basis. While successfully coping with this challenge depends on various factors besides HRD, such as corporate culture and managerial leadership, this chapter is confined only to the role of HRD.

The role of HRD in managing the challenge of diversity can be seen at Procter & Gamble, the consumer products giant. The firm employs more than 100,000 employees and operates in about 80 countries. In 1998, when Durk Jager took over as the new CEO, one of the first things he did was reemphasize his predecessor's view of the importance of diversity. "Unless you have diversity in thinking," said Jager, "you will never get real diversity—racial or gender or national diversity."[3] By this, he meant that diversity should be a conscious factor in the managerial thinking and decision-making process. Jager emphasized diversity in global organizational restructuring. He also utilized HRD programs such as mentoring and coaching both to help managers' awareness of diversity and to create a supply of potential managerial staff. Senior managers were expected to formulate specific plans for diversity and were held accountable for successfully coping with diversity in their units. Furthermore, a vice president was appointed to head a task force to deal with issues such as advancement of women. The lesson from P&G's experience is that leadership accompanied by actions is essential for success in diversity strategies.

HRD also helps alleviate gaps that may stem from the variety of the world's educational systems. For example, language and culture has an influence on organization of thought. In English-speaking educational systems, for instance, the hypothesis is stated at the beginning and the argument moves along to affirm the thesis. In French-language systems the hypothesis is at the end. Communication breakdowns or misunderstanding may at times also be due to nuances of using a language. Learning programs that are part of a firm's HRD strategy tend to fill skill gaps that may be due to different systems. Some organizations provide opportunities for improving English language and writing skills or learning non-English languages as well as programs that help employees work in different cultural and political environments.

Box 4.1 Disseminating Corporate Culture

Some firms also use HRD as a means to instill corporate culture so that employees, as members of a borderless firm, follow common corporate beliefs and values. British Petroleum (BP), for example, does this through its ethics program. BP is one of the world's largest petroleum and petrochemicals companies, active in more than twenty-four countries and employing about 115,000 people. BP's HRD program includes educating its employees on ethics both through e-learning and workshops. These programs are conducted regularly in every country where BP operates. To enable open discussions, the company also designs and runs programs designed specifically for work teams and business units. Additionally, the company's outside auditors independently review and certify these programs.[4]

Developing Leadership Capability

Human resource development has always been important as a tool for developing managerial and leadership capability. Globalization has made this even more important, because today managers work in an environment characterized by diversity, speed, and the complexities of technological, economic, and political changes. Furthermore, inasmuch as the market for products and services is global, the market for leadership and managerial talent is also global. The challenge for the transnational enterprise is twofold: first, to help its managerial cadre remain current in terms of knowledge and skills, and second, to ensure an effective system to develop future managerial and leadership talent.

The way McDonald's, the global fast-food chain, reacted in 2004 to the sudden death of its chairman and chief executive Jim Cantalupo is an excellent example of a firm that recognizes the importance of this challenge. Carol Hymowitz and Joan Lubin reported in the *Wall Street Journal* that hours after his death, the "directors announced that Charlie Bell, the 43-year-old president and chief operating officer, would succeed him. The swift decision gave immediate reassurance to employees, franchisees and investors that the fast-food giant has a knowledgeable leader in place who can provide continuity and carry out the company's strategies."[5]

Sun Microsystems, another global enterprise, confronts the HRD challenge in a somewhat different manner. The difference is on future management and leadership talent. An executive review process on current staff develops a pool of potential candidates for senior and managerial positions. However, unlike McDonald's, external recruitment supplements Sun Microsystems' pool. Generally, 10 to 30 percent of senior positions are filled through external sources.

Box 4.2 Learning from Success

The appointment of the CEO is just one feature of McDonald's that meets the leadership challenge. Leadership and management development at McDonald's is a strong, worldwide corporate system and an integral part of its business strategy. The company's policy is to promote from within the organization. In the United Kingdom, for example, about half of McDonald's managers were formerly kitchen crew members.[6] McDonald's researches best practices, including analyzing successful managers to develop profiles that can aid its future managerial staff. These profiles of success include leadership skills, the ability to manage in the restaurant environment, and high work standards. The main center for leadership and management development for both current and future leaders of the company, as well as franchisees, is the McDonald's Hamburger University based in Oak Brook, Illinois.[7] McDonald's also has centers in several other countries, and is able to conduct its learning programs in twenty-two languages.

Nonetheless, Sun Microsystems keeps current management cadre updated in the knowledge, skills, and experiences needed for its business. The system uses tools such as "leadership skill profiles," which include definitions of skills or knowledge (people skills, business management) that are unique to Sun Microsystems. This is supplemented with advice to employees on specific experiences that they should obtain for a particular career path, for example, technical, functional, or general management. Sun Microsystems supports this with a companywide system of performance reviews and leadership development programs. Technology is heavily relied upon for data collection, analysis, and reports on career and management succession planning. The HRD program is run with extensive employee involvement, with employees identifying their most important experiences, knowledge, and skills, and drafting their developmental and career plans.[8]

RETHINKING HRD

The challenges of continuous innovation, coping with diversity, and developing leadership and managerial capability are contributing to a rethinking of HRD. This shift has three aspects. First, firms need to see HRD less exclusively as training and more as a means to build human capital. Second, HRD should be approached as an integral part of the business strategy and expected to add value to the firm. Third, firms should endeavor to create a working environment where learning is part of employees' working life. This means adding value to the employee. The term "learning organization" is often used to describe firms characterized by this environment.

HRD as a Means to Build Human and Intellectual Capital

Knowledge is the key word in human or intellectual capital, and is in turn the basis for innovation and action.[9] The creation of knowledge and the management of that process are essential dimensions of HRD strategy. Individuals, however, create knowledge; HRD strategy provides the organizational means to facilitate and support the process.

Two dimensions of knowledge are necessary in HRD strategy: tacit knowledge and explicit knowledge.[10]

Tacit knowledge is in the minds of individuals (employees, customers, suppliers) and includes experiences, insights, and beliefs, which may not be easy to communicate. In describing the tacit dimension of knowledge, Michael Polanyi summarized this wisely by declaring, "We can know more than we can tell."[11]

Explicit knowledge is knowledge that is codified or expressed in manuals, rules, or procedures. Knowledge also becomes explicit when it is articulated in the form of theories or general principles that can be applied to a wide variety of situations. Explicit knowledge is often disseminated in a formal and systematic way, as in courses or books.

Nonetheless, tacit knowledge and explicit knowledge are not totally com-partmentalized as separate entities. As Nonaka and Takeuchi[12] argue, these two types of knowledge interact with and interchange with each other through human activities. In other words, tacit knowledge is converted into explicit knowledge and vice versa through interaction among and between individuals. Thus, knowledge is created and converted through human interaction.

The organizational environment is critical for the creation or conversion of knowledge (e.g., tacit into explicit), because intellectual capital is an asset as human capital only if knowledge is converted into a usable resource. If it is shared, it can be put into a form that can be useful to a firm (a mailing list, a database, an agenda for a meeting, a description of a process). Intellectual capital, therefore, is useful knowledge only when it is packaged.[13]

Many firms have taken a lead in introducing organization-wide interven-tions for knowledge creation and conversion. Hewlett-Packard (HP), for ex-ample, has long recognized the importance of HRD as the organizational means for knowledge acquisition and transfer. HP has research facilities (called "labs") in several countries. Communities of practice (discussed later under the learning organization) play a central role in enabling interaction among and between dispersed labs to create and share knowledge. Inputs from academia, industry, and government research groups as well as selected cus-tomers supplement the process.

Knowledge creation and knowledge conversion may also occur through personnel rotation and diversity (educational backgrounds or location of plants and offices). Some years ago, HP moved its process-engineering skills to

---

Box 4.3 Conversion of Tacit To Explicit Knowledge

Nonaka and Takeuchi[14] use the example of the tacit knowledge of a skilled baker (described by them as a master craftsman). They describe how, in the late 1980s, the Osaka-based Matsushita Electrical Industrial Company faced a serious mechanical-design difficulty in the manufacture of an automatic home bread-making machine. The problem centered on finding the best dough-kneading process (tacit knowledge possessed by master craftsmen). Analyses and tests comparing machine-made dough and that by master craftsmen were not helpful.

However, the head of the company's software development was aware that the best bread in the area came from Osaka International Hotel. In order to learn how the dough kneading was done there, she and several engineers apprenticed themselves to the hotel's head baker. Nonetheless, no one could explain how to make bread that tasted the same, until one day she noticed that the baker was not only stretching but also twisting the dough. This was the answer to the problem for Matsushita. This human interaction enabled the conversions of tacit knowl-edge of the master craftsman. Within the HRD context, this example has lessons for on-the-job-training, mentoring, trainee programs, and similar activities.

Singapore to manufacture calculators.[15] This triggered an unexpected knowledge-creation chain. The engineers at the Singapore HP plant altered calculator designs and related them to keyboards and eventually to inkjet printers. This knowledge was transferred, shared, and further developed, resulting in the design of new printers. Subsequently, printers became a key and profitable product for HP.

HRD as a Key Element of the Firm's Business Strategy

Firms that are successfully coping with the challenges of globalization regard human resource development as a critical element of the firm's business strategy. As business managers develop strategy, they should also focus on people by asking what value HRD can add to the firm's products and services. The answers should shape the role HRD plays in business strategy and in developing the firm's competitive advantage. They should show up as management innovations, improvements in products, services, and processes, and cost-effectiveness.

At Cisco, HRD (and all aspects of human resource management) is an integral part of the firm's business strategy. This California-based company employs about 30,000 employees in 50 countries. Its sales revenue is around $20 billion. It is the world leader for networking products and services for the Internet such as routers, and its employees, customers, business associates, and suppliers regularly interact and learn from each other. In this way Cisco is able to tap into the tacit knowledge not only of its employees but also of others, such as customers. It uses the same network for attracting new talent into its company. Measured by innovations, HRD at Cisco is value oriented and an integral part of its business strategy. It regularly offers new or improved products and services. A 2004 survey of 500 companies in 21 industries placed Cisco among the top 25 companies for innovation.[16]

The Learning Organization to Facilitate HRD

As mentioned earlier, individuals, not organizations, create knowledge. Firms should, however, create and sustain an enabling environment to stimulate learning and support knowledge creation and knowledge conversion (and packaging). The learning organization is the metaphor for this environment. Firms such as Toyota, Philips, and Hewlett-Packard have successfully used the learning organization. As part of human resources strategy, the learning organization facilitates knowledge creation and knowledge conversion. Peter Senge's[17] five dimensions (Senge calls them "disciplines") characterize the metaphor of the learning organization. These are:

1. **Personal mastery:** This is not just technical competence. It is a personal attitude to our everyday life, characterized by periodically clarifying

what is important and continuously learning to adjust to changes around us. Personal mastery is a principle and practice. Within the context of HRD, it involves continuous learning and sharing knowledge with the goal of making improvements.

2. **Managing mental models:** This helps managers to not be constrained by their biases or habits. Managing mental models implies that managers are more open to other views and consider alternatives (e.g., services, products). Within the context of HRD, it is being innovative.

3. **Building shared vision**: This fosters commitment and enthusiasm among people in an organization. It is a genuine leadership effort to make people part of the firm, connected and working in the same direction. Within the context of HRD, shared vision contributes toward an environment for learning and commitment.

4. **Learning as a team:** This enables learning from each other. Other dimensions of team learning include building trust and strengthening the skill of dialogue. Within the context of HRD, team learning creates an environment for creating knowledge and knowledge conversion.

5. **Systems thinking:** This helps managers to see the above dimensions as interacting elements of a whole that is more than the sum of its parts. In other words, systems thinking binds everything together. Within the context of HRD, a single issue is not treated in isolation.

At the heart of the learning organization is the "Community of Practice" (CoP). CoPs in firms such as Hewlett-Packard and Procter & Gamble lend reality to the learning organization, for example, through team learning with the focus on the practitioners. The practitioners—the people who actually do the work—know what knowledge or skills are needed for their work and how it affects their ability to perform. Nonetheless, the learning and knowledge of the practitioners is not the domain of the individual alone. The practitioner needs to interact with colleagues to reap the benefits from the stimulation. Furthermore, the CoP is a social structure that aids knowledge creation and knowledge sharing.[18]

In discussing earlier the notion of "explicit" and "tacit" knowledge, we noted that tacit knowledge is converted into explicit knowledge and vice versa through interaction between individuals. Hence, knowledge is created and converted through interaction between individuals. In the context of HRD, one way to enable this interaction for knowledge creation and knowledge conversion is through the CoP. Tacit knowledge might be a practitioner's experiences or knowledge about work processes that are internalized. It must become explicit to be useful to an organization. One way to enable the transfer is through the CoP.[19]

The CoP is a useful vehicle for interaction among and between individuals for knowledge creation and knowledge transfer. As part of the learning organization, it is a critical element of HRD strategy. The Xerox Corporation uses

Box 4.4 Informal Evolution of CoPs

The creation of CoPs need not necessarily be a formal organizational process.[21] They may also evolve informally, but can still be effective. For example, at Xerox the "Globalization CoP" started informally but with the support and encouragement of management. This was a community of specialists drawn from diverse areas such as marketing, design, software, and hardware, and document specialists involved in global product development. Their purpose was to learn from one another, improve communications among themselves, and strengthen coordination of global product launch. The success of the "Globalization CoP" was reflected in reduction of product revisions and delays in product launch, and led to the CoP becoming a formal organization for global product launch.

CoPs as a way to connect people for the purpose of learning, knowledge sharing, and development of ideas.[20] Its Corporate Engineering Center in New York state supports several CoPs focused on particular aspects of Xerox's business. The "Software Design CoP" is a community of engineers, and develops and shares best practices so that learning takes place across the organization and among all of its several hundred software engineers. This CoP contributed to the development and introduction of uniform competency levels for the company's software engineers, the practitioners. It also participated in the formal assessment and certification process of the company's software engineers.

CoP is one effective method to put the metaphor of the learning organization into practice. However, learning organizations take on many variations while maintaining the power of the metaphor. Many European companies conduct evaluation of investment projects, called post-completion audits (PCAs).[22] PCAs are independent reviews of how an investment project was implemented, assessing such things as actual results against planned objectives, and lessons in terms of design, supervision, and the responsible manager's performance.

Until a few years ago, however, management did not take PCAs seriously even when they were completed. The adoption of the learning organization created a new interest in PCAs as a source for knowledge. Heineken Nederland, the Dutch regional operations of the Heineken Corporation, began to use PCAs in this way for an investment project to replace the bottling line at one of its breweries. The managers of Heineken Nederland used the PCA report to discuss the lessons that might be learned. Among their conclusions was that variables in a project that are difficult to quantify (e.g., working conditions) must nevertheless be defined to enable ease of measurement. Another lesson was that some aspects of the investment were unnecessary because it was found during implementation that some of the old machinery could have been updated through modifications rather than replaced. This would have resulted in savings. Using subsequent PCAs in a similar way for knowledge generation, Heineken Nederland developed new procedures for investment projects. Furthermore, the discussion of PCAs became an agenda at the quarterly management meetings to make decisions for continuous improvement.

MANAGEMENT COMPETENCIES FOR HRD MANAGERS

HRD managers must of course possess basic knowledge of their field and related disciplines. In addition, three managerial competencies will assist HRD managers to address the management challenges they face from globalization: communication, team learning, and introspection.

The Power of Communication

Communication is a critical competency for HRD managers. HRD is often in a department perceived as a non–core technology or function in the organizational structure of the firm—that is, a department work process that is important to the organization but not directly related to its central mission.[23] Furthermore, HRD managers are required to interact with people from diverse knowledge or professional domains and sometimes with those who are skeptical about the benefits of human resources development. To be able to meet HRD challenges—by helping to create the learning organization or supporting a CoP—the manager should be able to convey ideas in a nonthreatening but persuasive manner. Whether the interaction is through discussions in a CoP, an e-mail, a telephone conversation, or a "show and tell" activity, communication must be clear and consider the audience, and, most important, the actions should mirror the words or written text for consistency and credibility.

Using the power of communication includes listening to and responding with empathy and reacting more like a coach in an environment of diversity. Stephen Covey summarizes this aspect of communication wonderfully when he says, "When I say empathetic listening, I mean listening with intent to understand. I mean seeking first to understand, to really understand. It's an entirely different paradigm."[24] Before it opens a restaurant in a new country, McDonald's requires its local managers, including those in human resources, to spend a learning period abroad at one of its established restaurants.[25] In China, the McDonald's HRD program for managers includes skills on how to give feedback and listen, and on what to do if they are faced with a person who becomes defensive.[26]

Learning as a Team

As discussed earlier, team learning is an important dimension of the learning organization. It includes building trusting work relationships and facilitating, coordinating, or leading groups in learning. A firm that has staff in many countries and cultures has a high potential for fragmentation of key pieces of knowledge, especially tacit knowledge. To minimize this fragmentation, HRD managers should be able to contribute toward finding innovative ways for knowledge creation and knowledge conversion. For example, at DaimlerChrysler, brake engineers might want to know how colleagues in different business units design brakes in big cars, trucks, or minivans.[27] The HRD manager may be the one to suggest a learning forum where an interaction could take place. The interaction might help avoid overlooking a unique piece of knowledge (which may be tacit); for example, information about the performance of brakes in sedans that may have relevance to minivans.

Team learning should be viewed at both the individual and organizational levels. At the individual level, team learning means not only being a team player but also welcoming feedback, seeking ideas from others, and sharing knowledge. It also includes the willingness to have others "lean on you" while they learn. PIMCO—one of the world's leading fixed-income managers, with about $445 billion in assets under its management—has offices in many countries and more than 600 employees, with 226 investment managers. Individuals like investment managers acquire lots of knowledge because of research on their clients, and at PIMCO it is corporate practice to share this tacit knowledge with other managers. "The quality and intensity of their interaction," according to Amin Rajan, "has put PIMCO in an enviable situation where it not only generates excellent investment performance but also provides top quality client service. Its client retention rate is exceptional by industry standards."[28]

At the organizational level, HRD leaders of transnational firms must be able to contribute toward the creation and maintenance of an environment for teamwork and team learning. Team learning cannot take place in isolation. It needs to be supported as part of a firm's management process. At McDonald's, human resource management and development take a frontline role even before McDonald's opens a restaurant. Customer satisfaction is always the criteria, stressed from the recruitment stage to throughout one's career at McDonald's. The emphasis is on skills and knowledge needed—interpersonal skills, systems thinking—for things such as being a team player. Nonetheless, the most important lesson to be learned from McDonald's is on the importance placed on human resource development, not the specific skills imparted. This led one commentator to conclude that McDonald's human resource management is a lesson for every business.[29]

Practicing Introspection

Introspection constitutes the skill to examine and explore one's experiences and to learn from them. Many writers refer to this competence simply as "reflection," following its usage by the philosopher John Dewey.[30] It is part of the continuous endeavor to improve.

However, the term is not used to suggest a manager sitting alone and meditating. Within the context of our discussion, the objective of introspection is knowledge. Knowledge acquisition and introspection are complementary processes. "According to the rationalist view," says Kujiro Nonaka, "human cognition is a deductive process of individuals, but an individual is never isolated from social interaction when he or she perceives things."[31]

One dimension of introspection is "thinking aloud" or "bouncing off ideas." At other times it might be talking about experiences or "talking things through," such as asking a colleague, "How did I handle the question at that CoP meeting?" Donald Schon describes this aspect of practicing introspection as "reflection-on-action."[32] It is exploring with colleagues, peers, and others why we acted in a particular way.

Another dimension is self-assessment of one's own impact on others, for example, one's leadership effectiveness. It is somewhat analogous to "talking to oneself." This internal dialogue is necessary for learning and improvement so that we gain from our experiences. Leadership style instruments and employee surveys are useful aids for individuals to reflect on their own impact. One large multilateral institution, for example, uses a survey questionnaire on an individual's management style, completed by his or her subordinates, peers, and supervisors, as a standard feature for its executive development programs. The questionnaire covers such topics as clarifying goals, providing feedback, time management, building trust, and teamwork. The responses are anonymous and analyzed by an independent external agent. The analysis is given only to the manager who is the subject of the survey. The individual uses the data to reflect on his or her own management style in light of the knowledge gained from the survey and as a guide for identifying new skills needed.

CONCLUSION

In summary, globalization demands continuous innovation in an environment of intense competition and the ability to manage diversity and develop managerial and leadership capability. These challenges require managers to reorient their thinking toward HRD in three distinct ways. HRD should be a means to develop intellectual capital; it should be an integral part of the firm's business strategy; and an environment of learning and knowledge creation should prevail. This requires that, in addition to basic knowledge on human resource development, HRD managers develop their competencies on using the power of communication, learning as a team, and practicing introspection. These managerial competencies will enable the enterprise to become a learning organization and thereby equip it to remain competitive in the rapidly changing environment.

NOTES

1. Bart Verspagen, "Large Firms and Knowledge Flows in the Dutch R&D System: A Case Study of Philips Electronics," *Technology Analysis & Strategic Management* 11, no. 2 (June 1999): 211.

2. http://www.newscenter.philips.com.

3. Margaret B. White, "Organization 2005: New Strategies at P&G," *Diversity Factor* 8, no. 1 (fall 1999): 16.

4. British Petroleum Corporate Information, "Raising Awareness: BP and Business Ethics: Setting Standards around the World," www.bp.com.

5. Carol Hymowitz and Joan S. Lubin, "McDonald's CEO Tragedy Holds Lessons," *Wall Street Journal* (Eastern Edition), April 20, 2004.

6. Christopher Adams, "Work Skills and McJob Training: Workforce Development: Fast Food Restaurants Manage to Combine Commercial with Development of Their Staff," *Financial Times* (UK), November 20, 2001.

7. Charlene Marmer Solomon, "Big Mac's McGlobal HR Secrets," *Personnel Journal* 75, no. 4 (April 1996): 46.

8. Howard Risher and William G. Stopper, "Succession Planning and Leadership Development," *Human Resource Planning* 24, no. 3 (2001): 3.

9. This section draws on Ikujiro Nonaka and Hirotaka Takeuchi. *The Knowledge-Creating Company*. New York: Oxford University Press, 1995, 59.

10. Michael Polanyi, *The Tacit Dimension* (New York: Anchor Books, 1967).

11. Ibid., 4.

12. Nonaka and Takeuchi, *Knowledge-Creating Company*, 61.

13. Thomas A. Stewart, *Intellectual Capital* (New York: Doubleday Currency, 1997).

14. Nonaka and Takeuchi, *Knowledge-Creating Company*.

15. Jose Santos, Yeves Doz, and Peter Williams, "Is Your Innovation Process Global?" *MIT Sloan Management Review* 45, no. 4 (summer 2000).

16. "Identifying the Innovators: How Are Companies Ranked?" *InformationWeek* (September 20, 2004); http://www.informationweek.com.

17. Peter M. Senge, *The Fifth Discipline: The Art and Practice of the Learning Organization* (New York: Doubleday Currency, 1990).

18. Etienne Wenger, "Knowledge Management as a Doughnut: Shaping Your Knowledge Strategy through Communities of Practice," *Ivey Business Journal* (January–February 2004): 1.

19. Paul Hildreth, Chris Kimble, and Peter Wright, "Communities of Practice in the Distributed International Environment," *Journal of Knowledge Management* 4, no. 1 (2000): 27.

20. *The Xerox Corporation* (2002); global services, digital perspectives, knowledge sharing; http://www.xerox.com/downloads/usa/en/k/kperspective_whitepaper.pdf (2002 update).

21. Ibid.

22. Mathijs Brantjes, Henk von Eije, Frans Eusman, and Wout Prins, "Post-Completion Auditing within Heineken," *Management Accounting* 77, no. 4 (April 1999): 20.

23. Richard L. Daft, *Organization Theory and Design*, 8th ed., Mason: Thomson South-Western, 2004), 604.

24. Stephen R. Covey, *The Seven Habits of Highly Effective People* (New York: Simon & Schuster, 1990), 240.

25. "McDonald's Serves Up HR Success...in 91 Countries around the World," *Management Development Review* 10, no. 1 (1997): 42.

26. Charlene Marmer Solomon, "Big Mac's McGlobal HR Secrets," *Personnel Journal* 75, no. 4 (April 1996): 46.

27. Wenger, "Knowledge Management," 1.

28. Amin Rajan, "Getting Tacit Knowledge to Work," *FT.com* (March 28, 2004): 1.

29. "McDonald's Serves Up HR Success," 42.

30. John Dewey, *How We Think* (New York: Dover Publications, 1997).

31. Nonaka and Takeuchi, *Knowledge-Creating Company,* 61.

32. D. Schon, *The Reflective Practitioner* (New York: Basic Books, 1983).

SECTION II

LEVERAGING THE ENVIRONMENT

The external environment of the far-flung enterprise is filled with enormous diversity, uncertainty, and volatility, which occur variously at the country, regional, and global levels. Moreover, even though the global economy is highly fragmented through the nation-state system, the economies of major commercial countries are sufficiently connected and interdependent that failures in one country can reverberate in domino fashion across a region or an industry and beyond. The dictum that countries don't default, which once guided international lending institutions, has not stood the test of time.

Thus, firms with global agendas need to understand and make the most of the national and international institutions that frame the commercial environment. Three of these institutional frameworks are considered in this section; a sound working grasp of each and how it is evolving enables firms to leverage or shape their environment in ways that mitigate risk and further enterprise agendas.

- The **Global Trading System**, managed through the World Trade Organization, ensures access to markets around the world on terms that are fair and predictable—at least in principle. It is this latter qualification

that requires firms to form international and regional alliances, to nurture
cooperative relations with multilateral institutions, to understand trade
negotiating processes, to appreciate the commercial and societal trade-offs
within the global system, and to think strategically about operating within
the emerging trade giants, China and India.

• The **Legal Environment** is much less a global system than a multilevel
and multiform aggregation of interacting legal systems. Like culture, every
country has its own, which it is loathe to compromise. These systems are
stacked next to and on top of each other in a makeshift manner. To enable
firms to integrate their operations across borders, corporate legal counsel need
to develop not only a working appreciation of how law cultures differ, but
also how they interact in ways that complement each other or at least
minimize the risk of conflict.

• **Country Risk** can manifest itself in economic, political, and cultural
terms. This risk can be minimized—and even become a competitive
advantage—if managers have the conceptual framework and tools to
perceive and come to terms with differing societal institutions and ideologies.
Countries should be understood as social systems, where the values and
heritage of their people shape markets, business culture and climate, and,
ultimately, public policy.

The overriding management question emerging from this group of chapters
is, how can an enterprise extract competitive advantages from the rich
diversity of social systems and cultures that characterize the global economy?

5

Trade and Government Relations

J. DAVID MORRISSY

INCREASING COMPLEXITY OF GLOBAL TRADE

Does globalization pose new challenges for corporate managers engaged in trade? Or is globalization, as Harvard economist Dani Rodrik[1] suggests, merely an uptick in trade expansion as it continues its two-century run? Economist Paul Streeten notes that, during that run, "between 1820 and 1992, world population increased 5-fold, income per head 8-fold, world income 40-fold, and world trade 540-fold."[2] Since 1992, trade has more than doubled again to $9.1 trillion, with developing countries' trade expanding more than twice the rate of industrial countries (Table 5.1).

The challenge of globalization for multinational firms is due less to the enormous growth in the volume of trade than to its complexity. Stanley Fischer, former chairman of the International Monetary Fund, describes that difference in trade flows as profound, because "the world's markets for goods and services are more integrated than ever before, though the pattern is different, with a rise in *intra-industry* trade, compared with the predominance of *inter-industry* trade in the earlier period of globalization"[3] (emphasis added). The earlier trade pattern consisted of exports of commodities (ore, rubber, coal) from colonies to industrial countries that used imported raw materials to manufacture the goods (sewing machines, capital goods) it exported. Today, raw materials and components crisscross national borders in complex trade

**TABLE 5.1. Merchandise Exports for Selected Trading Areas: 1992 and 2004
(Billions of U.S. Dollars)**

Selected Trading Areas	1992		2004		Percent Growth by Area 1992 to 2004
	Exports	Percent of World	Exports	Percent of World	
World	3,776	100.0	9,053	100.0	140
Industrial Countries	2,663	70.5	5,364	59.3	101
United States	448	11.9	819	9.0	83
Canada	134	3.5	304	3.4	127
Western Europe	1,681	44.5	3,570	39.4	112
Japan	340	9.0	566	6.3	66
Australia, New Zealand	53	1.4	106	1.2	100
Developing Countries	1,113	29.5	3,688	41.0	231
Africa	80	2.1	197	2.1	146
Asia	586	15.5	1,935	21.3	230
China (incl. Hong Kong)	204	5.4	852	9.4	318
India	20	.5	72	.8	260
Eastern Europe	160	4.2	686	7.5	329
Middle East	144	3.8	433	4.8	201
Latin America, Caribbean	148	3.9	459	5.1	210

Source: IMF, *International Financial Statistics Yearbook, 2004,* and *2005.*

patterns for processing, manufacturing, and assembling in the textile, electronics, computer, auto, aircraft, and other industries. As a result of these changes in the trade flows in the past decade, developing countries have increased their share of world trade by 31 to 39 percent while the industrial countries' share has fallen by 13 to 16 percent (Table 5.1).

　　The increasingly complex interconnectedness of global markets poses special challenges for business firms, prompts paradigm shifts in management thinking, and requires special managerial competencies for success. Therefore, managers of globalizing firms must develop fresh modes of thinking and new management competencies for dealing with the serious challenges they face in the emerging trade environment. These challenges and their management implications are summarized in Table 5.2 under four major themes: a still maturing supranational trade authority; regional trade agreement segmentation; technological proficiency; and asymmetries in trade patterns with the emerging trade giants, China and India. These themes are elaborated in the discussion that follows.

TABLE 5.2. Trade Challenges, Shifts in Managerial Perspectives, and Requisite Management Competencies

	Challenges	Shifts	Management Competencies
WTO: Supranational Authority	WTO creates uncertainty for member state trade policies	Develop dual perspective: private benefits and social burdens of WTO policies	• Master WTO procedures • Press government pursuit of trade remedies • Nurture cooperative relationships with multilateral institutions
Regional Free Trade Agreements	Regional trade pacts foster discriminatory trade relations	Perceive international trade as evolving: bilateral-regional-multilateral-global	• Understand trade negotiating structure/strategies and ratification process • Visualize RFTA expansion from sectors to country to region and to WTO global coverage
Technological Proficiency	Innovations neutralize distance, increase profits, and attract piracy	Telecommunications become delivery vehicles and cause difficult societal trade-offs	• Discern scientific applicability of, and market resistance to, innovations • Confront IPR piracy in the infringing countries and in the WTO • Convince governments of the developmental value of protecting IPR
Emerging Giants—China and India	Trade leverage of large and populous countries is rapidly increasing	Think strategically about competing and partnering with these complementary trading giants	• Conceptualize potential for cooperative/competitive strategies • Envision a hybrid market with large middle class amid vast poverty • Respond to stakeholder criticism • Support government efforts to secure full WTO compliance

WORLD TRADE ORGANIZATION: SUPRANATIONAL
TRADE AUTHORITY

Challenge: The WTO Liberalizes Trade
But Creates Uncertainty

Continued expansion of the World Trade Organization's scope and authority brought greater discipline and assurance of fair trade to corporations than its inauspicious beginning had indicated in 1948. A drafting committee representing twenty-three countries prepared the proposal for an International Trade Organization (ITO) charter, but when it was not ratified by the UN members, the committee decided to continue working together on a consensual basis as the General Agreement on Tariffs and Trade (GATT). Despite that fundamental weakness in decision-making authority, between 1948 and 2000 the GATT proceeded to liberalize trade by cutting tariffs from 40 percent to less than 3.9 percent.[4] Each liberalizing step, however, has had its domestic costs because the tariff cuts that benefit exporting firms came at the expense of those domestic industries whose protective tariffs were whittled down by the GATT. As if a Darwinian law of the global marketplace prevails, import-sensitive firms such as producers of footwear and textiles lose markets to low-cost foreign producers.

As corporate trade expanded, the GATT negotiations moved beyond reducing tariffs to adopting measures that discipline users of nontariff trade barriers. Those measures often reached within country borders into domestic jurisdictions to constrain certain internal government practices and corporate decisions. For example, in the 1979 Tokyo Round, a number of agreements, called codes, were adopted. One code forbade government grants of subsidies to its exporters; another required government procurement bids to be open to foreign suppliers. In addition, the Tokyo Round updated the antidumping code that forbade companies from engaging in the predatory practice of "dumping," that is, selling their exports at less than fair-value prices. The 1994 Uruguay Round agreement added Trade Related Investment Measures (TRIMS), a code that restricts host governments from imposing export or import performance requirements that foreign investors must meet, and the Trade Related Intellectual Property Rights (TRIPS), a code that protects innovations of corporations from commercial piracy. The General Agreement on Trade in Services (GATS) set forth a framework for services in general. All of these measures were designed to go beyond liberalizing merchandise trade, protecting firms from unfair laws affecting investments and services. Non-exporting firms, although exposed to greater foreign competition because of tariff reductions, benefited through protection from dumping, subsidies, and intellectual property rights (IPR) theft.

One critical change introduced in the Uruguay Round that sharpened the double-edged sword of trade liberalization was adoption of a clear Dispute

Settlement Understanding (DSU). With an appellant and enforcement process, the DSU can challenge and penalize foreign government practices and companies that are not in compliance. Legal scholar Gary Horlick describes DSU as follows: "The crown jewel of the Uruguay Round is the Dispute Settlement Understanding (DSU). The DSU, it is generally argued, brings quasi-juridical order to the General Agreement on Tariffs and Trade (GATT) regime maintenance system."[5] Countries that once could block the publication of unfavorable findings of a panel investigation now had to appeal, cease the unfair practice, or face penalties.

Nonetheless, firms still confront challenges because these remedial measures leave some areas of global applicability ill defined. Airbus and Boeing quarrel over definitions of subsidy—launch support versus military funding for research. Pharmaceutical firms that produce AIDS medications found their pricing policies undercut in South Africa by their own licensees in India. Music producers won the case against Napster's file-sharing only to have Kazaa, an international file-sharer, spring up to challenge anew the global vulnerability of IPR protection under the TRIPS code. Despite its imperfections, the international trading system offers the benefits of an explicit discipline and dispute resolution process for most firms. However, the WTO offers little protection to established firms that are in industries of waning competitiveness in developed countries, and has even less authority to deal with broad social issues of the environment, glaring income disparities, and worker rights that critics in Seattle, Genoa, and Cancún protest are exacerbated by trade.

The Doha Round initiated in 2001 took up the cause of trade liberalization. It set out to firm up and further extend its authority over agriculture, textiles, and specific services industry sectors. The Doha Round did not meet its scheduled deadline of January 1, 2005, but the WTO ministers held a meeting in Hong Kong in December 2005 to chart the stage for completion in 2006. Corporations involved in textiles and agriculture, which tend to be import-sensitive sectors, may be particularly challenged by the liberalizing results of the Doha Round. Dani Rodrik has summarized the challenge for the import-sensitive industries: "Gone are the days when trade policy negotiations were chiefly about interference with trade at the border—tariffs and nontariff barriers. The central trade issues of the future are 'deep integration,' involving policies inside the borders and how to manage it."[6]

Paradigm Shift: Firms Must Develop a Dual Trade Perspective

Firms must carefully develop a global trade perspective while being realistic about the impact of trade flows on the domestic economies. The progress made by the WTO to liberalize trade relations has improved global business potential and raised the living standards of billions of people. That progress has also fueled resentment in industries that fold because they are unable to compete with imports from foreign producers. Therefore, firms must play a constructive role in supporting their country's negotiating positions in the Doha Round that improve corporate access to, and competitive fairness in, global markets.

Determining the appropriate negotiating objectives for global firms has become more difficult because firms are structurally more complex and are present in more countries with disparate trade objectives. For five decades, changes in corporate product/marketing strategies evoked changes in corporate organizational structures: international, expanding globally from its home base; multinational, identifying with the national character of each major overseas market; and transnational, creating quasi-autonomous centers of special responsibility for the corporation as a whole. Firms with different corporate structures are subject in varying degrees to the influences of the national preferences of their components, making it difficult to craft an overall corporate trade policy that is consistent and globally realistic. However, there can be no return to the pre-WTO period when protectionist laws shielded domestic firms against unfairly traded imports. Today such protectionist trade practices will be successfully contested as being contrary to WTO principles. Adverse rulings by the WTO against the existing laws of a nation can cause corporate managers to be uncertain about which ruling will prevail on any given trade dispute. On occasion the WTO has issued such rulings. For example, the WTO found a decision on dumping damages under a 1916 U.S. law in violation of the WTO.[7] In another case, eight WTO members won an adverse ruling against the U.S. Byrd Law, formally known as the Continued Dumping and Subsidy Offset Act, which remitted $200 to $300 million to U.S. petitioners from the duties collected as penalties for foreign unfair trade practices.[8]

The European Union's value-added tax (VAT) was a source of much dispute in the WTO. The imposition of a European 15 to 20 percent VAT on all goods sold in the EU and a remittance of the tax on EU's exports troubled U.S. exporters who felt disadvantaged by the double taxation of paying U.S. income taxes and also the EU VAT. Congress responded by establishing in 1971 the Domestic International Sales Corporation (DISC) that deferred taxes on certain offshore earnings. In 1973 a WTO panel found that DISC violated the WTO export subsidies rules.[9] After the WTO rejected several revisions of the DISC and the EU threatened to impose retaliatory tariffs valued at $4 billion,[10] Congress finally relented and ended the DISC.

Managers must understand that a growing number of stakeholders perceive that WTO discipline expanded because country members derogated their sovereign authority to the WTO. Street demonstrators from around the world gathered in Seattle in late 1998 and at later trade policy meetings in Genoa, Quebec, and Washington to protest that the WTO authority lacks true democratic support. Some countries have trade advisory committees but, in truth, WTO members have never deployed procedures for gaining legitimacy on the basis of widespread public support. As a result, the WTO now finds itself unable to negotiate the compromises that could resolve some of the conflicts between trade and the public's concerns about poverty, labor exploitation, and environmental pollution. Rodrik states that "if the tension is not managed intelligently and creatively, the danger is that the domestic consensus in favor of open markets will ultimately erode to the point where a generalized resurgence of protection becomes a serious possibility."[11] He would counsel firms to realize that "reduced barriers to trade and investment accentuate the asymmetry between groups that can cross borders."[12] Managers take it for granted that their firms can cross borders to exploit low-cost labor. However, economic opportunities, language, and citizenship rights preclude workers from enjoying a similar advantage in relocating. Firms must find ways to heed Rodrik's warning that all stakeholders should be given a voice because "globalization delivers a double blow to social cohesion—first by exacerbating conflict over fundamental beliefs regarding social organization and second by weakening the forces that would normally militate for resolving these conflicts through national debate and deliberation."[13]

Management Competencies: Firms Must Master WTO Procedures and Nurture Purposeful Multilateral Relationships

Managers need a dual perspective on WTO activities—a short-term assessment of the risks and benefits of WTO rulings for their corporations, and a long-term view of how the WTO might address the trade-related issues of broad public concern such as the environment and the disparity of income both between and within the industrialized and the developing countries.

Instant comprehension of the implications of proposed changes in WTO trade rules is essential to prepare for the required adjustments in organizational strategy and resource deployment. The ability to nurture purposeful relations with representatives of nongovernmental organizations (NGOs), multilateral organizations (WTO, IMF, and World Bank), and member countries that have similar or complementary industry interests is critical.

Firms must have a clear focus on how their interests align with the objectives and procedures (executive, policy formulation, working parties, dispute resolution) of organizations such as legislative bodies and multilateral agencies. Knowledge of the structure and timing of each agency's decision-making process heightens a firm's potential for influencing its policy formulation.

Firms need to be familiar with the way the WTO structures its negotiating groups around major trade issues, when WTO reports on developing positions will be available for scanning, and what communication channels will be open to negotiators for conveying corporate concerns. Firms should also press for a forum in which the public can express its concerns. The absence of such a forum is a shortcoming that has led scholars like I. M. Destler to conclude that "means should be sought to *more effectively represent labor and environmental*

perspectives within existing trade policymaking institutions ... the current struc-
ture does not handle these well" (emphasis in original).[14]

Managers must quickly identify the use of unfair trade practices by foreign corporations and governments, and press the member countries involved to seek redress through WTO-approved remedies. In addition, they also must possess a thorough working knowledge of the WTO-authorized codes that govern the procedures for imposing retaliatory duties such as countervailing or antidumping duties to offset the margins by which imports are subsidized or dumped. When a country's investigation reveals that a subsidy has violated a WTO code, it consults with and requests that the subsidizing government remove the subsidy. If the subsidizing country fails to do so, the injured country may impose a countervailing duty calculated to offset the subsidy. Although the sovereignties of both countries are respected in that the subsidizing country can retain its subsidy, and the injured country can impose a countervailing duty, many trading partners object to the use of these remedies.

REGIONAL FREE TRADE AGREEMENTS

Challenge: Regional Trade Pacts Foster Discriminatory Trade Relations

The WTO has succeeded in reducing trade barriers among all of its 147 member economies because the WTO requires, as normal trade relations (NTRs), that any concession granted to one member must be granted to all on the same favorable terms. Notwithstanding WTO's success, some substantial tariffs on selected articles and significant other nontariff measures still remain to inhibit trade. As a result, many countries see the benefit of negotiating further reductions in trade and investment barriers exclusively with their neighbors. Since 1990, 275 trade arrangements to eliminate such trade barriers were signed by 72 countries with the United States. These arrangements, which take many forms and may involve just a single industry sector, are often triggered by a request from a firm seeking access to another country's market. More complex agreements include trade and investment framework agreements (TIFAs), bilateral investment treaties (BITs), and full-scale bilateral and regional free trade arrangements (RFTAs). Any concessions made to give more favorable terms to a limited number of countries must be reported to the WTO, which grants waivers from NTRs as steps en route to a broader application of the concessions.

The proliferation of NTR waivers for RFTA members threaten to degrade the integrity of the WTO global trade discipline by giving trade preferences to RFTA members that inflict competitive disadvantages on nonmembers. Not only are corporations from nonmember countries excluded from the benefits of the trade preferences, they also have little influence over the scope or the degree of reduction of the trade barriers involved. They do have access to a limited safeguard vis-à-vis countries that are granted NTR waivers by the WTO. The RFTA proponents must hold negotiations with non-RFTA members of the WTO to resolve their complaints about potential discriminatory treatment in the proposed RFTA. At such times, managers need to be sure that their concerns are understood by their own government negotiators and presented to the WTO before it approves of each RFTA. Even if there are no issues at the time the RFTA is signed, the longer RFTA status endures, the more formidable the insiders' advantages grow while the reductions in tariffs and other measures are phased in. Further, if additional neighboring countries join the RFTA, the market from which outsiders are excluded becomes wider. Whether the plethora of limited arrangements and RFTAs will smoothly evolve and meld into complete global liberalization, or devolve into selective globalization or even deglobalization, is a question that should greatly concern multinational firms. Skeptics abound, and complain that U.S. efforts to negotiate RFTAs "take resources and focus away from the multilateral system, divert trade, and create a patchwork of rules of origin that add complexity to the U.S. trade regime."[15]

Paradigm Shift: Firms Must Perceive Trade Relations as Evolving

Support for free trade agreements (FTAs) between two countries and RFTAs reflects a sea change in thinking that emerged in the last two decades. Many trading partners became persuaded that they could increase their trade revenue further by mutually reducing existing trade barriers regionally, even if the reductions are not applicable globally. Stanley Fischer cites supportive World Bank studies that "show that developing countries could reap income gains of more than $500 billion from full trade liberalization, which implies up to a 5 percent boost in incomes."[16] For those who fear that developing countries would fare badly in a free trade environment, Fischer notes "that at least half the gains from trade derive from intra-developing country trade, that is South–South trade."[17] In addition, beneficial breakthroughs can result from FTAs. As the U.S. Trade Representative (USTR) notes, "These . . . agreements also set modern rules for 21st century commerce. They break new ground in areas such as services, e-commerce, intellectual property protection, transparency, and in effective enforcement of environmental and labor laws."[18]

Managers must envision trade relations as a system of evolving trade agreements—bilateral, regional, global—and nurture a sense of how such agreements might develop to capture potential benefits for, or pose hazards to, their trade prospects. Often, regional negotiations have relatively obscure or even unlikely origins. In Europe, trade negotiations that began in 1952 illustrate how the challenge of a coal-and-steel sector agreement between six separate countries could expand to dominate the entire political economy of

> ### Box 5.1 EU: From Sectoral Agreement To Sovereignty, a Route for Other Regions?
>
> Although the European countries were initially reluctant to open their markets, the French foreign minister and political visionary Robert Schuman prevailed, and in 1952 the European Coal and Steel Community was established, followed by the Treaty of Rome in 1957 that established the European Economic Community, and the Brussels Treaty of 1965 that melded nine nations into the European Community with a commission, a council, a court, and a parliament. Subsequently, the Treaty of Maastricht in 1991 provided for adopting a common currency in 2002 for 350 million people; and the Treaty of Amsterdam in 1997 provided for the potential accession of other countries such as the 13 Eastern European countries, including Slovakia, the Czech Republic, Hungary, Poland, and Turkey.[19] The actual addition of 10 countries in 2003 brought the total number of countries in the European Union to 25.

a continent and have profound trade implications for corporations within and without its borders (see Box 5.1).

North American integration seemed unlikely in 1980, when neither Canada nor Mexico was inclined to seek closer trade relations with the United States. That attitude changed in the early 1980s when Canada began to negotiate a bilateral agreement on a sectoral basis with the United States that soon expanded into the U.S.-Canada Free Trade Agreement (USCFTA), signed in 1988. Mexico's view changed when it began bilateral negotiations with WTO members, which were required for its admission to the GATT in 1986. Later as an observer in the USCFTA, Mexico opted to participate in the three-way negotiations that emerged as the North American Free Trade Agreement (NAFTA) in 1994. Since then the three-way trade total has doubled to $623 billion.

As a result of that development, thirty-four countries in the Americas began negotiating for a hemispheric Free Trade Agreement of the Americas (FTAA), extending virtually from the North Pole to the South Pole, to be concluded by 2005. Dissension in 2004 among the countries stalled progress, and a strategic decision was made to revise the framework by creating two negotiating tracks. The first track would seek a balanced set of rights and obligations applicable to all thirty-four countries. The second track would go beyond the core commitments of the first to pursue negotiations on additional rights, benefits, and obligations.

Scores of countries are engaging in less publicized regional integration efforts. Regional trade negotiations between Brazil, Argentina, Paraguay, and Uruguay, with Chile and Bolivia as associates, resulted in the Common Market of the South, called MERCOSUR. Its members agreed to reduce tariffs in stages from 25.9 percent in 1991, the year of the agreement, to zero in 1995.[20] Exclusion from MERCOSUR could be costly for U.S. exporters, with losses estimated at $624 million, supporting "the well-known theoretical argument that even if external tariffs are unchanged by integration, nonmember countries are likely to be hurt by regional integration."[21]

Members of the Asia Pacific Economic Conference (APEC), which comprise the fifteen Pacific Rim countries whose two-way trade totaled $1.3 trillion in 2000, agreed to establish a free-trade area by 2010 for its developed countries, and by 2020 for its developing country members. Within the Pacific Rim countries, the six members (Singapore, Malaysia, Indonesia, Thailand, the Philippines, and Brunei) of the Association of the South East Asian Nations (ASEAN) initiated the ASEAN Free Trade Area (AFTA) in 1992. Subsequently, four other nations joined the AFTA: Vietnam (1995), Laos and Myanmar (1997), and Cambodia (1999), and invitations are being extended to Australia and New Zealand[22] with the objective of forming an economic community in 2020.

Africa's free trade regions are numerous and varied in their results. Some arrangements had promise but no permanence, namely Kenya, Uganda, and Tanzania. Others had promise and permanence but little performance, namely, the fourteen members of the Southern African Development Community. However, the Southern African Customs Union, comprising five countries, is concluding an FTA with the United States. The West African Economic and Monetary Union delivered integrated institutions for court and currency. In 2003 the Gulf Corporation Council formed a Customs Union consisting of six members (Bahrain, Saudi Arabia, Kuwait, Oman, Qatar, and the United Arab Emirates).[23]

Management Competencies: Firms Require Strategic Flexibility and Trade-Negotiating Expertise

Firms committed to liberalization on a regional scale and skilled in apprising their national trade negotiators of their interests will benefit from upcoming regional trade negotiations. This competency implies having an understanding of the scope of the agreements and how a firm's corporate priorities determine the concessions they seek in the RFTAs.

Managers should anticipate that regional trading blocs do, over time, extend beyond their initial reach to include more members and a broader array of trade issues. Therefore, they also must be proactive in seeking negotiations with countries granted WTO waivers to form an RFTA to preclude any problems early on.

Managers who understand the structure of the negotiating process can impel its momentum or thwart its potential damage. Internal preparations for negotiating sessions begin well in advance, and each country has its own way of organizing preparations. Some will seek the advice of the private sector, as the United States does through a three-tiered advisory committee system—a

TABLE 5.3.　Countries Chairing Major Issues in the FTAA Negotiations

Chairs	FTAA Negotiating and Consultative Groups
Colombia	Market Access
Uruguay	Agriculture
Costa Rica	Government Procurement
Panama	Investment
Peru	Competition Policy
Dominican Republic	Intellectual Property Rights
Caricom	Services
Canada	Dispute Settlement
Argentina	Subsidies: Antidumping/Countervailing Duties
Mexico	Technical Committee on Institutional Issues
Caricom	Consultative Group on Smaller Economies
Chile	Technical Committee on Institutional Issues
Ecuador	Consultative Group on Smaller Economies
Bolivia	Committee on Government Representatives on the Participation of Civil Society

Source: U.S. Trade Representative, 2002 Annual Report, 127.

President's Advisory Committee on Trade and Policy Negotiations (ACTPN); six policy advisory committees on trade-oriented issues such as labor, agriculture, and environment; and sixteen Industry Trade Advisory Committees (ITACs), each dealing with thirteen specific industries, ranging from aerospace equipment to textiles and clothing; and three topical issues, dealing with customs, intellectual property, and technical standards. Firms volunteer to participate and, if selected, meet periodically to formulate their industry concerns and to hear confidential briefings on government negotiating strategies. U.S. negotiating strategies are typically prepared by teams of government trade analysts who solicit the views of the ITAC members and other stakeholders. Firms involved in any of the FTAA issues keep informed about the ongoing negotiations by attending the public briefings given by U.S. negotiators and also by consulting the *Federal Register,* the official journal on government activities.

Preparations for the FTAA negotiations begin with a planning meeting of the participating countries to structure their collective negotiations around the major issues. Each country then volunteers to chair one or more of the negotiating committees or consultative groups. Table 5.3 illustrates the range of topics covered in such negotiating processes. Typically, the regional negotiating committees deal with the major issues covered by WTO negotiations such as the Doha Development Round (DDR).[24] In addition, several committees focus on issues of special relevance to the participating countries, for example, the Consultative Group on Smaller Economies chaired by Caricom and Ecuador.

Procedures for ratifying trade agreements vary with each country and depend on which government office or body a country's constitution grants the authority to ratify agreements. The U.S. Congress delegates Trade Promotion Authority (TPA) to the president to negotiate trade agreements for a limited time. If Congress grants "fast track" within TPA, the president is authorized to negotiate an agreement within a limited period of time and to submit the negotiated trade package to Congress for approval without amendment within ninety days. Legal scholar Ernst-Ulrich Petersmann describes the original purpose of the concept: "In the context of the GATT 1947, the U.S. and other GATT member countries had introduced special "fast-track legislation" facilitating reciprocal tariff liberalization agreements in GATT and their speedy incorporation into national implementing legislation."[25]

Under U.S. "fast track," Congress has bound itself to review the president's proposed agreement and decide whether to grant approval of the entire package without amendment within ninety days. Without "fast track" authority, trading partners are reluctant to negotiate an agreement because Congress might require the president to renegotiate any terms of the agreement, forcing other countries, in effect, to negotiate against themselves.

TRADE BASED ON TECHNOLOGICAL PROFICIENCY

Challenge: Balancing Global Marketing of Technological Innovations to Protect Intellectual Property Rights and Avoid Hazards to Society

Technological discoveries, particularly in telecommunications, deliver the competitive-edge benefits of global transparency and marketing immediacy, but they also introduce challenges—product piracy, global pricing disruptions, safety concerns, and accelerated competitive responses. Firms must recognize that one consequence of their pursuit of advanced technological proficiency is society's negative reaction to the potential displacement of the U.S. workforce due to outsourcing—not only of unskilled domestic workers but, increasingly, white-collar workers and skilled professionals.

The ease with which technology can be transmitted and adopted enables producers to pirate intellectual property rights in remote markets where enforcement of rights is erratic. For example, while the rate of pirating business software is estimated to be 38 percent worldwide, it is 98 percent in Vietnam and 95 percent in China.[26] Satellite transmissions enable global corporations to deliver movies, music, or special athletic events to TV sets around the world. Unauthorized broadcasters overseas, however, can easily intercept the signals and then rebroadcast the shows over their own commercial television networks without the permission of, or compensation to, the program originators. Similarly, the Internet file-sharing capability allows virtually any computer user to download the latest musical hits without paying the artists who produced the original CD.

The pricing policies of pharmaceutical firms that generate lifesaving remedies through extensive and costly research also have created contention. With millions of impoverished HIV-infected victims in developing countries, drug companies faced a Hobson's choice—sell overseas at drastically reduced prices that could undermine their pricing structure at home, or maintain their high-price marketing strategy overseas and be cut out of the market by their licensed low-cost overseas producers that cross over into markets without local producers. Cipla and Ranbaxy, two Indian pharmaceutical firms licensed by U.S. firms to sell proprietary HIV drugs in India, offered to sell to South Africa's Health Department a year's supply of generic antiretroviral AIDS drugs for $350, compared with $10,000 to $15,000 at U.S. prices.

Some technological breakthroughs can pose challenges for firms if the scientific research underlying the products prompts questions about health and safety hazards. For example, the EU ban on imports of beef from cattle that were fed DES, a growth hormone, was challenged in the WTO. The decision against the EU was based on the grounds not that "a product *might* be unsafe" (emphasis in original), as I. M. Destler pointed out, but that the EU did not prove that its claims were "based on scientific principles" and risk assessment criteria "appropriate to the circumstances."[27] Destler concluded, "This case is particularly difficult because it pits a plausible (but not now 'scientific') health and environmental concern against the threat of a de facto protectionist outcome."

Today's medical reports originating in the West are transferred overseas by the Internet, transcribed overnight, and returned to the physician by the next morning. In addition, x-rays taken on the night shift at hospitals in the West are sent to radiologists in Southeast Asia who return their analysis without delay to support quick decisions about the type of treatment a patient needs. Medical tourism has now evolved in response to the transfer of medical technology to Singapore, India, and Thailand. For instance, Indian hospitals with highly trained staffs hosted 150,000 medical tourists for cosmetic and critical surgery at prices one-quarter to one-tenth of prices in England.

Paradigm Shift: Technology Virtually Removes the Competitive Edge of Time and Distance

Telecommunications, computerized robotics, and the transcontinental time shift have given rise to virtually instantaneous competition worldwide from providers of a growing array of professional services from accounting to telesurgery. English-speaking operators at call centers in India have counterpart French-speaking operators at call centers in Africa. Technical professionals in such varied fields as computer science, finance, and medicine are increasingly outsourced to developing countries.

While technological innovations are increasing the prospect of outsourcing employment at very high skill levels, voices are being raised by renowned economists questioning the societal impact of pervasive outsourcing for higher-skilled employment: Dani Rodrik argues that increasing reliance on low-wage sources overseas tends to erode the implicit U.S. norm of fair-wage standards and undermines government commitments to provide adequate social insurance to counterbalance the job drain.[28] Paul Samuelson also believes that the effects of outsourcing need to be revisited:

> Mainstream trade economists have insufficiently noticed the drastic change in mean U.S. incomes, and in inequalities among different U.S. classes. As in any other society, perhaps a third of Americans are not highly educated and not energetic enough to qualify for skilled professional jobs. If mass immigration into the United States of similar workers to them has been permitted to actually take place, mainstream economists could not avoid predicting a substantial drop in wages of this native group while the new immigrants were earning a substantial rise over what their old-country real wages had been.[29]

Management Competencies: Firms Must Counter Unfair Trade Practices Overseas and Assess the Domestic Consequences of Outsourcing

Countering unfair practices such as barriers to markets and piracy of intellectual property rights requires discerning the different possible remedial approaches, each with benefits and drawbacks:

1. **Taking court action in the country of the offender** is usually costly, often ineffective, and alienating, as U.S. drug companies discovered in South Africa. In response to Indian producers selling proprietary HIV drugs in South Africa, thirty-nine U.S. drug companies sought redress in the South African courts, citing such practices as violations of the WTO TRIPS code.[30] However, when their efforts were censured in the court of public opinion, they withdrew their petition. Subsequently, with a $15 billion sweetener from the U.S. government to help health ministries make partial payments, the drug companies negotiated arrangements to supply the medicine at reduced prices.[31]

2. **Seeking recourse through one's own government** through its domestic courts or in its consultations with the offender's host government, however slow, can be effective. The home government may be willing to use its negotiating leverage, such as withholding benefits from the host government by withdrawing tariff preferences under the Generalized System of Preferences (GSP). Resorting to U.S. courts yielded a judgment that forced Napster to stop sharing copyrighted musical hits over the Internet without paying the original artists.

3. **Enabling IPR owners to seek retaliatory action** against unauthorized users may be achieved through a potential WTO remedy available under the TRIPS code. For example, countries such as China and Paraguay have been forced to destroy counterfeit copies of popular CDs. In countries that lack IPR protection, the threat of imposing WTO-approved sanctions can motivate those countries to implement IPR enforcement. However, gray areas exist, beyond the reach of WTO remedies, where successful pursuit of IPR protection can be elusive. For example, Napster lost its file-sharing case only to discover that others in Europe and Vanuatu took up free file-sharing over the Internet under the name of Kazaa.

Managers active in global markets must be conversant in applying scientific discoveries to the processes of production as much as to the goods and services they market. Whether trained in the sciences or not, managers require an innate sensitivity to the risks of adopting scientific discoveries that might be harmful to persons, societies, or environments. They also must appreciate the traditional values of foreign cultures and how innovative products and services might conflict with the values of host country cultures. The tension between the promoters of new products and the stewards of customs is well demonstrated by the social resistance to new discoveries such as generically modified organisms and growth-hormone-fed beef.

THE EMERGING GIANTS: CHINA AND INDIA

Challenge: Increasing Trade Leverage of China and India Intensifies Global Competition

China and India pose a unique challenge for multinational firms because of the enormous scale of their combined economies, the scope of their industrial coverage, and their swift adaptation to the global competitive market. Nonetheless, China and India differ in important trade characteristics. China's exports of $662 billion account for 90 percent of the two countries' combined merchandise trade, and 75 percent of their combined services exports of $102 billion. In the past decade, China's exports have grown fivefold, twice as fast as India's. China's trade encompasses a broad array of manufactured products, from textiles to metal fabrications and sophisticated electronics such as radio navigation equipment. Its progressive industrial growth is due in part to its superior infrastructure (highways, ports, power, industrial parks) and its ability to attract investment ($50 billion, compared with India's $4 billion).[32]

China's prowess in textile competition, the removal of textile and apparel quotas on January 1, 2005, and its undervalued yuan all threaten to exacerbate the poverty of twenty-four developing countries that export textiles. Of the twenty-four countries, seventeen export less than $5 billion of textile goods annually, but that trade accounts for 12 to 84 percent of each country's exports.

These small quotas could be swept aside by Chinese producers, who export nearly $100 billion of textiles and operate on such large-scale production that each of the fourteen towns on China's east coast is dedicated to making single articles of clothing such as socks, jeans, or wedding dresses.[33] In January 2005, China's first quota-free month, its shipments of cotton trousers jumped from 1.7 million to 27 million pairs, according to Cass Johnson of the National Council of Textile Organizations. He further stated that "the action the government takes or doesn't take will affect 30 million workers around the world."[34]

India, like China, has built up a substantial manufacturing capability well beyond its vaunted iron and steel industry. One-third of India's exports are in service industries, compared with 11 percent of China's exports. India derives its competitive edge from its workers who are educated in the Western tradition. Their fluent English and technical training enable them to compete with professional workers in industrial countries in service industries that pay high wages. Often with the help of multinational firms and the time shifts between continents, India's workforce can export from call centers on a round-the-clock basis such services as software development, consulting, financial analysis, industrial engineering, drug research, and mathematical analysis.

Here is how one commentator compared the two countries: "India is often portrayed as an elephant: big, lumbering and slow off the mark. Now investment bank reports are beginning to talk of it as a new Asian "tiger." If that is what it wants to be, it makes sense for it to study China: the tiger in front is Chinese."[35]

Paradigm Shift: Firms Must Adjust from Parenting To Competing and Partnering with the New Industrial Giants

The governments of China and India have profoundly altered their economic ideologies of a decade ago. China's command economy and India's protected economy are today emerging as more open-market economies. China's entry into the WTO in 2001 and India's struggle to recover from its financial crisis in the early 1990s signaled their readiness to comply with WTO trade discipline. Their trade growth—threefold for China and two-and-a-half-fold for India—attests to their ability to compete in global trade.

China and India are atypical trading partners in ways that are critical for understanding the future role of these two once-hostile giants. Not only are they vast in size, each with populations more than four times that of the EU or the United States, the two countries also signed an accord in 2005 to join in a "strategic and cooperative partnership of peace and prosperity."[36] Their cooperation and leadership in the IT industry, said China's prime minister Wen Jiabao, "will signify the coming of the Asian century in the IT industry."

China and India are hybrid countries with nation-sized developed segments within their massive developing-country economies. Multinational firms have been quick to outsource from China and India's extensive, low-cost, and competent manufacturing and service industries as part of an overall flow of industry from the West to the East. Initially, the challenge to Chinese and Indian competition was based on their enormous supply of low-wage labor. Middle classes that are the equivalent in size and income of large developed countries are rapidly emerging. China's middle class exceeds 100 million and is expected to reach 200 million by 2010. These large quasi-developed enclaves in each country magnify the scope of industrial output beyond a traditional developing country's capability.

Both countries are endowed with complementary economies. Chinese-made consumer goods from toys to television sets fill the shelves of Indian shops. India, in turn, exports to China such raw materials as iron ore, plastics, pharmaceuticals, and software products and training. In the energy sector, one of mutual deficiency, China's and India's state-owned oil companies are co-operating in producing oil in Sudan.

The two countries are acquiring the competence and capital to compete directly and seek cooperative ventures. What began as a symbiotic sourcing relationship between firms in industrial and developing countries is becoming a competitive relationship between the multinationals of the traditional industrial countries and the industrial producers of China and India. For example, Lenovo, a Chinese computer maker, acquired IBM's personal computer business to counter Dell's competitive dominance, and it has since catapulted itself into third place in world market share. The acquisition gave IBM access to Lenovo's clients while giving Lenovo a valuable strategic alliance with IBM.[37] In another case, the Chinese router maker Huawei was sued by Cisco for illegal use of its property. Huawei quickly dropped the contested component and now, through a venture with 3Com, Huawei sells its routers in direct competition with Cisco. In addition, Huawei made deals with a dozen other high-tech firms to sell in Europe, Asia, Africa, and Latin America.[38]

Management Competencies: Firms Must Be Ready to Compete, to Joint Venture, and to Press for Market Liberalization

Complex strategies are needed to capitalize on the competitive developments of the Chinese and Indian producers as they harness their potential complementarities in joint ventures, partnerships, or alliances. As in any joint enterprise, the advantages of collaboration may no longer favor the multinational firm, so preparations for an exit strategy must be in place. For example, General Electric Capital International Services (GECIS) pioneered in setting up a successful back-office operation in India in 1999 to leverage India's manpower and cost advantages. GECIS employs 13,000 of its 17,000 worldwide workers in India. (Other multinationals like IBM, American Express, Accenture, and Microsoft soon followed.) In late 2004, GE freed GECIS to take on other clients and freed itself from a labor-intensive operation by selling 60 percent of GECIS to two private equity firms for $500 million.[39]

Global firms with strategies that focus on China and India's emerging middle-class needs for products and services, not unlike those that firms market to their traditional middle classes, will enjoy a competitive advantage. Gaining access to these intramarkets of several hundred million will depend on a firm's ability to identify and communicate with those middle classes as cohorts that are scattered within these vast countries and then modify existing and innovative products and services to meet their needs. In doing so, firms need to heed criticism of their roles in increasing the effect these massive countries will have on displacing other countries from global markets and polluting the environment.

Firms need to be effective in pressing their governments, NGOs, multilateral institutions, and country representatives to urge China and India to liberalize access to their markets. China in particular needs to be persuaded, among other things, to revalue its currency in line with world market valuations. Firms must also be prepared to use WTO rules to sanction the unfair trade practices of China and India, but must expect China and India likewise to resort to WTO rules to vigorously challenge developed country practices that China and India regard as unfair.

CONCLUSION

Globalization challenges the traditional nationalist perspectives on trade and investment. The WTO discipline has become supranational in character; regional and global trade regimes are liberalizing at different rates; and technological innovations are extending the reach and speed of business transactions. Firms must have the organizational ability to continuously scan the trade environment for liberalizing trade opportunities, whether global or regional, that encompass broader country and product coverage. The continental embrace of twenty-five EU countries began with a six-country coal and steel pact. And a bilateral U.S.-Canada trade agreement launched pole-to-pole trade negotiations in the Western Hemisphere.

To capture the potential benefits and deflect the potential downsides of trade negotiations, firms need to field a team that is skillful in working the levers of the negotiating process. Firms face a dilemma in supporting globalization, one that requires a judicious prescience in balancing their industry benefits while simultaneously being attentive to the public policy needs of other segments of society that are vulnerable to trade liberalization. Firms must explore ways to assist trade dissidents to voice their concerns and encourage them to propose realistic remedies that address those concerns.

Technological proficiency enhances global competitiveness but also makes firms vulnerable to piracy, customer wariness, and unfair practices in global markets. Therefore, firms must be swift and persistent in pursuing remedies in country courts and in the WTO trading system. The populous emerging markets of China and India pose a unique threat of trade dominance not previously experienced in the WTO. To address these globalizing trends, successful firms need to master new competencies in trade discipline, regional diplomacy, and technological adaptation.

NOTES

1. Dani Rodrik, *Has Globalization Gone Too Far?* (Washington, DC: Institute for International Economics, 1997), 7.

2. Paul Streeten, "Integration, Independence, and Globalization," *Finance & Development* (Washington, DC: International Monetary Fund, 2001), 35.

3. Stanley Fischer, "Globalization and Its Challenges," *American Economic Review* (May 2003): 4.

4. John Jackson and William Davey, *The World Trading System*, 2d ed. (Cambridge, MA: MIT Press, 1998), 141.

5. Gary Horlick, "Problems with the Compliance Structure of the WTO Dispute Resolution Process," in D. Kennedy and J. Southwick, eds., *The Political Economy of International Trade Law: Essays in Honor of Robert E. Hudec* (Cambridge: Cambridge University Press, 2002), 636.

6. Rodrik, *Has Globalization,* 37.

7. "Iowa Court Hands Down First Ever Ruling in 1916 Act," *Inside U.S. Trade: An Exclusive Weekly Report on Major Government and Industry Trade Action* (December 19, 2003): 8.

8. "U.S. Seeks Arbitration to Resolve Byrd Law Retaliation Dispute," *Inside U.S. Trade* (January 30, 2004): 3.

9. Jackson and Davey, *World Trading System,* 355, 744–47.

10. "FSC Retaliation Downplayed Due To Rising Euro," *Inside U.S. Trade* (January 30, 2004): 4.

11. Rodrik, *Has Globalization,* 6.

12. Ibid., 4.

13. Ibid., 37.

14. I. M. Destler and P. Balint, *The New Politics of American Trade: Trade, Labor, and the Environment* (Washington, DC: Institute for International Economics, 1999), 59.

15. "WTO Members Express Alarm over U.S. Policy, Failure to Comply," *Inside U.S. Trade* (January 23, 2004): 10.

16. Fischer, "Globalization," 21.

17. Ibid., 20.

18. U.S. Trade Representative, *2005 Trade Policy Agenda*, Overview, 6.

19. Graham Bannock, R. E. Baxter, and E. Davis, *Dictionary of Economics* (New York: John Wiley & Sons, 1998), 135–40.

20. Won Chang and L. Winters, "How Regional Blocs Affect Excluded Countries: The Price Effects of MERCOSUR," *American Economic Review* (September 2002): 889–904.

21. Ibid., 901.

22. Jane Perlez, "Southeast Asia Urged to Form Economic Bloc," *Washington Post*, November 29, 2004, A8, www.ASEAN Free Trade Area (AFTA), February 20, 2006.

23. Michelle Wallin, "U.S.-Bahrain Accord Stirs Persian Gulf Trade Partners," *Washington Post*, December 24, 2004, W1.

24. "Draft FTAA Declaration," *Inside U.S. Trade* (November 21, 2004): 13.

25. Ernst-Ulrich Petersmann, "Constitutionalism and WTO Law," in Kennedy and Southwick, *Political Economy*, 53.

26. Medard Gabel and Henry Bruner, *Global Inc.: An Atlas of the Multinational Corporation* (New York: New Press, 2003), 74.

27. Destler and Balint, *New Politics*, 62.

28. Rodrik, *Has Globalization*, 6.

29. Paul Samuelson, "Where Ricardo and Mill Rebut and Confirm Arguments of Mainstream Economists Supporting Globalization," *Journal of Economic Perspective* (summer 2002): 144, 135–46.

30. D. McNeil Jr., "Selling Cheap 'Generic' Drugs, India's Copycats Irk Industry," *New York Times,* December 1, 2000, A1, A14; "U.S. at Odds with Europe over Rules on World Drug Pricing," July 20, 2001, A9.

31. Ibid., A9.

32. M. Kripilani and P. Engardio, "The Rise of India," *Business Week* (December 8, 2003): 72.

33. David Barboza, "In Roaring China, Sweaters Are West of Sock City," *New York Times,* December 24, 2004, A1, C3.

34. "With End of Quotas, Chinese Apparel Floods the U.S. Market," *New York Times,* March 10, 2005, A1, C6.

35. Simon Long, "The Tiger in Front," *Economist.com* (March 2005).

36. John Lancaster, "India, China Hoping to 'Reshape the World Order' Together," *Washington Post,* April 12, 2005, A16.

37. Steve Hamm, "Big Blue's Bold Step into China," *Business Week* (December 20, 2004): 35.

38. Bruce Einhorn and Peter Burrows, "Huawei: Cisco's Rival Hangs Tough," *Business Week* (January 19, 2004): 73–74.

39. Saritha Rai, "General Electric Sells 60% of Indian Back-Office Unit," *New York Times,* November 9, 2004, W1.

——— 6 ———

The Fragmented Legal Environment of Global Business

WILLIAM G. FRENKEL

The biggest hurdle for global companies from a legal perspective remains fragmentation of business law among nations whose legal systems function largely in isolation of one another. This chapter examines how the work of international business attorneys is shaped by varying and often conflicting jurisdictions and legal systems. We will review how globalization challenges the effectiveness of the legal function for enterprises with global agendas, then discuss the modes of thinking and competencies that corporate counsel need in order to work effectively in a global environment.

A LEGACY OF NATIONAL SYSTEMS

The international legal system is embedded in the principle of state sovereignty. This principle has given rise to national and local legal systems in two-hundred-odd countries that reflect a rich diversity of political, social, economic, and historical forces. Each country has the authority to regulate business activity. Perceived national and local interests predominate, not cross-border concerns. As a result, courts, regulatory regimes, and attorneys remain captive to their national or local perspectives and interests. While in some regions, such as the European Union (EU), the harmonization of laws is becoming quite important, harmonization remains the rare and limited exception. Moreover, the scattered network of bilateral and multilateral treaties—the backbone of international law—offers only a very limited attempt

TABLE 6.1. Multilevel Legal Systems Facing International Legal Counsel

Legal System	Decisional Authorities	Sources of Law
Public International Law, which governs relations among states and international organizations, including diplomatic relations, belligerency, and commercial relations.	International Court of Justice (Hague); International Criminal Court (Hague); ad hoc bilateral and multilateral tribunals, United Nations Security Council.	Treaties, customary law, general principles of law applied by civilized nations, and view of leading commentators. Decisions of the UN Security Council and Resolutions of the UN General Assembly are evidence of law.
Private International Law, **which** governs relations among individuals and legal entities from different countries.	National courts at all levels.	"Conflict of law" rules as adopted by legislatures and courts of each state and foreign and international law where relevant.
Supranational/Regional Law, which governs relations among states within a region as to specified activities and may apply directly to nationals in those states.	National courts at all levels as well as any supranational legislative and administrative bodies and courts. The European Union, for instance, has all three, while the North American Free Trade Area has none of these.	Treaties establishing the supranational authorities, implementing laws and regulations of governing bodies, and interprettive decisions of judicial bodies.
National Law, which governs all relations within a country as well as foreign policies, and typically is divided among different levels of government.	National legislatures, courts, and administrative tribunals, which may share authority with other levels of government as provided in national constitutions, e.g., federal systems of Canada, Germany, and the United States.	State constitutions, international treaties, legislation, judicial decisions, and relevant legal codes and other authorities. On occasion, certain courts may recognize in decisions foreign and international law.

to address the multijurisdictional conflicts that challenge transnational business operations.

The legacy of national sovereignty has practical outcomes for legal counsel and their corporate clients. First, cross-border business transactions are subject to widely differing rules and practices, due to varying legal and judicial philosophies, court and administrative systems, and attorney practices. Basic differences among legal systems make multinational legal planning and compliance extremely difficult (see Table 6.1).

International private law is often classified into several major legal systems. These include common law, including in England, the United States (except for Louisiana), Canada (except for Quebec), South Africa, Australia, and New Zealand; civil law, including much of Continental Europe, Latin America, and former colonies of European powers; socialist law, including the former Soviet regimes of Russia and other nonmarket systems; and Islamic law systems, including many nations where Islamic law or *Shari'ah* forms the jurisprudential base.

In general, the more developed legal systems offer firms a greater degree of protection of private property and private enterprise, more certainty in conducting sophisticated commercial, financial, trade, and investment transactions, and more impartial and effective dispute resolution. In less developed legal systems, firms often seek to compensate for the lack of adequate legal protection through other, extrajudicial means, which may involve some self-help remedies (contractual right to seize property), intermediaries (escrow account holders), or private arbitration procedures. But these makeshift remedies can be both uncertain and costly.

Within each legal system, moreover, the legal profession is locally (some would say parochially) regulated. This presents yet another type of legal risk to a global management. Attorneys may find themselves unable to serve the full scope of their clients' multinational business operations because bar associations, law societies, and other legal licensing bodies frown upon local attorneys going outside their "domestic" jurisdiction and dispensing advice on matters of "foreign" law. These national regimes are only now beginning to take account of the simple fact that an increasing number of economic actors present in their respective jurisdictions are doing business on a global scale and may require a different legal treatment than purely domestic business entities. Second, states have radically different ideologies and approaches to regulating business activity. The same type of business transaction or business entity may be treated differently, regulated, restricted, or banned altogether. Hostility to private business activities and foreign ownership, uneven enforcement of law, political, and foreign affairs considerations, favoritism, and government corruption can distort the application by courts and administrators of relatively sophisticated legal regimes, even when laws on their surface seem to favor commercial activities. Thus, for example, some of the newly independent post-Soviet states have adopted en masse various pieces of well-drafted and well-meaning commercial legislation but continue to remain largely inhospitable markets for private entrepreneurs and foreign investment due to the problems of enforcement, weak political will to implement reform, and pervasive corruption. Although a strong and independent judiciary with the power to review government decisions is essential, many political systems do not recognize the separation of powers, or do not provide the judiciary with the practical means of enforcing judicial decisions against government or state-owned entities.

Third, the central role of "jurisdiction" and limited role of comity and reciprocity in international private law generate both uncertainty and complexity

TABLE 6.2.   Principal Bases of Jurisdiction

Territoriality. This is a fundamental principle inherent in the sovereignty of every independent state that allows it to assert jurisdiction over all matters within its borders. It is not without limits, however, some of which are expressed in the other bases of jurisdiction below.

Nationality. Complementary to the territoriality basis, the right of an independent state to adjudicate disputes involving its nationals (and, in some instances, residents and domiciliaries) rests on the principle of sovereignty subject to certain limits.

Universality. One example of universal jurisdiction is premised on the inherent right of any independent state to address problems of such gravity and global nature that they affect the fundamental interests of the international community as a whole.

Protection. This jurisdictional basis emphasizes harm to a state's own national interests and focuses on the effects on a state of an activity occurring outside the state's borders.

Passive Personality. In criminal or tort cases, the nationality of the victim or the injured party may give rise to the jurisdiction of the state in which such person is a citizen or resident.

Extraterritoriality. This is a term given to the consequences of states exercising jurisdiction over foreign nationals, residents, or transactions as well as of legislation explicitly or implicitly targeting such foreign nationals, residents, or transactions.

for firms' cross-border operations (see Table 6.2). Aside from a few international conventions, such as the U.S. Convention on Contracts for the International Sale of Goods of 1980, and bilateral tax, trade, and investment treaties, states are reluctant to limit their right to regulate international business activities within their borders.

It is important to emphasize that these jurisdictional bases overlap and that in some circumstances no single basis may be sufficient to sustain valid jurisdiction under international law (which exerts some tempering influence in most national courts). Most developed legal systems have established the means to mediate among jurisdictional conflicts. Commonly known as "conflicts of laws," these rules attempt to help courts and lawyers determine which national law should govern a specific transaction or dispute out of two or more possible legal systems that may be applicable but offer different results. Nevertheless, "conflict of law" rules are the creature of national legal systems. Their application is subject to the interpretation of local courts and political or ideological interference. This fact can lead to unexpected results.

STRUCTURING TRANSACTIONS TO HARMONIZE
LEGAL REQUIREMENTS

There have been few changes in the legal environment of the multinational firm that serve to harmonize divergent national laws. Some of the few exceptions can be seen in the treaty requirements imposed by the World Trade Organization (WTO), within major regional trading blocs, and in the areas of intellectual property law, taxation, and certain other specialized legal areas.[1] A lawyer advising a multinational enterprise generally must still consider: (1) the law of each jurisdiction with authority to regulate the firm's activities within and, sometimes, outside its national borders; (2) international law (including treaties and conventions, international customary law, and so-called "general principles of international law") that has been accepted by each jurisdiction into its domestic laws; and (3) "unwritten law" or a combination of commercial cultures, practices, and norms that exist outside the confines of written law.

Bridging the fundamental differences among these three components, however, sometimes offers enterprises special opportunities that originate far from national parliaments, courts, or regulators. They lie in the realm of new technologies, business patterns, and global political, economic, and environmental trends (such as technological innovation, cheaper transportation and communications costs, lower trade barriers, and emphasis on trade in services rather than goods). To take advantage of these opportunities, enterprises are being driven to integrate and innovate, which in turn is intensifying global competition.

Nevertheless, the necessity of integrating or reinventing cross-border operations has not been accompanied by adequate international coordination among national legal regimes in matters of trade and investment. This has resulted in:

- Inefficiencies and confusion in interpreting applicable law. Many legal systems lack the transparency needed to handle complex commercial transactions, including poor access to judicial, regulatory, and administrative documents;
- Failed regulatory efforts, as firms manipulate diversity among the legal systems in the never-ending search for cheaper sources of production and lower taxes, customs duties, and other trade barriers and restrictions; and
- Inequities in the conduct of business overall, whether due to government corruption, monopolistic markets, or discriminatory treatment of foreign investors.

Some countries, including major emerging markets such as China, India, Russia, and Brazil, continue to espouse significant foreign investment and trade restrictions. Many other countries resist the idea of having open access to their markets and put various obstacles on the way of globalization. As a result, the very benefits of the liberalization of international trade and investment achieved through recent multilateral and bilateral mechanisms are often put at risk through the application of poorly harmonized or developed national laws. Policies and practices designed to buffer and protect local ("vested") interests from foreign incursion and the demands of global competition place substantial obstacles in the way of foreign companies, often at the expense of local consumers.

Developing economies are not the only ones plagued with this type of protectionist obstructionism. Foreign direct investment (FDI) restrictions and protected industries are common in most every country, including the European Union (at least for non-EU firms) and, to a much lesser extent, in the United States, where foreign ownership restrictions are relatively narrowly drawn and mild.

Other noneconomic, international problem areas also call for harmonized laws among nations. Terrorism—not unlike piracy in previous centuries—is resulting in the broadened application by national courts of universal jurisdiction to criminal, military, and immigration law. Universal jurisdiction, accompanied by intensified enforcement, is also being applied to trafficking in people, arms, and illicit drugs. Commercial operations of legitimate business are seriously affected by the increased vigilance of law enforcement in such areas as customs clearance, foreign labor, and banking transactions. While these threats spell increased costs for firms dependent on the physical movement of cargo, it has opened up new opportunities for other firms and new technologies.

MINIMIZING LEGAL RISKS TO BUSINESS OPERATIONS

Corporate managers often view legal and regulatory concerns as key obstacles to efficient global trade and investment. As a result, managers have grown to rely on input from attorneys to ascertain what the law requires and how to stay in compliance. However well-versed these attorneys might be, there are always significant risks, both for local and foreign counsel, in accurately interpreting foreign laws, regulations, and court decisions, and in anticipating how these will be applied by tribunals and government officials in the future.

Because law depends so much on its application by government officials and administrative tribunals, foreign companies often need local counsel to assist them in interfacing with the host country's government authorities on many different levels. As experienced managers know, knowledge of the law is just a starting point. There is often a sizable gap between written law and actual regulatory practice. Many countries do not have a complete or well-versed civil service in place to support foreign investment and trade, and may suffer as well from pervasive corruption. Foreign companies doing business in emerging-market economies cannot take existing institutions and business practices for granted, as they are still evolving and inexperienced. Even in developed economies, the task of dealing with the government bureaucracy is formidable as businesses must deal with ever-expanding and burdensome regulatory requirements. Below are some of the common areas of legal concern to global business.

Intellectual Property and E-Commerce

One of the most formidable challenges to global business lies in generating and protecting intellectual property (IP). Because IP is the foundation of the knowledge, software, and Internet economies, substantial losses are incurred from piracy and other types of infringement. Theft and counterfeiting of intellectual property around the world have grown to truly catastrophic proportions and is occasionally advocated and practiced by states as well as by organized crime.[2] A major portion of this theft occurs in the emerging nations where IP protection is weakest.[3] (See Box 6.1.)

While the law could easily regulate and protect manufacturing and sales activities of a traditional nineteenth-century corporation, it has been struggling with pharmaceuticals, digitized music, and video, and such late-twentieth-century innovations as e-commerce and bio-engineering, none of which fits neatly into existing property and contract doctrines. In the virtual world of Internet or e-commerce, entities may enjoy a significant slice of the economic pie without having a legal "presence" in any jurisdiction in the conventional sense, that is, physical address, office, plant, warehouse, or even bank accounts. They, therefore, become a much tougher target for government regulators.

Box 6.1 Chinese & U.S. Authorities Cooperate to Convict Counterfeiters

U.S. Immigration and Customs Enforcement (ICE) hails U.S.-Chinese cooperation that led to the conviction and sentencing in Shanghai of two U.S. counterfeiters and two Chinese accomplices. In an April 19, 2005, news release, ICE announced the successful conclusion of "Operation Spring" and described the joint U.S.-China effort as a "landmark" that will serve as a road map for future cooperation on intellectual property rights (IPR) investigations. A Shanghai people's court sentenced the offenders to jail terms and ordered them to pay fines for illegally selling and distributing more than $840,000 worth of pirated DVDs (digital versatile discs) via the Internet to buyers in more than twenty countries. The case began in September 2003 with an ICE official's purchase of counterfeit DVDs at a flea market in the southern United States. It "led to the conviction in China of a global distributor of counterfeit products, thanks to the hard work of Chinese authorities and ICE agents," said Michael Garcia, the U.S. Department of Homeland Security (DHS) assistant secretary for ICE. Chinese law enforcement personnel seized more than 210,000 counterfeit motion picture DVDs and approximately $67,000 in U.S. currency as well as 222,000 Chinese renminbi. [approximately $27,500] Chinese authorities also located and destroyed three warehouses that were being used to store counterfeit motion picture DVDs. Overall the operation utilized the efforts of various U.S. law enforcement organizations as well as China's Ministry of Public Security and Shanghai's Public Security Bureau.[4]

New network-sharing technologies enabling the redistribution of text, graphics, music, video, and other content to millions of individuals across the world in seconds are among the new challenges facing legal systems. The campaigns of the music and film industries against Internet file-sharing networks have proven to be a difficult challenge for American courts.[5] These developments signal a need for a major overhaul of the business law that has been heeded in some countries and ignored or neglected in others.

Government Regulation in Host Countries

Legal regulation of business varies greatly across the world. The scope of regulation ranges from relatively laissez-faire jurisdictions with minimal governmental intrusion (such as industry self-regulation) to very pervasive regulatory regimes that subject business operations within their borders to administrative mandate and require licensing and adherence to specified statutory norms and agency rules. In general, more open market economies tend to intervene less in the majority of business activities that do not pose a clear threat to the national economies or represent economic crimes. However, even those market economies that for ideological and pragmatic reasons give businesses significant freedoms in the questions of formation and liquidation (or market entry and exit) may subject certain areas of the economy to massive regulation.

Thus, aside from a few "hard-core" proponents of a command economy, such as Cuba, Burma, and North Korea, a large number of national economies continues to feature significant state-dominated sectors and many state-owned enterprises.[6] Both nonmarket and mixed-market economies use the law and the threat of criminal punishment or administrative sanctions as a means to further ideological, political, and possibly personal goals of government leaders to manipulate the private economic sector. Even within the clearly capitalist economic system there are degrees of state intervention in the affairs of private companies based on the "public interest." The "public interest" covers a wide range of social policies, that is, (i) competition, consumer protection, and unfair trade practices; (ii) employment and workplace safety; (iii) data protection and privacy; (iv) business licensing; and (vi) tax, financial reporting, accounting, and currency controls.

Laws of business regulation occasionally have "teeth" beyond the civil relief ordinarily available to private litigants in contract and commercial disputes. For example, antitrust laws impose individual criminal liability on corporate officers and employees for willful violations of their provisions. Legal entities may also be found guilty of violating criminal provisions of business regulation laws, although the only penalty applicable to legal entities in most jurisdictions is monetary fines (as opposed to jail time for executives). They provide for treble damages and other types of punitive damages, which in some instances may be catastrophic to the company found guilty of violating such laws.

Resolving Business Disputes between Local
Parties and Governments

International dispute resolution is fraught with many more risks and uncertainties than an average domestic civil process. Enforcing judgments across
national borders is difficult, if at all possible, and litigating in foreign jurisdictions may be subject to undue pressures, corruption in the judicial process,
and outright duress. Usually the biggest obstacles to litigating abroad, especially in less developed countries, are (1) unfamiliarity with the local civil
procedure governing court actions, and (2) the shortage of qualified trial lawyers who are also familiar with the laws and business practices of the multinational enterprise's home jurisdiction.

The nature of civil litigation in the United States, Britain, India, and other
common law jurisdictions is radically different from that of much of the rest of
the world. It relies on a rather prolonged, costly, adversarial procedure with
litigants having some role in influencing the pace of the process. Civil code
jurisdictions have a much smaller incidence of litigation and a simplified,
streamlined civil procedure where judges control the process almost exclusively and litigants have little input. Litigation, even if successful, also suffers
from very limited international recognition of judgments, which then have to
be enforced through additional court proceedings in one or several countries
where enforcement of the judgment is sought.

International arbitration offers many advantages over litigation and is used
increasingly in transnational business disputes as a kind of alternative dispute
resolution process. Its principal strength is in the ability to avoid the risk of
having to litigate in the other party's courts and thus to avoid potential bias and
unfairness. With the main international arbitration centers now established in
London, Paris, Stockholm, and New York, among others, international arbitration also offers a process led by competent arbitral bodies and arbitrators
with significant commercial experience. Indeed, the parties may be able to
select an arbitrator or arbitration panel that has expertise in a particular
technical or business area. Arbitration in general tends to be less expensive and
more expeditious than litigation, although much depends on how the dispute
resolution process is designed by the parties to a contract that provides for
arbitration. Some also believe that arbitrators in well-established commercial
arbitration centers can be more competent and proficient adjudicators than
judges who typically hear a wide range of cases. Arbitration is also final and,
with few exceptions, there is no right of appeal from the arbitration award
(something that may be both an advantage and a disadvantage). Finally, arbitration proceedings are typically nonpublic and provide often-sought confidentiality to the parties involved in a dispute.

Most international arbitration contracts today contain clauses providing for
arbitration in a neutral forum, often on the basis of institutionally designed and
administered rules (such as those promulgated by the American Arbitration

Association and the United Nationals Commission on International Trade Law). International investment disputes with host jurisdictions are commonly arbitrated at the International Center for the Settlement of Investment Disputes. Arbitral awards are intended to be a final, judicially enforceable decision. This is achievable if the countries of the parties are signatories of the New York Convention on the Recognition and Enforcement of Foreign Arbitral Awards, to which over one hundred nations have subscribed.

In an international context, arbitration rules and procedures may be complex, and the application of various national laws may not be avoided altogether, especially when enforcing arbitral awards. Moreover, in a number of countries that subscribe to the so-called Calvo Clause, courts may refuse to enforce mandatory arbitration clauses in commercial contracts but instead require the parties to agree to arbitration only after their dispute arose. Special conditions apply to litigation or arbitration involving state-owned or controlled entities.

Laws with Extraterritorial Reach and Conflicts of Law

Multinational enterprises and other companies involved in transnational business are by definition functioning in a multijurisdictional environment. They are exposed to legal risks from each host country where they are "present" or "doing business." Yet determining which laws of what countries apply can be complex. Courts, therefore, ask whether a company is "doing business" (maintaining certain minimal contacts) in its jurisdiction. Though this phrase in law has a distinctly technical meaning, it usually refers to the fact that a firm has voluntarily submitted to the jurisdiction of a host country by undertaking certain activities within the state's borders.

The challenges raised by laws operating across frontiers are real and potentially devastating due to the fact that jurisdiction may be asserted by two or more sovereign governments at the same time over the same company and its activities (see Table 6.2). A company incorporated in one country (jurisdiction by "nationality") may conduct sales activities within a nation's borders (jurisdiction by "territoriality"), while defects in its products may injure someone within another country (jurisdiction by "protection"), and the injured party may be a national of a third country (jurisdiction by "passive personality"). This has led the United States and the European Union to assert extraterritorial jurisdiction over firms whose actions outside their territories adversely affect activities and polices within their territories (see Box 6.2).

Conflicts of laws (which mandate which national law should govern) and conflicts of international jurisdiction (which interpose a certain location or forum in which a dispute is to be brought for resolution) impose additional costs on companies doing business internationally and prevent multinational enterprises from realizing greater efficiencies in their global operations. One consequence of these conflicts is that laws of one nation may (by contractual

Box 6.2 The Russian Gas Pipeline Dispute

In the early 1980s, during the Cold War with the Soviet Union, the United States sought to prevent the French engineering subsidiary of a U.S. enterprise from providing pump technology to a European consortium intending to import natural gas by pipeline from Russia. U.S. authority was based on U.S. Export Control Regulations, which banned the export of U.S.-source technology without government approval of the use of the technology. These regulations applied to affiliates owned or controlled by U.S. corporations. American policy-makers chose to extend United States export controls on oil and gas equipment to the fullest extent possible under the law so as to restrict exports from the United States and from Europe. This option embodied the most expansive interpretation of United States power to apply its laws extraterritorially. Regulations were promulgated, pursuant to the Export Administration Act (EAA), which stated that for the purpose of those controls, persons subject to the jurisdiction of the United States included: (1) citizens or residents of the United States; (2) persons within the United States; (3) corporations organized under United States law; and (4) any partnership, association, corporation or other organization wherever organized or doing business, that is owned or controlled by persons specified in (1), (2), or (3). The Commerce Department began enforcement proceedings in the United States and denied export privileges to firms in France, the United Kingdom, Italy, and West Germany. The ministers of the European Communities complained, and the British and French governments took steps to prevent their firms from complying with U.S. law. On November 13, 1982, approximately five months after extension of the controls to Europe, the U.S. president announced that the United States had reached agreement with several European states on regulating relations with the Soviets, and the controls on European exports were lifted. The issue became moot and no U.S. court has ruled on the legitimacy of the expansive jurisdiction contemplated in the EAA. European objections to the United States controls had been expressed in terms of international law principles. They had claimed that that exercise of jurisdiction was contrary to international law and that the United States' actions had been an infringement on European sovereignty. American policy-makers justified the extension of export controls and argued this was legitimate under international law. Both sides justified their positions in terms of the traditional bases for extraterritorial application of law and the more recently articulated *Restatement* reasonableness analysis.[7]

choice or by a decision of a judge) be applied outside its borders in a foreign state—a phenomenon known as extraterritoriality. The following categories of substantive laws have been known to apply outside the home jurisdiction when the company in question is deemed to be a local national or where adverse effects of an overseas transaction are deemed to reach the home country in one way or another.

Box 6.3 Differences in Antitrust Philosophies

The European Commission's controversial decision to block a proposed merger between U.S. firms General Electric and Honeywell is an example of antitrust or competition laws invoked to thwart a pending transaction between firms not even organized under European laws. The EU Commission feared that the combination of these two corporate strengths would have given the merged firm almost complete control over the market in aviation equipment. This is the first time that the European authorities have vetoed a U.S.-only merger that had already been given clearance by the U.S. Justice Department. The EU Commission also blocked a proposed merger between WorldCom and Sprint and a proposed takeover by AOL Time Warner of Britain's EMI. From these cases it would appear that European government authorities are tougher on big mergers than is the United States. This action has provoked anger in the United States and the threat of retaliatory action from senior American politicians. The United States has retaliated against Europe in international trade matters before—most famously in a recently resolved row over bananas. It remains unlikely, though, that Washington would regard the failure of a corporate merger—even one involving a firm as large and well known as GE—as serious enough to warrant souring international relations.

Antitrust Laws. These laws may be invoked, for example, with the acquisition of a company, product line, or business operations/productive assets that are located in several different nations and where approval of each national competition authority may have to be sought. Another example relates to distribution, licensing, and various other commercial agreements that may have anticompetitive clauses. It is worth noting that the EU Court has employed the concept of "extraterritoriality" in an antitrust case below (see Box 6.3).

Securities Regulation. Issuing and trading securities, soliciting investors, and similar investment activities commonly trigger the application of securities laws in every nation where such activities are undertaken. There is a wide divergence in securities regulation among different nations, and less developed economies may not have significant government oversight of securities transactions.

Financial and Tax Reporting. This obligation is typically triggered in connection with the company laws of every nation where subsidiaries, affiliates, and sometimes branches and representative offices of a foreign company are domiciled and wherever the company is found to be "doing business" for tax purposes.

Foreign Corrupt Practices Act. The Foreign Corrupt Practices Act is a U.S. statute that, with some minor exceptions, proscribes bribery of foreign government officials. The statute was followed by a recent Organisation for Economic Co-Operation and Development (OECD) initiative targeting some of the same activities. Although laws banning bribery in the domestic context are fairly common, other nations may or may not have similar legislation that targets corruption overseas.

Employment and Labor Laws. These laws are triggered anytime a company employs local nationals. Occasionally employment and labor laws may be invoked with respect to persons otherwise considered independent contractors; protection of agents and distributors is a common theme in many developing nations.

Fraud and White-Collar Crimes. Jurisdiction over fraud and white-collar crimes can sometimes be very far-reaching and predicated on the nationality of an officer or a director as well as the domicile of the company, regardless of where the crime was committed. While fraud is proscribed in many legal systems, effectiveness of prosecution of white-collar crimes varies greatly from one country to another, depending generally on the strength, integrity, and efficiency of the rule of law in that society.

National Security. Many nations seek to regulate commercial transactions of private firms when they concern national security, defense, or other industries deemed of "national importance." Some countries, including the United States (with the Exon-Florio Act[8] as one example), restrict acquisition of domestic entities in such industries by foreign companies.

From economic and political perspectives, extraterritorial jurisdiction creates a number of problems with respect to international trade and investment. Arguably, it increases the burden of legal and regulatory compliance and generates conflicts among national laws. Naturally the existence of such extraterritorial jurisdiction does not mean that the state will choose to exercise it in every instance. In reality, states have little practical influence in enforcing compliance outside their borders. However, extraterritorial jurisdiction is more than a mere theoretical dilemma for free trade. As a practical matter, firms have no choice but to seek full compliance with the applicable laws of their home country as well as the nations where they do business. The threat of penalties (including, in some instances, criminal penalties), loss of government contracts, and resulting bad publicity usually deter business from ignoring the extraterritorial jurisdiction of their home countries.

Structuring Foreign Investment

The laws applicable to the formation of commercial entities constitute one area of transnational law where practitioners may find a relative common approach. There is commonality, if not actual harmony, among the basic principles and doctrines employed in the law of business organization in some countries, though with significant divergences in other countries (see Box 6.4). Thus, at least within a single family of jurisdictions (such as a common law or a civil law system), corporate entities and their formation, organization, capitalization, management, and reorganization or liquidation are—despite

Box 6.4 Structural Considerations in FDI Transactions

In structuring an investment transaction in a foreign country, several preliminary considerations should be carefully analyzed. First, a decision must be made whether to structure the investment as an acquisition of shares or assets or as a merger or consolidation and whether a new enterprise is to be formed with the assistance and participation of the local partner, involving a joint venture entity or contractual alliance. While business requirements are an important part of these decisions, tax and regulatory requirements typically play a major role.

Apart from the level of investment itself, the principal legal risk in acquiring rather than forming a new company ("greenfield") in a foreign country is undisclosed tax or other liabilities. Although this risk can be managed to a large extent through an appropriate due diligence examination of the target company, where the risk of nondisclosure is unreasonably high, consideration should be given to formation of a new company, a limited purchase of assets, or subcontracting for the needed components or services. Another possibility is to interpose a shareholding entity that can buffer against unknown liability. Often, a special-purpose subsidiary is established to achieve that purpose.

Foreign investors envisioning a holding company structure with operational units in multiple foreign markets should also consider how "functionally distinct" or "industry distinct" divisions of the company should be organized. Most legal systems provide a fairly broad selection of legal entities from which to choose the juridical form of a foreign business entity, including forms of stock companies or corporations, general and limited partnerships, and limited liability companies. Initial entry into foreign markets is also feasible via branches and representative offices of a foreign company, both of which can be formed without forming a local entity.

differences in terminology and local practice—grounded in the same general principles.

Even beyond a single legal system, company laws share many fundamental similarities among the nations of the world, and business lawyers from virtually all jurisdictions would be generally conversant with the principal features of legal entities such as corporations, limited liability companies, and partnerships. Company laws of less developed countries often mirror either common law or civil law traditions, although in practice their legal provisions may be enforced quite differently from what was intended by the legislator.

A critical disclaimer is in order here. As the saying goes, "The devil is in the details," and the legal work that goes into determining the actual rules applicable to foreign direct investment activities and the ways of achieving legal compliance must obviously be done with each new foreign market a firm enters. Important distinctions are normally found in foreign investment laws, which restrict or vary the requirements for enterprises with some foreign ownership or control. Probably the biggest element of divergence and surprise relates to taxation, because tax laws and regulations of individual countries bear little resemblance to one another beyond the common motivation of the tax authorities to maximize tax revenue. Virtually every business transaction involves issues of corporate income tax and, possibly, withholding tax, and may also involve sales or value-added tax, payroll taxes, capital gains tax, and other taxes. A network of bilateral tax treaties provides some limited relief from "double taxation," or multiple profit taxes, which may be imposed by several jurisdictions on the same cross-border trade or investment transaction.[9] Many other categories of taxes are not regulated by treaties and tend to vary greatly from one market to another, thus complicating both financial planning and tax compliance for the business taxpayers.

FORGING A PRO-ACTIVE MINDSET

The challenges described above require attorneys to think more comprehensively and creatively about their work on behalf of enterprises with global agendas. This shift in thinking has less to do with the traditional tools of legal analysis (such as interpreting statutes, rules, and judicial opinions) than with developing a broader perspective on the interaction of different legal, economic, and political systems.

Clearly globalization is making the work of business lawyers everywhere increasingly multijurisdictional and multidisciplinary. With many more firms venturing into foreign markets and some of them also making equity investments abroad, their legal advisers are no longer able to cling to the traditional notion of practicing law in one or more jurisdictions. Many law firms and in-house law departments, therefore, have been aggressively expanding overseas to establish "one-stop shopping" for their clients. Business lawyers are also asked for more comprehensive, strategic legal advice and must be prepared to handle questions previously reserved for a particular legal specialty or even for nonlawyers. They also must be prepared for much closer cooperation with accountants, finance professionals, general management, and other experts.

Legal counselors to transnational enterprises have to approach their work differently. They need to understand their business clients' global objectives and strategies, their competitive strengths and weaknesses, their strategic competencies, and the impact of new technologies on global business. When they fail to do this, they risk being viewed essentially as legal technicians and being consigned to narrow and technical tasks far from the boardrooms where corporate strategies are plotted and executed.

In coming to grips with the challenges of globalization for enterprises, therefore, corporate counsel must shift their perception of their tasks in five critical ways. These should be viewed as an addition to—and not a replacement for—the high standards of legal craftsmanship traditionally expected of attorneys.

Shifting from an ethnocentric to a **geocentric view of law**, corporate counsel need to understand how legal systems differ and the distinctiveness of their underlying values and practices. For example, to understand why EU and U.S. competition laws differ, or why certain cultures do not hang everything on rules and contractual provisions, corporate counsel need to appreciate the history and rationale of particular laws and legal systems. Despite some common objectives among EU and U.S. antitrust law, the European Union must overcome a long history of cartels, protected markets among its member states, and dominant national enterprises that the United States—with over a century of antitrust experience and a continentwide market—has never faced or no longer faces.

Shifting from a single to a **multilevel jurisdictional practice**, corporate counsel need to appreciate critical institutional differences that exist among judicial systems, whether due to their unitary, federal, confederal, or supranational structure. All legal systems reflect jurisdictional differences among their courts and administrative tribunals that enterprises can ignore only at their risk, as they typically reflect a deeply embedded check and balance of national power. Most legal systems recognize the fundamental principle that judicial remedies must be exhausted at one level before proceeding to the next, but this can become extraordinarily complex when tribunals from different states are involved. Within one jurisdiction, rules usually exist that determine which court rulings take precedence and when an appeal may be taken from one court to another. Once foreign court rulings on the same matter become involved, however, there is little specific judicial guidance apart from general principles of comity.

Shifting from a unilateral to a **multilateral, complementary view of law**, corporate counsel need to broaden their perspective, shifting from a unilateral view of law where legal systems compete with each other for the authority to resolve disputes to a multilateral view that recognizes the complementary roles of differing systems and of multilateral and regional agencies. This entails the ability to see how, through careful analysis and thoughtful draftsmanship, differing legal requirements can dovetail or be aligned with each other.

Shifting from a purely transactional to a **strategic view of legal practice**, corporate counsel need to view every transaction within the larger framework of a globally integrated enterprise and the vision and policies that drive it. Thus, it may be feasible to drive hard bargains on individual transactions to achieve lower costs, but this practice may give the firm a reputation that hampers its operations worldwide.

Shifting from a purely craftsman to a risk manager view, corporate counsel need to develop their expertise in the service of managing risk. While it is critically important to do things right in a professional sense, limited time and resources compel counsel to focus on minimizing business risks. This entails an ability to recognize and prioritize risks and to provide others in the organization with the guidelines, workable rules, and procedures for carrying out their tasks in the most efficient and effective way. Corporate counsel should see themselves as facilitators of enterprise operations, rather than as primarily naysayers or road blocks. Equally important are the qualities of practicality and pragmatism related to the exercise of judgment, such as looking for cost-effective, politically viable, and socially responsible ways to solve legal issues.

KEY MANAGEMENT COMPETENCIES
FOR CORPORATE COUNSEL

The challenges of today's global business environment place very special demands on corporate counsel in advising senior management. In responding to these challenges, corporate counsel act both as purveyors of legal advice and as intermediaries between outside counsel and the firms employing them. As such, they must combine the analytical skills of international attorneys and the organizational and communication skills of managers. The legal management competencies proposed here reflect the "proactive mindset" noted above.

Working Appreciation of Interactive Legal Systems

Legal counsel to transnational businesses are primarily responsible for minimizing the legal risks of entering and operating in multiple jurisdictions. While knowledge of foreign laws can be helpful to this end, this task is generally better left to local counsel who appreciate the legal nuances. Much more valuable is an understanding of how different legal systems interact in regulating global business and how to resolve any conflicts that result from the clash of these systems.

A spirit of legal pragmatism is an especially valuable trait when seeking to accommodate differing or competing legal requirements. Contracts, for instance, must realistically reflect the environment in which they will be performed (or breached), possibly renegotiated, and enforced through the judicial process. In the international environment, counsel need to find a balance between two extremes. "Overlawyering" matters can be costly, both in terms of legal fees and, more important, of business relationships. Negotiating and drafting "ironclad" agreements that purport to protect firms against all possible risks can easily be seen by potential partners as signs of mistrust and inflexibility or as attempts to intimidate or lock in an unfair advantage. This can endanger long-term partnerships and alliance relationships. "Under-lawyering," by contrast, is equally undesirable. This may be done in the mistaken belief that "to keep things simple" will be less likely to offend the local partner or possibly confuse local government authorities. While the rationale of civil code systems may well obviate the need for lengthy U.S.-style agreements, there are no excuses for failing to perform appropriate due diligence or to accurately document critical points.

Some happy medium is always needed when translating practices from advanced legal cultures, such as centers of international capital like New York, London, Frankfurt, and Tokyo, to other territories and circumstances. Nothing sours a deal faster than having an aggressive New York–style lawyer disregard rules of negotiation—for instance, in a Continental European or East Asian milieu—and hammer the other party with unreasonable demands in order to secure a "killer contract." Being aware of foreign commercial and corporate cultures, understanding their institutions and practices, and being open to original, creative solutions to cross-cultural deadlocks are all qualities of a good international business lawyer.

"Fluency" in Cross-Cultural Lawyering

Despite some convergence in the legal practices and protocols of cross-border deals, differences still abound among nations –especially among countries with fundamentally different legal systems, as noted in the Box 6.5. Fluency in working with these differences is an important skill needed by corporate counsel, for legal systems incorporate the social, economic, and political values of the country. Thus, rule-oriented lawyers need to think in terms of relationships to get things done in most foreign jurisdictions. In many civil code systems, moreover, the law can be understood only within the context of a highly refined, conceptually integrated legal system. Outside the United States, attorneys should understand that various forms of non-judicial dispute resolution are far more prevalent than litigation. This is especially true

---

Box 6.5 Different Styles of Agreements among Legal Systems

European acquisition agreements tend to be much less detailed and comprehensive than their U.S. counterparts. Europeans are more keen to consider the most obvious risks beforehand and to discuss how they would be addressed in a contract, though they would be relying on general answers from the civil code, commercial code, or some other general business legislation and would be less likely to provide for such specific contingencies in the document. Asian parties tend to put a lot of faith in the personal dynamics of their business relationship and, instead of agreeing on all possible minute aspects of their deal, would rather leave them open, hoping to resolve potential disagreements through mediation and continued negotiations. Americans favor very detailed contracts in which any possible contingencies and future rights and obligations of the parties to a contract are spelled out in advance as much as possible to minimize uncertainty and to allocate risks of breach of contract in advance. There is also a greater tendency in American legal documents to be self-contained and not rely on outside sources such as statutes or regulations.

of commercial and regulatory disputes with states, governmental agencies and other sovereign entities. Continental European, Latin American, and other attorneys schooled in the civil legal tradition should realize that their customary reliance on civil and commercial codes and other legislation in lieu of comprehensive documentation may not be sufficient to fully protect corporate interests.

Working Effectively in Teams

Corporate counsel need to work effectively as a full member of the management team in order to contribute effectively to a firm's decision-making process. Counsel must foster and effectively use communications channels within management at all levels, as well as with outside attorneys and the entire range of corporate constituents around the world, if he or she is to benefit from the immense cultural and political diversity at work in the multinational environment. As much as for other areas of senior management, corporate counsel must also be cognizant of the full range of possibly diverse corporate objectives at work in a far-flung enterprise and how they are being pursued, so that these can be factored into legal analysis. Most larger multinational organizations are managed by groups of executive managers, often with different national and cultural backgrounds, working out of widely scattered affiliated entities. They are likely to have perspectives and operating issues very distinct from those at corporate headquarters.

A work ethic for the law function that incorporates teamwork not only enables effective communication, but also protects corporate counsel against being blindsided. Might General Electric's bid to acquire European Honeywell, for instance, have been successful had GE's European counsel had the opportunity to lay groundwork with the European Commission before GE's CEO launched a full-court press? (See Box 6.3.) While the precise scope of corporate counsel's functions varies greatly from country to country and from one firm to another, it is absolutely necessary for lawyers to work alongside functional managers and technical experts from other fields in order to understand and minimize risks in transacting business, protecting tangible and intellectual property, and complying with industry regulations. Indeed, the legal function is arguably the business function closest to the executive boardroom because of its role in shaping corporate strategy as well as in ensuring legal compliance in day-to-day operations.

Working Effectively with Outside Counsel

Perhaps the most critical competencies for corporate counsel are hiring outside counsel and using these counsel cost effectively. Although heavily staffed in-house law departments are not unusual in major corporations, it is rare that multinational enterprises have the resources or need for full-time attorneys from all countries where an enterprise does business. Retaining out-side counsel, therefore, is essential to guide and protect firm interests around the world. It is equally essential to systematically structure, manage, and mon-itor working relationships with outside counsel, since legal fees can be ex-pensive and legal practice standards can vary widely.

The task of identifying local counsel around the world is somewhat sim-plified by retaining an international law firm that has branch offices in major countries. This gives some comfort that all attorneys in branch offices meet a commonly accepted standard of craftsmanship and professional ethics. Be-cause the branch approach can be expensive for law firms and clients alike, many more law firms are simply establishing working relationships with a network of locally independent counterparts in a variety of countries. In any event, these relationships need to be carefully managed.

Managing Risk from a Strategic Organizational Perspective

For in-house counsel in particular, managing organizational risk is a critical competency in delivering effective legal services. This applies whether the task is drafting or negotiating an agreement, advising on a regulatory matter, prosecuting civil litigation or arbitration, or implementing an organizational compliance plan. It requires counsel to be well informed about the business environment and be astute in assessing its impact on legal issues facing the enterprise—risks that are much more diverse and difficult to define for transnational than for comparable domestic enterprises. The manner in which counsel advises managers and, in effect, educates them about risks must reflect the relative sophistication of the organization and its managers, management's strategic objectives and capacity for risk-taking, and the nature and extent of the organization's assets and risks. Counsel also must be able to balance risk between the short and long term and between any given transaction and the organization as a whole.

Whatever the situation, the foremost task of corporate counsel is to struc-ture a relationship or settlement, or to position the enterprise within the legal environment so that risks are minimized or certainty is improved consonant with the enterprise's operating requirements. The goal of effective counseling is managing legal risks (which range from contractual to regulatory) efficiently and effectively within a firm without exposing it to undue legal exposure and, to the extent possible, without disrupting its business operations.

Much of the legal counseling in practice focuses on the "gray areas" of the law—where precise interpretation of the law is not possible and conclusions cannot be drawn definitively. The judgment that corporate counsel is called on to exercise in evaluating and managing such legal risks thus requires a solid understanding of the firm's business model, commercial environment, regu-latory enforcement patterns, and other nonlegal factors in addition to the "law," whether it is a contract negotiation, potential civil litigation matter, or a possible antitrust investigation by a government prosecutor. For example, an attorney advising on an antibribery compliance program for a client has to consider a wide latitude of risks shaped by the actions or nonaction the firm may choose to take with respect to dozens, maybe hundreds, of different parties and situations and to "weed out" material risks from trivial ones. To do that, counsel must take an active role in designing and monitoring the program, speaking to the managers who deal with government officials firsthand, educating the executive management, and performing other work that serves the twin goals of managing (minimizing) risk and facilitating the operations of the enterprise without undue burden.

In many jurisdictions, corporate counsel are considered to be officers of the court as well as of their firms. As such, they may be charged with special fiduciary duties to act as guardians of their companies' ethical positions and to "police" internal compliance. In this capacity, counsel can contribute a great deal by designing self-regulatory measures to be adopted by management, thereby responding to the worldwide criticism of what is widely perceived as injustices committed in the name of greed. Given the limited capacity of government to regulate effectively on a global scale, support for self-regulation is a low-cost way to change corporate behavior, restrain the backlash against globalization, and further the gains inherent in a competitive global economy.

CONCLUSION

In conclusion, globalization is bringing many challenges and calling for changes in the law function of transnational firms, significantly expanding the scope of the legal responsibilities from the traditional functions of an attorney practicing in a single national or state/provincial jurisdiction. These changes affect the way corporate counsel think about their tasks and the competencies they need to accomplish them, which include cross-cultural, multidisciplinary, and strategic skills. The principal reason for seeking out new approaches to legal counseling of the players in the new global business community is that the "rules of the game" made by national states have hardly changed since the dawn of the industrial age and are poorly suited to the information age. Until international private law takes more than baby steps toward a meaningful standardization of business law, business attorneys will have to find new ways of bridging the gap between the demands of global business and the limitations of the world's fragmented legal systems.

NOTES

1. Reich, "The WTO as a Law-Harmonizing Institution," *25 U. Pa. J. Int'l Econ. L.* *321* (spring 2004). For the texts of the WTO treaties, see http://www.wto.org/english/ docs_e/legal_e/gatt47.pdf.

2. U.S. Chamber of Commerce Report, "What Are Counterfeiting and Piracy Costing the U.S. Economy" located at http://www.uschamber.com/issues/index/counter feiting/default.

3. Allison Cychosz, "The Effectiveness of International Enforcement of Intellectual Property Rights," 37 J. Marshall L. Rev. 985 (spring 2004).

4. This press release can be located online at http://usinfo.state.gov/ei/Archive/ 2005/April/21-61764.html.

5. Jennifer Norman, "Staying Alive: Can the Recording Industry Survive Peer-to-Peer?" 26 Colum. J.L. & Arts 371 (summer 2003).

6. The World Bank, "Bureaucrats in Business: The Economics and Politics of Government Ownership," (1995): 32–33.

7. Comment: Extraterritorial Application of United States Law: The Case of Export Controls, 132 U. Pa. L. Rev. 355 (January 1984).

8. 50 U.S.C.A. app. section 2170 (West 1991 & Supp. 1993) (enacted August 23, 1988).

9. OECD, Model Tax Convention on Income and Capital (July 23, 1992), 1 Tax Treaties (CCH), p. 191.

7

Managing Country Risk

CLARENCE J. MANN

MANAGING RISK ENTAILS AN APPRECIATION OF SOCIAL DYNAMICS

Managing country risk is a perennial issue for even the best of companies. It stems from conditions in the foreign country as well as international factors impinging from outside. Thus, when Microsoft first entered China in 1989, it saw a tantalizingly enormous market. Yet after fifteen years and well over a billion dollars in expenditures, and despite the fact that 60 percent of China's computers now run on Microsoft's operating system, the company's China operations continue to run losses. Microsoft's Windows XP operating system, priced at US$245, is equivalent to four months' salary for an average Chinese worker but can be purchased on the street for $5.50. When the company pursued its usual aggressive tactics to combat software piracy, Microsoft was labeled a "foreign bully" and, reportedly, blacklisted by various government agencies, which began turning to Red Flag Linux. Despite China's international trade commitment to protect intellectual property, enforcement is weak. Widespread piracy is penalized at best by modest fines. Instead of withdrawing, however, Microsoft has toned down its combative style. It now funds basic research at Chinese universities and collaborates with government agencies to establish an indigenous software industry from scratch. As Microsoft's chief China strategist acknowledges: "There was a degree of naïveté in how we entered the country. . . . You either help [China] emerge and reap the long-term benefits or you have to make the strategic assumption that someone else will."[1] Or, to put it somewhat differently, the "common sense" that guided Microsoft to dominance in the West was not making sense in China.

For a wide variety of economic, political, and cultural reasons, firms doing business in foreign markets face a level of complexity and uncertainty to which they are unaccustomed at home. In screening countries for future operations, firms typically first consider **macroeconomic indicators**. These encompass international factors, reflected in analysis of shifting exchange rates, balances of payments, and trade policies and practices. They also include such macro-domestic factors as GDP growth rate, governmental stability, loan repudiation, various forms of direct or creeping expropriation, and rules restricting trade, remittances, and foreign investment. As a next step, firms investigate **micro-economic aspects**—those factors determining the competitive structure of the industry in the country and the policies and state practices that affect the free functioning of the commercial and market system for the firm.

There is a third aspect, however, that rarely receives sufficient attention; too often it is only fully appreciated once firms have committed resources and commenced operations. It consists of **country dynamics** reflecting distinctive mindsets and ideologies that animate attitudes, thought patterns, and behavior of a country. These dynamics influence everyday business operations. They shape markets and marketing channels, commercial institutions, and business culture and practices. As a result, they decisively affect a firm's operating performance over the long term. Taken together, these factors and dynamics constitute the risk management framework of any country.

Country Economies Are Evolving
Socioeconomic Market Systems

Conventional country risk analysis tends to focus on go/no go market entry decisions and macroeconomic indicators that affect them. This stems largely from the fact that country risk analysis has been dominated during the last half century by lending institutions, corporate financial officers, and money managers making or assessing financial commitments. Major crisis periods have shaped their views of risk analysis: "political risks" in the 1960s and 1970s, "debt risks" in the 1980s, and "financial risks" in the 1990s.[2] The crises over the past two decades, incidentally, refute the dictum frequently heard in banking circles that countries don't fail. The emphasis on sovereign debt and financial risk, moreover, has tended to skew risk analysis toward quantitative methods. But as the Microsoft experience indicates, entry analysis—however well founded in macroeconomic analysis—may have limited value for assessing the microeconomic aspects and country dynamics that affect a firm's performance. Both quantitative and qualitative analyses are needed to assess the full range of country risk on an ongoing basis.

Today's unremitting pace of globalization calls for a dynamic understanding of country risk, one that views country economies as **evolving socioeconomic market systems**. There are several reasons for this. First and foremost, market capitalism has become the dominant standard worldwide for measuring economic performance. It is the companion of the international trading system, whose principles over the past five decades are dedicated to lowering trade barriers of every kind, thus limiting the scope for governmental intervention. This standard is evident, for instance, in the annual World Competitiveness Report, initiated in 1989,[3] as well as in the World Bank's World Development Report 2005,[4] which employ both quantitative and qualitative metrics. The former employs 323 factors to rank the competitiveness of 60 country economies, while the latter compares policies and institutional factors affecting business operations among 143 countries. Indeed, the World Competitiveness Report posits enterprise competitiveness as the major determinant for raising prosperity worldwide.[5] The World Bank Report includes a variety of institutional factors that define the business climate for investment and provide incentives for firms to invest productively. As a result, whether or not a nation fully accepts the discipline of market capitalism, its industries are being measured by those standards and, to a significant extent, by the ability to function as a market capitalist system.

Cross-Border Activities Are Shaping a New "Geo-Economy"

Secondly, **cross-border activities** through market systems are penetrating and becoming embedded more or less in all economies. The primary bearers of these interpenetrating activities are transnational enterprises of various types, seeking out comparative advantages among countries. The intrafirm trade of their affiliates accounts for at least one-third of international trade. Equally indicative, industry clusters are becoming multicountry networks as advances in information technology enable greater specialization through outsourcing at various points along the value chain. This is resulting in a new global division of labor, transforming the world in important respects into a new "geo-economy."[6] Moreover, as national economies integrate and competition intensifies, nations are forced to align many of their institutions and practices, such as banking, commerce, property rights, and judicial systems, in order to benefit from increased global intercourse. The pace and intensity of this process will be widely uneven across the world, but no country and few industries can escape for long its demands for change.

Market Systems Differ Widely by Country

Finally, while the forces of market capitalism dominate the economics of globalization, these forces in turn are channeled and configured into a wide variety of **country-specific market systems.** As Microsoft found in China, no firm can neglect the socioeconomic differences among these systems—of how they function and are evolving to accommodate, or possibly resist or shape, global market forces. The differences in these market systems reveal themselves in their institutions, business cultures and practices, and regulatory regimes as well as in the mindsets and ideologies that govern policy, thought, and action. Various topologies seek to classify differing systems of market capitalism around the world. They draw distinctions, for instance, between liberal economic and coordinated market economies,[7] among five forms of market capitalism: Anglo-Saxon, Asian, Continental-European, Social-Democratic, and Mediterranean,[8] and among different patterns of industrialization.[9] Firms should expect significant differences among countries in their market systems, how they function, and the extent to which they embrace capitalism.

For these various reasons, firms need to assess and manage country risk from the **socioeconomic systems perspective**—and not as lists of macro or even microeconomic factors. In "systems" terms, to paraphrase Talcott Parsons, this means grasping a country's environment as a dynamic or interactive "network of interrelationships," such that the "evolution of [any element of society] triggers a revolution of the whole, and any modification of the whole has repercussions on each element."[10] The social system itself—through the institutions, mindset, and ideologies that anchor it in history—has a certain internal logic and inertia of its own but is constantly subject to change due to internal innovation and outside forces. While an intrinsic part of any social system, macro and microeconomic factors need to be grasped holistically within the context of a country's evolving economic, political, and cultural systems. This becomes painfully clear to firms whose expectations and "bargained for" benefits upon entry somehow dissipate or are offset by unforeseen factors or changes in the country environment.

The framework presented here for assessing and addressing country risk, therefore, augments conventional risk management through a qualitative model that focuses on a country's **social system**. It seeks to do this in a way that is at once comprehensive of the socioeconomic environment as well as simple enough to be manageable. In keeping with open systems thinking, this framework is designed to enable firms to:

- View any society **holistically** (economically, politically, and culturally) to discern the risk in its market system and business environment from both within and without;
- Analyze the **underlying dynamics** of any society in order to gain insight into differing mindsets, values, and institutions that shape country risk; and
- Monitor emerging risks in terms of how **society is changing** to accommodate the forces of globalization.

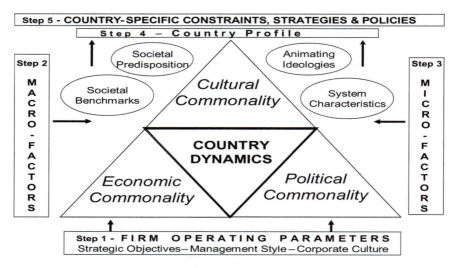

FIGURE 7.1. Country Risk Framework

The country risk framework centers on an analytical model, consisting of the "social process triangle" (SPT) and its corollary the "corporate process triangle" (CPT). These lie at the heart of a five-step methodology (Figure 7.1). Both the model and the methodology are presented here. Because of the complexity involved in understanding and analyzing societal dynamics, country risk analysis—to be manageable—should focus throughout on the operating parameters of a particular firm. This is the task outlined in Step 1. Once these parameters are established, Steps 2 (Macro Factors) and Step 3 (Micro Factors) provide an initial screening of country risk levels, possibly among a number of target countries. Therefore, Steps 2 and 3 provide a conventional, top-down analysis for arriving at a go/no go entry decision. See chapter 9 for this analysis.

For operational purposes, however, firms must take the next step of building a "country profile" from the bottom up (Step 4). The country profile is based on an analysis of the primary dynamics of society as they are refined and interpreted through the application of **four lenses**: societal benchmarks, system characteristics, societal predisposition, and animating ideologies. Taken together, these four lenses clarify how a country functions as a socioeconomic system. Finally, by juxtaposing the firm and country profiles (Steps 1 and 4), the firm is able to identify the specific constraints and impediments it faces in the foreign country and develop strategies and policies to address them (Step 5). Steps 4 and 5, moreover, establish a baseline for a firm to monitor social change in the country on an ongoing basis and to formulate strategies and policies to accommodate change.

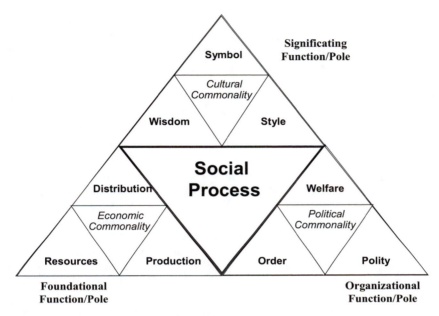

FIGURE 7.2. Social Process—Major Realms

The Social Process 'Triangle' Model (SPT): Basis for Analyzing Country Risk

The social process model is built around a trifold division of social dynamics,[11] portrayed in Figure 7.2. The triangle divides society into **three major interdependent realms**—economic, political, and cultural.[12] Each realm in turn is subdivided into three interrelated dynamics, which are used to develop country profiles and assess country risk. This section summarizes the rationale for SPT before proceeding to its application in the five-step analysis that follows.

Rationale of Social Dynamics

The three SPT realms are constructed around three fundamentally different social functions and perspectives, entitled foundational, organizational, and significating.* Like fractals, the subdivisions of each realm mirror the rationale of the whole, thus achieving nine subtriangles at the second level that

---

*In this chapter, distinctions are drawn among the social dynamics themselves (divided into three **major realms**), the overall functions they serve (foundational, organizational, significating), and the perspectives (or ideologies) through which they are interpreted or employed in a given society. In this model, the term "social" refers to society at large, while "cultural" refers primarily to one of the three societal realms and the dynamics at work there.

maintain a comprehensive depiction of society. The lower left triangle of each realm always refers to its **foundational function,** for example, resources, order, and wisdom. These are the basic building blocks of each realm as well as of SPT and of society as a whole. The lower right triangle of each realm always refers to the **organizational function**—production, polity, and style. These are the ways in which society transforms its resources, common values, and beliefs into usable products, governance, and social relationships. Without it, no society—indeed, no social unit—is possible. Its collapse typically results in social chaos or civil war, as occurred in the former Yugoslavia during the 1990s.

The top triangle of each realm always refers to the **significating function** or the value-giving aspect of each dynamic—distribution, welfare, and symbol. These are the ways society infuses all aspects (realms) of common life with value. Ultimately every society consists of values that freight its heritage, its sense of purpose or destiny, its thought process and daily patterns of interaction. The loss or weakness of this identity may lead to cynical resignation, social stagnation, or civil strife, as Samuel Huntington points out.[13]

These dynamics are embedded in and acted out through societal institutions and practices. Of course, these dynamics play out differently for every society due to history, geography, and chance events. Whatever the particular societal circumstances, SPT provides a disciplined framework to **think comprehensively across all social dynamics,** whether at the local, national, or regional levels—and whatever values, ideology, or societal heritage they reflect.

Major Realms at Play

The three overarching realms both complement and stand in tension with each other. They **complement each other,** as seen in Figure 7.3, through the distinctive functions that each realm performs. While the economic realm generates resources to satisfy society's needs, the values emanating from the cultural realm largely define these preferences, providing direction to producers and governmental decision-makers alike. For its part, the political dynamics establish and enforce the rules for channeling and ordering social behavior in the other realms. A legislative decision to increase the minimum wage or provide health benefits, for example, entails an exercise of political will that both redefines an economic benefit and expresses the value society places on the participation of the less fortunate in the economy.

Despite the apparent harmony among the three realms, they also stand in tension with each other (Figure 7.4). As Daniel Bell suggests about American society, such tension is endemic, for "the different realms respond to different norms, and have different rhythms of change, and are regulated by different, even contrary, axial principles of change."[14] Whereas at work we obey the functional rationalistic principles of a techno-economic, hierarchical order, outside in our political lives we recognize the principle of equality and equal treatment, and in our personal (cultural) lives we pursue self-realization and

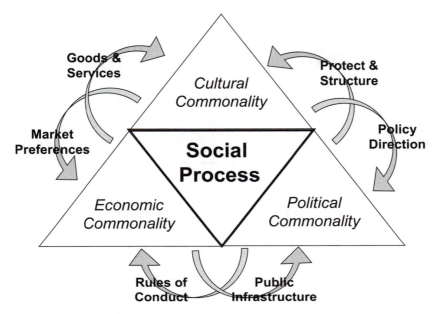

FIGURE 7.3. Complementary Relationships among the Major Realms

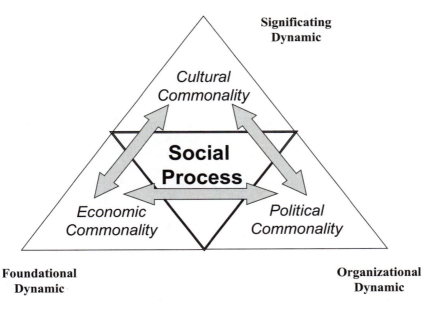

FIGURE 7.4. Tensions among the Major Realms

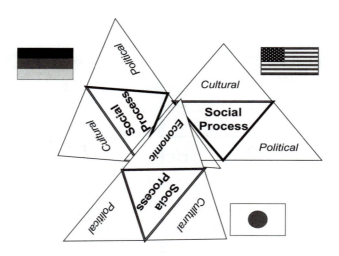

FIGURE 7.5. Globalization: Economic Convergence

self-fulfillment. As a result, tension among the realms also will be evident in policy decisions. It is evident in trade-offs among stakeholders, for instance, as countries shift from command to market-based economies, and as they seek to shield their culture, class structure, and industries from the competitive demands of the globalizing economy. In fact, social issues typically can be traced to different perspectives rooted in these three realms.

This juxtaposition of the three realms helps explain why globalization—grounded in the economics of a market-oriented discipline—has become the bête noire of many diverse groups. As Figure 7.5 indicates, its economic dimension single-mindedly challenges and may simply bypass or overwhelm existing state authority (political realm) and the folkways (cultural realm) of many countries. Indeed, even more so than English, the language of the international marketplace is dominated by monetary, financial, cost-benefit, and exchange rate analysis as well as by the metrics of socioeconomic growth. The international political system remains rudimentary, dependent largely on ad hoc treaties and institutions and the willingness of states to honor them, while the cultural realm remains largely passive and highly diversified among countries and localities—except where religious ideology takes hold.

Corporate Process Triangle (CPT)

In keeping with the organizational complexity that accompanies global business operations, SPT rationale can be transposed to **organizational dynamics of the enterprise** itself (see Figure 7.6). Like social process analysis, the analysis of organizational dynamics is first and foremost systems analysis. Indeed, in most respects, organizations are society writ small, except that

FIGURE 7.6. Organizational Profile Indicators

a firm's focus is much narrower, has a more limited duration, and seeks to achieve a more purposeful integration of people, assets, and goals than is true of most societies. They are creatures of societal norms and practices. Over time, of course, the practices and operating philosophies of firms and their industries can influence the mindset, institutions, and ideologies of society.

Organizational profiles are built around nine indicators, which track the second-level dynamics of the CPT. The CPT, like society as whole, possesses three distinct realms: corporate operations (economic), corporate organization (political), and corporate culture (cultural). The realms are defined in much the same terms as the SPT, for the same dynamics are present in CPT. Like society, a firm's overall effectiveness depends largely on the extent to which these three realms complement and reinforce each other in building and extending core competencies and in enhancing the firm's value proposition. The questions posed around the perimeter of the triangle provide nine indicators for developing an organizational profile of a firm. As will be seen in Step 5 of the model presented below, the juxtaposition of a firm's profile to that of a foreign country environment can be instructive in fashioning entry strategies.

Five-Step Methodology for Analyzing Country Risk

Step 1: Firm Operating Parameters. Applying the nine indicators of the Corporate Process Triangle, develop a profile of the firm's operating parameters.

When first undertaking operations overseas, a firm needs to specify its operating parameters by reference to its home country environment in the context of the competitive structure of its industry. Firms that have substantial international experience may choose to perform the same step by reference to a country environment more akin to the type of environment they are targeting. To accomplish this step, a firm should clearly state its global or regional strategic objectives (both scale and scope) for the relevant businesses. Then it responds to the nine questions—one for each of the second-level CPT questions—posed in Figure 7.6. This ensures that the country risk analysis that follows will be highly focused on those aspects most critical for the firm. Without a sharp focus, there is danger that country analysis becomes lost in irrelevant data collection and interpretation. The firm profile, moreover, enables the firm to develop a clear understanding of its strategic objectives and its most critical operating assumptions. Firms can be blindsided when unarticulated assumptions don't materialize.

Step 2: Macro Factors. For entry decisions, employ public and proprietary sources to assess the overall political stability and economic growth expectations of the country needed to achieve the firm's business objectives.

Because macro risk factors cover a wide range, they need to be tailored to the strategic objectives and operating flexibility of the firm. See chapter 9 for a discussion of these factors. While firms always are concerned about these factors, some are more critical than others depending on the mode of operations in the country. Thus, export or insourcing operations are particularly sensitive to changes in exchange rates, while manufacturing or banking operations are also highly exposed to government instability. Technology licensing will depend heavily on the effective enforcement of intellectual property laws. For assessing macro factors, firms have available a wide variety of professional country-risk rating services, for example, Geneva-based Business Environment Risk Intelligence, S.A., whose index covers over 50 countries; the bimonthly information letter Nord Sud Export rates 100 developing countries; the USA-based Political Risk Services Group's periodic political and country risk guides covering 100 countries; and the Economist Intelligence Unit (The Economist Group), whose quarterly risk ratings aggregate political, economic, and liquidity risk for 100 developing countries.[15]

Step 3: Micro Factors. Determine the attractiveness of the competitive structure of the country's industry for the firm's operations.

This analysis establishes industry-specific differences a firm will face in a foreign country compared to its home or other country reference. It is concerned with the competitive structure of the industry, whether in terms of Michael Porter's "five forces" or "diamond" model.[16] Whichever Porter model is used, the analysis should assess whether the industry is expanding or stagnating and determine the existence and stage of development of "industry clusters" (i.e., related and supporting industries) that would contribute to the firm's operations. Comparing industry structure to the firm's home or reference country will expose the existence of any constraints or advantages that the firm otherwise might not recognize and should be prepared to address.

Step 4: Country Profile. By reference to the major country dynamics as interpreted through four lenses, determine the dominant societal themes and characteristics that distinguish the country vis-à-vis the firm's operating parameters and industry.

Country profiles capture the dominant themes of a society and provide benchmarks to assess areas of country risk and track societal change over time. Four lenses are used for this purpose: societal benchmarks, system characteristics, societal predispositions, and ideologies. These lenses, overlaying the SPT dynamics, act as "filters" for interpreting different aspects of the country environment and for identifying potential issues. Their choice and sequence can be adapted as appropriate to the firm and the country in question.

Capture Critical Data on Societal Benchmarks. As a starting point, SPT provides nine practical benchmarks for assessing a country's business environment. These benchmarks provide a comprehensive map of any society. They are derived from the second-level triangles (three for each realm), whose titles have been rephrased somewhat in Figure 7.7 to reflect primary areas of concern to any enterprise. Moreover, the benchmarks themselves can be customized to fit firm-specific interests and industries.

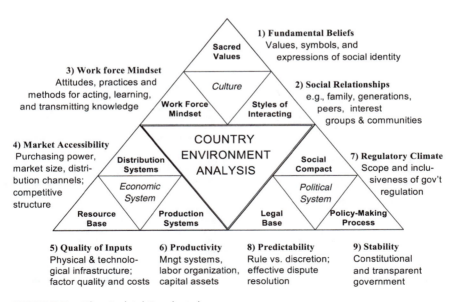

FIGURE 7.7. Nine Societal Benchmarks

Taken together, these benchmarks provide a "bottom up" approach to country analysis and a tool for capturing critical data. While each benchmark should be examined independently to ensure comprehensive coverage, real insight comes from aggregating the benchmarks by their realms and defining specific types of risks in a systems context as suggested by Figure 7.8. Alternatively, all nine benchmarks may be used to analyze a particular issue, topic, or scenario that cuts across the three realms. Thus, markets can not be well understood apart from appreciating the effects of societal values on product preferences and of regulatory requirements; productivity is often affected by the workforce mindset and well as the effect of the tax system on incentive pay; and effective management may depend as much on building social relationships as on aligning the firm's policies with the country's social compact.

Identify System Characteristics. A second lens views the economy as a socioeconomic system—that is to say, as an integral part of society as a whole. While market capitalism appears at first glance to dominate the global economic landscape, in fact everywhere economies are mixtures of three fundamentally different economic systems, that is, traditional, command, and market economies. Not only does each constitute a distinctive economic system,[17] each also embodies a distinctive **social system** and **mindset** that distinguishes it in large part from the other two. Figure 7.8 illustrates the differences—albeit somewhat stereotypically—by listing key aspects of the major SPT realms down the left-hand column and the three systems types across the top.

Viewing economic systems through the eyes of SPT offers several insights. First, each type of system is based on a different set of economic, political, and

	TRADITIONAL (Cultural)	COMMAND (Political)	MARKET (Economic)
Dominant Traits			
Static	◄ – ►		Dynamic
ECONOMIC COMMONALITY			
	Past Practices	**Planning Procedures**	**Market Mechanisms**
Production	— Custom/status	— Bureaucratic elite	— Monetized markets
& Distribution	— Barter	— Favors/suasion/force	— Market competition
Decisions	— Patrimony	— National interests	— Consumer demand
POLITICAL COMMONALITY			
Social	— Custom/tribal	— Administrative fiat	— Private property
Compact	— Status	— Entitlements	— Individual rights
CULTURAL COMMONALITY			
Wisdom -	**Status**	**State Ideology**	**Wealth**
Applied	— Craftsmanship	— Planning	— Efficiency
Scientific	— Universal truth	— Orthodoxy	— Relativity
Social Morality	— Perpetuate past	— Party line	— What works
Life Style	**Fealty**	**Power**	**Achievement**
Social Units	— Extended family	— State groups	— Nuclear family
Recognition	— Royalty	— The party	— Interest groups
Sacred Values	**Aristocracy**	**Social Manifesto**	**Productivity & Growth**

FIGURE 7.8. Comparative Framework for Socioeconomic Systems

cultural assumptions. Each solves the economic problem differently, and each operates out of a different mindset and social morality. As a result, the three systems exhibit different—and sometimes incompatible—decision-making cultures and perspectives that affect the way firms do business.

Second, these three types of systems coexist—often uneasily—in every society. Thus, countries such as China and Russia demonstrate a kind of societal schizophrenia between their emerging market economies on the one hand and their autocratic governments and networks of state enterprises on the other. But advanced market economies like the United States also have their share of traditional and command elements, whether in terms of family firms, bureaucratically managed enterprises, or sizable portions of the economy that are managed pursuant to centralized or politically driven "command" decisions. This fact suggests why business executives and their public sector counterparts often fail to appreciate each other—even though (or, despite the fact that) they profess the same general values and may work with each other on a daily basis. Differing systems function according to differing decision-making rationale.

Third, country economies may differ substantially depending on the mix and proportionate influence of these three systems. A significant shift in resources from the private to the public sector, significant growth in state subsidies or entitlements, or the absence of a vigorous antitrust regime, for instance, may well dampen the influence of free market signals as well as stifle international trade. By the same token, country economies dominated by large conglomerates or favoring business relationships built around personal, family, ethnic, or nationalistic ties may be protective and less open to the free play of market forces. Thus, at least until recently, *kereitsus* in Japan, *chaebols* in Korea, and the "houses" of India have exercised significant influence over foreign direct investment and technology transfer.

However economic systems are configured, there are three primary rules or "bottom lines" for assessing their potential effects on firm operations. Each rule, reflecting a benchmark for each realm (Figure 7.9), provides a standard for measuring a critical aspect of country risk. Thus, the "rule of the market" confirms whether there is transparency and a level playing field within an industry. The "rule of law" indicates whether there is political stability, due process, and evenhandedness in the exercise of governmental power. For the cultural realm, the "rule of effectiveness" is equally important—though most frequently neglected. It assesses the ability of firms to function most productively by respecting fundamental values and harmonizing their operations at all levels of society. Ignoring or not adequately addressing these benchmarks, as Microsoft discovered in China, can result in serious setbacks.

Societal Predispositions. The third societal lens reflects the residual effects of history on a society's socioeconomic system. It is shaped over time by any number of defining historical events, geographical circumstances, and demographic factors, among others, as well as by the accumulation of choices made

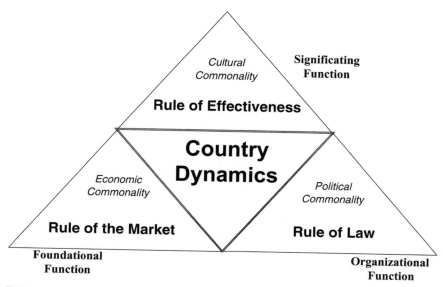

FIGURE 7.9.   Three Rules for Assessing Socioeconomic Systems

by society to accommodate both exogenous and endogenous events and factors. Societal heritage or predispositions consist of social patterns embedded in the institutions and mindset of society. They pervade every socioeconomic system to some significant extent. "Institutions" should be understood in their broadest sense. They are, says Rosabeth Moss Kanter, "taken-for-granted patterns of everyday behavior" that "endure because they become socially accepted ('institutionalized') whether or not they are the theoretically optimal response to a particular need."[18] "Mindset" means more or less fixed attitudes and patterns of thought that tend to guide the outlook, behavior, and action of a people. Because of their path-dependent nature, institutions and mindsets are slow to change over time and tend to define a distinctive character of society.

The three functional poles of the SPT (foundational, organizational, and signficating) can be used to capture the attitudinal (mindset) and institutional predispositions of society, for the dynamics of societies tend to be oriented toward one of the poles. To appreciate the pervasive nature of a societal predisposition, keep in mind (as previously discussed) that the three functions (functional poles) are replicated in each of the three major realms (economic, political, and cultural) and in their subordinate dynamics (fractals). As a result, all three functions are integral to every social structure. Further, given the interdependent structure of the three realms, there is a kinship among dynamics from different realms as related to a particular function. Thus, the **significating function** is reflected in the top subtriangles (distribution, welfare, symbol) of each of the major realms, just as the **organizational function** is reflected in the lower right subtriangles (production, polity, style) and the **foundational function** in the lower left subtriangles (resources, order, wisdom) of each realm. To the extent parallel dynamics (having the same function) in each of the major realms reinforce each other—or converge in some respects—this functional perspective becomes embedded in a society's mindset, customs, and related social structures. It reflects dominant themes in the life of a society. Conversely, the failure of parallel dynamics to reinforce each other may indicate a weakness or dysfunction in society. Dominant themes and dysfunctions, therefore, also provide markers for understanding how and why societies differ.

A comparison of the United States, Japan, and Germany—three sophisticated market economies—illustrates how different functional predispositions are reflected in their institutions and mindsets. These are depicted in the second-level (bold) triangles in Figure 7.10. The dominant themes running through U.S. society, for instance, are anchored in the *significating function* of each of the three major dynamics, that is, symbol (individual liberty), distribution (consumer sovereignty in a free enterprise market system), and welfare (human rights guaranteed by the Constitution). Reinforcing each other, these themes give full vent to individual choice in goods, services, and lifestyles, and the opportunity for individual risk-taking and entrepreneurship. They

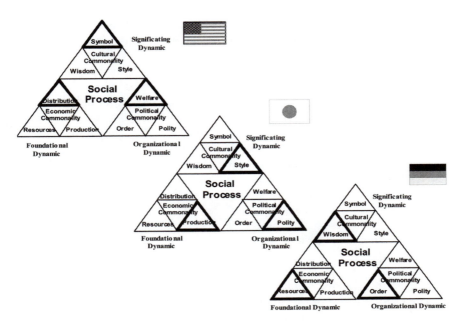

FIGURE 7.10.   Functional Predispositions: Comparing Three Market Economies

establish a predisposition in the United States for a relatively classless society, favoring individual freedom and success based on merit and perseverance. Confirming these traits, Geert Hofstede's research ranks the United States first among fifty countries in individualism, while being strongly egalitarian and risk-taking.[19] The result is a convergence of institutional strengths around common ideals, integrating all three realms of the social fabric.

By contrast with the individualism and ethnic diversity of the United States, Japan and Germany reflect much more homogeneous communitarian societies less comfortable with risk. In Japanese society, the *organizational function* dominates the three major realms. As this suggests, the Japanese mindset and institutions are predisposed toward an "organizational" or political perspective rather than a "cultural" or "economic" perspective as is sometimes suggested.[20] This predisposition reflects, as in previous centuries, a deep-seated desire among the Japanese people to maintain societal harmony—at least on the surface—through a variety of control mechanisms that pervade the country's economic, political, and cultural realms. Not surprisingly, therefore, Hofstede's research ranks Japanese medium for individualism, somewhat more egalitarian, but quite shy in risk-taking. Somewhat surprisingly, the Japanese scored first among other nationalities in the "masculine" dimension, that is, revealing a bias toward being assertive and competitive.[21]

While Germany shares a number of communitarian attributes with Japan, it is less risk-shy and more egalitarian than Japan. As a whole, its societal predisposition is oriented predominantly toward the *foundational function*. In contrast to the United States and Japan, Germany's history is replete with the ravages of religious and territorial wars, becoming united relatively late as a European nation through the leadership of autocratic Prussia. During the three previous centuries its numerous autonomous principalities developed cultures rich in music, philosophy, and literature. This combined experience has engendered a German predisposition toward caution, respect for authority, tradition, and the intellect, and a deep-seated yearning for political order, stability, and social cohesion. In the economic realm, Germany prides itself in workforce training and skills (resources dynamic) while culturally it has been a world leader in meritocratic education, vocational training, research, and intellectual endeavors in all spheres and at all levels—both applied and theoretical science (wisdom dynamic). In the political realm, the foundational emphasis is on "order" and domestic harmony (order dynamic)—on an orderly, well-run society, showcased by a healthy respect for key stakeholders, an egalitarian welfare system, and the highly refined German civil and commercial codes. "*Ordnung muss sein*" is frequently voiced about most every aspect of life.

These three country examples indicate how the convergence of comparable dynamics toward one or the other functional poles point to societal strengths. These predispositions are embedded both in societal mindsets and institutions, and therefore the overall functioning of society. Thus, for the United States the convergence of social dynamics around the significating function solidified its role as a stable leader of constitutional democracy and market capitalism throughout the West. For Japan, the convergence of social dynamics around the organizational function has enabled it over the decades through a single-minded discipline to modernize, industrialize, and become an economic powerhouse. For Germany, the convergence of social dynamics around the foundational function ensured its preeminence in R&D and craftsmanship, and its leadership in industrial machinery, chemicals, and auto manufacturing. It has been the economic backbone of the European Union.

At the same time, it is important not to be doctrinaire or stereotypical about either a society's predisposition or its changeless character. While societies reveal dominant integrating themes, there also are likely to be at least latent tensions among the major realms. This fact points to possible institutional weaknesses, difficulty in aligning social values, and, as a result, the presence of dysfunctions at work in various aspects of society. Thus in striving for the ideal of equal treatment (the significating function of the political realm) among a highly heterogeneous population, U.S. elementary and secondary education appears in many respects to favor socialization at the expense of meritocratic education (the foundational function of the cultural realm). Recognizing potential societal dysfunctions enables firms (as well as governments) to develop compensating strategies.

Equally important, dysfunctions among the major realms may reflect more fundamental and, possibly, destructive tensions within society. Using Samuel Huntington's classification, these tensions may be endemic to societies though they share a common civilization (e.g., Czechoslovakia, Canada); because they reflect different civilizations and, therefore, deeply held cultural values ("cleft" countries, e.g., India, Kenya, Nigeria, Sri Lanka, Malaysia, Singapore, Philippines, Indonesia); or because they are "torn" by transition or being challenged to change (e.g., Australia, Mexico, Russia, Turkey) due to different visions of society or different views of how to arrive at a common vision.[22] These societal tensions are reflected as well in societal ideologies, considered next.

Animating Role of Ideology. As socioeconomic systems, countries also are defined by the ideologies that dominate their economic, political, and cultural realms. Ideology provides a fourth lens for assessing country risk that overlays societal benchmarks, system characteristics, and societal predispositions. Ideologies are value-oriented perspectives or "social blueprints" that infuse institutions, programs, and everyday activities.[23] Says George Lodge: They constitute "a set of beliefs and assumptions about values that the nation holds to justify and make legitimate the actions and purposes of its institutions."[24] It gives direction to policy, freights programs of action, and provides institutions with an operating raison d'être.

Ideology differs from a societal predisposition primarily in its point of reference and the proactive role it plays in social change. Societal predispositions, like any heritage, embody the accepted way of thinking about or doing things. In essence, they look backward, building upon tradition and, typically, occur intuitively without forethought. By contrast, ideology tends to be deliberate, advocative, and coupled with a program of action—even when it is voiced to retain or resurrect the past. It may be rooted in many if not the same values that underlie a society's predisposition, but its programmatic orientation provides conscious rallying points for special interests—whether for change or the status quo. This enables ideology to play a benchmarking role for understanding the operating environment of socioeconomic systems—both how they function and dysfunction. In the sense used here, ideology provides a tool of analysis rather than a utopian "call to arms" such as dominated much of late-nineteenth and twentieth-century thinking. Given the complexity of modern industrial and postindustrial societies, ideology provides a reference point for appreciating how societal values play out in everyday life and how societies are coping with forces of globalization.

For ideology to serve a benchmarking role in analyzing country environments, its parameters must be clearly delineated. The parameters portrayed in Figure 7.11 are tied to distinguishing marks of a modern or modernizing society—and especially pluralistic, open societies—that are shaped by multiple value perspectives. Most socioeconomic systems are blends of varying and often divergent ideologies.[25] Insight into country risk comes from identifying the dominant ideologies at work in the economic, political, and cultural realms of society and from appreciating how these may diverge, complement, or clash, and are given to change and evolve in the course of a country's development.

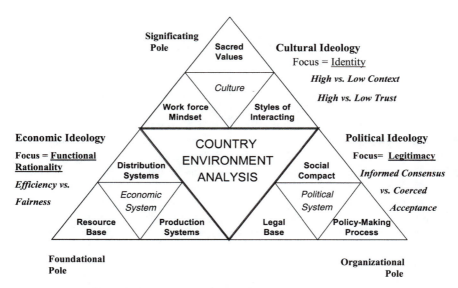

FIGURE 7.11. Ideological Parameters of the Major Realms

TABLE 7.1. Distinguishing Marks of Ideology

Distinguishing Marks	Economic Commonality	Political Commonality	Cultural Commonality
Purpose Served	Functional Rationality	Legitimacy	Identity
Range of Values	Efficiency ↔ Fairness	Informed Consensus ↔ Coerced Acceptance	High ↔ Low Trust High ↔ Low Context
Operating Principle	Economizing	Bounding Power	Creating Workable Harmony
Organizing Principle	Technical Specialization Hierarchical Roles	Modes and Channels of Decision-Making	Social Protocols, Unifying Stories and Symbols
Change Principle	Decreasing Productivity and Benefits-Cost Ratio	Unenforceability of Laws & Regulations	Internal Strife Among Fundamental Values

By reference to each realm, as indicated in Table 7.1, it is possible to identify the purpose and range of values served by an ideology as well as the principles that define how it operates in society, how it organizes to accomplish its role, and ultimately what shifts in the environment may undermine an ideology and cause it to change.

Within the limits of this chapter, it is possible to illustrate only briefly how ideology may be employed as a tool of analysis. Figure 7.12 shows U.S. ideologies in terms of the social process triangle. Thus, U.S. economic ideology is dominated by free enterprise capitalism, emphasizing notions of efficiency and free play of market forces; political ideology broadly emphasizes participation and choice for the individual in most aspects of social policy; and cultural ideology focuses on individual liberty in a highly diverse society (low context) with maximum leeway for individual aspiration and expression and voluntary collaborative action (high trust).

By comparison, Table 7.2 shows how the three realms of ideology in two other market-oriented countries, Japan and Germany, differ from the United States. Because space is limited for discussing the nuances of these ideologies or to rehearse their rationale more fully, suffice it to say that each society deeply embeds differing ideologies and that these pervade the mindset and institutions of that society and underpin its social policies. Moreover, while the ideologies of the three countries differ, the dominant ideologies for the three realms of each society tend to complement and reinforce each other. This is not true for all societies, however, as Huntington suggests with respect to "cleft"

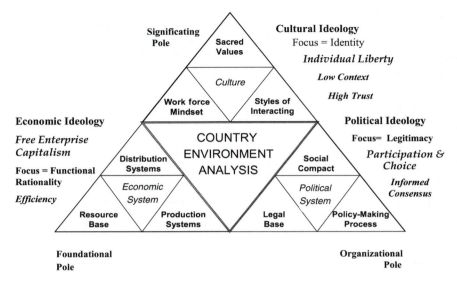

FIGURE 7.12. U.S. Ideologies

and "torn" societies, where realm-specific ideologies may clash or compete for dominance.[26] The clash may provide benchmarks for monitoring change within each society. Thus, China's "socialist market economy" reflects a growing market ideology[27] that is challenging the autocratic Communist Party ideology of state-owned and controlled enterprises dominating the political realm, while both are at odds with the ideology of Confucian familism in the cultural realm.[28] Conflicting ideologies signal potential pitfalls for foreign firms to address as they negotiate China's complex environment.[29]

Beyond pointing to underlying societal conflicts, the dissonance among realm-specific ideologies may also provide insight into the process of societal change. Because by nature ideology embodies an action plan, it must be effective in order to endure. When shifts or discontinuities in the environment

TABLE 7.2. Comparing Ideologies among Three Market-Oriented Economies

Ideologies/of Three Countries	Economic	Political	Cultural
United States	Free Enterprise Capitalism	Participation and Choice	Individual Liberty
Japan	Developmental Capitalism	Stakeholder Nationalism	Societal Harmony
Germany	Social Market Economy	Universal Welfare State	Structured Meritocracy

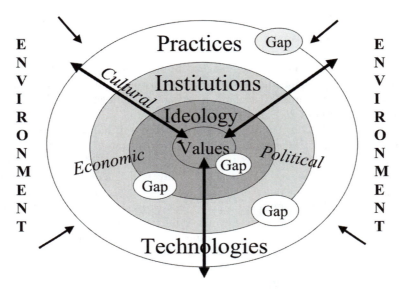

FIGURE 7.13. Dynamics of Social Change

undercut its efficacy, ideology is subject to change. It is useful, therefore, as Lodge suggests, to understand ideology also as a "bridge by which timeless values are connected to the surrounding reality in various cultures at different points in space and time."[30] This can be seen in the American West, where the political ideology of the "gunslinger" gradually gave way to an ideology of "law and order." Or in Japan, which relinquished its self-imposed isolation and vastly modified its feudal system to adopt its own form of constitutional government and market capitalism. Moreover, Soviet Communism collapsed due to its inability to deliver on the economic promise of its political ideology.

Through its bridging function (see Figure 7.13), ideology links deeply held societal values with institutions and, through them, administrative practices and systems that have evolved for interfacing effectively with the environment. As change or substantial dissent occurs in the environment, however, existing practices and systems may begin to change in order to be effective. At that point, "gaps" or constraints emerge—initially at the interface with the environment, then between practices and the institutions they support, and ultimately over the course of time, between institutions and the ideologies that animate them. These changes in ideology may be relatively minor and adaptive, as when business practices adopted consumer-oriented and environmental protection, or they may be historic as with the collapse of Communist systems. Societal ideology, therefore, provides a means for firms to identify the values and assumptions that guide societal policies, institutions, and decision-making as well as to appreciate the source of societal tension and analyze the impact of environmental change. As a practical matter, ideology provides three reference points for assessing country risk.

- First, risk can arise from **dissonance among realm-specific ideologies**. In market-oriented systems, for instance, trade-offs between efficiency and fairness often mark points of tension, whether exemplified by child labor or minimum wage laws, or collective bargaining.
- Second, risk stems from **dissonance within and among institutions** as they seek to deal with the escalating forces of globalization. This dissonance is due in part to the sheer complexity of these forces and the difficulty of grasping the nature of their impact, but also to the built-in inertia of the ideologies that guide institutionalized practices. Even when external change has been correctly diagnosed, the legislative and judicial processes may not address this change for years, if not decades. Business culture may be equally impervious to change, such as the personalized lending practices that made many financial institutions so susceptible to the 1997–98 "Asian contagion."
- A third type of risk comes from **differences between societal ideologies and a firm's operating values and culture**—in a sense a firm's own ideology. This risk is inherent in any international operation, although it is frequently overlooked by firms and ignored largely by host country agencies. Because firms are products of their home environments, including reigning ideologies and societal predispositions, it is understandable that they may not readily appreciate the extent of the potential conflict between their operating philosophies and the foreign country or how, as a practical matter, conflict could impact their operations.

Step 5: Country-Specific Constraints, Strategies and Policies. Determine what measures the firm should take to address country-specific risks to its operations.

As indicated previously in this chapter, the social process framework can be employed to address the management as well as the assessment of country risk. This requires, first of all, a profile of the firm's normal operating parameters and of the competitive structure of its industry (Steps 1 and 3). By juxtaposing the firm and country profiles, it is possible to uncover and address areas of dissonance between these two profiles (see Figure 7.14).

Note: Because of the derivative nature of the CPT, the organizational profile of a firm is likely to reflect in some significant respects the management style, cultural predispositions, and ideology of its home environment. Its operating philosophy and structure also will tend to complement the regulatory and industrial practices of that country. These facts provide a baseline as firms contemplate the opportunities and impediments they face in another country environment. An analysis of this sort was clearly in Toyota's mind, for example, in its NUMMI alliance with General Motors. There it sought to determine whether Toyota's manufacturing processes could be replicated with an American labor force.

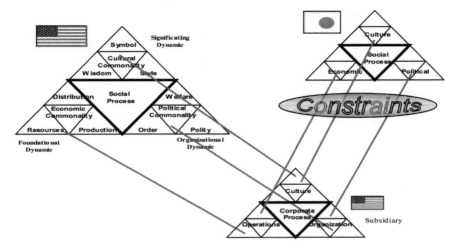

FIGURE 7.14. Juxtaposing the Firm with Country Dynamics

Step 5, therefore, consists of a two-part analysis to develop a country-specific action plan.

• **Firm-Specific Constraints**. In light of the firm/industry and the country profiles, identify the major issues and foreseeable constraints or impediments specific to the firm and its existing and anticipated future country operations. These constraints have also been termed "liabilities of foreignness,"[31] although this terminology carries a negative connotation that is not necessarily warranted. The necessity of adapting a firm's accepted practices to the new environment may as well result in improvements to the firm's operations. As noted in chapter 1, for example, while Siemens' decision to establish an R&D center near Beijing countered its long practice of relying on engineers at its Stuttgart headquarters in Germany, the result is a more cost-effective design and production of cell phones in keeping with Siemens' high standards and the Chinese market.

Constraint analysis typically begins by surveying the various issues and relating them to one or more of the nine societal benchmarks indicated in Figure 7.7. At that point it is critical to appreciate the broader societal origin of each issue by tracing each issue to its source or root cause in all three realms of a country's socioeconomic system in terms of the four lenses. It is now possible to articulate the underlying societal constraint specific to the firm. Sometimes these constraints are fairly obvious, such as weak intellectual property protection or state-controlled competitors, but at other times they can become highly complex, as when differing work ethics, cultural diversity, and competing in-country political regimes are at play. Whatever the case, it is necessary to uncover the various root causes of each constraint for analysis to be successful.

• **Firm Strategies and Policies.** Next, the firm formulates country-specific strategies and policies to address the constraints. These strategies and policies will have implications for all three realms of the firm's organizational dynamics. In some cases, for instance, strategies and policies will need to counter gaps through negotiations with local authorities or complement weaknesses through training programs or insourcing initiatives. At the same time, firms will undoubtedly need to revise their organizational processes in order to take advantage of the new environment. Thus, as Microsoft discovered in China, it may be counterproductive to launch legal and political attacks on intellectual property infringers, if the economic and cultural concerns of customers and entrepreneurs and their perceptions of the value of protecting intellectual property are not addressed as well.

CONCLUSIONS

In both assessing and managing country risk it is imperative to think and act in terms of socioeconomic systems. The models and methodologies presented in this chapter are intended to provide managers with the means for accomplishing these tasks. This approach does not by any means negate the utility of quantitative analysis where data is available and relevant, but it does suggest that qualitative analysis is equally valid and probably more useful than quantitative analysis once firms have committed themselves to country operations. At that point, the societal benchmarks outlined here enable firms to discern underlying societal dynamics and appreciate how these dynamics are shaping and possibly changing the socioeconomic system. The four lenses—the nine benchmarks, system characteristics, societal predisposition, and ideological analysis—are simply tools for better understanding the mindset and values that shape the institutional framework and the business climate and culture of society. They also provide the means—especially as globalization proceeds—for spotting societal tensions and monitoring societal changes that are likely to affect a firm's operations.

NOTES

1. R. Meredith, "(Microsoft's) Long March," *Forbes* 171, no. 4 (2003).

2. Michel H. Bouchet, Ephraim Clark, and Bertrand Groslambert, *Country Risk Assessment* (West Sussex, England: John Wiley & Sons, 2003), 15.

3. IMD, *World Competitiveness Report* (2004).

4. World Bank, *World Development Report, 2005*.

5. Stephane Garelli, *IMD World Competitiveness Yearbook, 2003*, p. 702.

6. Peter Dicken, *Global Shift: Reshaping the Global Economic Map in the 21st Century* (New York: Guilford Press, 2003), 75–80, 116–18.

7. P. A. Hall and D. Sockice, *Varieties of Capitalism: The Institutional Foundations of Comparative Advantage* (Oxford: Oxford University Press, 2001).

8. Bruno Amble, *The Diversity of Modern Capitalism* (Oxford: Oxford University Press, 2003).

9. R. Whitley, *Divergent Capitalism: The Social Structuring and Change of Business Systems* (Oxford: Oxford University Press, 1999). Alfred Chandler's early study (1977), moreover, distinguishes between "competitive managerial capitalism" (United States), family-owned or "personal capitalism" (Britain), and "cooperative managerial capitalism" (Germany). Other narrower, more topical bases of comparison, like Transparency International, rank countries in terms of the extent to which corruption skews market-based decisions.

10. J. Ellul, *The Technological System* (New York: Continuum, 1980), 77, citing Talcott Parsons, *The Social System*, 1951.

11. The social process triangle as well as the corporate process triangle were created substantially in their present form during the early 1970s by the Institute of Cultural Affairs, a nonprofit organization dedicated to strengthening grassroots communities around the world. The author, who participated as part of a larger work group in their original formulation, has adapted them to the business context, expanded on their theoretical foundation, and formulated the country risk framework for their application.

12. The tripartite division of society has been adopted by others, even though the terminology and the content of the realms they depict differ somewhat from the approach taken here. See Daniel Bell, *The Cultural Contradictions of Capitalism* (New York: Basic Books, 1976); and R. L. Heilbroner, *The Making of Economic Society*, 9th ed. (Englewood Cliffs, NJ: Prentice-Hall, 1993).

13. Samuel P. Huntington, *The Clash of Civilizations and the Remaking of World Order* (New York: Simon & Schuster, 1996).

14. Bell, *Cultural Contradictions*; and Heilbroner, *Making of Economic Society*, 10.

15. See Bouchet et al., *Country Risk Assessment*.

16. M. E. Porter, *Competitive Strategy*, 1980; and M. E. Porter, *The Competitive Advantage of Nations* (New York: Free Press/Macmillan, 1990).

17. Heilbroner, *Making of Economic Society*.

18. R. M. Kanter, *The Institutional Perspective on Management* (Boston: Harvard Business School Press, 1997), 4, note.

19. G. Hofstede, *Culture and Organization: Software of the Mind* (New York: McGraw-Hill, 1991).

20. See E. F. Vogel, "Japan: Adaptive Communitarianism," in G. C. Lodge and E. F. Vogel, eds., *Ideology and National Competitiveness: An Analysis of Nine Countries*, chapter 6 (Boston: Harvard Business School Press, 1987); K. van Wolferen, *The Enigma of Japanese Power* (New York: Vintage Books, 1990); and N. Yoshimura and P. Anderson, *Inside the Kaisha: Demystifying Japanese Business Behavior* (Boston: Harvard Business School Press, 1997).

21. Hofstede, *Culture and Organization*.

22. Huntington, *Clash of Civilizations*.

23. Gerald F. Cavanagh, *American Business Values*, 3d ed. (New York: Prentice Hall, 1990).

24. G. C. Lodge, "Introduction: Ideology and Country Analysis," in Lodge and Vogel, *Ideology and National Competitiveness*, 2.

25. Bell, *Cultural Contradictions*.

26. Huntington, *Clash of Civilizations*.

27. K. Chen, "A See-Through China? Leaders Aim at Transparency," *Wall Street Journal*, August 13, 2000, A8.

28. F. Fukuyama, *Trust: The Social Virtues and the Creation of Prosperity* (New York: Free Press, 1995).

29. G. J. Gilboy, "The Myth behind China's Miracle," *Foreign Affairs* 83, no. 4 (July–August 2004): 33–48.

30. Lodge, "Ideology," 4.

31. S. Zaheer, "Overcoming the Liability of Foreignness," *Academy of Management Journal* 38, no. 2 (1995): 341–63.

ADDING ENTERPRISE VALUE

A critical issue for all firms with global agendas is how to build value within their far-flung operations. In one sense this task is addressed by all chapters in this book, but more specifically it involves the management of knowledge flows in general and of financial data and knowledge in particular. Both these disciplines are necessary to integrate diverse operations across geography and to build a common identity. Without the former, an enterprise lacks memory and the ability to learn from its successes and mistakes. Without the latter, it will find it difficult to gauge and communicate the extent of its accomplishments, to comparatively assess and allocate scarce resources among diverse operations, and to attract working and investment capital. Like strategy, both of these business functions help the enterprise establish a working identity and pursue a singleness of purpose amid the cascade of threats and opportunities found in the global environment.

The three chapters in this section assemble perspectives on how firms can add and consciously track value for their extended operations:

• **Knowledge Management**, as will be seen, enables the firm to know what it knows. As self-evident as this task may seem, in fact firms often overlook the breadth and depth of experience and intellectual capital within their organizations. This may be because they do not recognize its value, do not have the processes and common culture for capturing and sharing it across the organization, or do not motivate employees to employ it for learning and continuous improvement. Instead, managers need to develop knowledge holistically from all parts of the enterprise, coordinate it effectively using the advanced tools of information technology, and employ it strategically as a competitive advantage.

• **International Accounting and Corporate Governance** contributes to enterprise value using quantitative tools. In the global business environment, accounting provides the means for firms to standardize and track enterprise accounts across a wide range of geography. Externally, it reflects differing state taxation systems and fluctuating currency values. While worldwide accounting standards are evolving for financial reporting, accounting principles still vary measurably among countries. The increasing transparency that accompanies these standards should strengthen both accountability in corporate governance and the willingness of investors to participate in the global capital market.

• **International Financial Managers** need a broad road map for their tasks due to the complexity and volatility of capital markets. They are faced not only with monitoring the ebb and flow of enterprise value but also with managing financial risk and creditor and investor expectations as well as the firm's relations with a wide range of governmental institutions. Given currency volatility and the significant differences among tax systems, major responsibilities of the financial officers of any far-flung enterprise are to manage its foreign exchange and tax exposure.

The question to consider in these chapters is how to organize and manage the enterprise so that it is enabled to learn and coordinate its operations in the volatile global environment.

8

Managing Knowledge in the Extended Enterprise

VINOD K. JAIN

"If TI only knew what it knows."
—Jerry Junkins, ex-CEO,
Texas Instruments

"I wish we knew what we know at HP."
—Lew Platt, Hewlett-Packard

ORGANIZATIONS AS REPOSITORIES OF KNOWLEDGE

An organization is a repository of knowledge—knowledge that is embedded in its routines,[1] stored in its memory (e.g., paper files and computer databases), and carried in the heads of its individual members. Over time, the repository expands through learning and experience and because obsolete knowledge tends not to be deleted. It is hard for a manager to know what knowledge the organization possesses and where in the organization it is located. The larger and the more established an organization, the greater its repository of knowledge and the more difficult it is for any individual or group to know what knowledge exists in the organization, who has it, and where it resides. In such a situation, managers, unable to fully leverage their human and knowledge assets, may be continually reinventing the wheel.

Top management now recognizes the importance of knowledge to organizational success and competitive advantage. Ray Stata, former chairman of

Analog Devices, Inc., observes: "The rate at which individuals and organizations learn may become the only sustainable competitive advantage, specially in knowledge-intensive industries."[2] The purpose of this chapter is to explore knowledge and knowledge management in organizations, the challenges, and the paradigm shift that occurred in the last decade or so in how organizations view and use knowledge to gain competitive advantage, and the managerial competencies needed to address the challenges. First, consider some preliminary concepts.

THE BASICS OF KNOWLEDGE MANAGEMENT (KM)

What Is Knowledge?

Does knowledge differ from data and information? According to Thomas Davenport and Laurence Prusak,[3] the term "data" refers to simple, discrete facts and figures, whereas "information" is data organized for a meaningful purpose, and "knowledge" is a mix of values, experiences, contextual information, and expert insight. Hence, **data** are facts someone collects for some purpose. For instance, when you make a purchase at a supermarket, the item you buy is scanned and "data" about the purchase (e.g., product, price, quantity, purchaser) are collected at the point of sale and stored in the supermarket's databases. At this stage, data are merely numbers, without much meaning attached. When a marketing analyst begins to analyze these data, he or she might separate or combine the numbers in many ways and into many different categories, with a view to deriving some meaningful conclusions about customers' purchase behavior. The analysis produces **information**, which could be used by the supermarket's management in many ways. So, information is data after they have been analyzed for a specific purpose. The term **knowledge** refers to data and information, supplemented by organizational values, experiences, and employee insights.

Information and knowledge do not deplete with use; they cannot be used up! The value of information and knowledge actually increases as more people use them. This principle is the economic counterpart of the principle of **network externalities**, also known as Metcalfe's Law,[4] which states that the utility of a network equals the square of the number of users. As the number of users of a network increases, the utility of the network to its owners and users goes up exponentially. (Examples are the Internet, operating systems such as Windows and Linux, an algorithm, a song, etc.) The principle applies equally to information and knowledge.

There are many dimensions of knowledge. One of the more useful dimensions classifies knowledge into two categories—tacit and explicit. Knowledge is **tacit** when it resides in the heads of one or more organization members and may be difficult to articulate and document. In olden times, tacit knowledge was what craftspeople passed down over generations. Even today, much of the knowledge in organizations is tacit, and the challenge for managers is to know who has what knowledge, how to use it for the good of the organization, and how to perpetuate it. If knowledge is tacit and cannot be articulated and documented, it will be extremely hard to store and transmit it to others inside or outside the organization. There is no "market" for tacit knowledge, that is, there is no systematic way to price such knowledge, and hence it cannot be traded. Knowledge is **explicit** when it is articulated and documented by some means, as in a standard operating procedure. Such knowledge can be stored, reused, traded, and transmitted economically.

What Is Knowledge Management?

There are many definitions of knowledge management (KM). In this chapter, we define it as follows: **Knowledge management involves concerted efforts to identify, capture, organize, contextualize, store, share, and leverage organizational knowledge to gain competitive advantage.** Notice that the definition is independent of any reference to technology. While technology is important, competitive advantage based on KM comes more from organizational routines and culture than from technology.

What Is the Organizational Value of KM?

Knowledge management has both operational and strategic value, as summarized in Table 8.1. At a very basic level, knowledge management enables better decision-making and improved operational efficiency. It places up-to-the-minute decision information in the hands of employees as needed. How a firm uses its knowledge assets can be a valuable source for establishing and sustaining competitive advantage. Competitive advantage based on tacit

TABLE 8.1.   The Organizational Value of Knowledge Management

Operational	*Strategic*
• Easy, 24/7 access to company policies, directories (e.g., who knows what), latest prices, etc., to employees	• Identifying best practices
	• Inculcating a culture of learning, knowledge-sharing, and continuous improvement within the organization
• Automated, self-service administration of financial, personnel, and other information for employee support	• Cost reduction
	• Product differentiation
• Automated, self-service administration of core business transactions, e.g., customer orders, payment processing, etc.	• Speed to market
	• Competitive intelligence
	• Customer relationship management
• Employee collaboration in virtual teams	• Data-based marketing
• e-Learning	• Competitive advantage
• Productivity enhancement	

knowledge is more enduring than advantage based on explicit knowledge, which can be bought, replicated, or even stolen. Knowledge management also can facilitate innovation in organizations by helping employees located anywhere and everywhere to brainstorm together effectively. It improves operational efficiency by automating processes that required human interface in the past. Knowledge management can train new employees via e-learning, passing on the knowledge of both in-house and external experts cost effectively. It can provide new knowledge and skills to existing employees and help them monitor and react quickly to changes in the organization's internal and external environments. Overall, when used effectively, therefore, KM can help improve organizational productivity and competitive advantage.

WHAT IS AN EXTENDED ENTERPRISE?

Over the last decade or two, organizational boundaries have continued to expand to include not just overseas subsidiaries and joint ventures, but also nonequity alliances, licensees, suppliers, and even customers.[5] These developments are a result of globalization, technological change, and adoption of new management practices by corporations. An **extended enterprise** is "an enterprise that has located business-critical operations outside its direct control through outsourcing, alliances, licensing or other arrangements . . . In an extended enterprise, suppliers, manufacturers, distributors, and others are not only providing products or services to one another. They are opening up their databases, allowing partners an unprecedented level of access to previously sacrosanct information."[6] At Wal-Mart, for instance, vendors have access to the company's sales databases so that they may forecast what Wal-Mart would need during the next quarter or the next month and supply exactly that. If a vendor over- or undersupplies, it is his (and Wal-Mart's) loss, and could even affect his business with the company in the future.

HOW KM CHALLENGES MANAGERS

The challenges of knowledge management for managers are to use the organization's existing knowledge for building and sustaining competitive advantage and to continue to add to their knowledge base through innovation and learning. These challenges can be further classified into seven specific challenge domains. All organizations face some or all of these challenges. In global organizations, the challenges are exacerbated.

Knowing What We Know

The first challenge most managers face is knowing who in the organization knows what and where certain knowledge might reside. This challenge is especially true of extended organizations. Tacit knowledge is often the hardest to place one's fingers on, though it may be equally hard to locate explicit knowledge. Visualize a large multinational corporation with autonomous foreign subsidiaries, where the information flow has traditionally been from headquarters to subsidiaries. If a subsidiary were to develop certain valuable knowledge (e.g., a new process), it is unlikely that the headquarters or other subsidiaries would learn about the existence of such explicit knowledge easily or quickly. The problem of not knowing who knows what, of course, can exist in organizations of all sizes, except possibly in very small organizations.

Capturing and Retaining Knowledge

Capturing the tacit knowledge of employees for possible future use is a big challenge in both small and large organizations. For instance, when a customer calls a company's helpdesk or service center with a specific problem, the service person attending to the call may or may not have a readily available solution. If the problem is rare, the service person may need to access other company resources and use his or her ingenuity and expertise. When another customer calls in with the same problem, another service person may have to go through the same routine and may or may not be able to resolve the customer's problem. If the company had a means of capturing the tacit knowledge of its service personnel for reuse when needed in the future, these difficulties could be avoided.

Organizations are also under increasing pressure to retain the knowledge and experience of the employees who leave. According to a major study (*The War for Talent*) conducted by McKinsey & Company in 1997 and 2000, organizations' most important resource over the next two decades will be talent— smart, sophisticated, technologically literate, and agile employees.[7] When these talented employees leave their current employers, their unique knowledge walks out the door to the detriment of the organizations. Unlike their predecessors, today's smart, talented, and creative people have a wide world of opportunities to choose from. Increasingly, they are finding Canada, New Zealand, Scandinavia, and other countries more open and more inviting than the United States.[8]

According to David DeLong, America's aging workforce places additional pressures on organizations to capture and retain the knowledge that baby boomers will take with them when they retire.[9] These individuals have often stayed with the same employers for many years, accumulating a great deal of knowledge and expertise that is largely tacit within the individual. The departure of these retirees, if their knowledge and experience has not been captured by their organizations, could cause major competitiveness challenges for their employers in the coming years. It is therefore critical for organizational continuity and success that managers find means to capture and retain the knowledge of all employees, especially those who leave, or could leave (which is about everyone in the organization).

Making Knowledge Accessible and Usable

Making knowledge accessible and usable to organization members is a key function of knowledge management. This typically involves some or all of the following operations: (a) finding ways to codify tacit knowledge so that it can be stored and accessed by others; (b) transcribing knowledge from diverse sources (e.g., private libraries of country managers, trade fairs, journals, etc.), formats (paper, computer files, CD-ROMS, microfiche, etc.), and languages (not just the languages we speak but also computer languages and the jargon of different functional areas) into a standardized format that everyone could understand; (c) contextualizing knowledge obtained for some specific purpose in the past for use by people who may not know the original context; (d) indexing, categorizing, and storing knowledge for ease of retrieval; (e) ensuring consistency, accuracy, recency, and quality of the knowledge being added to the knowledge management system; and (f) removing items of knowledge from the KM system that become obsolete. All of these factors pose KM challenges for managers.

Securing Knowledge

Knowledge in the wrong hands can be devastating for an organization. With growing threats to the security of computers, corporate intranets and extranets, and intellectual property, and the rise of the competitive-intelligence industry, securing knowledge assets is a major challenge for organizations of all sizes. This challenge also involves providing access to information and knowledge repositories based on need of individual members, bearing security and confidentiality issues in mind, and safeguarding knowledge from unintended spillover to competitors. In addition, with growing outsourcing and offshoring, the issue of the security of information sent overseas to partners and subcontractors has become very important.

Sharing Knowledge

Once an organization establishes a KM system, it may still find that the system is worthless if organization members are not be willing to contribute to the system or to use it. For some people, knowledge is power, and they tend to keep their knowledge to themselves. On the other hand, members suffering from the Not-Invented-Here (NIH) syndrome are often unwilling to use knowledge available from other sources. And, then there are the free riders— people who benefit from using the KM system but do not contribute to it. According to Bill Gates, power comes not from knowledge kept, but from knowledge shared. KM is often a big challenge for organizations without a sharing culture.

Leveraging Knowledge

Leveraging knowledge to build and sustain competitive advantage requires more than a KM system and a sharing organizational culture. It requires organizational capabilities and managerial competencies that enable managers to leverage their and others' knowledge to the organization's advantage. These needs are the focus of the section on managerial competencies needed to effectively utilize the organization's KM system.

Learning and Continuous Improvement

Challenges of knowledge management go beyond capturing, retaining, and leveraging an organization's existing knowledge. In the digital economy, the sheer volume of human knowledge is doubling every four to five years. Learning and continuous improvement are the biggest challenges organizations face to their competitive advantage, even to their very survival. Some organizations have a learning and continuous-improvement culture, while others do not. According to Bill Gates, Microsoft is a living example of a learning organization: "We read, ask questions, explore, go to lectures, compare notes and findings... consult experts, daydream, brainstorm, formulate and test hypotheses, build models and simulations, communicate what we're learning, and practice new skills."[10]

Challenges to KM from the Global Environment

How is globalization affecting knowledge management? Challenges are developing largely as a result of four key forces—the rapid proliferation of globally extended enterprises, the increasing pace of technological change, the emergence of highly competitive markets for most goods and services, and changes in management and organization practices. Figure 8.1 shows the four *drivers* of knowledge management. Note that the arrows in Figure 8.1 are bidirectional. Not only are all four factors impacting knowledge management, knowledge management is impacting them as well.

Extended Enterprise

Managing an extended enterprise entails working with entities and strategic alliance partners not necessarily under the direct control of the organization. This process involves: (a) working with geographically dispersed individuals and work units; (b) learning from "partners" in the extended enterprise while they are also trying to learn from you; (c) shielding knowledge from them that you do not want them to have; and (d) integrating knowledge and information

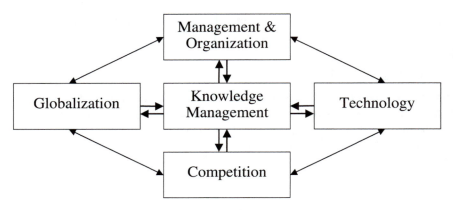

FIGURE 8.1.   Drivers of Knowledge Management

systems located in different time zones and using different technologies. All of these factors have necessitated the development and use of KM tools appropriate for distributed environments.

With more and more **cross-border mergers and acquisitions** taking place, the need for knowledge management increases by orders of magnitude. Unlike other entities in an extended enterprise, acquired organizations become part of the organization's boundaries and are under management's direct control. The biggest need here is to consolidate not just the operations of the merging units, but also their organizational cultures. For instance, one of the merging parties may have a culture of sharing knowledge, while the other may not, and this difference can cause serious challenges to the very survival of the combined organization.

Moreover, **strategic alliances** of various kinds are supplanting the classic joint venture. For decades, companies from developed countries entered into joint ventures with junior partners from developing countries to obtain access to those markets. The joint ventures were used for disseminating the technology of the senior partners in the home markets of the junior partners. Now, modern strategic alliances are often between major companies from developed countries; they are designed to develop technology rather than disseminate the senior partner's technology overseas. These changed business relationships have led to a greater need for effective knowledge management, including the need to safeguard one's knowledge assets from unwitting leakage to partners.

Increasing Pace of Technological Change

Technology, like globalization, is having a pervasive impact on how we live, work, and manage organizations and has been a key driver of KM. The increasing pace of technological change, increasing technological complexity, and concerns of security and business continuity have all been drivers of knowledge management. The next subsection highlights some of today's more common KM technologies and their application, most of which were not available a decade ago.

Intensifying Competition

Extended enterprises everywhere face much more serious competitive challenges in an increasingly digital and interconnected world (the **borderless cyberjungle**)[11] than ever before. This reality is a result of globalization, but also of factors such as the existence of excess global capacity in most industries and shorter product lifecycles. Increasing competition has therefore made knowledge management an imperative for most organizations.

Rise of Efficient Markets. One of the key revolutions resulting from the Internet and the World Wide Web is that, with declining transaction costs,[12] markets are becoming more efficient. As a result, customers and partners are demanding greater transparency in their business dealings with organizations, which they will be hard-pressed to meet without effective KM systems.

Multipoint Competition. In the global arena, major companies meet and compete with each other at different places at the same time, so a multinational company competing in a specific country must have information systems to alert it to its interactions with the same competitors at other locations. A more holistic and integrated competitive strategy is needed than in the past, and these strategies necessitate good KM systems.

Sequential versus Simultaneous Entry into Foreign Markets. The pattern of internationalization followed by major multinationals in the past was that they would enter one foreign market in a specific region (e.g., Asia-Pacific), followed by sequential entry into other countries in the region. Now, with growing competition, companies are simultaneously entering several markets in regions of interest to them, lest their strategic plans be preempted by major competitors from the host country or other nations. This new pattern places an extra burden on companies to have KM systems that inform them of competitive dynamics in different markets in real time.

Pressure on Profits. Increasing competition is continuing to place great pressures on corporate profits, and organizations are focusing on cost reduction and cost control like never before. As a result, their challenge is to begin using knowledge much more strategically than ever before to establish and sustain competitive advantage, or simply to stay in the game.

Management and Organization Practices

Management and organization issues are often primary drivers of knowledge management in organizations. Increasing organizational complexity, fragmentation of organizational activity into geographically dispersed units, and global distribution of work drive organizations to seek knowledge management systems. Three aspects of management and organization especially relevant to KM are organizational culture, organization structure, and management practices. Organizational culture can make or break KM initiatives in organizations. Organizations that have a learning culture are more likely to have success in implementing knowledge management systems than organizations that have a Not-Invented-Here or Knowledge-is-Power syndrome. Similarly, flat organization structures and two-way communication are more conducive to knowledge management than are hierarchical structures and one-way communication.

With downsizing, rightsizing, reengineering, outsourcing, and unfunded pension plans, the employer-employee contract is no longer what it used to be. Employees facing such an environment may not be fully committed to the organization, much less to knowledge management. It is simply not enough for an organization to want its people to share and leverage their knowledge for the good of the organization. What the organization needs are appropriate management practices (such as performance appraisal systems and incentives and rewards programs) that encourage knowledge-sharing and effective knowledge management. It is also absolutely essential that top management displays the behaviors that they want their employees to inculcate.

PARADIGM SHIFT IN VIEWING, MANAGING, AND USING KNOWLEDGE

Due to these significant challenges from globalization, managers must rethink their perspective and practice of knowledge management. This is true in five respects:

- Managers need to take a **holistic view** of knowledge, including both internal and external knowledge, and tacit and explicit knowledge;
- KM requires both an **operational and a strategic focus** on knowledge as a basis for establishing and sustaining competitive advantage;
- Knowledge managers must adopt and promote the use of **technologies and applications** that were neither available nor thinkable a decade ago;
- Knowledge managers must offer **24/7 solutions and gateways** to employees who are armed and on-the-run around the world with only a computer with a browser; and
- KM thrives in an **organizational culture** that supports learning, continuous improvement, and sharing of knowledge.

Knowledge Management Tools

As suggested earlier, technology has been a major contributor to the paradigm shift in knowledge management. What are some of the more common technologies that have led the paradigm shift? Following is a short list of the core technologies and their applications that permit organizations to manage their knowledge assets efficiently and effectively.[13] These technologies were either not available, or not mature enough to be useful in KM, just a decade ago. In addition, new KM technologies and applications are continually evolving.

Corporate intranets and **portals** offer a single point of 24/7 access to employees on company policies, information, milestones, and many other resources. They facilitate automated, self-service administration of financial, personnel, and other information for employee support as well as processing of core business transactions such as customer orders and payments. At the Ford Motor Company's portal, for instance, an employee can access knowledge from both internal and external sources—internal information such as warranty and technical information about company products and external information and knowledge from universities and research institutions. An employee can also order a Ford vehicle online at the employee price.

Knowledge databases support a variety of analyses and elaborate queries requiring extensive data searches as well as provide access to the staff experts that created them. Service technicians at the Xerox Corporation, for example, have access to the Eureka "tips" knowledge base, which allows them to learn from the experience of other technicians in the field who came across similar problems. The knowledge base is built on tips submitted by the service technicians themselves—identifying machine problems, proposing solutions, and then documenting their tacit knowledge about these problems and solutions. Currently the knowledge base has over 50,000 tips, available in eight languages, and is used regularly by over 20,000 Xerox service technicians worldwide.

Document management tools allow employees access to key information in a variety of formats. At Newport News Shipbuilding, the second-largest shipbuilder in the United States, over 2,000 employees have electronic access to custom-tailored information from the company's Knowledge Delivery Architecture, which helps them save time spent compiling and distributing corporate documents. The system captures, indexes, and archives business-critical documents automatically and allows employees to search, retrieve, compile, and distribute documents electronically. The company estimates that it will save them 6 million pages of computer printouts every month in addition to achieving other major efficiencies in the document management process.

Search engines offer text-matching and analytical capabilities, pinpointing specific information on the corporate intranet or the Internet. At Newport News Shipbuilding, for instance, employees can search for specific documents on their intranet, just like you and I search for information on the Internet via search engines such as Google.

Web conferencing allows employees located anywhere and everywhere opportunities to interact with each other inexpensively and in real time. Web conferencing facilitates sharing of documents, making presentations, and collaborating with people around town or around the world without leaving one's office. Agilent Technologies, for instances, uses Web conferencing for holding about 4,000 meetings per month, an average of 200 meetings per day, with major savings in time, travel expenses, and other cost.

Online collaboration permits teams to work on projects virtually irrespective of where team members may be located, eliminating the need for people and documents to travel. Ford uses online-collaboration software in virtual computer-aided design. In Europe, for example, Ford vehicles are designed jointly by engineers based in Germany and the United Kingdom. Buell Motorcycle, a Harley-Davidson subsidiary, uses Web-based collaboration in brainstorming sessions and for component design jointly with parts manufacturers worldwide.

Online communities (communities of practice) bring together individuals sharing a common professional interest in a virtual environment, using message boards and listservs, to share information and advice. Schlumberger, an oil field services company, has about twenty online communities covering a range of businesses and technologies. The communities help spur innovation and promote employee motivation through greater team cohesiveness within the company. The World Bank has more than one hundred communities of practice across geographic and functional boundaries. In one of its latest efforts, the World Bank Institute is developing a community of practice of e-leaders from numerous countries. This community includes the heads of information technology departments (such as CIOs) from both donor and beneficiary countries.

E-learning helps employees acquire new skills without leaving their desks—using a variety of tools such as discussion boards, computer-assisted instruction, and Web conferencing. Countrywide Financial, a *Fortune* 500 company that provides financial services all over the world, uses e-learning to train hundreds of employees at the same time, which eliminates offsite training sessions and employee and trainer travel and saves the company $4 million a year. The Ford Learning System at Ford Motor Company has over eighteen hundred Web courses available to employees via the company's corporate intranet.

Business intelligence tools, such as budgeting, forecasting, and data-mining applications, can provide a better understanding of business operations to both employees and management. For example, customer relationship management (CRM), based on data-mining tools, can help employees with insights about customer behavior and preferences. Dow Chemical has a searchable Web-based database of all critical documents relating to archived research projects. Text-mining at the company allows employees to more fully explore complex relationships among documents in its text databases.

Organizations typically make such technologies and applications available to employees via their corporate intranet, a single point of access to multiple knowledge sources, available anytime from anywhere. These self-service, instant, and automated applications were simply not available a decade ago.

These technologies contribute greatly to the paradigm shift in how organizations view, manage, and use knowledge.

PREREQUISITES TO EFFECTIVE KNOWLEDGE MANAGEMENT

We shall now discuss what an organization needs in order to have an effective knowledge management system, including how managerial thinking needs to change as a result of the paradigm shift in knowledge management. Ideally, an organization should create an internal work culture where people can share ideas and lessons learned, provide each other with updates, contribute their tacit and explicit knowledge to organization repositories, and willingly reuse prior work—theirs as well as others.

In a 2001 survey of corporate KM initiatives, *Knowledge Management* magazine and International Data Corporation found that the main KM implementation challenges relate to organizational culture and related issues.[14] The survey, based on 566 responses, found the following implementation challenges for knowledge management, shown in Table 8.2. (The numbers in the second column indicate the percentage of respondents who gave a particular response.)

In an Ernst & Young survey of 431 companies worldwide, 54 percent of the respondents indicated that creating a knowledge culture was the biggest obstacle to establishing a successful KM system.[15] Looking at survey results, it is easy to surmise that KM implementation can be a daunting task for any organization. However, given the business environment organizations face today, knowledge-management initiatives are important not only for building and sustaining competitive advantage, but for their very survival as well.

TABLE 8.2. Implementation Challenges for Knowledge Management

Challenge	Percentage of Respondents Who Believed This Is a Challenge
Employees have no time for KM	41.0%
Current culture does not encourage sharing	36.6%
Lack of understanding of KM and its benefits	29.5%
Inability to measure financial benefits of KM	24.5%
Lack of skill in KM techniques	22.7%
Organization's processes not designed for KM	22.2%
Lack of funding for KM	21.8%
Lack of incentives, rewards to share	19.9%
Lack of appropriate technology	17.4%
Lack of commitment from senior management	13.9%
No challenges experienced	4.3%

Source: G. Dyer and B. McDonough, "The State of KM," *Knowledge Management* (May 2001); available at: http://www.destinationkm.com/articles/default.asp?ArticleID=539.

Implementation of a knowledge management system requires certain **organizational capabilities, management practices,** and **cognitive and managerial skills.**

Organizational Capabilities

Since knowledge management is implemented based on modern KM technologies, the organization must have an appropriate information technology infrastructure. The previous subsection on knowledge management tools provided a list of some of the core technologies used in knowledge management. Which specific technologies an organization will need depends on the specific KM applications it wants to have. For instance, if the organization wants to use KM for employee collaboration, as in a decentralized R&D environment, it should invest in a collaboration platform, including Web conferencing, listserv, and message board software. If the organization wants to build a virtual repository of its unstructured information and knowledge, it should be looking for an enterprise content management system, including authoring tools, tagging and indexing software, storage, and a search engine.[16] Most such applications also require a corporate portal or intranet, which provides access to employees worldwide to the company's information.

It goes without saying that the organization must also have the absorptive capacity needed to effectively implement and use the new KM technologies. An organization is better equipped to absorb KM technologies if it already has a corporate intranet and employees are up to speed with information technologies. Other organizational capabilities needed for effective KM implementation are an organization structure and routines that allow quick response to changes in the external environment. Flat organization structures and two-way communication are more conducive to KM than are hierarchical structures and one-way communication.

Management Practices

Having appropriate technology is of course, a requirement for KM implementation, but the most important element of successful KM implementation is the organization's management practices, including its human resources (HR) policies, which must be designed to encourage the desired knowledge-sharing behaviors. When Daimler-Benz merged with the Chrysler Corporation in 1998, one of their earliest decisions made was to implement a KM system for the merged DaimlerChrysler organization. In 1999 the company began adding KM competencies and behaviors to their performance appraisal process to ensure that employee performance was judged on the basis of behaviors the company wanted them to practice. In fall 2000, a new senior-manager appraisal process was installed that included five desired behaviors, one of which was knowledge sharing and management.[17]

The importance of having appropriate management practices designed to elicit desired employee behaviors cannot be overstated. For effective knowledge management, it is absolutely essential that there be no disconnect between the behaviors espoused by management and the behaviors actually reflected in management practices such as performance appraisal, as illustrated above, and incentives/rewards programs. Organizations have formal and informal incentives and rewards programs that are typically designed to encourage desired employee behaviors. David DeLong cites several examples of companies, such as Quaker Chemical, that tied their incentives programs to employees' knowledge-sharing behaviors.[18]

As mentioned in an earlier section, organizations must find means to capture and retain the knowledge of all employees, especially those who leave, or could leave, to ensure that valuable knowledge does not walk out the door as well. Succession planning and career development are needed to retain employees (and their knowledge) within the organization and to build long-term employee capabilities. Organizations generally undertake succession planning only for the top management positions, but it is imperative that they also involve professionals, managers, and other employees with key skills in succession-planning initiatives. The McLane Company, for instance, does an inventory of its employee skills every six months—to identify current and potential knowledge gaps at all levels in the corporation. Once employees with critical knowledge and skills are identified, McLane uses succession planning and career development to not only try and retain those people within the company but also to develop others to take over these roles in the future.[19]

Managerial Competencies

Having appropriate technology and management practices is a necessary, but not a sufficient, condition for knowledge management. It has been suggested that knowledge management is 10 percent technological and 90 percent social and cultural. In fact, that statistic is what positions KM as a source of competitive advantage. Technology is something practically anyone with resources can buy, but how it is actually used depends a great deal on management practices and the organization's social and cultural milieu. Technology can be bought, management practices can be imitated, but an organization's social and cultural setting and interactions are not transferable. Hence the role of organizational culture in the success of KM programs in organizations, and the role of KM in establishing competitive advantage!

The managerial competencies needed for knowledge management revolve largely around an organizational culture that supports KM. In organizations that have such a culture, knowledge-acquisition, sharing, and reuse are things employees do everyday as a matter of course. At Schlumberger, for example, "knowledge responsibilities" are part of employees' daily work routines.[20]

Thus, a knowledge culture includes employee behaviors that seek out new knowledge, find and use existing knowledge, share knowledge, and learn from others' experiences.

Developing a KM culture is not something an organization can easily do. Depending on the organization's existing culture, changing to a KM culture can be very time-consuming and expensive, as can all culture-change initiatives. At Ernst & Young (E&Y), for instance, culture-change implementation incorporated training, internal marketing, thought leadership, communication, measurement, and reward mechanisms. *Every* practitioner at E&Y was assigned responsibilities for contributing to and using the KM system. System use was made one of four dimensions of the firm's Balanced ScoreCard, which became a key performance metric for all employees. Designed to make knowledge-sharing an integral part of what everyone at E&Y does, the effort involved one-fifth of total knowledge budget over many years.[21]

Managers need to create the right organizational environment (culture) and mechanisms (e.g., organization structure and management practices) to institutionalize knowledge-sharing by everyone, and they must lead by example. It's the working environment managers create as well as their own actions that determine employees' knowledge-sharing behaviors. David DeLong lists five specific knowledge-sharing practices that need to be institutionalized and embedded within organizations to encourage knowledge capture and sharing.[22] These are: interviews, training, storytelling, mentoring, and communities of practice.

Interviews are used by many organizations, including the World Bank, to capture employees' tacit knowledge that might be otherwise lost. The text and video clips of interviews with veteran staffers returning from long overseas field assignments are stored in the bank's repositories and can be accessed by employees through their intranet.

Training of employees, both new and old, is a time-tested method of imparting explicit knowledge from the organization and external sources. It can also be used to impart the tacit knowledge of experienced employees when they are leading the training sessions.

Storytelling is another method used by some organizations in an attempt to codify employees' tacit knowledge. Storytelling is actually something we all do to some extent in our everyday organizational lives. In stories, we share our knowledge and impressions of the organization, leaders, colleagues, customers, and general perceptions about how things are. They can be a powerful means of capturing employees' tacit knowledge, provided managers take the time to listen to stories as a matter of course. Some, however, question the validity of storytelling since one cannot always be sure if a story being told truly reflects how things are.

Mentoring involves one-on-one coaching of employees and new hires by the more experienced employees. It is a valuable technique for imparting technical, operational, and managerial skills as well as knowledge of cultural norms and behaviors.

Communities of practice bring together individuals with common professional interests to share information and advice with each other in a virtual environment. These groups are another useful method of sharing tacit and explicit knowledge with community members.

In addition to knowledge-sharing and management through approaches such as those discussed above, managers and employees need a facility with computers and the Internet, since most of their KM work will involve using these tools. Most individuals already have these competencies, as they already use these tools as a normal part of their day-to-day responsibilities.

CONCLUSION

Knowledge management has clearly come of age and is here to stay. However, it is no longer "the next big thing" or "the killer app" that it was touted to be in its early years. As we saw, successful KM implementation involves 90 percent sociology and culture, and only 10 percent technology. Implementation can be time-consuming and costly. Technology was a key driver in many KM implementations in the early years of the paradigm shift, but future developments will be driven more by human factors and strategy than by technology. Even today, an organization may begin its KM journey with technology investments, but the real enabler (and bottleneck) of knowledge management is organizational culture and people. Since there are no cookie-cutter approaches to knowledge management, every organization attempting to implement knowledge management will need a system that is more or less custom-designed for its use.

Knowledge management is firmly established as a determinant of competitive advantage, especially employees' tacit knowledge, rather than their explicit knowledge, which can be bought, stolen, or even replicated. Already in use by large organizations, KM is increasingly being used by small and medium-sized enterprises as more cost-effective technologies become available. The return on KM investments is not measured in terms of dollars, though some have attempted to do so, but in terms of expertise developed and retained, speed to decision-making, and improved operational efficiency.

Globalization will continue to challenge organizations to become better at knowledge management. In fact, the scope of knowledge management is already going beyond internal knowledge-sharing to external knowledge-sharing via extranets and knowledge networks with suppliers and customers, as in the Wal-Mart illustration. More and more companies will need to take on the challenge of extending their KM systems to include customers and suppliers for improved performance.

NOTES

1. The concept of routines was popularized by Richard Nelson and Sidney Winter (1982) in their evolutionary economics framework. Routines is "a general term for all the regular and predictable behavior patterns of firms" (R. R. Nelson and S. G. Winter, *An Evolutionary Theory of Economic Change*, Cambridge, MA: Belknap Press, 1982: 15). A routine is thus a set of rules and procedures for performing a certain task (such as writing software code or assembling a finished product); it may or may not have been explicitly articulated. Writing about routines in the 1992 edition of their classic 1963 book, *A Behavioral Theory of the Firm*, . . . Cyert and James March had this to say: "Organizations develop, stabilize, and follow routines. The routines may change over time, but in the short run they function as carriers of knowledge and experience" (224).

2. R. Stata, "Organizational Learning: The Key To Management Innovation," *Sloan Management Review* (spring 1989): 63–74.

3. T. A. Davenport and L. Prusak, *Working Knowledge* (Boston: Harvard Business School Press, 1998).

4. Proposed by Robert Metcalfe, founder of 3Com.

5. Jack Welch, the former CEO of General Electric, even created a term for such an organization—the boundaryless organization.

6. "Extending the Enterprise: A New Model of Growth," a white paper from the Economist Intelligence Unit, 2002.

7. McKinsey & Company, *The War for Talent* (2001); http://www.mckinsey.de/_downloads/knowmatters/organisation/organization_war_talent.pdf.

8. R. Florida, *The Flight of the Creative Class: The New Global Competition for Talent* (HarperCollins, 2005).

9. D. W. DeLong, *Lost Knowledge: Confronting the Threat of an Aging Workforce* (New York: Oxford University Press, 2004).

10. Microsoft case study on sharing knowledge: http://www.1000ventures.com/business_guide/cs_inex_microsoft-kbe.html.

11. K. Ohmae, *The Next Global Stage: The Challenges and Opportunities in Our Borderless World* (Philadelphia: Wharton School Publishing, 2005).

12. An organization incurs *transaction costs* whenever it makes a purchase. These include search costs, information costs, bargaining costs, decision costs, and policing and enforcement costs (L. Downes and C. Mui, *Unleashing the Killer App: Digital Strategies for Market Dominance*, Boston, MA: Harvard Business School Press, 1998).

13. This discussion is adapted from Economist Information Unit's "Leveraging Knowledge: Business Intelligence in the Global Corporation," 2002.

14. G. Dyer and B. McDonough, "The State of KM," *Knowledge Management* (May 2001); available at: http://www.destinationkm.com/articles/default.asp?ArticleID=539.

15. D. Webb, "Corporate Culture Blocks Use of Knowledge," *Computing Canada* (September 1, 1998).

16. L. M. Orlove, "When You Say 'KM,' What Do You Mean?" (2004); available at: http://www2.cio.com/analyst/report2931.html.

17. Based on the author's discussions with KM managers at DaimlerChrysler headquarters in Germany (Stuttgart) and the United States (Auburn Hills, MI) in the summer of 2000.

18. D. W. DeLong, *Lost Knowledge: Confronting the Threat of an Aging Workforce* (New York: Oxford University Press, 2004).

19. Ibid.

20. "Leveraging Knowledge: Business Intelligence in the Global Corporation," a white paper from the Economist Information Unit, 2002.

21. P. Harkins and L. Carter, *Linkage, Inc.'s Best Practices in Knowledge Management & Organizational Learning Handbook,* Linkage, Inc. (2000).

22. This discussion is adapted from D. W. DeLong, *Lost Knowledge: Confronting the Threat of an Aging Workforce* (New York: Oxford University Press, 2004).

9

International Accounting, Taxation, and Corporate Governance

SAAD LARAQUI

THE WORLD ACCOUNTING ENVIRONMENT

For firms with international operations, the world accounting environment is changing at a quicker pace than ever before. Accounting is shifting in favor of a single international standard. In many countries the burden of taxation is shifting from corporations to individuals. Globalization of capital markets is demanding more transparency in corporate governance.

The interests of corporate stakeholders vary significantly. Bankers seek comfort in their credit decisions, governments establish varying tax standards, and bond and stock holders want reliable investment information. Internally, financial reports are the primary control mechanism available to the management team.[1] Developing consistent financial information in formats useful to all stakeholders has been the principal challenge to practitioners of accounting of all persuasions—private, public, and regulatory—in all corners of the globe.

Today's Approaches Stem from Four Traditions

Over the course of the last two centuries, four methods of accounting have evolved:

Commonwealth. Encompasses the United Kingdom (UK) and most of the former colonies that rely on British common law as the foundation for commercial dealings;

Continental. Used in most of Continental Europe and former European colonies adhering to tenets of Napoleonic Civil Code;

Soviet. Grounded in concepts unique to centrally planned economies;

United States. Used by a number of countries in Asia and Latin America where US business interests have been active; rooted in American commercial law, which itself evolved out of British common law.

These classifications are not absolute. Many hybrids have evolved, reflecting transitions into different spheres of influence and changes of political systems. Sometimes the distinctions between the accounting treatments are very subtle and require a detailed understanding of accounting practice, applicable law, and legislative history.[2] For example, at first glance the annual reports of Canadian and U.S. companies appear nearly identical in presentation of their financial statements. On further reading, material differences in approach are disclosed in the footnotes concerning recognition of some types of income, certain expenses, and most depreciation and depletion allowances.

Changes to established accounting practice often come as a reaction to financial scandals erupting in periods of economic downturns. In the modern era, global outrage and charges of fraud resulted when the "dot com" crash occurred in first half of 2000, accompanied by allegations of improperly booked sales as well as misclassification of incurred costs. "Bubbles" are not new to the investment community. Although others are lost to antiquity, the "South Sea Bubble" of 1720 involved the stock runup and subsequent collapse of the British-chartered South Sea Company, established in 1711 to trade with Spanish colonies in the West Indies and Latin America. It duped investors as smart as Sir Isaac Newton.[3]

Over time, nearly a dozen influential "accounting standards" boards have emerged among more than 250 organizations representing well over 1 million professional accountants who provide guidance to perhaps 100 million finance managers, company accountants, and bookkeepers around the globe.[4] Most United Nations (UN) member countries now have some form of domestic association representing practicing accountants, sponsored by local commercial, governmental, and international interests.

CHALLENGES TO ACCOUNTING FROM GLOBALIZATION

Language and other purely cultural aspects aside, the greatest difference that the average business experiences outside its home country is the level of permits, regulations, reporting requirements, and other "red tape." Since accounting is how a business keeps score, knowing the local rules of the game is critical to long-run success. With globalization, challenges to established accounting practices are the following:

The Global Harmonization Challenge

Understanding the differing rules of disclosure, audit standards, and corporate governance as well as the convergence in global financial reporting demands a higher skill level among accountants and finance industry professionals than at any other time.

At an operating level, risks stem largely from measuring and managing floating exchange rates, different levels of inflation, and varying capital costs, including interest rates. A universal accounting approach is needed to handle the impact of inflation and changing interest rates as well as for plant and inventory valuations. This is the key factor driving the adoption of International Accounting Standards (IAS).[5]

The Accounting Technology Challenge

Sole proprietorships have access to accounting software that once required an IBM 360 or other legacy system computer and a roomful of technicians. The Internet enables managers to develop real-time financial information for domestic and international operations, programmed to meet local, national, and parent reporting country accounting standards. However, as powerful as accounting software has become, the cardinal rule of computer-assisted data processing still applies: GIGO = Garbage In yields Garbage Out.[6]

Web-based data processing products greatly facilitate the ability of an accounting manager to generate better and timelier financial information than ever before. Nonfinancial managers read reports generated in several currencies, in multiple languages, and in graphic as well as numeric formats, distributed around the world via e-mail to authorized recipients.[7]

Despite the advances in accounting software, bringing a fully conforming general ledger and financial reporting package online using experienced information technology (IT) professionals can consume a considerable amount of time and money. System updates to account for rules changes issued by local accounting standards boards and government authorities as well as changes to the business processes can be difficult to program while maintaining system functionality and interoperability.[8]

The Reporting Standards Challenge

Reporting relationships are being redefined as traditional areas of responsibility for the controller, treasurer, and country manager as they focus more on business lines and less on local business units. Maintaining working financial controls and stringent audit trails is made more difficult by having a greater reliance on outsourcing key elements of production processes to suppliers half a world away. The workload of internal auditors and independent outside audit firms has never been greater.[9]

With the development of global instantaneous communication networks, there is a trend toward outsourcing accounting functions. Specialized firms like ADP have long processed payrolls for small- and medium-sized enterprises (SMEs) as well as for multinational enterprises (MNEs). Business process outsourcing (BPO), as it has come to be called in India, is a fast-growing element of accounting services offered through facilities like the Accenture Delivery Center in Bangalore. While BPO greatly cuts the cost of processing items like sales tickets, credit card invoices, and delinquent invoices, it also introduces new dilemmas for audit professionals as they seek to minimize fraud and overbilling by contractors.

The Challenge of Adopting International Accounting Standards (IAS)

The International Accounting Standards Committee (IASC) developed a set of IAS standards in 1998, greatly aiding cross-border securities registrations. The standards were quickly adopted by most countries of the EU. The London-based successor to the IASC, the International Accounting Standards Board (IASB), made the adoption of IAS mandatory for all publicly traded companies headquartered in the EU beginning with the 2005 reporting year.[10] Additional countries, with some notable exceptions like the United States, are adopting IAS as the basis for uniform financial reporting. For a global firm, IAS will decrease accounting complexities and produce reports that are recognizable to accountants, business managers, financial analysts, and shareholders around the world. However, the transition process from reporting in national GAAP (generally accepted accounting principles) to financial reporting under IAS is likely to be painful for some firms, as earnings and asset values, particularly with respect to mergers and obsolescent plant and equipment, are restated in a uniform format. Some firms may find that IAS imposes limitations on dividends and on compliance with previously negotiated loan covenants.[11] Despite trends toward international harmonization on reporting to shareholders, changes in reporting for tax purposes is meeting much more resistance, principally due to perceived adverse revenue impacts to the tax collectors.[12]

For a variety of complex historic and political reasons, the level of external financial reporting and disclosure differs from country to country. In the United States and some other industrialized countries, business accountants and managers have long been accustomed to maintaining two sets of books—one for financial reporting purposes and one for tax purposes. Under the law of a number of countries, this is permitted and generally reflects differences in income recognition, depreciation periods, and tax credits.[13]

In many other countries, however, there is a single system of accounts used for both reporting to stakeholders and to tax authorities. This concept is difficult to accept and understand for accountants and general managers who have grown up in a U.S.-oriented environment. In a globalized setting the implications can be quite profound. Since most tax systems are progressive, local business managers may have a disincentive to report increases in reportable earnings. This can make it difficult to compare reported earnings and cash retention among countries. In a few instances, like contemporary Russia, large segments of economic activity occur outside the regulated economy, due to uneven application of tax policies and outright confiscation of cash and other reported assets by local and federal tax authorities. Even as Russia adopts IAS, enterprises that bother to file tax reports are required to maintain their books on a cash basis, which generally increases their tax liability.[14]

For U.S.-based MNEs there are many challenges. In the United States, the Securities and Exchange Commission (SEC) and the Internal Revenue Service (IRS) have been slow to embrace IAS, citing budget constraints. Adoption of IAS by U.S. businesses could well undermine revenue intake in an era of unprecedented government deficits and the need to fund both military and social programs.[15] Continuing resistance in the United States to the adoption of IAS may limit access to globalized capital markets if the growing number of non-U.S.-based institutional and private investors spurn issues reported solely using the U.S. GAAP standard. Interestingly, the adoption of IAS in the European Union is likely to synchronize financial reporting and tax accounting into a single set of books as EU members move toward a harmonized income tax code. This is likely to improve collection of EU member states' tax revenues.[16]

Another accounting complexity is the fact that the United States is one of only a few countries that compels the reporting of worldwide income. While U.S.-based MNEs have mounted a successful lobbying effort to minimize the competitive effects of US tax policy on their foreign earnings, challenges from the IRS on issues like the level of reported profits on transfers of goods produced between onshore and offshore divisions have compelled some major firms to reincorporate in jurisdictions like Bermuda and conduct business in the United States as a foreign corporation.[17] Just as production jobs can be exported to the lowest-cost bidder, the headquarters function and state of incorporation can be moved on resolutions by the board of directors to the most favorable tax jurisdiction. Companies that are home-based in jurisdictions that adopt IAS will gain a competitive advantage over those based in countries that do not embrace the change.

The Currency Exposure Challenge

Many transnational business decisions rely on accounting data and an understanding of transnational accounting issues such as "translation exposure" and "transaction exposure." Currency exposure in general refers to the effects of changing currency exchange rates, particularly on currencies that govern a firm's consolidated accounts. Translation exposure occurs when financial statements of the foreign subsidiary of an MNE are consolidated with the parent financial statements. Transaction exposure results from the possibility of exchange gains and losses on transactions that have already been entered into and are denominated in a foreign currency. In the absence of a single world currency, weighing the impact of these exposures is crucial to understanding the accounting statements of an MNE on a global or regional level. With the creation of the Euro, the EU eliminated the currency exposure problems for many thousands of European companies in a single stroke of the pen. EU companies listed on a U.S. exchange still need to report using U.S. GAAP standards. The SEC, however, allows accounting prepared in accordance with IAS to be reported to U.S. shareholders.[18]

The complexity of currency exposure varies with the number of countries in which the MNE operates and its relative exposure to foreign currencies in local business units. A large U.S.-based energy producer pumping oil from Angola, Indonesia, and Norway may have relatively low exposure to currency swings, because both the oil being sold and most of the costs associated with the production side, except locally employed labor, are in U.S. dollars. A UK-based tobacco company selling tobacco products in the developing world where people still take up the habit may have significantly different exposures on the value of the sales in a given country, the cost to produce the product in a nearby country, and the cost of imported primary inputs like tobacco and fine paper. An emerging Chinese MNE producing white goods such as refrigerators and stoves in China and the United States may have relatively less exposure if the principal sales area is North America than if sales are expanded into South America.

To mitigate against the earnings impacts, financial managers have adopted hedging strategies both on the currencies and on the primary commodities involved in the production process. A Cyprus-based shipping company moving iron ore between Brazil and China may be working currency hedges against the reminbi and the real as well as the euro, whether or not the pricing of the contract is U.S. dollars. In an era of volatile energy prices, the company's managers may be engaged in a hedging strategy to minimize the cost effect of fuel bunkering on multiyear contracts and sixty-day voyages. The level of sophistication may vary among the managers, but the financial strategy is the same.

A third type of exposure is economic exposure, also known as operating exposure. It measures the extent to which firm value is affected by **unexpected** changes in currency rates. Where changes in currency rates are expected, investors factor this information into their evaluation and these expected changes would not be included in the definition of operating exposure. Potentially, economic exposure can have more severe implications on the long-term financial health of a business than changes caused by translation and transaction exposure. For all these exposures, the role of accounting managers is crucial, as they can lead to different strategies or accounting methods to deal with the trouble.

KEY FORCES OF CHANGE

In today's business climate, operating, financing, and investment decisions are colored by their international implications and the growing irrelevance of borders for MNEs as we witness a transition to truly global firms. Although politicians and tax authorities in most countries resist the pace of change, policy-makers around the world have been compelled to rethink old approaches as they relate to accounting, economic regulation, and taxation. Key forces for change are: (a) the emergence of the EU as a major economic force; (b) the awakening of China and India; (c) the development of globalized financial institutions; (d) recognition of shareholder value; and (e) calls for better corporate governance.

Emergence of the EU as a Major Economic Force

The EU, an economic association of some twenty-five countries has created the single greatest force for changes in accounting, taxation, and corporate governance standards. In a world formerly dominated by British, German, Japanese, and U.S. business interests, there was little demand for change. Today, with the increasing unification of Europe, a second force of consumer power has emerged, which has the potential to surpass the United States in economic dominance as a function of more prudent fiscal policies, higher savings rates, and lessened dependence on out-of-zone imports. By mid-2005 the combined buying power and economic activity of the EU constituted approximately one-third of global output, while the remainder is about evenly divided between the North American Free Trade Association (NAFTA) and the rest of the world, including the fast-growing regions of Asia. As part of its drive to harmonize reporting standards for shareholders, most EU countries have adopted IAS standards, and have been instrumental in gaining acceptance of the IAS standard by other countries around the world. As the EU continues to integrate its monetary and fiscal policies, it will become increasingly difficult for any business to operate exclusively under GAAP. As a result, U.S. firms may find their access to capital limited unless the IRS and SEC can be persuaded to embrace IAS standards.

The Awakening of China and India

A second force is the emergence of China and India as influential economic and political powers. With a combined population approaching 2.5 billion—over one-third of world population—and high sustained economic growth over the foreseeable future, the economies of these two giants are likely to outdistance the EU and the United States over the next five decades. At the same time, Chinese and Indian companies and brands will become well-known in world markets just as Western firms and their brands have penetrated

Chinese and Indian markets. While Chinese and Indian accounting systems may present some challenges to a Westerner, the strength of these accounting systems will progressively and subtly be absorbed into IAS standards. The beauty of the leveling of the business field across emerging markets and mature economies is the synergy that takes place and results in a more robust global system. Both China and India have long traditions in international trade and commerce and, as such, have developed capabilities in their accounting systems that over the long term can contribute to strengthening IAS standards.

The Development of Globalized Financial Institutions

A third force for change has been the emergence of globalized financial institutions, with shareholders in many countries and portfolio managers as comfortable trading on the Bolsa in Mexico City as they are on the London Stock Exchange, the NYSE, or NASDAQ. Large financial services firms operate across international borders as readily as MNEs engaged in automobile manufacturing, consumer products, and energy. Their product, capital, is capable of near instantaneous transfer around the globe. Increasingly, hedge funds and similar institutions are locating in tax havens such as Curacao or the Isle of Man, where the tax on investment transactions is minimized. The power of the globalized capital market is forcing changes on management, presenting new challenges to meeting earnings expectations, and maintaining the price of the stock on an increasingly global playing field.[19]

Recognition of Shareholder Value

The movement to increase shareholder rights is slowly gaining momentum. The diversity of jurisdictions makes it difficult for shareholders to force changes to such issues as voting rights, standards of disclosure, and adoption of IAS. Stock exchange listing requirements, often reflective of national laws governing the regulation of exchanges, have continuously been improved, requiring a greater degree of accounting data capture and comparable accounting standards. Approaches such as the UN code of conduct for MNEs have not been nearly as effective at compelling changes at large companies as the promulgation of some regulation by the U.S. SEC or the outcome of a lawsuit involving one of the major auditing firms. Many of the changes are reactionary, resulting from scandals in the wake of stock market crashes, corporate bankruptcies, and shareholder lawsuits.

Calls for Better Corporate Governance

Corporate governance has become a very visible issue in the U.S. press as a result of several well-publicized business collapses such as Enron, Global

Crossing, and WorldCom in the economic recession of 2001–2002. It is less of an issue in most other industrial countries. Unlike the United States, which only recently resorted to compelling senior executives of publicly traded companies to sign financial statements, most other countries require a company to have a designated "accountable manager." Being the accountable manager takes on a meaning totally unfamiliar to an American financial officer. Under Chilean law, for instance, the accountable manager can be jailed when the company has not paid the customs duties on imported parts or failed to make a quarterly payroll tax payment within the statutory time period. This is nearly unheard-of in the United States. In sharp contrast to Chile, which scrupulously adheres to accounting standards and law, is the environment in Russia, where corruption permits the circumvention of nearly every applicable law and where the cash economy thrives.[20]

The control required for consolidating financial reports will compel changes in accounting standards, even when the current IAS system is phased in. For instance, U.S. authorities uniformly require over 50 percent ownership of a subsidiary to permit consolidation. Canada, Bermuda, and many others permit consolidation if control can be demonstrated, which can be established well below an 80 percent ownership threshold, particularly in large, publicly traded entities where "control" of the board of directors can be effected with as little as 5 percent of the outstanding stock. Within the EU, the polyglot of tax policies between individual, corporate, and trust holdings has given rise to complex interlocking relationships between "sister" companies within a "group," whose meaning can vary from country to country. As a result, some of the standards issued by the IASB have been subject to protracted negotiation before being promulgated.[21] Around the globe, the burden of taxation is shifting from corporations to individuals.

SHIFTS IN THE INTERNATIONAL ACCOUNTING PARADIGM

A series of perceptible shifts in the international accounting paradigm is occurring as world business practices become more integrated. The pressure to change is compelling the following adjustments to practices.

IAS: The New World Standard

Conformity to IAS is becoming an integral feature of the international business and finance arenas. Standardized approaches to accounting and the concept of risk-shifting are being adopted by most publicly traded MNEs that report earnings to the same group of securities analysts who can link themselves with trading desks, portfolio managers, and institutional and private investors in near real time. Those firms whose financial statements are not easily understood are likely to rapidly fall out of favor with market-makers and find that their access to capital markets is increasingly limited.

The basic purpose of accounting information such as sales revenue, cost of goods sold, interest costs, and taxes is to provide management the information it needs to evaluate and monitor financial performance. As such, accounting systems are by definition control systems. Although the chart of accounts may vary widely, the function of accounting is the same in a small business operating on Main Street as it is in an MNE operating around the globe. The level of sophistication increases as local complexities are introduced. Measurement of results for U.S. firms is governed by an accounting standard last revised and issued in 1981 by the Financial Accounting Standards Board (FASB). EU based MNEs are transitioning to IAS, which take a different approach on several key aspects of international accounting. Rather than historic value, the focus of IAS is on fair valuation, which concerns itself more with timely recognition of impairments to cash flow, earnings, and assets values. Given present trends, most countries will adopt IAS, at least for MNEs, by 2010. In the United States, there will be a much slower transition, pulled along by the efforts of the NYSE and other major U.S. exchanges, to remain competitive relative to the Euronext, Frankfurt, London, Mumbai, or Tokyo exchanges.

At an operating level, conducting business outside a familiar domestic environment means taking on additional risks due to measuring and managing accounting exposures within an environment of floating exchange rates, different levels of inflation, and capital costs, including interest rates. Developing a universal approach to accounting for the impact of inflation and changing interest rates as well as plant and inventory valuations is the key factor driving the adoption of IAS.[22]

Securities Markets Are More Global

Broadly speaking, the number of publicly traded firms is now evenly split between the United States, the EU, and the rest of the world (ROW). There are about 10,000 publicly traded firms on U.S. exchanges, including the NASDAQ (National Association of Securities Dealers Automated Quotation System). More than 7,000 firms are listed on exchanges in EU countries, and nearly 33,000 are listed in the ROW on exchanges as diverse as Casablanca, Melbourne, Tokyo, and Toronto. Billions of dollars of securities are traded every day, and in some measure, the value of the underlying security is reflected in the perception of the quality of earnings of the company. For a small natural resource company listed on the Toronto Venture Exchange, the value of its common stock is more likely to be linked to a discovery of a diamond pipe in southwestern Africa or northeastern Canada than any historic earnings. For a U.S. airline traded on the NYSE, a quarterly earnings report showing a significant change in seasonal losses or quarter over quarter losses can compel it to seek protection in bankruptcy courts as its credit sources dry up. An EU-based insurance company may see its securities rise in value simply because the Euro has moved up in value in relation to the U.S. dollar, depending on whether or not it has significant earnings exposure to the U.S. dollar or another currency, such as the Chinese reminbi or Mexican peso, closely linked to the dollar.

Accounting Technology Is Much More Powerful

Advances in IT have allowed accounting systems to be standardized between business operating units as never before, and most have the capability of being programmed to deal with translation and transaction exposure as well as the local country practices on taxation, currency repatriation, and capital reserve ratios. Although they are not foolproof, modern audit controls can be built into an advanced accounting system typically installed by a large MNE. Variance reports can be generated to allow managers to compare actual results with anticipated ones and trace the variance to a decrease in production, inventory slippage, or other usually readily identified cause. With the trend toward carefully monitored global supply chains, almost no input or output of any process escapes the ability to be monitored. Maintaining the integrity and security of the IT system is emerging as a greater challenge than the customary shrinkage of finished goods inventory on the production line by employees, or criminal gangs, or payoffs to government officials.

The Big Four Prevail, Usually

The increasing transparency of accounting statements across industries around the world is having a direct impact on capital market valuations and access to credit. Credit analysts and stock researchers are better able to understand relative cash flow and quality of earnings as well as the overall creditworthiness of the firm. The emergence of the "Big Four" accounting firms with global reach and high standards has facilitated capital market valuation but has not proved to be foolproof. Burned by accounting embarrassments such as BP's overstatement of proven oil reserves, Enron's understatement of liabilities, and WorldCom's overstatement of revenues, the profession is ever more vigilant in maintaining rigorous audit standards and testing. The dismembering of Andersen Accounting in the wake of the Enron failure was a sharp reminder to the accounting profession of its responsibility to shareholders.

Increasingly, the "big four" global accounting firms—Deloitte Touche Tohmatsu, Ernst & Young, KPMG, and PricewaterhouseCoopers—are taking on more aspects of the accounting function than providing an independent audit of the numbers making up the annual report to shareholders.[23] Table 9.1 illustrates the global reach of the "big four" accounting firms, each of which has established a worldwide network of offices, usually by acquiring a stake in a local accounting firm. The "big four" have experienced an annual growth of 5 to 10 percent since the mid-1970s, with significant increases in business

TABLE 9.1.   Global Reach of the Big Four Accounting Firms

Firm	2004 Billings (Billions-USD)	Countries	Offices	Employees	Average Billings/ Offices (Millions/ USD)	Average Billings/ Employee (Thousands/ USD)
Deloitte Touche Tohmatsu	$16.4	148	670	117,000	$24.5	$140,000
Ernst & Young	$14.5	140	670	100,000	$21.6	$145,000
KPMG	$13.4	148	717	94,000	$18.7	$143,000
Pricewaterhouse Coopers	$17.6	144	769	122,000	$22.9	$144,000
Total or Average	$61.9	144	2,826	433,000	$21.9	$143,000

Source: Compiled from financial, location, and personnel information disclosed on each website in March 2005.*

*Extracted from the "big four" websites from the "about us" sections; each website also has growth statistics; United States and the rest of North America is running at 8 percent, but overall firm growth is running at 15 percent, with Asia running at 25 to 35 percent year after year

coming from the faster-growing regions of the world, such as Asia. Part of the growth has come about as a result of a requirement of many countries for businesses to maintain separate audit and accounting consulting relationships with public accounting firms. Whereas a business may once have had only a relationship with a single firm like KPMG, today it is more likely to retain KMPG for its annual audit and maintain a relationship for accounting consulting with Deloitte Touche Tohmatsu as well as outsourcing an accounting function to Ernst & Young or PricewaterhouseCoopers.

In such a dynamic environment, operating, financing, and investing decisions are colored by their international implications and the growing irrelevance of borders for MNEs as we witness a transition to truly global firms.

Companies Use an Array of Tools to Minimize Tax

No area generates as much litigation for MNEs as the nexus of local, regional, and federal taxation as various government tax authorities try to apply regulations as fully as they dare on local and foreign income. MNEs have always worked hard to minimize the tax bite of their operations on both a local and home-country basis. Offsetting the U.S. taxation of worldwide income is the ability of U.S.-based MNEs to benefit from taxation treaties aimed at eliminating double taxation and the ability to engage in the trading of goods between offshore and onshore subsidiaries. While the rules change from time to time, almost every change that an affected U.S.-based MNE has experienced is met with an effort to minimize the change. If a lobby cannot be mounted to get the offending tax regulation amended in the legislative process, then more aggressive solutions can be put into play. The threat by a large MNE to move its headquarters out of a small state like Connecticut to Grand Cayman will likely spur the local and federal politicians into a meaningful dialogue, if not positive action. Some countries are less responsive to such approaches. A Chinese MNE is likely to be state-sponsored and not as able to flex its muscles at this stage of Chinese economic evolution. As offshore-resource-oriented China-based MNEs emerge this could change, and it may be politicians in Beijing protesting the re-incorporation of a Chinese mining company in Bermuda rather than an American or British one. As the Russian "oligarchs" find ways to repatriate capital to their non-Russian-based companies, the federal government in Moscow may be compelled to undertake reforms in corporate accounting, taxation, and corporate governance.

Standards of Corporate Governance Vary Widely

The requirements of establishing corporations and corporate bylaws can differ among industries as well as among political subdivisions within a nation. Large MNEs can afford the costs required to understand the accounting and legal complexities of doing business in a particular jurisdiction. For larger MNEs, the overall size of the market, expectations of returns to capital, and an in-house law department tend to mitigate these transaction costs. Smaller firms, understandably, may find these costs to be untenable.

It will be many years before issues relating to taxation and corporate governance are harmonized among countries. However, it is important to realize that very few MNEs operate in all or almost all of the countries of the UN. Most operate in fewer than 50 of the world's nearly 200 countries. Many operate in North America, some in South American countries, most of the EU countries, and select Asian, African, and Middle Eastern companies. Some, such as gasoline marketers, limit their exposure to local concessionaires who pay a licensing fee or other royalty to an offshore franchising entity. While the globally recognized brand name may adorn the service stations and fuel storage tanks, their local investment and local costs may be zero. The product sale is booked offshore when the receiving agent's signature is recorded as the chartered tanker connects to the wharf and the letter of credit supporting the purchase is drawn down per the contract terms. All local accounting, taxation, and governance issues are transferred to the local concessionaire.

The accounting challenges presented by doing business inside China or Russia cannot be taught in a classroom. Many auditors from headquarters cannot readily determine which accounts conceal bribes and other facilitation payments to customs officials, politicians, and suppliers when dispatched to a subsidiary or joint venture in the developing world. Home country laws and official corporate policy may make it illegal to make such payments, but in the practical world, the local managers are likely to engage in local practices if they are expected to maintain production at budgeted levels.

Tax Policy and Practice Have Become Very Complex

The manager responsible for maintaining the relationship with tax authorities has no less of a challenge. The interface with tax authorities occurs at the local, national, and home-country level. At a local level, in the absence of special exemption, local authorities attempt to tax the value of on-site inventories, buildings, land, and improvements as well as services such as water provided by the community. In some cases the value of a new plant can significantly alter the revenue base of a community. Politically, local authorities may be limited in their ability to get any offset to local tax revenues lost to a grant of special tax-exempt status by the national government intent on attracting a MNE to invest in the country. Not paying the local tax bill as presented may result in the water to the plant being shut off, interrupting the production process. In some cases, as in Bolivia with its attempts to export natural gas, local political events can lead to an abandonment of significant investment in facilities after they have been built. In other countries, like Russia, changes in the royalties paid to the state for resource extraction can result in curtailment of investment, with a consequent write-off of the assets on the balance sheet.[24]

Many countries have adopted a value-added tax (VAT), which is the major provider of revenue in nations with few reporting taxpayers. Some countries maintain high customs duties on certain classifications of imports, and in other cases, on exports. At issue almost always is what happens to goods undergoing a transformation process where they are in the country on a temporary basis. Oftentimes, unless produced in a "duty-free" or "special economic zone," the national tax authorities will seek to collect the highest possible levels of VAT, customs duties, and excise taxes as well as applicable income tax. In some cases the global firm may have enough influence within the national political structure to make the tax authority see the errors in its approach. However, in other cases, such as in the mining business, where billions of dollars can be invested in a facility before the first ton of ore is mined and processed, the political leverage may not be as great, because only the very largest MNEs can afford to take the write-down on assets resulting from a "walk" from a failed project.

Even in the least controversial environments, the great challenge continues to be accounting for the value of the goods produced or transformed in the national political entity and the level of income tax owed to the national government. The debate on "transfer pricing" has been one of the longest-running in the age of globalization. In some industries, such as mining, almost all sales take place in tax havens, with minimal profit being reported at the shipping sites. In other industries, such as aircraft assembly, the value added to the transformation process is determined to be at the final stages of assembly, where corporate overheads are assigned, reducing reportable profits at delivery and minimizing reported profits at foreign branch facilities. In the case where foreign subcontractors are used, the margin of profitability is often determined in the contract negotiation phase, and the burden of taxation falls to the subcontractor in his jurisdiction.

Universal agreements on taxation are unlikely given the diversity in approach to what constitutes income and what is taxable. Similarly, largely due to a resistance of U.S. lawmakers to participate in global forums, it will be some time before there are universal standards on corporate governance. Those companies whose shares are listed on a U.S. exchange will be subject to SEC regulation. Foreign companies reporting to their EU and non-U.S. shareholders will have to report differences in reported earnings under U.S. GAAP to its U.S. shareholders. Those non-U.S. companies that have more than three hundred U.S. resident shareholders will be forced to comply with the U.S. Sarbanes-Oxley Act, requiring senior management to personally sign the financial reports developed for its public shareholders, unless they take steps to limit U.S. purchases of their securities.[25] Compliance required by the 2001 USA Patriot Act has prompted non-U.S. banks to curtail lending to U.S. companies.[26]

ACCOUNTING COMPETENCIES

The challenges of globalization continue to test traditional managerial approaches, especially those relating to accounting, taxation, and corporate governance. In business or at a public accounting firm, accountants involved in international spheres need a broader set of skills than those of the traditional "bean counter."

Learn to Work with Tougher Auditors and Tax Collectors

The "big four" accounting firms have taken steps to structure their businesses in such a way as to conduct their professional accounting practices in as many countries as are determined to be worthwhile by the senior partners. The U.S. entity is usually quite separate from the rest of the global practice, which is often managed from London. For this reason London has reemerged as a major financial center in a networked world where English has become the global language of business. To the extent that global firms are outsourcing specific accounting functions to the overseas accounting consulting arms of the "big four," a more standardized consensus on industry-specific accounting practices may emerge. The fate of the Andersen accounting firm is compelling a more conservative and consistent approach among accounting firms' audit standards, reporting of income, valuation of assets, risk assessment, and limitations on professional liability with audit clients.

The ability of an individual accounting manager at any firm to influence the outcome of an audited financial statement signed off by a "big four" accounting firm is greatly diminished over the level it may have been in the mid-1990s. Relying on a less-well-known audit firm to generate an audited financial statement may diminish acceptance of the company's securities in the marketplace, including lenders as well as any other stakeholders. Small nonpublic enterprises in developed economies may well be able to continue to rely on the smaller professional accounting firms. In developing countries, the "big four" have made tremendous strides in capturing a significant share of the accounting business, usually by establishing a business relationship with a well-regarded local firm and augmenting its audit and accounting consulting capabilities, as well as cultivating a firm-wide approach on accounting standards and ethics.

The fact that state-of-the art software and talented global accounting firms have emerged has not diminished bad accounting practices, fraud, or tax-cheating. The challenge to auditors at all levels has never been greater. A challenge to the revenue booking practices of an accounting officer at a high-flying communications firm like Global Crossing may be easier to issue than uncovering the artful practice of a Chinese factory manager duplicating all of the work time cards and coaching the employees on what to tell the auditors from headquarters when they periodically show up. Staring down the black-hooded Russian tax police armed with AK-47s is not a challenge welcomed by most accounting professionals when confronted with a demand for several years' worth of tax payments exceeding the reported gross revenue according to company records, with business practices signed off by competent local legal advisers and tax professionals.[27] Equally, testifying before a U.S. congressional committee can have a chilling career effect.

Accountants Must Know IAS Standards as Well as GAAP

By walling itself off and asserting the supremacy of its regulations over harmonized global standards, the United States is in danger of playing a diminished role in a world of free capital flows when almost all other countries adopt IAS and most MNEs begin to report financial results in directly comparable terms. U.S.-trained accountants, schooled only in U.S. standards as issued by the FASB and the IRS, will find themselves at a significant disadvantage when seeking employment at global firms, particularly those in the Global 1000 headquartered outside of the United States. By contrast, an accounting professional schooled in IAS as well as U.S. GAAP is likely to have a great advantage over one knowledgeable only in IAS.

Stay Current with Technology Capabilities

With greater overseas activities, it is critical to have a keen understanding of the interactions of the global components of accounting, finance, and production. The demands on accountants to provide "the numbers" for decision-making will not diminish, and it is not likely that less financially oriented members of the management team will grasp the intricacies any more in a complex world environment than they do in a multiplant domestic entity. As a professional, an accountant needs to stay current with advances in accounting software and all its capabilities. Software suites will continue to evolve, especially with input from practitioners, who are ultimately the consumers of the product.

Master the Tax Rules Where You Do Business

Although taxation is often a specialized field within the domain of accounting, most accountants involved with global enterprise come across tax issues that affect record-keeping and decision-making. It is essential to recognize the tax implications of proposed multinational transactions. Running a model and developing a workable solution to the taxation issue is most likely going to fall into the domain of accounting managers, even at MNEs with a tax department staffed by lawyers and other experts. At a practical level, having a solid knowledge of the tax approaches of each of the major countries in which one is conducting business is key to being able to deal effectively with local, regional, and national tax authorities. Developing a "win/win" solution has a different complexion when working at the international level, especially in developing countries where MNEs may be a very large factor in the national economy and government budget.

Accountants Have a Bigger Role in Maintaining Corporate Ethics

The old chestnut that a good accountant is one who "makes $2 + 2$ equal anything I want" has been permanently retired. Yesterday's "hero" is today's liability. Those days are over, and the competencies required of accountants within business and public accounting firms have changed accordingly.

As periodic financial scandals like Enron demonstrate, the responsibility for good corporate governance comes home to roost among accountants. Although the government has attempted to compel greater personal responsibility among officers and directors through legislation like Sarbanes-Oxley, it is too often the professional accountant who is tried and sent to jail. With the expansion of business on a transnational basis, accountants have multicountry exposure to alleged violations of law. The challenge of demands for greater transparency from a wide cross-section of stakeholders around the globe inevitably comes to the desk of a financial manager. In addition to being conservative in the doctrines of accounting, one needs to champion the need for the global enterprise to conduct itself according to high standards and best practice. Acquiring the ability to communicate company ethics standards on a worldwide basis, across many cultures, will test the competency of accountants as never before.

The pressures on maintaining high-quality numbers and high standards of conduct will not diminish at any level within the accounting profession. Within a global enterprise, the obsession of improved quarterly profitability and better returns to equity may need to yield to realistic numbers. Whistle-blowers are not likely to be any better received in the boardroom than in the past, but at most publicly held global enterprises the personal consequences for senior management have never been greater. Forfeiting multimillion-dollar compensation packages and becoming a corporate pariah can have as chilling an effect on a senior executive at an MNE as the prospect of jail when informed that bribing senior government officials or counting inventory consigned to customer locations as sales still requires double-entry bookkeeping.

CONCLUSION

Accounting as a discipline continues to evolve. As international standards are adopted, there is less divergence on accounting theory and practice. Paralleling the professional movement to one set of standards is the adoption of a narrow range of powerful accounting software suites. As accounting technology advances, many of the transactional issues which consume the time of accounting managers at global enterprises become routine, freeing capacity for more analysis, which in turn allows for greater fine tuning of the business and reporting systems. The challenges to maintaining integrity of accounting and best business practices will not diminish with the availability of real time data from worldwide operations. Issues like equitable approaches to multinational taxation will move to the forefront as others such as inventory exposures become more manageable under a single set of IAS rules. In time, harmonization of accounting standards may lead to greater uniformity in tax codes and standards of corporate governance. Countries whose governments and business leaders resist are likely to become economic backwaters as greater transparency among the others allows for freer flows of investment and commerce.

NOTES

1. Attributed to Wanda Wallace in the *Handbook of Internal Accounting Controls*, 2d ed. (Prentice-Hall, 1991).

2. Attributed to Shahrokh M. Saudagaran, *International Accounting: A User Perspective*, 2d ed. (Thomson South-Western, 2004), 52.

3. Attributed to Christopher Reed "The Damn'd South Sea," *Harvard* magazine (May–June 1999).

4. Attributed to Patrick McCarthy in "Unnecessary Complexity in Accounting Principles," *CPA Journal* (March 2004).

5. See Ken Milani article in *Management Accounting Quarterly* (winter 2004).

6. Attributed to William S. McNamara in *Comptroller's Handbook in Internal Controls*, publisher *Management* (January 2001).

7. Disclosure of program features is voluminous and best found on Oracle or SAP websites.

8. For discussion see "The Cart Pulling the Horse," *The Economist* (April 9, 2005), 53.

9. See Ernst & Young website, "Thought Center Webcast Recap: Keeping in Tune with Financial Instruments," program broadcast date January 21, 2004; similar information can be found in Deloitte, PWC, and KPMG.

10. Attributed to John Ver Bockel in "Accounting World: International Accounting, Convergence, and Principles-Based Financial Reporting Standards," *Insight: The Magazine of the Illinois CPA Society* (August 2004).

11. Other EU companies are discovering these limits on ability to issue dividends while pensions are underfunded under IAS, in FT.com site (August 5, 2005).

12. In "A Question of Measurement—no byline," *The Economist*, October 21, 2004 edition.

13. G. Siciliano, *Finance for the Non-Financial Manager* (McGraw-Hill, 2003), or chapter 2, *Harmonizing Financial Reporting Standards Globally*, summary on p. 51.

14. See Deloitte Country Update, Russian Federation (November 2004).

15. News provided in accountingWeb, national accounting news, week of June 21, 2002, Texas Society for CPAs.

16. IAS and National Account Statistics (ESA95) assess the impact of IAS application on the various statistical domains in International Accounting Standards (IAS) and EU statistics.

17. See Ernst & Young website, "Thought Center Webcast Recap: The American Jobs Creation Act of 2004."

18. In *Insight: The Magazine of the Illinois CPA Society*, Accounting World; international accounting, convergence, and "principles-based" financial reporting standards by John Ver Bockel.

19. See articles by Ken Milani ("The Rigorous Business of Budgeting for International Operations: Managing Global Risk is at the Center of Budgeting for Overseas Subsidiaries," *Management Accounting Quarterly*, January 1, 2004), or class presentation of Professor W. J. Hunter on multinational finance.

20. Ibid., 23.

21. In "Key Changes from IAS 35," Standard, IAS 35, IFRS 5, address link: www.iasplus.com/standard/ifrs05.htm.

22. Milani, *Management Accounting Quarterly* (winter 2004).

23. See PWC website on their history of contract accounting/outsourcing, beginning with BP Exploration in 1991 at Aberdeen, total turnkey operation.

24. Work done by the Heritage Foundation, "The YUKOS Affair: Protecting Democracy, Private Property, and the Rule of Law" by Ariel Cohen, Ph.D.; Research: Russia and Eurasia, Executive Memorandum #906.

25. Summary of Sarbanes-Oxley Act of 2002 in the American Institute of Certified Public Accountants. http://www.aicpa.org/info/sarbanes_oxley_summary.htm.

26. Attributed to study prepared in connection with the International Monetary Fund seminar on current developments in monetary and financial law, held on "The Impact of the USA Patriot Act of 2001 on Non-U.S. Banks," May 7–17, 2002, Washington, DC.

27. Attributed to President Putin of Russia in his annual address to the Federal Assembly, April 25, 2005, the Kremlin, Moscow.

10

Road Map To the Changing Financial Environment

SAAD LARAQUI

No aspect of international business has become as global or as dynamic as finance. Increasingly, global managers need to be knowledgeable about the broad spectrum of international finance because it plays a critical integrative function for the global enterprise. Constantly improving communications technologies have made money more fungible and capital more fluid.

This chapter highlights broad challenges, evolutions in approach, and emerging skill sets required to succeed in today's global finance environment. Given the development of highly specialized disciplines within banking, brokerage, leasing, trading, and other financially oriented sectors as well as within global enterprises, it is by no means exhaustive. It discusses pivotal elements in the changing financial environment, ranging from seeing the "big picture" of the global economy to risks in foreign investment. The chapter then summarizes the changing face of international financial management. It concludes with a discussion of the tools needed for success in the new international financial management.

SEEING THE "BIG PICTURE" OF THE GLOBAL ECONOMY

From a corner office in a building in London, or a cubicle in an office campus in Silicon Valley, or a desk on a factory floor in Guangzhou, it is difficult for global managers to stay abreast of their industry or specific job function, much less to understand the world economy. This is as true for a highly specialized trader at a hedge fund as it is for a chief financial officer at a software firm, or the general manager at a manufacturing firm conducting business on an international scale.

Currently there are some 6.5 billion people populating 191 officially recognized countries of the United Nations (UN) and about 40 more less independent territories, each with a Gross Domestic Product (GDP) contributing to an annual Gross Global Product (GGP) estimated to be more than US$41 trillion.[1] Reflecting the uneven distribution of people, natural resources, and wealth, some countries play a more prominent role in the global economy than others. The United States, European Union (EU), and Japan produce nearly $31 trillion, or 75 percent of the world's economic output, with about 885 million or 13 percent of its population.[2] Despite the offset of a decade-long recession in Japan, China's 9 percent average annual rate of growth since the mid-1980s has not materially altered this set of facts. The United States, with 298 million people, or 4.4 percent of global population, alone accounts for more than $12 trillion, or nearly 30 percent of the world's economic output. Together, the EU and the USA, currently accounting for about $25 trillion, or 61 percent of GGP, are pulling ahead faster economically than the rest of the world, including China and the other so-called Asian Tigers—India, Indonesia, Korea, Malaysia, and Thailand.[3]

While much media attention focuses on China's booming economy and its role in the offshoring of jobs, driving up prices of natural resources, and growth in global trade, the available data on Foreign Direct Investment (FDI) suggests a more nuanced story. To be sure, China's share of FDI is increasing, appearing to come at the expense of additional investments in other Asian Tigers and other developing countries like Mexico. Having attracted significant outward FDI from the United States in the early 1990s following the establishment of the North American Free Trade Association (NAFTA), by 2004, Mexican assembly plant jobs were being outsourced to China, where weekly wages were equivalent to one day's Mexican wages or two hours of pay of the average U.S. factory worker.[4] Similarly, computer component manufacturers such as Maxtor are shifting manufacturing from Singapore to China, resulting in significant job losses on the Asian island, which saw major investment by U.S. high-technology firms from the late 1980s onward.[5]

One Thousand Enterprises Dominate
World Trade and Investment

Just as the bulk of the flow of trade and investment is between few nations, the number of global enterprises that transact most of the business is much smaller than one might think. Although the United Nations Conference on Trade and Development (UNCTAD) estimates that there are some 60,000 "multinational" enterprises that control about 500,000 affiliates around the globe, a group of about 1,000 global enterprises generates economic activity equal to nearly 40 percent of GGP. Most of these companies—ranging from aircraft manufacturers to banks to oil companies to transportation conglomerates—are publicly traded and make up just 2 percent of the companies listed on the world's exchanges, but represent nearly 75 percent of total market capitalization.[6] Closely analogous to the *Fortune* 1000 list compiled each year by *Fortune* magazine, within the group is a smaller core of about 200 companies that generate economic activity equal to about 25 percent of GGP, many of whom are larger economically than all but the most developed countries. For instance, Wal-Mart Stores, Inc., with 2004 sales of US$285 billion, would rank just behind Austria and ahead of Indonesia as the twenty-second-largest "economy" in the world. Wal-Mart's non-USA international sales of $56 billion (20% of total sales) would give it the fifty-fifth largest GDP, ahead of Morocco and behind Bangladesh.[7]

Although the relative positions of the leading global enterprises change each year as individual fortunes rise and fall, a worldwide trend in mergers and acquisitions continues to concentrate economic activity. The 1,000 leading global enterprises appear to account for as much as 75 percent of global trade, estimated at $9.5 trillion in 2005, with an increasing level arising from intracompany shipment of goods across international borders.[8]

UNDERSTANDING THE REGULATORY ENVIRONMENT

Regulation from International Agencies

Another critical challenge for global managers is understanding the regulatory environment in which the business operates at transnational, national, and local levels. Globalization is resulting from changes in regulatory philosophy across a wide range of industries and between nations. Known in various parts of the world as "deregulation," or "liberalization," or "privatization" or "reform," all speak to an abandonment of previously accepted standards of economic governance, ranging from airport ownership to banking practice to labor protection to tariffs to utility regulation. A series of events—from President Nixon's abandonment of the "gold standard" in 1971 to President Carter's deregulation of the U.S. airline industry in 1978, to UK prime minister Thatcher's privatization of British Petroleum (BP) in 1979 to USSR general secretary Gorbachev's policy of perestroika in 1986, to a series of reforms introduced in China in 1986 by Deng Xiaoping—contributed to a near universal repudiation of protectionist systems, which had developed in the twentieth century in the aftermath of two world wars.

Both proponents and opponents of globalization hold up the UN-sponsored agencies—International Monetary Fund (IMF), Organisation for Economic Co-Operation and Development (OECD), UNCTAD, World Trade Organization (WTO), and World Bank—as icons of the "liberalization" movement. The Bank for International Settlements (BIS) escapes notice, but it has played a crucial role in standardizing international banking practice, permitting a free flow of funds on a global basis, especially between central banking organizations.[9] Similarly other far-reaching organizations such as the International Telecommunications Union (ITU) and the International Standards Organization (ISO) are playing vital roles in revolutionizing global business practices. In most cases, only practitioners in highly specialized fields have any direct contact with these agencies and their regulations. However, the policies of three—IMF, World Bank, and WTO—have generated the most public recognition and controversy at a global level.

A financial manager of a global enterprise must be concerned about the IMF or the international monetary system because when operating in a country subject to an IMF loan package agreement, long-standing financial rules may be suspended. The business may become subject to new limitations on its ability to export currency, repatriate earnings, and maintain current levels of indebtedness to local banks, whose interest rates and lending conditions suddenly may become less favorable. In the absence of fixed exchange rates based on reserves of gold at the central bank, a relatively stable currency may drop quickly in value, as the Forex market seeks to establish equilibrium. As experienced in Argentina in the late 1990s, long-profitable business operations suddenly became candidates for radically scaled down operations, closure, or divestiture when the peso was untied from parity with the U.S. dollar as a condition for an IMF loan package that was ultimately rejected by the national government.[10] Conversely, an IMF-backed financial "rescue" package may provide a major stimulus to the local economy and cause a foreign-owned factory in a country like Thailand to outperform budgetary expectations.[11]

Just as financial managers often loathe the red tape of IMF intermediation, the policies of the World Bank have become contentious. Since its reconstruction role of Europe and Japan following World War II, the bank has shifted its focus to the developing world, providing about $20 billion worth of loans annually to build infrastructure, alleviate poverty, and promote good governance with the aim of generating capitalistic development.[12] In some countries—Guatemala for instance—the World Bank is the target of environmentalists as one of its units seeks to partially fund a gold mine aimed at providing local employment.[13] Conversely, many global business managers do not like the rules of the World Bank, such as meeting OECD targets on environmental pollution when the World Bank agrees to participate in financing a project in a developing country where standards are not as rigorous and compliance can add significantly to the initial construction costs. For a global manager, particularly those working in developing countries, being able to weigh the pros and cons of potential financial participation by the World Bank and its business units may be critical to success.

Less controversial to most businesspeople is the WTO, for it assures compliance with the rules of trade between member nations. While mainly focused on tariff reduction and less restrictive trade, the WTO, with its 142 members, has developed a wide-ranging series of standards covering such items as agricultural subsidies, food safety, intellectual property rights, and industrial standards.[14] Equally important for trade are international production and management standards established under the auspices of the International Standards Organization (ISO). These standards greatly facilitate the ability of even very small enterprises to subcontract manufacturing of their products to lower-wage countries for export back to higher-income countries.[15] The combined successes of the WTO and ISO have contributed greatly to globalization. Subtle changes to regulations from either organization can have a major impact on global enterprises, altering financial requirements substantially.

Transnational agencies like the IMF, WTO, and BIS, however, have not been able to achieve a completely standardized approach to financial gearing, bank reserve ratios, capitalization, and taxation. Even in an age of globalization there is wide variation among nation-states on all aspects of doing business within a specific country. Most tax treaties are negotiated on a state-to-state bilateral basis. The general requirements for simple incorporation, minimum capitalization, and responsibilities of corporate directors and officers vary widely from country to country. Although there is a trend toward adopting international accounting standards, legal systems are not harmonized.

Local Regulation

Equally challenging to many global managers is the local regulatory environment. In "greenfield" developments—such as building a new factory on a virgin site—most issues such as local tax abatements, surcharges for infrastructure improvements, and compliance with building and zoning codes can be resolved in the Front End Engineering Development (FEED) phase. If accommodation cannot be reached, the managers of a global enterprise are usually in a position to "walk," and relocate the project to a jurisdiction where it can proceed and come on line according to plan. Confrontation with local regulators often comes about as the result of an acquisition, where time constraints do not always allow for full evaluation of the condition of existing production facilities prior to closing the deal. Tremendous liabilities with costly financial implications can arise, making unplanned demands on management time and the corporate treasury.

For finance managers, the challenge is to identify the transactional risk associated with potential problems and then seek to minimize the exposure for each. The objective is to limit each identifiable risk to as short a time or as small a potential financial outlay as possible, including local and national taxation. For multinational enterprises (MNE), the tax playing field is not equal. Although double taxation treaties have eliminated some aspects of the problem, no global tax standards are emerging as in the accounting profession.

Part of the problem is the fact that tax rates on corporations vary materially between countries, and part of the problem lies in different approaches to taxation of profits earned outside the home country. For instance, the United States is one of a relatively few countries that taxes worldwide income. To avoid some of the more onerous aspects of U.S. taxation, a number of large U.S.-based MNEs have reincorporated themselves in tax havens like Bermuda.[16] While operating in a simplified tax environment where depreciation is obviated by a lack of taxation on income, there has been some shareholder and political backlash against such companies. At the same time as the WTO challenged U.S. tax practices with respect to extraterritorial income exclusion of foreign sales corporations, the U.S. Congress passed the American Jobs Creation Act (AJCA) in late 2004, which contained a provision reducing the tax on repatriated foreign earnings to 5.25 percent from the standard U.S. federal corporate tax rate of 35 percent.[17]

PARTICIPATING IN GLOBAL CAPITAL MARKETS

Accessibility to third party sources of credit is usually directly related to the size of the enterprise and the scope of its financing needs. To established MNEs, the capital markets have become truly global. To small and medium-sized enterprises around the world, they remain mostly local. The relative transparency of fully audited financial statements of publicly traded or large private MNEs, with recognized credit ratings, generally guarantees access to the global capital markets. Besides direct lending by commercial banks, global capital markets have evolved to include: (a) equities placed by investment bankers; (b) bonds and other fixed income securities sold on a private and public basis; (c) commercial paper sold by corporations; (d) trade finance instruments such as letters of credit, guarantees, forfeiting, and factoring; (e) commodity and securities-based futures and derivatives; and (f) Forex.

Global capital markets growth is a direct response to demands for capital across all sectors around the world. The demand for equity and debt comes from globally expanding companies like Wal-Mart as well as from financing infrastructure in both the industrialized and developing world. Such companies and financing organizations support trade expansion and stabilize central bank activities. To protect individual private investors, equity pools now are controlled by institutional investors such as hedge funds, mutual funds, and pension funds as well as income and other unit trusts. Traditional commercial lending remains the domain of regulated deposit-taking commercial banks like Citibank, less regulated private banks like Bank Julius Baer, and finance companies like Mitsui. A combination of investment banks like Goldman Sachs, nonbanking arms of multinational banks like Deutsche Credit, commodities trading firms like Refco, and hedge funds like Citco participate in the less traditional emerging sectors of the financing marketplace.

Equity Markets

The evolution of global trading of stocks and bonds is inextricably linked to the gradual development of MNEs over the past 150 years. By the late 1960s the emerging global enterprises began to access foreign equity markets by taking parts of foreign subsidiaries public on local stock exchanges, or listing certain classes of securities of the parent.[18] Although U.S.-based multinationals are not widely listed on foreign exchanges, it became commonplace in the 1990s for major EU-based and some Asia-based companies to obtain listings of their common stock on the New York Stock Exchange.

A stock listing on at least one of the major exchanges of the world is available to the 1,000 largest global enterprises. Globally, about 50,000 entities maintain a public listing, of which about 12,000 are mutual funds and other securities-based investment pools. Since the mid-1980s, electronic linkages have been developed to permit greater and greater levels of inter-exchange trading, permitting 24/7 access to market-makers, and, increasingly, private securities traders. Market volatility has increased as a function of the reduction of trade settlement periods from T+5 (five days) towards T+0 (instantaneous recognition/settlement of trades) on major exchanges. Although the finance department of global enterprises has greater access to stock trading than ever before, the flotation of new issues of shares, particularly in the United States, continues to suffer from losses in confidence following the dotcom crash in late 1999 to mid-2001. Since that period, most initial public offerings (IPOs) have been launched on the London, Mumbai, and Toronto exchanges.

A growing source of additional equity in the global capital marketplace is the specialized buyout firm like Kohlberg Kravis Roberts & Co., or a hedge

---

**Box 10.1 Depository Receipts Offer Alternatives
To the Stock Market**

The most popular alternative to direct listing on a U.S. stock exchange is for a non-U.S.-based MNE to issue an American Depository Receipt (ADR), which is a negotiable instrument issued by a U.S. bank, representing the underlying value of the shares of the foreign-issued stock, held in trust at a custodian bank in the country where the MNE is directly traded on a stock exchange. Similarly, there are European Depository Receipts (EDR), generally denominated in U.S. dollars, trade on the Euromarkets, typically on the London Stock Exchange (LSE) or the Luxembourg Bourse. The EDR has become very popular since the passage of the U.S. Sarbanes-Oxley Act in July 2002, with its onerous and expensive reporting requirements. In the case of an EDR, the issuing bank is European rather than a U.S. one in the case of an ADR.[19] More recently, the Global Depository Receipt (GDR) has emerged, which can be denominated in any currency, although the U.S. dollar and the Euro dominate. GDR is often listed on more than one stock exchange in more than one country.

fund like Citco. Working generally in concert with other, similar private institutionally backed funds, these organizations become partners with MNEs in acquisitions of foreign companies, or in joint ventures in emerging markets like China. Although the expectations on return on capital are higher than those of commercial lenders, institutional funds have the flexibility to participate in a mix of equity and debt, usually with fewer covenants and limitations. The challenge to the senior management of a global enterprise is to strike a balance between the funds expectations and those of the corporation, particularly with respect to total return and exit strategies.

Debt Markets

Global enterprises have been beneficiaries of the trend in the internationalization of banking as well as the consolidation of money center banks. Most financially successful MNEs maintain banking relationships with key money center banks like Bank of Tokyo-Mitsubishi, Citibank, BNP/Paribas, and HSBC. With increased deregulation of banks, the major banks have added many specialized divisions, allowing them to lease, place securities, trade Forex, and to advise on mergers and acquisitions, which serve to allow them to expand the business relationships.

Apart from traditional debt and equity, global enterprises have access to other more specialized markets like the "Eurocurrency" market. About 75 percent of the Eurocurrency market is composed of Eurodollars, and Eurobonds make up about 75 percent of the total international bond market, with U.S. issuers—both private and public—making up about 50 percent of the total offering in terms of funds raised.[20] In 1989 the World Bank introduced the "global bond," an issue that is registered in each national market according to local regulations, issued simultaneously on major stock markets. Due to the complexities of registration, global bonds have been sold by a few large government-backed issuers like China Development Bank, and the largest global enterprises like DaimlerChrysler.

The expansion of global capital markets is not related solely to the expansion of international business by MNEs. Other factors have been at play in the marketplace, including increasing ease of data transfer. Moody's, the investment rating service, began rating commercial paper in 1973 and expanded its ratings to include significant offshore issues effected by ratable issuers. Beginning in the early 1980s the United States began financing large government budget deficits at the same time it was running growing trade deficits with most of its international trading partners. The volume of securities offered greatly enhanced the viability of non-U.S. offshore banking centers, already strengthened by petrodollars from each spike in the price of oil from 1973 onward. Contemporaneously, the development of the EU into a single economic unit created new sources and new demands for capital. Similarly, fast-paced economic development in Asia increased available funds as investors discovered emerging markets as well as the appetite for more funds. Then China awoke—creating an insatiable demand for funds to develop new factories, which then began to generate funds as Chinese enterprises sold low-priced goods to the United States, EU, and nearly all parts of the world. Adding to demand was privatization of formerly government-operated entities in many parts of the world, including the countries of the former Soviet Union in the wake of its 1991 collapse. Combined, truly global capital markets emerged.

Trade Financing

As entrepreneurs know, capital has always been scarce. Pioneers in the development of MNEs, like Harold Geneen of ITT, were early users of the Eurocurrency markets because access to U.S. capital markets was difficult and comparatively more expensive. Politics can play a role as well. Until the collapse of the Soviet Union in 1991, Soviet issuers were largely shut out of the marketplace due to repudiation of prerevolutionary debt, undermining sovereign guarantees made on behalf of state-owned enterprises. Comparatively, more than a dozen of the more successful Russian companies like LUKoil have been able to raise capital on the London Stock Exchange since 2000.[21]

An emerging area of the global capital markets is trade finance, driven by the sheer growth of international trade, and a desire to use "off balance sheet" financing whenever possible. With "supply chain management" and "just-in-time manufacturing," the capital requirements to build, ship, and maintain inventory has been reduced. Nonetheless, financing the shortened production and shipping cycle still requires short-term financing instruments. Letters of credit issued by major international banks, sometimes supplemented by standby letters of credit issued by a trading company to offload the lending risk, covered by insurance where available, finance the much-shortened cycle. For those making the transition to financing trade on a cross-border basis, the customs bonding and shipping requirements can be bewildering, even in an era of "free trade" and greatly reduced tariffs under the WTO.

The mushrooming exports of finished goods such as construction equipment, machine tools, and medical equipment have led to greater reliance on guarantees extended by the export development agencies of most OECD countries and their counterparts in developing countries. Agencies like Australia's Export Finance and Insurance Corporation, Germany's Hermes, or U.S. Export-Import Bank (Ex-Im) have the capacity to mitigate much of the payment risk to exporters who meet their criteria. With local divisions in many countries, global enterprises are well positioned to maximize the availability of such risk-reducing finance vehicles once managers become familiar with program offerings.

Islamic Law Considerations

As managers at global enterprises try to meet expanding trade finance requirements, they are being introduced to concepts not well known in developed countries. For instance, as the world's petrodollars are recycled from Muslim countries to pay for imports, traditional Western bank credit may not be available to the purchaser. Under Islamic or *Sharia* law, earning interest or *riba* on the lending of money is forbidden. Central to Islamic finance is the concept that money has no intrinsic value, and that wealth is to be derived from trade and investment in assets. Any trading activity has to involve legitimate risk, with the provision that the gains realized from the trade have to be shared between the provider of capital and the one providing the trading expertise. While it may seem complicated to a nonpractitioner, there is virtually no aspect of conventional Western finance that does not have a counterpart in an Islamic bank. Leasing, known as *ijara*, is very similar, with the bank acquiring the asset in a sale/leaseback transaction with a defined basis for rental and term. Mortgaging, known as *ijara* with diminishing *musharaka*, or limited duration partnership, works by making a capital principal reduction in addition to an agreed rental payment, with ownership in the asset when all agreed payments have been made. A fully collateralized loan, or *qard,* is effected on a service charge basis, with repayment made to a pledged current account at the financial institution. Most major Islamic banks are part of a larger group of financial companies operating under *Shari'ah* law where required, and under other applicable law elsewhere. A Saudi-based financial institution operating in Morocco, where *Shari'ah* law does not govern banking transactions, would lend conventionally, as it would through any U.S. or EU establishment not specifically retailing to the local Islamic community.

Financial Impact of Market Trading

Although commodities and securities-based derivatives as well as Forex are commonly included under the header "global capital markets," if only for their relative volume, it can be difficult for managers at global enterprises to recognize that these are elements to financial transactions that can be used to enhance credit and mitigate risks, but are not sources of financing. Trading in commodities and derivatives can generate returns to capital. Earnings from Forex, and derivative-enhanced trading can improve cash flow from operations. Working to maintain 10 to 20 percent returns on publicly traded equity, the finance departments of global enterprises routinely engage in such transactions, but rarely does it become the primary focus of the firm. At hedge funds, aiming to achieve 25 to 50 percent annual returns on their private capital pool, market trading is often as much a part of the earnings mix as returns from operations in portfolio companies, and other securities transactions.

COMPREHENDING THE FOREIGN EXCHANGE MARKET

In an era of greater transparency with multiple sources of data from commercial and government sources, foreign exchange ("Forex") markets are more real-time, hence, more volatile than ever, creating new challenges for financial managers at global enterprises. Acting as an around-the-clock clearing mechanism, the global Forex market establishes a near instantaneous market equilibrium for the world's currencies. Forex traders execute transactions in a climate of billions of U.S. dollars, euros, UK pounds, and yen with a spread measured in thousandths of a percent within a finely negotiated fee structure.

Although currency exchange has been going on for centuries, the current phenomenon can be traced to the decision by U.S. government to abandon to the "gold standard" in 1973, and to let the U.S. dollar "float" on the world market. In short order, most of the major currencies of the world were unpegged from the gold-based exchange mechanism of the IMF. The Forex market continues to evolve as participants—individual and institutional traders, investment funds, bank currency operations, corporate treasurers, and government agencies and central bankers—seek to reduce trading risks as free-floating currencies rise and fall on economic news, trade data, and rumor. It operates 24/7, networked via the Internet and specialized banking links such as the Society for Worldwide Interbank Financial Telecommunication (SWIFT). The growth of daily SWIFT transactions from 10,000 among 239 founding banks in 15 countries in 1973 to nearly 10 million among 7,600 participants in nearly 200 countries in 2003 is one measure of the rate of Forex growth and other interbank transactions.[22] By 2004, the value of traditional Forex transactions averaged $1.9 trillion per day, fluctuating between $1.5 and $2 trillion per day. When foreign-exchange derivatives and interest-rate derivatives are included, the daily Forex volume is averaging over $3 trillion.[23]

Forex volume is huge, nearly 150 times the value of NYSE daily trading. Although broadly correlated to growth in global trade, Forex transactions have grown exponentially. First, there is a buy and a sell component to every single trade. Second, with the advent of hedging through money market futures and other derivatives, an increasing percentage of the total trades represent multifaceted exchanges. Third, the playing field is very broad—with individual traders permitted since 1998 as well as specialized hedge funds. In addition, traditional banks and corporate treasury operations add to Forex trading, which has become a market occupation in its own right. Fourth, the cost of technology in the form of 24/7 trading links and sophisticated trading software continues to decline, rapidly increasing turnover as it becomes easier to trade. Lastly, major international banks, institutional funds, and MNEs have perfected daily sweeping of their worldwide accounts, generally through London, New York, or Tokyo, as extensions of cash management systems, allowing them to better comply with regulatory requirements and internal treasury policies.

To a senior manager at a global enterprise, increasingly greater focus is being given to exchange gains and losses. Improving the business results in the home-country currency is possible by skillfully trading the mixed basket of foreign currencies in which it operates. Losses are suffered at increasing degrees of discomfort as their magnitude becomes known and reportable in the monthly, quarterly, or annual financial statements. Coca-Cola, with sales of over $20 billion, earns as much as 80 percent of its income from outside the United States. The company has long been engaged in very sophisticated Forex trading, aimed at reducing its currency translation exposure.[24] On an annual basis, its finance department may churn $50 to $100 billion worth of currency swaps and derivatives to manage what might reflect $500 million to $1 billion worth of earnings improvement at its current level of sales and earnings.

Many other factors influence the relative demand for the currencies being traded: (a) central bank intermediation; (b) interest rates; (c) inflation rates; (d) foreign reserves; (e) trade balances; (e) perception; and (f) volatility of trading for other securities. The ease with which Forex transactions can be made ultimately affects the liquidity and volatility of the most frequently traded currencies. Pure arbitrage plays in major currencies such as the gains made in 1992 by George Soros's Quantum Fund against the pound are less available to traders in much larger and much broader markets.[25]

While currency futures exist, as do other derivatives such as those tied to interest rates and other aspects of currency, Forex is not traded on an exchange like commodities such as cotton, gold, or oil. Hedging is trading strategy involving a two-or-more-step process, even when the transaction is done as a "simultaneous" trade, and results cannot be guaranteed. Moreover, Forex is not a market one can borrow capital from like an asset-backed loan, or an equity security. Although for some, Forex trading has become an occupation in its own right, for the manager of a global enterprise, it is but one relatively small cog in the financial gearing of the business.

MANAGING RISKS IN FOREIGN INVESTMENTS

Determining where to invest and when to fold continues to be the major challenge for senior managers in all enterprises, and international investment decisions add to the complexity. They need to balance the likelihood of achieving sales numbers, profitability goals, and internal rates of return targets against the risks presented in each country they elect to operate in. Simplified, the global finance function is risk management. And these risks change over time. Risks associated with foreign investment fall into two broad categories: (a) country; and (b) operating. While these risks are discussed extensively in chapter 7, they are reviewed here from the perspective of the financial officer.

Country Risks

On the front end, the principal risk to the firm is a "planning" risk—determining that the business objective can be achieved in the targeted country. The manufacturing and distribution of most products will require some front-end investment, even in a globalized environment with multiple sources of supply and eager in-country distributors.

Where the project is justified, the next risk is having the project become strangled in "red tape" risk. Bureaucracy can feed on new foreign-sponsored enterprises, with many new hands held out with every necessary permit or agreement required by the national, state, and local officials. Even when one of the government-controlled parastatals is a partner in a project such as an oil field, there is no guarantee that needed construction materials will not get hung up in customs. Each step of a project involving construction or establishing distribution can present small daily challenges, none of which may singularly overwhelm the project, but together can serve to delay the start-up. This is why it is so critical for management to have a good understanding of the macroeconomic and regulatory factors as early as possible in the planning stage of an international investment.

Political stability is another country-related risk. In countries where the risk can be identified early, planners tend to assign a high hurdle rate to the project, to minimize the time before the parent gets its invested cash back out. In countries like Angola and Nigeria, the major international oil companies have worked to minimize the risk of business interruption from domestic political upheaval by concentrating their rigs as much as possible offshore, even to the exclusion of developing perfectly viable onshore oil deposits. The risk of "nationalization" is one, which, within the limits of the premium cost, can be insured against in most cases. In extremis is the case where civil order breaks down completely as in Liberia or Sierra Leone, where assets are not nationalized, and property and any business interruption insurance claims are not paid under "war risk" limitations.

Risk is also associated with *economic stability*. Global enterprises operating in the developing world face devaluation of the local currency. Exporting from a country that has experienced a significant devaluation, for instance, has both an up and a down side. The firm immediately enjoys a onetime reduction in labor costs, but this tends to be offset over time by higher wage demands arising from inflationary pressures. To the extent local assets are financed in local currency by local banks, there is little pain. However, if the loans underpinning the local assets are denominated in a home-country currency like the euro or U.S. dollar, even the export-oriented entity may have a difficult time servicing its obligations to domestic and foreign financial institutions. Devaluation can be fatal for import-oriented companies, as the suddenly more expensive imported goods move beyond the reach of the average consumer, whose buying power declines. Prudent managers need to constantly reassess the risk profiles of their investments in each country.

Operating Risks

Once the project comes on line, the nature of the risks shifts to daily operations. At the big-picture level, achieving internal investment targets becomes the driving operating risk factor. For a factory established to manufacture subassemblies for a plant in a different country, different criteria will apply than for a factory built to fabricate products for sale to local consumer markets. In some industries, like the international airline business, it is easy to pull the plug very quickly on a project that does not make the numbers. In others, like automobile manufacturing or electric power generation, the risk at the financial level is that the parent firm may need to commit more capital or otherwise increase its obligations to the project.

Once the project is up and running, the challenge for local management is to meet the marketing and financial targets of the enterprise, as agreed in the annual budget review with headquarters. The ongoing risk for both the local managers and those in the treasury department in the home country is a "measurement" risk.

Advances in Forex management techniques allow global managers to mitigate better than ever translation- and transaction-related measurement risks. For companies engaged in extractive industries such as gold mining or oil production, the underlying "commodity" risk is likely to cause volatility to earnings rather than "measurement" risk, particularly as most commodities are transacted in U.S. dollars. For a UK-based company like BP, measuring its performance in UK pounds, or an EU-based MNE like Total-Elf, measuring its performance in euros, a finance department will constantly work Forex hedges against changes in the relative relationships of the home currency to the dollar-denominated commodity.

At companies like Airbus or Boeing, where a single airliner can cost US$200 million, sales contracts and most cross-border production sharing agreements are written in U.S. dollars, leaving the treasury departments of all parties to manage the Forex risk.

THE CHANGING FACE OF INTERNATIONAL FINANCE

Revolutions in communication, computer technology, supply chain management and transportation have changed the face of international finance. Still, the goals of maximizing returns to capital and minimizing risks remain unchanged. Discerning what has changed and mastering new approaches is critical for financial managers at all levels of international business. The following sections summarize key changes that affect the finance function.

Financial Controls Have Improved

Financial managers at a global enterprise need to interact with their counterparts more often and more quickly than most others in the firm. At major international firms, accounting systems are now standardized around an Oracle or SAP platform, linked into virtually all offices in the organization with a need for up-to-date financial information.

Accounting platforms have the capability to manage supply chains to tight "just-in-time" limits. A financial manager in Hamburg, Germany, for instance, has the authority to work with the production manager and the expeditor to tweak the inputs of supply when a shipment misses the UPS cutoff in Toulouse, France, or a production line in Harbin, China, comes to a halt, or, alternatively, cuts shipments in half because more than $500,000 is suddenly tied up in inventory on the factory floor because someone forgot to factor in the Chinese New Year holiday into factory production targets. Never before in history has this degree of financial control been possible, and the technology is being improved all of the time. Over the last decade, astute financial managers at MNEs have been able to wring hundreds of billions of dollars of cash savings, freeing up redeployable capital, lessening the requirement for additional equity and lines of credit. Purchasing over the Internet on a business-to-business ("B2B") basis is now routine at global enterprises like GE, and, with manufacturing conducted to ISO standards, a bidder in Korea is as likely to win a contract as one in Colorado or Italy, especially if they have the capacity to finance the order to delivery.

Capital Favors Developed Countries More Than Ever

As barriers to trade have come down, global enterprises must think in terms of opportunity costs and benefits. They seek to improve internal enterprise growth by focusing on the regions of the world where measured economic growth has been greatest. As a result, the trend toward globalization has seen a general slowdown in FDI inflows to developing countries viewed as risky by EU and U.S.-based MNEs. Countries like Nigeria, with a reputation for corruption, find it particularly difficult to attract FDI, even in sectors like energy. As a consequence, Nigeria imports refined petroleum products because no MNE will put its capital at risk to build a new onshore refinery, despite growing local demand, and the country's status as a leading oil producer. Other countries, like Russia, whose government periodically has changed the business rules for MNEs overnight, have experienced even sharper slowdowns in FDI when investor confidence is shaken. Capital simply flows to safer havens.

Although media in the developed world tend to focus on job losses to emerging economies like China and India, capital flows are mostly among developed countries. Two factors are contributing to this phenomenon. First, affluent consumer markets exist in the developed countries like Canada, the

Box 10.2 Market Wins and Losses of VW's Low-Priced Cars

A German company like Volkswagen (VW) is perfectly comfortable buying Skoda in the Czech Republic, and modernizing the assembly line. It thereby gains low-priced Skoda models for customers unable to afford a VW Passat and achieve enterprise-wide savings by importing components from Chinese, Brazilian, German, Mexican, and Spanish VW-controlled operations. Conversely, although it was one of the first major foreign automobile manufacturers to establish a complete assembly line in China, VW-China is scaling back production and laying off workers for the first time, as its sales are being undermined by competition from new Chinese domestic producers and GM offerings.[26]

EU, Japan, and the United States. Second, the political and legal rulebooks are easily understood by MNEs seeking to undertake FDI. A third factor is also emerging: local incentives to steer a particular plant to a specific location within one of these areas. States like Alabama, South Carolina, and Tennessee have given foreign automobile manufacturers like DaimlerChrysler, BMW, and Honda incentives amounting to $100,000 per new job created to build new plants in areas far from the traditional automobile manufacturing centers in the United States. Similarly, Canada and the Province of Ontario are contributing hundreds of millions of dollars toward upgrading General Motors facilities to preserve existing jobs. Within the EU, the Flemish region of Belgium competes with Wales for the location of a new factory by a Paris-based MNE.

Information Technology Has Created a Level Playing Field

The international playing field is being leveled by the widespread ability to acquire expertise and put it to work in an international financing transaction. Everybody around the global business table works with the same spreadsheets on laptop computers from the same manufacturer and seeks a "win-win" solution. The days of quick negotiation with the local sheikh by a MNE seeking an oil concession are long over. Even transactions involving the privatization of electricity generation in former Soviet Union (FSU) countries, or for airport operation in Mexico, are developed on a well-advertised bid basis by experienced professionals, often paid by the IMF, World Bank, or European Bank for Reconstruction and Development (EBRD).

Betting Is an Option

The explosion of Forex, currency derivatives, and commodities trading marks a seismic shift in the development of global capital markets. The

Box 10.3 Mittal Steel: Where There Is a Will, There Is a Way

Mittal's adroit deals helped make it the world's largest global steel firm. The Mittal Karmet structured trade finance deal illustrates how managers in global enterprises, big or small, can work creatively with enterprising bankers to overcome obstacles that would normally result in a rejected loan application, as most could not get past the transaction risk, let alone the country risk, and the then credit risk of the proposed borrower, now an NYSE-listed firm.

Formed in 1989 by Indian-born entrepreneur Lakshmi Mittal to acquire the steelmaking operations of a parastatal (a company owned at least partly by a government) in Trinidad, the highly leveraged firm caught the attention of the steelmaking world when it emerged as the successful bidder for a nearly bankrupt steel producer in Kazakhstan in 1995. Mittal perfected its interest in the 6-million-ton annual capacity Karmet mill in 1997 using structured trade finance. Operating in the barter environment common the post-1991 FSU, the mill was trading its steel at a deep discount to obtain coal and electricity and spare parts, slowly choking to economic death, just as the worldwide steel market began to turn around from a prolonged slump in the 1980s as Asian demand soared. Based on the evidence of eighteen months of progress toward a turnaround under new management, Mittal obtained a $45 million revolving credit line from a consortium of European banks, without an EBRD guarantee. The transaction was secured by contracts with creditworthy EU-based steel purchasers as well as letters of credit backed by output consigned to less creditworthy purchasers in FSU countries and elsewhere, with an escrow account established in Amsterdam. Each time steel was sold, a percentage of the cash was applied to the interest on the credit line, and the rest turned over to Mittal to meet its obligations in Kazakhstan. Subsequently, with positive cash flow, the Karmet steel mill was able to acquire local electricity generation and coal-mining facilities, further reducing its operating costs, with margins improving as the price for steel products increased, and the operation became more efficient. Using this template, Mittal has acquired parastatals in Algeria, Mexico, and a half dozen other countries, acquiring International Steel Group (ISG)—which had been put together from the remnants of the former Bethlehem Steel operations and several other U.S. producers—in 2005, creating the world's largest steel group, with combined sales of over $22 billion.[27]

conventional wisdom suggests such trading is best left to investment professionals and foolhardy day traders. That view has changed markedly within the finance departments of global enterprises as more and more managers recognize the problems of trying to keep score in home currency, and meet investment objectives and earnings targets on a consolidated worldwide basis. International finance managers, therefore, need to keep pace with the Forex market to minimize any unsystematic risk.

In some industries, particularly those involved in commodities, such as cattle, gold, or oil, it is possible to leverage future production of the asset base as a means of securing financing to develop a project that produces the pledged asset base. No company has had greater success with this approach than Barrick Gold, in developing its gold-mining operations in Nevada. Armed with geologists' reports on core sample drillings, Barrick predicted, with a fair degree of accuracy, its future gold production levels once its mining operation came onstream. Since there are few, if any, forward buyers for mined gold as there are for finished steel, as in the case of Mittal Karmet, Barrick and its financial advisers developed a hedging strategy, selling gold forward at about a five-dollar discount per ounce to market for every one hundred tons under contract. By selling the future production forward to gold traders who worked the commodities markets, Barrick was able to raise all of the capital it needed to bring the mine onstream. The technique was widely copied by other gold producers. The discount rate was increased as the price of gold became more volatile in the wake of the dotcom crash and the worldwide increase in petroleum prices, decreasing hedging as a means of financing new gold mines. For Barrick, then a junior mining company, betting the mine on future production provided the cash to allow it to become one of the world's largest gold producers, now growing by acquisition of other gold producers.[28]

Options-based hedging strategies are useful as a means of pledging a receivable as a means of securitizing a loan obligation. Since commodities are usually more volatile than true receivables, which can be factored at a 10 to 15 percent discount from face, the advance rate is not as great, and there is significant trade-off in future profitability as reported to shareholders. When less tangible "rights" and other "synthetic commodities" are substituted for something that can be readily cleared on an exchange-based market like oil, the risk may be higher than prudent financial managers of a publicly traded corporation would be inclined to accept.

Not Everybody Plays the Same Game

Competition has been intensified by the adoption of near worldwide standards with respect to bank settlement practices, manufacturing, and tariffs. As a result, managers at broadly held global enterprises are more accountable to shareholders than at any time in history. But anyone who thinks that the world marches to the beat of a single drummer is likely to be disappointed. Managers at global enterprises face exposure to subtle differences in culture and misunderstandings arising out of different levels of fluency in the operative language of business. In the financial area, the numbers can nominally speak for themselves, but different people in different parts of the world still measure business results by different accounting techniques. As the events on Wall Street, which led to requirements under Sarbanes-Oxley in the United States, prove, transparency is more a "wish list" item than a deliverable fact. Vast differences exist in the legal systems of countries, particularly with respect to business practices, intellectual property, and the rules under which businesses are established.

NEW TOOLS FOR SUCCESS IN INTERNATIONAL
FINANCIAL MANAGEMENT

Understanding the new reality is at the core of developing solutions to financial challenges. Changes in management philosophy brought on by the emergence of institutional investors as "owners" with greater demands for accountability to shareholders begins to shape the approach at publicly traded global enterprises. Managers at hedge funds, insurance companies, mutual funds, and pension funds are equally accountable to their stakeholders and have the resources to make informed decisions about investing in any corner of the globe. This shift in the paradigm is no longer confined to a few "sharks" in New York. Investors in Hong Kong, London, and Dubai all have access to the same technology and the same fast-paced flow of information. Globally, more managers are being trained at the undergraduate and MBA level using the same textbooks covering the same course material, acquiring the same basic knowledge and skill sets.

Coping with the changes with respect to financial expectations is basic to achieving results. To accomplish this requires a new set of competencies:

Develop a Broad Worldview

Most critical to managing in the smaller world of globalization is to acquire and maintain as broad a perspective as possible. Too many financially oriented managers stop learning beyond what is required of them to perform their job, narrowly specializing in accounting, taxation, and treasury. When dealing in Australia, China, the EU or other countries, global financial managers need to develop cross-cultural competencies. Competent managers need to learn how their global counterparts manage technical aspects of their financial enterprise system. This allows everybody to speak and understand the same financial language, irrespective of how tortured one's command of the local language might be.

Running Wal-Mart as a global enterprise requires a different set of financial competencies than running a single "five and dime" store in northwest Arkansas. Its early expansion was financed by regional banks, with personal guarantees by Sam Walton. Today Wal-Mart is courted by financiers from around the world. Internally, its needs for financial products have changed from supplier-provided credit and receivables factoring to complex Forex hedging strategies and support of its intricate supply chain stretching across some twenty countries. Similarly, although 80 percent of total sales in 2004 came from its U.S. operations, Wal-Mart's future growth is tied to its ability to successfully introduce its retailing concepts to emerging markets like China and the EU. Not every new international operation has met its financial plan. In Germany, for instance, the company has had greater difficulty promoting Wal-Mart "culture" across its customer, employee, and community base than in China and elsewhere. Given the buying power of the EU market, financial managers need to have the capacity to keep a broad perspective in working solutions to achieve local unit earnings goals.

Stay Abreast of Regulatory Changes

For a financial manager, staying abreast of the changes in the regulatory environment and the consequences for the financial position of the firm is one of the most complex and dynamic aspects of managing a global enterprise. In addition to home-country considerations like Sarbanes-Oxley, the financial manager needs to develop a good understanding of the accounting, banking, and other commercial rules of the countries where the firm generates significant activities. As the case of Mittal Steel illustrates, sometimes being able to triangulate between regulatory limitations, credit risk perceptions, and market fundamentals is the very key to success in financing the growth of an emergent global enterprise.

Depending on the overall direction of the firm, which can change from time to time, based on overall corporate performance, new senior management, and being acquired, the level of commitment to foreign operations can change. With the increased focus on quarterly earnings performance, decisions affecting financial performance have a shorter time horizon. This fundamentally challenges the risk assessment criteria and rate of return considerations of the global enterprise, where it is rare that all units are performing uniformly well at any one point in time. Major capital investments, such as a new oil refinery built in the United States by Royal Dutch Shell, may be deferred in favor of using the same capital to achieve short-term gains trading in crude or increasing the output at its Canadian tar sands project.

The burden of making any investment outside of the home country is going to fall to the local country managers and the team in the accounting and treasury at headquarters. Typically, when overseas units do not "make the numbers," all of the former champions in marketing, planning, and senior management quietly melt away from the problem. Establishing the tipping point to shut down and write off is the arena of financial managers at global enterprises. The skill set of knowing "when to hold them, and when to fold them" is going to distinguish successful financial managers from those caught up in a cyclical reduction in force or worse.

Cultivate Flexibility

As the cases of Barrick Gold or VW-China demonstrate, the forces of the marketplace require tremendous flexibility. The once tried-and-true strategy of Barrick's financing mines with hedges on future production gave way to acquisitions of the shares of operating gold mines when it became more lucrative to buy undervalued securities than finance gold ore in the ground. The erosion of VW's dominant position in the Chinese domestic market requires a complete assessment of its financial strategy within the country. If it cannot make a profit selling cars locally as local Chinese producers bring less expensive vehicles into dealer showrooms, then the financial managers at VW have to assess whether they have enough of a labor advantage in China to scale up parts production there while reducing it in Brazil, the Czech Republic, and Mexico. Conversely, if the output of the new Chinese competitors proves to be less durable than the high-quality German-designed product, the situation in the marketplace could reverse itself in a few years, requiring a major step up in investment in China to keep up with demand.

As global capital markets continue to evolve, it is necessary to reexamine traditional relationships. Few know that the Mumbai stock exchange has nearly double the listings of the NYSE. While the daily trading volume is much smaller than the NYSE, this could change over time, requiring a reassessment of one's approach to such markets. It is important to remember that the ADR was developed in response to a onetime British limitation on ownership of foreign stocks. The marketplace adapted, and one of the first derivatives was born. In a world of instant communication, the pace of financial innovation has quickened. It is not likely to slow down, and what is demanded of financial managers at global enterprises is not likely to slacken.

CONCLUSION

Finance in the international arena is likely to remain as dynamic in coming decades has it has been in the recent past. Understanding the "big picture" of the global economy, with its subtle shifts in opportunities, will remain challenging. The interwoven complexity of changes in financial regulation and the responsiveness of global capital markets will assure the expansion of derivatives and other instruments of financial leverage. With greater volatility of currency and instantaneous flows of capital, managing risks in foreign investments will not become easier. Managers must master the range of financial tools to deal with these risks. Recognizing the challenges and staying on top of the latest approaches are nearly as critical as broadening one's network of contacts in the global finance arena.

NOTES

1. Compiled from *CIA World Factbook,* "Rank Order, GDP, Per Capita" (www .cia.gov/cia/publications/factbook/rankorder/2004rank.html), U.S. Census Bureau World POPClock Projection (www.census.gov/ipc/www/popclock.html), and World Bank Total GDP 2004 (www.worldbank.org/data/databytopic/GDP.pdf).

2. See note 1 above, plus Eurostat (epp.eurostat.cec.eu.int/portal). For an extended discussion, see Lester Thurow, *Fortune Favors the Bold* (New York: HarperCollins, 2003), 7–12.

3. See note 5. For an extended discussion, see Thurow, *Fortune*, 33–38.

4. See Sarah Anderson and John Cavanaugh, "Outsourcing: A Foreign Policy Agenda," *Foreign Policy in Focus* 9, no. 2 (Washington, DC: International Relations Center, April 2004). Downloadable at www.fpf.org/briefs/vol9/v9n02outsource.html.

5. See March 7, 2005, press release by IDG News Service entitled "Maxtor to Cut 5,500 Jobs in Singapore (http://storage.itworld.com/5035/050307maxtor/).

6. Data is extrapolated from the 2004 *Fortune* 1000 list, building on the themes of a paper by Professor Paul H. Dembinski, director, Observatoire de la Finance, Geneva, "Can Very Big Enterprises Help Bridging the Gap?" Presented in April 2003 (wbln0018 .worldbank.org/eurvp/web.nsf/Pages/Paper+by+Dembinski/$File/DEMBINSKI.PDF).

7. See notes 1 and 11. Wal-Mart Stores, Inc., 2004 sales data is from its *2005 Annual Report*, at www.walmartstores.com Home/Our Company/Shareholder Information.

8. See Dembinski, "Can Very Big Enterprises ... ?" Also see *World Trade Report 2005*, which can be downloaded at www.wto.org.

9. See BIS Seventy-fifth Annual Report, June 27, 2005, at www.bis.org/publ/ar2005e.htm.

10. Thurow, *Fortune*, 149, 230, 235, and 290.

11. See Press Information Notice (PIN) No 98/44 issued by the IMF, "IMF Concludes Article IV Consultation with Thailand," at www.imf.org/external/np/sec/pn/1998/pn9844.htm.

12. See web.worldbank.org for a detailed description of World Bank organization, policy, and projects.

13. See above. Go to Home/Topics/Oil, Gas, Mining & Chemicals, "Glamis Gold Ltd.'s Montana Exploradora Marlin Project in Guatemala" for a more extensive discussion of the issues.

14. See www.wto.org for a description of the World Trade Organization, its functions, history, and key agreements and suborganization.

15. See www.iso.org for a description of the now renamed International Organization for Standardization, or more commonly, ISO, its history, and its programs.

16. See "Bermuda-Bound?" *Business Week* (June 3, 2002): 14.

17. For more information on WTO position, see www.eurunion.org/news/press/2005/2005079.htm, Press Release Number 79/05, issued 9/30/05, entitled: "FSC: WTO Condemns US Subsidies To Exporters; Recipients of Illegal Support Include Boeing." For more information on AJCA, see http://webcast.ey.com/thoughtcenter/interface on subject "Repatriation of Foreign Earnings Under Section 965."

18. See D. John Daniels, Lee H. Radebaugh, and Daniel P. Sullivan, *International Business: Environments and Operations*, 10th ed. (Prentice-Hall), 2003, chapter 20, 606.

19. Ibid., 612.

20. Ibid., 606.

21. See www.londonstockexchange.com Newsroom/Press Releases. Various since 2002, when LUKoil was listed.

22. See www.swift.com, About Swift, for an account of the evolution of interbank wi system.

23. "The Buck Doesn't Stop Here," *The Economist* (September 30, 2004).

24. See www.BusinessWeek.com/investor. BusinessWeekOnline, "Insight From Standard & Poors; Updates on Coca-Cola Co.," by Richard Joy, as posted October 20, 2005. See also *Annual Report 2004*, Coca-Cola Co.

25. See www.Businessweek.com, "Failed Wizards of Wall Street" (September 21, 1998).

26. See www.chinadaily.com.cn/english/doc/2005/07/13/content_459845.htm, "VW Sees China Sales Slump as Rivals Soar," July 13, 2005, article.

27. See www.mittal.com, various news releases in 2005, and *2004 Annual Report*.

28. See www.barrickgold.com, History and Annual Reports 2004, 1999, 1998.

MOBILIZING CREATIVITY AND COMMITMENT

I n the globalizing economy, cultural diversity has become the norm for enterprise operations. It is present at every level of business—if not in every unit, then across the geographically dispersed units of the enterprise. It has ramifications up and down the value chain, from marketing and sales to product development and from effective working relationships among employees to the firm's partnering network. These relationships establish the context for effective management.

Cultural diversity offers both challenges and opportunities for management. The challenges, of course, arise from differing and, at times, conflicting perspectives, languages, and life and work styles that coexist in the workplace. These can easily produce communication miscues and other problems that cost time and resources. In the worst cases, they can embarrass or possibly jeopardize the firm's operations. At the same time, diverse perspectives and mindsets—when constructively channeled—can stimulate creativity and keep the enterprise in tune with disparate and changing markets. This requires firms to establish the corporate culture and channels of communication that promote intercultural creativity and commitment.

Four chapters in this section address issues that arise from the multicultural environment of any far-flung enterprise:

• The **Global Leader** epitomizes the challenge facing all enterprises as they expand transnationally. What qualities and skills are required to lead in an enterprise as it builds global perspective, seeks to cope with a continuously changing and risky environment, and strives to build a culturally diverse network of partners? While leadership qualities should not be reserved for chief executive officers, three CEOs are discussed here to exemplify the critical roles of facilitator, integrator, and partner.

• **Cultivating Global Teams** is the ultimate test for effective decision-making and action in the workplace. Here, the challenge of diversity plays out in the most intense way, for not only do teams embrace multiple cultures and varying professional and technical perspectives, but their work and interaction must be conducted increasingly through the Internet. This virtual dimension requires a multifocus mindset in order to navigate all stages of a team's development and work. The challenge lies in cultivating these skills among all team members.

• **Transnationalizing Corporate Culture** presents another view of the diversity challenge. There is general agreement that country culture affects business culture and that business operations within far-flung enterprises routinely encounter cultural barriers. In what ways, then, can an enterprise build a corporate culture and identity that overcome this diversity, thereby enhancing communication and collaboration and contributing to operational effectiveness? Business experience suggests that, while building this culture and identity are certainly possible, it requires firms prepared to train their employees with this in mind.

• **Ethics and Corporate Social Responsibility** provides a capstone for this discussion of cultural diversity, corporate identity, and employee commitment. In a real sense, these two topics constitute the pinnacle of manager and corporate commitment to business success in a global market economy. Without them, business is engaged in a "race to the bottom" and, ultimately, to the defeat of market capitalism itself as a viable economic system. This brings us full circle in this book, for ethics and corporate social responsibility need to be seen now as integral parts of corporate strategy.

The key issue to consider in the following chapters is how to shape corporate leadership and culture so that it nurtures creativity and commitment around the priority values of the global enterprise.

———— 11 ————

The Global Leader

LINDA L. SMITH

THE COMPETENCIES OF SUCCESSFUL GLOBAL LEADERS

Leadership within a global business is not a defined skill set. It is a cluster of overlapping competency roles that executives must have. Global leaders confront high-stake challenges that require expanded roles and a shift in mindset for effective leadership performance. Chief among their challenges is the boundarylessness of economies, industries, and organizations, while executive management continues to focus on prescribed traits and skills, guided by hard-to-see culture. When Carlos Ghosn, president and CEO of Nissan and more recently-appointed president of Renault, SA, began turning Nissan away from bankruptcy, he knew that he had to implement strategy in direct opposition to Japanese culture. Ghosn faced determining how to facilitate his plan for Nissan's transformation while navigating the cohesive, lifetime employment traditions of Japan. Daniel Vasella, chairman and CEO of Novartis emphasizes the best strategy and structure in his quest of leading the global company. His leadership identifies the need for skillfully integrating often conflicting information over wider and wider ranges of people and products to meet expectations for company growth. As CEO of Hewlett-Packard, Carly Fiorina executed the largest merger of technology history. She sought partnerships for transforming HP into a global marketing competitor. Fiorina's story will be remembered, however, for failing to lead many stakeholder groups, and as such illustrates the need for developing the right partnerships.

While it is easy to understand that senior managers hold major responsibilities for communicating the work of their companies to the world, there is limited understanding that these leaders also have work of their own.

This chapter probes the leadership styles of Ghosn, Vasella, and Fiorina to identify the twists and turns of their successes and failures. The material emphasizes their experiences that reflect more of the art and less of the prescribed techniques that accompany the complexity of leading a global company. The author hopes that readers find ideas in these leadership stories that help them envisage the emergent challenges and risks of leading globally, and then frame a new mindset toward acquiring these leadership competencies. These competencies lead managers to ongoing learning about the "soft" issues of culture, communication, and a trustworthy style as critical factors for global leading in addition to holding the accepted, traditional "hard" skills for budgets, manufacturing, marketing, and profit.

The new paradigm for global leadership defines broad roles for being a facilitator across cultural differences, an integrator of the right strategy and structure, and a partner who can build trusting relationships among diverse groups. And each of these roles, as will be seen in the following profiles, entails a shift in the leadership perspective (see Table 11.1). The facilitator role requires leaders to shift from relying purely on positional authority to being consensus builders within the enterprise and among its stakeholders. As integrators, leaders must be able to align at times highly diverse functions and operations across geographical divides to serve a common purpose. And the partnering role calls upon leaders to forge working relationships among stakeholders with diverse and competing expectations—both within and outside the company—that are mutually beneficial for the long-term future of the firm. These are demanding roles for leaders to play. As the following discussion demonstrates, sometimes they succeed and sometimes they don't.

TABLE 11.1. The New Work in Leading Globally

New Roles	Challenges and Issues
Facilitator—builds consensus across geography and cultural beliefs.	Cultural beliefs are intrinsic and implicit. They limit a global perspective and present resistance to the positional authority of leadership.
Integrator—appropriately combines strategy and structure	Diverse sets of functions and information grounded in cultural expectations set up high risk environments
Partner—builds trustworthy relationships	Commitment is required from multiple sectors with diverse, competing expectations.

BECOMING THE FACILITATIVE LEADER:
CARLOS GHOSN AND NISSAN

In 2002, a sleek 350Z rolled off the Nissan assembly line, but three years earlier few would have predicted that. Carlos Ghosn was the driver and he was also Nissan's chief executive officer, and even fewer business analysts would have predicted that.

Nissan faced bankruptcy in 1999 with an $18 billion debt. Carlos Ghosn— born of Lebanese parents, raised in Brazil, educated professionally as an engineer in France—was not the typical Japanese leader. Also in 1999, Renault SA became the largest shareholder of Nissan, and its leadership intervened for Ghosn. Given the bankruptcy danger, Nissan's Japanese directors were willing to try a different leader. In looking back at this beginning, Ghosn noted he needed to "explain what we had to undertake and why we had to undertake it and then outline the best way."[1] But Ghosn had to work within Japanese society, which is recognized for its strong emphasis on lifetime employment.

Mastering Cross-Cultural Intelligence

While a global leader's credibility is based on results, the leader must pool knowledge, grounded in powerful and diverse cultural beliefs. These beliefs shape countless activities and decisions. The concept of the leader knowing how to do it all—coming up with the compelling vision, driving its implementation through the authority of his or her executive position—is an idea from time past. In contrast, the global leader facilitates by first recognizing what he or she does not know, then asking questions of those who do, to identify a strategy that leverages the cultures of the firm and its markets.

Cross-cultural intelligence, such as the artful skill demonstrated by Ghosn in working with Nissan workers, is a complex competency. Studied systematically for almost thirty years, this intelligence requires knowledge about cultural symbols, rituals, and public behaviors, which frame the surface level of influence for business-leading. Paying attention to having a proper setting for corporate events is an example of the cultural surface. But leveraging culture for business requires an understanding of deeper beliefs. These sets of beliefs serve as signals for "getting it right" in developing strategy. Geert Hofstede, in *Cultures and Organizations*, has identified these beliefs as knowledge of power or authority dynamics and their translation into organizational structures; orientation for individual or collective mindset; masculine (competitive) or feminine (collaborative) approaches for leading; proper timing and uncertainty avoidance in determining decisions; and whether there is emphasis on longer-term relationships or shorter-term contractual results.[2] Beliefs vary from country to country, and define different expectations for effective leader communication across country boundaries and their markets.

Straightforward tactics are not easy for a foreigner to carry out in Japan. Early in the Nissan revival, Ghosn perceived that restructuring operating costs was the place to start. Ghosn recalled: "As a first step I engaged in what I call active listening with as many people as I could. . . . People told me, 'You can't go fast in Japan. You can't close plants. . . .' I listened carefully even to the opinions that totally contradicted my own beliefs to make sure that when I made my decisions, I hadn't missed anything."[3]

His attention to listening at this stage is supported by cultural research. Howard Gardner has identified recognition, respect, and reconciliation as values for developing leader facilitation options;[4] the findings of Fons Trompenaars and Charles Hampden-Turner in their study of innovative leaders indicate the value of reconciling opposing values by applying the "unwritten rules" of culture.[5] This was the case for Nissan and Ghosn. He reviewed his plan numerous times with Nissan employees, then listened to gain informal knowledge focused on operations and also picked up cues about less visible cultural expectations that could lower resistance to his plan.

Ghosn determined that effective facilitation of the proposed plan hinged on an appeal to the rational, practical thinking of the company's engineers. "My goals were to find existing assets in the culture that I could use to leverage change. The Japanese people are very pragmatic. They are always a bit suspicious of big ideas, but they believe in results . . . so we said that the quality of management can be measured, and we are going to measure based on performance. Car manufacturing is mainly a culture of engineers, they understood this."[6] By providing sufficient data for an engineering work culture, he established credibility and set the stage for the necessary facilitation of the more difficult cost-cutting measures within his plan.

Reinforcing Facilitative Leading

Ghosn went on to lead a three-year strategy that included reducing parts purchasing, lowering the number of suppliers, selling off stakes in affiliates, and shedding 21,000 jobs worldwide, including 16,500 in Japan.[7] To gain commitment for his strategy while also attending to cultural expectations, Ghosn took the management debate to the workers themselves. He provided significant amounts of data and scenario projections. By communicating effectively with many, Ghosn demonstrated—to his workers specifically and to the Japanese more generally—that he recognized and respected the need for Nissan to work well. Ghosn's reviews of the plan also tapped into another strongly held Japanese cultural attribute—the shared motivation to compete and win. Ghosn offered this challenge: "Judge me on results . . . Look at the profits, the debt, the market share . . ."[8]

He then reinforced his facilitative leading. "If you ask people to go through a difficult period of time, they have to trust that you are sharing it *with* them" (emphasis added). "So I said that if we did not fulfill our commitments, I would resign."[9] This public statement helped the Japanese see that Ghosn saw himself as sharing the risk, and as such he was a part of the collective. By the end of 2000, Ghosn and Nissan had accomplished the following: trimmed supply costs by 10 percent, lowered the number of suppliers by 22 percent, and reduced the number of jobs by 8,800.[10] Two years later Nissan posted a profit that was $1.6 billion higher than rivals Toyota and Honda.

Ghosn is now a hero in Japan. Throughout the negotiations of the change strategy, he acted as a facilitator who recognized and reconciled issues of restructure. Ghosn knew that he needed to leverage Japanese culture while also selling his strategy of turnaround. He appealed to the practical, competitive culture of Japanese workers to communicate clearly the risks of failure if radical change did not happen. He then understood that using the professional, analytical language of engineers would build the needed facilitation bridge. Throughout, Ghosn showed respect for Nissan workers by holding multiple reviews and allowing for a proper pace of information-sharing and deliberation. As a result, he lowered the resistance to cultural issues while facilitating a growing Nissan-Japanese commitment to change.

INTEGRATING THE RIGHT STRATEGY AND STRUCTURE: DANIEL VASELLA'S ONGOING QUEST FOR NOVARTIS'S GROWTH

Global leaders are both magicians and weavers. They demonstrate a competency for strategic business acumen that focuses and expands while also foreseeing broad changes and trends—a highly diverse set of skills and tasks. Under the leadership of chair and CEO Daniel Vasella, the European-based pharmaceutical firm Novartis was named one of the "10 Great Companies to Work for in Europe" in 1994 by *Fortune* magazine.[11] Vasella himself has earned the most influential businessman in Europe award from the *Financial Times*.

As Vasella has remarked, "It is a question of how can you be big and small? How can you create the environment with a spirit of small and have the advantages of scale?"[12] While attending to profit-making for Novartis, Vasella is navigating a course for the company and the industry that consistently integrates drug research and a human rights responsibility, a stance that counters public perceptions of profit and greed often associated with the prescription drug industry.

Incorporating Innovation Management

Novartis, the third-largest pharmaceutical company, was formed from a merger of Sandoz and Ceiba-Geigy in 1996 and specializes in oncology, cardiovascular disease, and transplant drugs. Headquartered in Basel, it employs 82,000 people in 140 countries.[13] Pursuing Vasella's vision, which emphasizes drug development, in 2003 the company had 64 drugs in the middle to late stages of research development, a rate that compares well to Roche, with 34 new pharmaceuticals, and Merck, with 14 for the same time period.[14]

Global leaders must integrate juxtapositions. The development of Gleevec (which arrests chronic myelogenous leukemia, a blood cancer) illustrates Vasella's leadership as an integrator. Early on he received development reports for the drug from Novartis researchers; the tests showed extraordinary promise. After discussing the results with Novartis researchers, Vasella drove the needed review process. This included clinical trials followed by a two-and-a-half-month U.S.-based review and approval process, the fastest in Food and Drug Administration history.

Throughout these steps, patients with the disease and their families and physicians were kept informed; the company often answered two-thousand-plus inquiries per day. As Novartis prepared to produce the drug, Vasella insisted that the company incorporate a patient assistance program for people with limited financial resources. This approach aided Novartis in working with patients and health providers, and the attention to ongoing communication helped avoid media criticism that has accompanied recent therapeutic discoveries.[15] As Vasella described the Gleevec process, "We incorporated what I call innovation management. It requires a host of skills, including the willingness to take great risks." In developing Gleevec for market, there were "pressures, various groups competing for time and attention, while making contradictory demands."[16]

Vasella's acumen for drug innovation comes from his particular commitment to research and development while also being entrepreneurial. Novartis spends 20 percent of its profit on research, which is above the industry standard. Vasella has said that he does not believe in setting a fixed budget for research and development, an unconventional position.[17] Equally important is that Vasella has no use for bureaucracy and secrecy, and that view is transforming the internal dynamics of the company. In the 1990s, Novartis implemented a pay-for-performance system; up to 50 percent of managers' pay is tied to performance and up to 10 percent of factory workers'. Much of this transformation is attributed to a state-of-the-art training program and paying attention to informal learning. Vasella also advocates a more informal communication structure, in contrast to other drug companies where the expectation is that management socializes with management and lab people with lab people. Novartis takes pride in having different people from different departments and levels eating lunch together.[18]

Building on Multiple Knowledge Bases

Methods of action science and collaborative inquiry can help illuminate the dynamics of strategy and structure integration.[19] This research emphasizes informal conversations and experience for developing appropriate integrating of strategy and structure.[20] Vasella has been singled out for the amount of time he spends in the laboratories, as a research scientist among colleagues, and for being curious and using inquiry. Successful development of complicated technical therapies such as Gleevec require new levels of strategic critical thinking to work through the multiple risks they present. Not only must Vasella as CEO publicly assure quality and patient safety, but as a leader he must also integrate the organizational goals of production efficacy and profit. To achieve these goals Vasella moves back and forth, finding and then discussing relevant research and product information, modeling communication from one sector to another, so that the company's workforce builds the structure it needs.

Coupling the goals of growth for a global business with a responsibility toward the larger society is another lens through which to view the global leader in the role of strategic and structural integrator. Vasella serves as chair of the Business Leader's Initiative for the United Nations, and indirectly, through that responsibility, Vasella positions Novartis as a global corporate actor. His leadership uses the company's medicine to expand its markets by tying Novartis medicines to places of human need throughout the globe. "Human rights, we are all agreed to apply to all people throughout the world. They should guarantee everyone a life in freedom and dignity. Our medicines help to cure disease, relieve pain, and reduce the length of stays in hospitals," writes Vasella.[21] Examples of Novartis's social and business integration measures include programs of free access to diagnosis and treatment in parts of Africa and Asia. Vasella also emphasizes responsibly integrating hard business goals into that social response: "In concrete terms this means we create and preserve attractive jobs and pay our employees competitive salaries and wages. We ensure our shareholders a reasonable interest on the capital they have invested."[22]

In summary, the global leader's role as integrator is one that uses multiple sets of information trends and needs, inside and outside the company, to drive growth. Vasella leads the Novartis workforce by communicating company research while incorporating market trends, alongside addressing global public health needs—knowledge bases not often linked. Through ongoing attention to company structure, he aligns his plans across sectors of research, manufacturing, and distribution by continually inquiring into the work taking place. Novartis workers in turn use this highly integrated model provided by Vasella's leadership, and as a result the company has ongoing informal communication that strategically advances its medical products to improve health for many while meeting stockholder interests.

SEEKING TO BE THE RIGHT PARTNER: LEARNING FROM CARLY FIORINA AND THE HEWLETT-PACKARD EFFORT

The case of Carly Fiorina illustrates the global leader's role as a partner; however, unlike the stories of Ghosn and Vasella, it is the lack of success that helps us better understand the importance of that role. Fiorina's task was to develop a trusting relationship and partner across diverse sectors of workforce, media, and stockholders to turn around Hewlett-Packard. Her efforts elucidate the competencies of reciprocity, inclusion, and trust, which are the "softest" of required leader dynamics but without which the global leader cannot succeed.

Fiorina faced a dilemma she could not navigate. The first years of the twenty-first century were brutal for those leading technology businesses around the world, with the media focused on the theme of the dotcom bust. In the middle of the bombast was the issue of whether or not Carly Fiorina could, in fact, use Compaq's merger into HP as the springboard for competing successfully against Dell and IBM.

Reaping Strategic Information from All Stakeholders

In 1999, Hewlett-Packard was a technology company employing 145,000 workers in 178 countries. Founded in 1939 by two engineers, Bill Hewlett and Dave Packard, the company evolved from manufacturing oscillators, voltmeters, and atomic clocks to producing computers, printers, and other technology products.[23] When Fiorina became CEO, management wanted to turn a reliable but staid company with high-end products into a visionary, global technology competitor. In choosing Fiorina, Hewlett-Packard became the first large, well-established corporation to select a woman chief executive, which brought forward assumptions and questions about women as leaders. Fiorina leaped into her executive role with a competitive plan for purchasing Compaq. In launching this strategy, Fiorina encountered intense scrutiny at multiple levels, which did not help her in building relationships. As a result, she did not attract followers or commitment, not only among HP employees but also from stockholders and others necessary for future alliances.

The global leader's authority must encompass power-sharing at deeper and wider levels, as companies need business from multiple local markets and face increased competition from almost anywhere. Fiorina was known for her wizardry as a master salesperson, with talent for knowing what pieces to put into place before anyone else. However, Hewlett-Packard, like other global enterprises, had invisible cultural rules driving expectations for strategy and operations. Critical information, particularly observations on challenges, needed to be retrieved from managers. That retrieval process was dependent on trusting relationships, or a sense of partnering to bridge corporate cultural challenges. But the partnership was not there, and strategic information was lost.

In the beginning Fiorina listened carefully. She hunted for good strategies buried in the Hewlett-Packard bureaucracy, asked questions, and gleaned ideas and practices that were diamonds being left behind on the floor. She found a focus in the original Palo Alto garage story of the founders, Bill and Dave. They shaped the early company culture around doing more than what was promised, a principle that evolved to be a part of "The HP Way." Fiorina turned the original principles into a video fable using black-and-white footage from the garage days, combining history and the future to help workers understand and accept her strategic message.

Looking back after Fiorina's departure, the video is a signal of the fundamental cultural differences not discussed by Fiorina and her reports, or by Fiorina and her board of directors. The video was an imaginative marketing approach, but its broad message missed the mark for engineers accustomed to and seeing the need for a hands-on operational strategy. Unlike Ghosn, who had repeated face-to-face sessions with workers to build relationships for transforming Nissan's structure, Fiorina used a video, which did not build a sense of worker inclusion. Although inventive, the video added a perception of distance, not relationship.

Fiorina proposed the merger with Compaq shortly after arriving at Hewlett-Packard. For eighteen months negotiations continued without closing, and the strategy appeared doomed. On a Sunday morning in December, Fiorina held a conference call to discuss the merger with the current chair, Richard Hackborn, and a half dozen directors. She asked the directors to consider three questions and then listened. The questions were: Should we stop? Should we go on as is? Or should we go on in a modified way? Hackborn began by saying, "Let's get back to the question, why are we doing this?" And then he answered, "It's the best solution for fixing the whole computer business."[24] The directors responded, and there was energy, commitment, and a consensus for going forward with the merger. It appeared that Fiorina had the necessary partnership from her board, but that effort would not be enough.[25]

Aligning the Firm's Vision with the Leadership Model

Outside of Hewlett-Packard, Fiorina was a charismatic spokesperson and leader of business partnerships. Like Vasella of Novartis, Fiorina adeptly used Hewlett-Packard's culture for altruism and its powerful foundations to expand or build partner initiatives for opening markets. For example, Hewlett-Packard developed multiyear i-community programs in Kuppam, India, and Mogalakwena, South Africa. These were micro-enterprises, but served several thousand people to increase technology applications linked to local economic development. In addition to these larger sites, Hewlett-Packard expanded its total e-inclusion projects to 34 by 2004, in 19 countries on five continents. With Fiorina's leadership the e-inclusion work moved from altruistic strategies to serving as a partnering resource for projected HP business goals.[26]

Under Fiorina, Hewlett-Packard also touted its low-cost supply chain as a resource for business partnerships. In 2004 this supply chain was a $52 billion resource and offered economies of scale for the company's business customers. Partnerships included Citrex Systems, for adding management software technology; Apple Computers to expand iPod distribution; and an alliance with Foxconn, the leading Taiwan electronic manufacturing service, to develop new technologies and products.[27] Hewlett-Packard and 7-Eleven partnered to roll out a technology system designed to transform convenience retailing, notorious for its mismanagement, and Intel and HP spent two years developing a research initiative to make the Internet more adaptable and intelligent.[28] Fiorina was adept at sponsoring external partnerships for business.

Within Hewlett-Packard, however, Fiorina was not finding the right partnerships. With eighty-seven fairly independent divisions, HP was a uniquely collective corporate culture, revered by workers as the strategy for achieving invention. When Fiorina aggressively pitched consolidation of divisions following the Compaq merger, she overlooked this cohesive but autonomous set of structures within the company. As a part of the merger she proposed a new five-division structure that could better focus on developing HP markets. Instead of relying on autonomy of the various divisions to meet business goals, Fiorina planted a critical question in the minds of HP employees: How could just a few consolidated divisions possibly give enough attention to each and every product line in ways that promoted quality? This perception separated Fiorina from her workforce.

Later, Fiorina spoke of the relationship-building challenges. In an interview with the author she said, "The soft stuff of people working with people is really the hard stuff, not the technology."[29] Similarly, Fiorina explained, "Employees tend to soft-pedal their remarks when the CEO enters. That is why companies need to foster an atmosphere in which employees at all levels can broach difficult-to-talk-about topics. Business is much more than facts. It's also about powerful emotions and how people react to them."[30]

The Compaq acquisition brought 65,000 new workers into the company. "Part of what we've done is to inject new DNA," reported Fiorina.[31] While her leadership had expanded HP resources, questions about her leadership style grew. Fiorina had advanced in marketing within the telecom industry; HP was a technology-sector company dominated by engineers, and Fiorina was outside that profession. She easily admitted that she was not a technology expert; she was a savvy marketer and a quick study. Fiorina's vision for HP growth was slow to take hold. The company failed to meet financial goals. Wall Street investors were disappointed and Hewlett-Packard stock fell, which brought more criticism of Fiorina as HP's leader.

Hewlett-Packard's board of directors deserves additional scrutiny for its inability to foster an honest, reciprocating relationship with its outsider CEO. While Hackborn and others were supportive of Fiorina in the merger with Compaq, there was a pattern of delaying needed communication that muddled the relationship. It began before her arrival. For much of the 1990s technology boom, HP's leaders did nothing strategically to position the company for growth. When there were hints of a technology-sector implosion in 1999, the directors acted to hire Fiorina, who had the charisma and focused ambition of leaders from that sector. But as the economy weakened, that style became suspect. The business press readily questioned her style, but the board appeared to pay little attention. In the chaos of the Compaq merger, the board rewarded Fiorina by making her its chairman. A year later, when there were no indicators of Hewlett-Packard's turnaround, the board increased her salary from $3 to $9 million, overlooking the gap between performance and reward.[32]

Fiorina's speeches as CEO consistently used compelling stories. Examining those stories throws light on how she perceived her leadership and also identify the partner gaps that were developing. She often told the story of her professional education, which was a nontraditional pathway into business leadership, and was clear in viewing herself not as a female executive, but as a business leader who happened to be a woman.[33] Her story continues to offer hope to diverse workers, particularly women, but may have prompted questions about following an outsider among HP employees, who held a cohesive, inside-the-company culture.

Further, her charismatic style of communicating was in direct contrast to practical engineering ways. Fiorina told several stories of the Hewlett-Packard future, suggesting imaginative opportunities for HP growth. But the stories emphasized markets coupled with new inventions—a broad view. One of these focused on two young women in India who, with the help of HP engineers, developed solar-powered digital equipment that they transformed into a photography business. And Fiorina sometimes shared a story that highlighted her forceful drive, in which she negotiated a business proposal while eating lunch in a stripper lounge, a setting many would have refused. The story demonstrated her will to push change, and perhaps points to the biggest issue within the faltering employee partnership for her leading Hewlett-Packard. A corporate cultural assessment, completed just as Fiorina became CEO, showed HP workers revolting if faced with major changes too quickly. No matter how attractive Fiorina's stories were when first told, they did not help develop or sustain a trusting relationship with her workforce or address HP's need for operational strategy.

On hearing and reading stories, listeners and readers alike evoke their imaginations, seeing heroes and villains. Leaders of complex systems, such as global enterprises, increasingly have the task of changing the minds of those who are managing the enterprise as well as of the customers the business seeks in order to have effective relationships.[34] This was the case for Fiorina and Hewlett-Packard. She had to tell the stories that communicate the vision, including the compelling reasons and solutions. And the story of the life she projected needed to model the leadership she was offering. Equally important, the two sets of stories must be complementary.

Fiorina's charismatic personal story did align with the need for a marketing vision and strategy at Hewlett-Packard. The future of HP will suggest the extent to which her imaginative ideas took hold. But complementary stories were missing that the HP workers could see and use from their practical, operational perspectives. Workers were not empowered and aligned with Fiorina. As a result, the story of Carly Fiorina and her relationship with Hewlett-Packard assists in illustrating how challenging but necessary it is to have the right internal partnership between leader and followers of any company, but particularly in a global enterprise with its many units and diverse workforce perspectives.

NECESSARY SKILLS OF THE GLOBAL MULTICULTURAL LEADER

Expectations about what is required for executive leading continue to be informally bounded within a unicultural belief system, seeded by the corporation and its history and linked to the country in which the business is headquartered. In this more traditional landscape of corporate belief systems, the executive traditionally learned to organize his or her executive leadership around three skill sets: (1) excellent technical skills, which include business and governance models; (2) conceptual skills from which to analyze and be proficient in strategy decisions and problem-solving; and (3) interpersonal skills from which to direct followers.[35]

The experiences of the Ghosn, Vasella, and Fiorina suggest a shift in an understanding of the necessary skills. First, the global leader facilitates strategy among various cultural belief systems instead of directing strategy. He or she is deeply mindful of the paradox that while the business mission is global, much that is important remains rooted in particular cultures. Not only do Ghosn and Nissan exemplify aptitude for facilitating and leveraging culture to meet company goals, but they also navigated through multiple cultural realms. Vasella continues to facilitate the use of a research culture to add credibility to production and profit for Novartis stakeholders. He also integrates options for wider social responsibility, a third cultural sphere. Fiorina made visible a global marketing strategy to the existing Hewlett-Packard culture. Her outsider leadership points to the risks involved when a global leader strives to change inside-company culture and communicate across different cultures simultaneously.

Global leadership requires defining the best structure for strategy, but the leader does so in a way that expands the familiar structure of governance, to aid the workforce in navigating diverse cultures and emerging trends. Vasella's leadership of Novartis provides an example in the risky but successful push to place Gleevec into market, accompanied by an attentive research structure and worldwide patient-focus strategy. Ghosn also demonstrates the competency to integrate strategy and structure. In turning Nissan from bankruptcy to profit, Ghosn has led the company to a more accountable structure, one that has more flexibility and options for a smaller workforce, a strategy new to Japanese business. Fiorina's story reveals the need for structural strategy. She focused on vision and strategy for marketing while the HP workforce needed operational plans that aided in seeing beyond individually focused work units.

The global leader must pay greater attention to social relationships to define a partnering role for leadership. Carlos Ghosn applied active listening and sincere attention as a foundation for a highly effective relationship to thousands of workers in turning around Nissan. Daniel Vasella is known for his ongoing commitment to spending time in the research labs, where he seeks engagement and challenges from his science colleagues as a means of adding partnership resources for the best strategy and structure. Carly Fiorina, in contrast, was not perceived as partnering with the many diverse groups she needed to lead. That diversity of expectations escalated misperception and distrust.

CONCLUSION

The knowledge base for defining global leadership is dynamic, aided by innovation and the challenge of diverse contexts. Like a kaleidoscope, the three primary roles and competencies discussed here—facilitator, integrator, and partner—overlap in various ways to form patterns for global leaders that greatly extend the artistry of leading. Indeed, the roles present leaders with substantial challenges, for they can not be mastered without serious commitment.

As a facilitator the global leader takes on and takes advantage of overlapping and often invisible knowledge that makes up cultures bounded by geography. The leader is artfully and mindfully aware of facilitating various cultures around the globe to accomplish his or her tasks. Ghosn convinced a Japanese workforce to set aside group interests, and also met the demands of Renault, a primary partner with a European mindset, while simultaneously expanding markets in a U.S. change-focused culture. The facilitator competency contrasts with the skills needed by an executive who uses a unilateral culture determined by the primary location of company headquarters. In that more unilateral, in-country setting, leading is simpler. The corporate culture dominates, with a familiar professional pathway serving to credential the advancement into general management based on technical skills that include attention to business and governance models. The corporate culture that shapes decisions, communication, and commitments is intrinsic or embedded and there is very little awareness of it in daily operations. As a result, general managers experience shocks and resistance as they lead negotiations that span multiple cultural belief systems defined by geography.

Thus, the global leader's work must incorporate internal and external dynamics that encompass the world's many languages and cultural beliefs. How does the global leader gather the wisdom to master this complexity? One strategy is to gain experience in multiple cultures. Carlos Ghosn combined multiple country experiences with a very simple listening and questioning approach that continued to keep his mind open. Within the facilitating competency is a Zen

Buddhist solution of finding a simple, but reflective answer—listening more widely and deeply in order to act. Didn't Carlos Ghosn do so in helping turn around Nissan?

The global leader is required to gather and pool knowledge across widely diverse functions, which is an integrator role. In contrast, the executive who leads the unilateral culture of a company stays focused on analysis and the logic strategy as a primary general management role. The proper alignment of strategy and structure is perceived more easily because corporate cultural beliefs are homogeneous. These beliefs emphasize doing what is necessary to compete and win market share; thus, strategy for directing and controlling is focused and communicated through directives and management.

But a global leader's credibility is based on the strategy he or she promotes, while much of the company structure is shaped by many local operations with diverse, country-centric cultures. In some countries the role of leader is autocratic, while in other local markets the leader must consult. The cultures shape perceptions, negotiations, and decisions to gain results for the company. Just as the global leader requires artful facilitation as a competency, the alignment of strategy and structure for global leadership demands the mindset of an integrator whose approach is curious, inquiring, and nimble. In the global leader setting, the work of leadership brings forward the strategy and structure question asked by Daniel Vasella: "How can you be big and small? How can you create the environment with a spirit of small and have the advantages of scale?"

Successful global leadership addresses complex social connections to achieve business results. The partnering competency encompasses a wide array of external and internal relationships that both challenge and engage the other parties. The leader acts as spokesperson for the company externally, while also developing the appropriate, trustworthy relationships internally among the company's workforce. The partner role manages diverse, competing interests.

The profile of Fiorina outlines what happens when a global leader does not achieve the needed partnership. As Hewlett-Packard CEO her charisma captured external attention and goodwill. Yet she failed to gain the commitment of HP workers.

A unilateral corporate culture is bounded more easily by a primary set of values, perceptions, and rituals. There, the leader communicates a vision that directs the general managers and technical workers, while corporate culture provides control informally. Intrinsic to this setting is the concept that appropriate authority appears and acts in a familiar manner using the same or similar values. For instance, Hewlett-Packard's workforce expected that leaders would develop through long-term experience as general managers. There was also an undiscussable factor of male leadership. That set of expectations provided an ongoing corporate framework for the company's workforce. Carly Fiorina was not a match for the powerful influence of HP's corporate culture.

Carly Fiorina's experience as Hewlett-Packard's CEO suggests the need for not only a deeper and wider competency for appropriate relationships, but also work as a trusted partner. It suggests the need as well to continuously stay open and gain access to useful information from relationships within the company as well as outside of it. This poses a useful question: How does the leader develop partner relationships that ensure the ongoing information and feeback essential for the company and its people to thrive?

The competencies for global leadership can be framed as deeper, wider roles for facilitation, integration, and partnership. However, identifying and developing these competencies also point to the larger need for curiosity, communication, and cultural awareness among those who seek global leading. These needs suggest an emergent, artful, imaginative approach that must accompany the acts of leading as well as learning about it. Global leadership is not static; it cannot be easily prescribed by formulas, processes, or mental models. Inquiry, the ongoing attention to compelling questions to engage imagination, aids in recognizing the continuous development required for global leadership. The answers are found by examining and questioning the experiences of the emerging global leaders themselves.

NOTES

1. L. Tischler, *Fast Company* 60, Nissan Motor Company online magazine (July 2002): 80–82, at http://pf.fastcompany.com/magazine/60/Nissan.htm.

2. Geert Hofstede and Gert Jan Hofstede, *Cultures and Organizations: Software of the Mind*, 2d ed. (New York: McGraw-Hill, 2005), 1–227.

3. Tischler, *Fast Company*, 80.

4. H. Gardner, *Changing Minds: The Art and Science of Changing Our Own and Other People's Minds* (Boston: Harvard Business School Press, 2004), 1–12.

5. F. Trompenaars and C. Hampden-Turner, *21 Leaders for the 21st Century: How Innovative Leaders Manage the Digital Age* (New York: McGraw-Hill, 2001), 20–25.

6. Tischler, *Fast Company*, 81.

7. *Nissan Annual Report, 2003*, para. 8 (cited 28 October 2004), at http://www.nissan.com/annualreport/htm.

8. Tischler, *Fast Company*, 81.

9. Ibid.

10. *Nissan Annual Report*, para. 10.

11. "Novartis Recognized as a Top Company," cited 19 September 2004, at http://www.novartis.com/special/fortune_survey.shtml.

12. *Wall Street Journal* editors, *Boss Talk: Top CEOs Share the Ideas That Drive the World's Most Successful Companies* (New York: Random House, 2002), 155–58.

13. "Novartis Recognized," para. 6.

14. F. Hawthorne, "Keeping the Pipeline Full: Thanks To Its Indefatigable CEO, Novartis R&D Effort Is Paying Off," *Chief Executive*, online magazine, cited 27 October 2004, para. 8–11; at http://www.chiefexecutive.nnet/depts.innovation/200.htm.

15. Ibid., para. 12.

16. D. Vasella and R. Slater, *Magic Cancer Bullet: How a Tiny Orange Pill Is Rewriting Medical History* (New York: HarperCollins, 2003), 32.

17. Hawthorne, "Keeping the Pipeline Full," para. 5.

18. Ibid., para. 6.

19. J. Bray, J. Lee, L. L. Smith, and L. Yorks, *Collaborative Inquiry in Practice* (Thousand Oaks, CA: Sage Publications, 2000), 141–55.

20. W. Torbert, "Organizational Transformation as a Function of CEO's Developmental Stage," *Organizational Development Journal* 16 (1998): 11–14.

21. Vasella, *Magic Cancer Bullet,* 35.

22. Ibid., 110.

23. Hewlett-Packard, "HP Fast Facts," 2004 para. 3–8, cited 27 December 2004; at http://www.hp.om/hpinof/newsroom/facts.htm.

24. G. Anders, "The Carly Chronicles: An Inside Look at Her Campaign to Reinvent HP," *Fast Company* 67, as cited 19 September 2004, at http://www.fastcompany.com/magazine/67/carly.html.

25. P. Burrows, *BackFire: Carly Fiorina's High-Stakes Battle for the Soul of Hewlett-Packard* (New York: Wiley & Sons, 2003), 157–245.

26. Hewlett-Packard, "HP Fast Facts," para. 24–36.

27. Ibid., para. 55.

28. Ibid., para. 42.

29. "Fiorina Interview," with L. Smith and E. Dent, audio clip as cited 6 October 2004, at http://UMUC.edu/graduateschool/25anniv.htm.

30. M. Lagace, "Carly Fiorina: Heed Your Internal Compass," *HBS Working Knowledge* para. 4, online report of Harvard Business School Seminar, March 5, 2003, as cited 19 September 2004, at http://hbswk.hbs.edu/item.jhtml?id=3384&t=entrepreneurship&noseek=one.

31. Anders, "Carly Chronicles," 67.

32. Burrows, *BackFire,* 245–61.

33. Anders, "Carly Chronicles," 67.

34. Gardner, *Changing Minds,* 15–25.

35. G. Yukl, *Leadership in Organizations,* 3d ed. (Upper Saddle River, NJ: Prentice Hall, 1994), 1–33.

——— 12 ———

Cultivating Global Teams: Diversity Management Squared (DM²)

GLENDA J. BARRETT

Taking time to reflect on the important issues underlying daily activities is a mark of an astute manager and a practice encouraged by genuine learning organizations. In the following case, the executive discovers a useful metaphor for developing global teams as she reviews her own company's experience and identifies the competencies managers and teams need to succeed.

THE DECISION TO GO GLOBAL

Jill Ricci laid her wet spoon across the saucer and leaned back in the cushioned chair to sip her coffee. A faint whiff of jasmine floated by and the morning air bustled with bird chatter. The sun had not yet stretched over the roof into the corners of the garden, but she could see the bursts of color—tall reds, bunches of yellow, short stalks of orange, bright pinks, and soft purples—among the greenery. She gazed at a patch of white towers toad lily, wondering what the development she had learned of yesterday would really mean in practice. Like many other companies in the high-tech industry, Jill's organization,[1] a leader in designing and installing security systems, had decided to globalize. Would managing the people really be so different? What new competencies would the managers need in order to succeed?

Jill watched a bumblebee cross paths with a monarch butterfly near the azaleas as she began to reflect on the implications. The company's employees were already considerably diversified. All levels of management and employees were well on their way to valuing those differences and had learned to look for the opportunities they offered—creative problem-solving, better understanding of the customer base, and reduced legal risks. They had stopped thinking that people were uniform units of equipment that could be easily exchanged when one piece burned out, or that people had fewer rights than a disk of software. As indicated by Jill's own promotion to Vice President of Human Resources, executive management had also embraced the fact that HR policies and procedures must be integrated with other dimensions of the strategic plan. It had not been easy to foster this understanding; it took years of constant lobbying and learning. Surely all the hard work would position them well to move into the global environment.

Still, Jill could feel a cloud forming. Is there any chance they could avoid cross-border staffing? The promise of a worldwide labor pool has many strings attached. She smiled at her own naïveté. There were several reasons why multinational staffing would be necessary. The executive board will expect to capitalize on lower labor costs in other locations. Local employees will also help the company better understand the new customer base and local infrastructure. Indeed, in some cases, the government will require employment of its citizens in order to award a contract or approve a business development. Moreover, any shortage of critical skills will undoubtedly require expatriation or immigration, virtually if not physically. No, avoiding cross-border staffing is not a real option; perfecting it is. Jill placed her empty cup on the table and nodded in agreement as she arose from her chair to face the day.

That was three years ago. Sitting again on the deck at home, Jill noted that the garden had grown considerably since then. She drew a cup of English Breakfast tea to her lips. On the teak table, next to her toast, lay the debriefing report, a standard evaluation exercise for any corporate-level project. This morning she fingered the cover page pensively. In the document, she knew, the review team identified several "best practices," numerous "lessons learned," and many "areas for improvement." She would need them all.

Despite the groundwork that had been laid in managing domestic diversity, the global work teams—of employees, of employees and subcontractors, suppliers, customers, community agencies, and government representatives—had experienced significant problems. The research and development groups had exceeded their budgets and delivered later than scheduled; the sales and marketing teams experienced inopportune turnover. Moreover, the customer service groups had significant interpersonal conflicts and, on a few occasions, created bad publicity.

In the executive summary, the report concluded that they had:

underestimated the differences in cultures and laws and the impact those differences could have. We were dealing with Diversity Management Squared (DM^2), diversity times itself to a new level. We needed more sophisticated tools—an inclusive compass framework and a multifocus mindset—to navigate all the stages of group development.

In its overview, the report outlined a close relationship between HR systems and group development by mapping the common connections that support line management.

THE SIX STAGES OF GROUP DEVELOPMENT

Jill recognized the modified Tuckerman model[2] of group development and noted that even domestic teams are seldom as linear in their life cycle as Table 12.1 indicates. She knew, too, that HR functions may be involved in stages other than the predominant ones listed. Nevertheless, she thought, it was a helpful chart for the purposes of the report.

A sneaky, sharp wind flipped the divider page for her. She anchored the corporate binder between the teapot and her briefcase then creased the page open to the next section. Yes, she needed more detailed information; highlighting the key points in each group stage would be useful.

First Stage: Preparing

Jill clicked her pen and began to read:

In this initial stage, cultural and legal factors impacted all the HR functions—strategic planning, job analysis and design, as well as recruitment and selection. For strategic planning, to align the group work with the business objectives, we began at the end. How would we know if the group succeeded?

TABLE 12.1. HRM Support in Group Development

Group Stage	Human Resource Management Function
Preparing	Strategic Planning Staffing • Job Analysis and Design • Recruitment and Selection
Orienting	Employee Relations • Communication • Training
Adjusting	Employee Relations • Conflict Management • Grievance Systems
Performing	Performance Management • Appraisal • HR Development • Reward Systems
Readjusting	Change Management
Terminating	Employee Relations

As we discovered, cultural concerns help determine which outcome measures are most important and who the relevant constituents are. We found, for example, that managers in China, where unemployment is high, were pressured to hire more people than would normally be needed to accomplish the work.[3] Not surprisingly, the extra staff presented problems in group coordination and motivation as well as the budget. Although the local team may have been inefficient by our standard measures, in fact, at a global level it was a success; the excess labor was an acceptable price to pay in order to obtain and retain the contracts. Understanding the larger role labor played in the business venture was critical.

In job analysis and design, there were several cultural and legal considerations. For instance, we reverted to task simplification in areas where the educational level was inadequate (and concomitantly planned for increased training and development). In China, we emphasized more group interaction in the workflow to meet the needs of a collectivist culture.[4] We also used traditional, top-down authoritative group structures in countries with a high power distance norm, such as in France, where the employees expect the supervisors to give direction.[5] On the other hand, we were able to use self-directed teams with our suppliers in Sweden, where, with a low power distance cultural norm, employees were quite comfortable with participatory management.[6]

Jill recalled the power distance problem that Sweden's Electrolux encountered when it acquired Italy's Zanussi. Sweden's top management expected the Italian managers to solve their own problems, but the Italian managers thought particular tasks should be handled by senior management and the system should "force" resolution. Both sides were frustrated by the unmet expectations.[7] Fortunately, her own company had prepared to reduce similar dynamics by structuring the groups in accordance with their cultural preferences.

The report continued:

In designing the jobs, we also considered legal parameters. We analyzed and revised all our employment contracts with hiring agencies and renegotiated our collective bargaining agreements to be sure we would not violate those terms or create public relations problems at home with the new developments overseas. We avoided much of the union resistance we experienced several years ago when we opened facilities in South Carolina.

Yes, thought Jill, we knew the union would see offshoring as being even worse than moving to a greenfield site within the United States. It's a sensitive issue. She recalled that IBM experienced negative publicity when the *Wall Street Journal* reported part of its internal analysis for offshoring;[8] and, EDS, which calls it "best shoring," restricts the practice to commercial accounts since it might cause extra problems in government work.[9] Thankfully, so far, Jill's company had balanced the pressures at home with the needs offshore fairly well.

In addition [the report continued] we compared U.S. laws to those of the other countries to identify acceptable working conditions. As expected, we had to accommodate a variety of provisions for holidays, religious observances, working hours, health and safety measures, and employee security in the wake of 9/11. Although the differences complicated the cultural and administrative aspects of team management, we also found that they were a welcome source of flexibility. We were, for instance, able to create a "follow-the-sun" operation, wherein the work passed along time zones to provide continuous customer service to our clients across the globe.

Jill noted in the margin that the global variety, in fact, had encouraged the company to alter its benefit program: Instead of specific religious-related holidays, people now have a designated number of personal days to take whenever they choose.
She read on:

Staffing was more complex than anticipated and took much longer than planned. Cultural and legal factors impacted the hiring philosophy, the labor supply chain, and the screening methods. Equal Employment Opportunity (EEO), a primary scaffolding for domestic diversity in the U.S., is not a universally accepted principle. In some leadership positions, for instance, despite having appropriate knowledge and skills, women and younger employees were not welcome.[10] Instead, nepotism, a practice that our company restricts domestically, was a predominant hiring strategy in Asia.

In other instances, culture voiced which knowledge and skills were important. For example, in Germany, the technical abilities of the leader seemed more significant than the interpersonal abilities considered valuable in the U.S. In other cultures, such as Japan, knowledge or skills may not be as important as seniority or the person's position in the wider community. In all cases, group members had both subtle and blatant ways of protesting cultural violations. The breaches of social status frequently impacted the group dynamics negatively.

Jill shifted in her chair. The tall black walnut tree in the far west corner caught her eye. It is such a bully, she thought. The beautiful pink peonies and three other flowers she planted wouldn't grow near it. She had finally selected a bed of lunaria, the money plant, which was compatible. Finding the right combination was as challenging as staffing a team, she mused. How could she have known the roots of the walnut tree exerted juglone, an allelochemical that was toxic to so many plants? She flinched mentally at the feeble excuse; the information had been available since Roman times.[11]

In addition to the social norms [the report continued] the governing laws were often confusing. Who had legal jurisdiction was not always clear. National employment laws, such as the Civil Rights Act, that play a dominant role in the U.S. can be overridden elsewhere by local provisions or trade agreements.[12] Even the

European Union, with its push toward regional consistency, often allows each member country, via Directives, to determine its own form and method for implementing EU employment principles.[13] International laws and standards, while developing, are still relatively embryonic.

The labor supply chain of eligible people also differs by country. We were quite successful in linking with universities in Russia and China to identify and develop potential staff.[14] The academic avenue was blocked in Japan, however, because the Japanese have traditionally fostered the school-to-work transition. Since local firms monopolized that labor market, we often competed instead for returning nationals and employees of temporary agencies.[15] We did notice, however, that local Japanese women are increasingly interested in joining our corporation. Our preference for knowledge-based (versus gender-determined) selection and reasonable working hours are attractive to new graduates.[16]

Several times we expatriated American staff to fill the leadership positions. Unfortunately, a high percentage of those appointments ended early. We understand better now how cultural and family issues can cause overseas assignments to fail and why American companies are increasingly designing expatriated positions to include training a local successor.[17] This planned transition to local leadership, of course, sows expected change for the work group. Screening the local staff for appropriate positions proved cumbersome as well. For instance, in some countries, the applicants' credentials are not reliable,[18] the use of technology is limited, and/ or cross-cultural communication makes the validity of the interviewing process questionable. We also discovered a significant difference in the laws regarding employee privacy. When we tried to hire a Senior Technical Manager from Germany to work in our Bangalore, India, office, we had difficulty obtaining his employment information. Due to a significant difference between U.S. and European Union standards, the agency could not release his personal data to us.[19]

Given the differences in hiring philosophies, labor supply chains, and screening methods, it proved wise to contract with local consultants and agencies to help us get "the right people in the right place at the right time." It was also extremely important to consult immigration and tax specialists since, for domestic purposes, we did not have that expertise in-house.

In short, we know that selecting the right people is a major success factor. While we did several things well in forming the groups, we discovered several hurdles to overcome. These barriers increased both the amount of time and money needed to complete the preparation.

Second Stage: Orienting

Jill scribbled several notes about group composition. Hearing a rustle, she glanced across the rolling landscape toward the gate. She saw nothing except the morning glories drooping on the trellis by the gazebo. She silently promised to give them some water soon. Then, pouring another cup of tea, she turned the page.

As the first interaction of the team members, the Orienting stage introduces three key components: the people, the task, and the ground rules. All facets are impacted by culture and/or law. We managed many of the differences well by emphasizing effective communication principles. For instance, we designed more feedback loops, such as bilingual summaries of critical decisions, to verify that we had not missed something important due to the low context vs. high context communication styles.[20] Using cultural interpreters also helped us understand the nonverbal signals and environmental cues that our word-oriented, low-context approach often overlooks. Without their help, we would not have realized how many ways someone can mean "no" without directly saying it.

We also allowed more time for people to become comfortable with one another. We know there is a cultural dichotomy about task vs. relationship. Americans prefer to "get down to business" right away; they learn something about the people through addressing the task. In fact, they may interpret a delay as an unwelcome lack of commitment. By contrast, people in other countries, such as Asia, the Middle East, and Latin America, want to focus more on the relationships first and understand the people in greater depth. For them, rushing to discuss the task casts doubt on the sincerity of the individual.[21] We discussed this beforehand in the cross-cultural training.

During training, we also discussed the cultural aspects of the group's ground rules. The perceptions of time, in particular, received attention. Monochronic time (M-time), which prizes punctuality, and polychronic time (P-time), which favors completion of the task-at-hand before proceeding to another activity,[22] were especially explored to avoid problems in planning and meeting deadlines. In addition, we explained the zero-tolerance policy for sexual harassment and discussed possible cultural differences in defining that behavior. We also included a discussion about intellectual property after we discovered that people in collectivist cultures may believe that ideas are "public goods" for everyone to share rather than competitive proprietary assets that need protection.[23]

In short, we recognized the importance of this second stage and its potential for establishing primacy norms for group behavior. We allocated additional travel money for face-to-face kickoff sessions, even for groups that would work virtually throughout most of the project. We estimated more time for the groups to move through this stage, and we designed training to address key cross-cultural issues. With the exception of the meeting in Estonia, we prepared the people well for this start-up, trust-building phase.

Jill tapped her pen on the rim of her cup. She recalled the intense debriefing session she had had with the group leader for that project. The short, heavy-set woman had bent over the desk, hammered her hand against the blotter, and choked back tears as she threatened to file a lawsuit. The cultural interpreter had neglected to explain in advance that it was customary in Estonia to alternate dining throughout the evening with sitting in the spa. When the time came to move from the table to the sauna, the American visitors were shocked. Sensitive about their weight as well as public nudity, they were visibly conflicted between wanting to respect their colleagues and feeling appalled. Two men finally joined their hosts in the sauna without vocal fanfare, but the others were too overwhelmed by the surprise to be tactful; they rudely protested the custom. While the Estonians understood the problem, the subsequent group interaction was strained by the rejection.[24] No, Jill agreed, that had not gone well. Damage control is an exhausting and time-consuming endeavor. She dog-eared the page before continuing.

Third Stage: Adjusting

> There is a high potential for conflict—and creativity—in this third stage. Team members experience a more detailed reality of interaction. They are "settling in"; the honeymoon, if they had one, is over. If the team does not process conflict productively at this pivotal juncture, further group development may be impeded.
>
> We found that the basic sources of conflict in global groups were familiar: Insufficient resources, poorly defined workflow interdependencies, a mismatch of people's capabilities with the job requirements, miscommunication, violation of ground rules, incompatible goals, and divergent role expectations are all still likely culprits. However, identifying when conflict exists and resolving it satisfactorily is more difficult in multicultural teams. Cultures express problems or disagreement differently, and the variety of face-saving norms complicates the matter.

Jill underlined "face-saving" and jotted a side note. She recalled an American colleague who, returning from Korea, complained that workers would not report problems occurring in the plant or, when they did, they waited until the end of the day to notify him. He didn't understand until later that conflict was so damaging to one's *kibun*, or self-esteem, that the workers delayed telling him so they would have the evening for everyone to restore face.[25]

> Furthermore [the report continued] a virtual environment adds another layer of difficulty in handling conflict, especially with people who use high context communication. Linda Beamer and Iris Varner, prominent authors in cross-cultural studies, explain the steep divergence of approaches to this important issue:
> "The whole idea of managing conflicts is a low-context notion.... In high-context cultures, conflict is a part of life.... In individualist cultures ... conflicts are looked upon not only as inevitable, but sometimes as necessary and even healthy.... In collectivist cultures, however, conflict may be viewed as one dimension of the ongoing relationships among group members, not something outside the relationships. Conflicts are part of collective life. But conflict that is openly identified threatens the harmony of the group. Indeed, when conflict is out in the open, it is almost always destructive in collectivist cultures. Instead of verbalizing conflict, high-context cultures use actions to compensate, show goodwill, and restore harmony to the group.... A low-context person who insists on 'talking it out' with a high-context person may feel resolution is being achieved. But the other person may feel the open admission of conflict is an irreparable rupture in the relationship."[26]
>
> With such polar strategies, we had to design creative ways to address the issues. Often, informally, we were able to involve third-party "facilitators" (family or friends) to help. Of course, conflict that cannot be processed informally may invoke the formal grievance systems. Like legal systems, formal grievance

channels also differ in structure and tone since the history of and trends in labor relations are considerably different across the countries.

In short, conflict occurs normally in this refinement phase of a group's start-up process. The cultural and virtual dimensions make identifying and resolving disagreements or problems more complicated. Finding creative methods that will enable the group to build an inclusive environment and allow them to direct their energies as quickly as possible to the group's mainstream activities is crucial.

Jill left her pen in the bend of the binder to mark her page then stood up to stretch. The sun flooded the lawn now. Avid sunbathers, the blue-eyed daisies lifted full-face toward the light. The shade-loving impatiens, however, seemed to squint in the brightness. Jill marveled at the range of responses. Reading the flowers' other, more subtle signals had taken long, constant effort— almost, she smiled, like learning to interpret Mr. Fujimura's weekly status reports.

Fourth Stage: Performing

Jill grabbed the watering can then followed the stone path. She sprinkled the drooping morning glories. At closer range, she could see the periwinkles and roses needed weeding. Inefficiencies, she thought, weeds were. Like naysayers on a new project, why did they grow so well? She uprooted a handful of the unwelcome visitors and tossed them on the ground. She would tend to those later, she promised, returning to her chair.

After the group has answered basic organizing questions and members have found ways to work together without disruptive conflict, the team moves into a more mature phase, the Performing stage. It is a period of synthesis and increased productivity, upheld by sound knowledge management. It is a culmination of group development, the crest of the wave.

In this fourth phase, Expectancy Theory is an underlying framework. The model asserts that people are motivated to work only if they believe the effort they expend will be sufficient to achieve the required performance and that, when they do accomplish the work, they will be adequately rewarded.[27] Thus, managing performance involves several key functions: goal-setting, training/ human resource development, performance appraisal, and reward systems/ compensation. We found that culture influenced all of them.

The idea of goal-setting itself is culturally bound since it implies an ability to control one's environment and time, ideas that are not universally shared. Work/ life balance norms and work ethics, too, shape acceptable goals or standards for the group. For instance, the Protestant Work Ethic,[28] which views work as a noble use of one's time, is a prominent thrust in American culture but not everywhere else.

People also have different learning styles and preferences. E-learning, which we are emphasizing in the United States, is not always technically possible or immediately accepted elsewhere. To be most effective, online courses need to be translated into the local language, accompanied by culturally appropriate examples.

Plus, the method of delivery needs to address cultural norms. For instance, in Japan, a high-context culture, we found that blending face-to-face instruction with virtual classrooms works well. In France, using a prescribed online curriculum supplemented by mentoring helps to preserve the high power distance norm.[29]

Similarly, we know that providing feedback about how well a team is doing vis-à-vis its goals and versus benchmark groups is often useful in the United States.[30] However, feedback may be perceived differently across cultures.[31] In particular, monitoring and evaluating performance at the individual level requires reconsideration; the philosophy and administration of performance appraisal varies widely throughout the world. In India, for example, we found that formal performance evaluations were not emphasized, perhaps because they threaten the personalized nature of supervisor-employee relationships.[32] In Japan, however, the *satei* is used regularly to determine the rate of promotion and the level of monthly pay.[33] When individual appraisals are used, we found, it is important to consider carefully the purpose (i.e., for employee development, to document problems, to determine compensation), who will conduct the evaluation (i.e., home office and/or host staff; 360-degree or immediate supervisor), and the logistics (i.e., forms, schedule) to ensure that all pertinent cultural concerns are addressed.

Jill penciled another side note: Americans don't relish performance appraisals either, but what are the alternatives? What can we learn from cultures that don't use formal evaluations?

We also saw that culture impacts the link between performance and rewards in the motivational chain. We found, for instance, in countries where "being" is more significant than "doing," an incentive-based philosophy faces an uphill challenge. We did discover, however, that some companies that traditionally used seniority-based wage structures are experimenting with merit-based systems.[34]

For example, some Japanese firms that experienced harsh economic times in the 1990s are worried about the expensive impact a graying workforce could have on future labor costs if age and seniority are predominant factors in determining wages. Thus, in the compensation formulas, they are shifting the relative weight of time and performance factors measured in the *satei* to emphasize productivity.[35] Still, although changes are under way, as we expand globally we need to consider a variety of compensation strategies.

Moreover, we must review the types of compensation we use as well. Knowing what someone values—what would serve as an effective reward—is difficult even domestically. The unwritten expectations in psychological contracts and the personal assessments of the Equity Theory factors (inputs, outputs, and comparison references)[36] make identifying intrinsic and extrinsic rewards difficult. To accommodate our diversity in the United States, when possible, we have used cafeteria programs so people can select what matters to them. We found, in the global environment, the variety in cultural values and legal stipulations—especially tax structures[37]—demand even greater overall flexibility. Without adequate reward systems, groups either underachieve or lose members prematurely.

To recap, in this culminating stage of group development, as in the others, we need to craft flexible, dual-focus strategies—umbrella programs and policies that can simultaneously protect the corporation's global interests (such as incentive pay strategies) and also be tailored to suit local needs and customs (such as tax-free housing subsidies versus higher wages as currency). Finding the macro-micro balance in the motivational chain of goal-setting, learning, performance evaluation, and rewards—especially in a dynamic world—requires artful management.

Fifth Stage: Readjusting

Jill shifted her weight in the chair and continued reading.

The Readjusting stage, the fifth phase, is actually an artificial linear construct for incorporating into group development the fact that environments are not static but chaotic. Whenever groups evaluate their status, such as they do in the Performing stage, they may discover they need to make modifications. Also, when the conditions for the group change significantly, such as having a new delivery deadline, obtaining a new technology, or altering group membership, a period of readjustment may occur. During this time the group may revisit some of the issues prevalent in any of the previous stages. For instance, resources may need to be secured (Preparing stage), members may need training (Orienting stage), or role conflict (Adjusting stage) may arise again.

We have not yet found a long-term group that has not had to cope with some type of change during its life cycle. We have found that change is usually accompanied by some form of resistance: objection to an expected "net loss" generated by the nature of the change itself, negative reaction to an individual change agent, and/or reluctance fostered by the change management strategy. Cultural norms interplay with each of these factors. For instance, cultural values help determine what is perceived as a "net loss" (i.e., whether a pay raise is deemed more important than a heavier workload). Similarly, cultural stereotypes—about age, gender, race, or nationality—impact how well the group members accept the person acting as a catalyst for the change.

In terms of management strategy, we recognized two pertinent cultural dimensions that have not been specifically discussed previously: locus of control and uncertainty avoidance. While in the United States we often assume that people have considerable influence over their environment, other cultures have less confidence in human autonomy. For instance, in Muslim societies many people believe that Allah guides everything and that planning a change is an affront to Him.[38]

Destiny-oriented cultures are not the only ones to resist managing change at a philosophical level. We found in Russia, for example, that uncertainty avoidance played a role; some managers defined the purpose of their jobs as being "to stabilize" the organization. As such, they saw change as a step in the wrong direction.[39]

In short, as in the first Adjustment stage, this Readjustment period—an unfreezing, altering, and refreezing process[40]—has a high potential for conflict, dressed as resistance. Like before, the resolutions must accommodate face-saving issues.

Sixth Stage: Terminating

Most of our teams are still working. We have, however, learned important lessons from the few that have disbanded. For instance, if completion of the project
equals termination from the organization, an immigrated individual may be
deported.Termination can also become a serious face-saving issue if it is not
handled properly.

The company may also incur additional costs for unwelcomed unemployment, since most countries do not subscribe to the employment-at-will doctrine
that serves as the default in U.S. employment law.[41] Instead, they often require
"just cause" for termination[42] and attempt to prevent job loss via penalties and
complicated procedures. We also found that celebrating the completion of a
project requires cultural sensitivity. From the way groups are recognized to the
foods that are served at parties, protocols and preferences abound.

In summary, given the web of psychological, economic, and legal factors, the
final stage of group development actually needs to be considered thoroughly at
the beginning of a project. In fact, prudent managers ask how each person can be
terminated—or whether the individual can leave prematurely—before hiring
him/her into the group. Such planning allows astute managers to use this adjourning phase not only to provide positive closure to the project but also to lay
the foundation for future cooperation.

REQUIREMENTS FOR GROUP DEVELOPMENT IN
THE GLOBAL MANAGEMENT PARADIGM

Jill closed the binder and sat back to let all the ideas about the six stages
simmer in her mind. Exactly what has changed? The number of perspectives
has multiplied. Moreover, given the legal and cultural differences, those additional perspectives breed higher possibilities for conflict, both in terms of
degree and volume, in all aspects of group development. Even organizations
that are accustomed to working in diverse and virtual environments discover
an increased intensity, a greater complexity. Diversity Management Squared
does indeed capture the essence of the shift.

Yes, she thought, the complex systems require more sophisticated analysis
and action. Managers must focus on multiple dimensions simultaneously—
must think both globally and locally—in accelerated time. Isn't it ironic that
when managers need to be more adept, they actually have less assurance in
their position? They must question their infrastructure, their assumptions;
what has worked well before may not be valid in multicultural domains. Since
managers no longer know the terrain, they must learn again how to navigate.
Unfortunately, the available maps are sketchy; proven guidance for the global
manager is currently limited.

Jill recognized that, all things considered, her company had made a good
deal of progress in three years. They had learned much about cultural differences and had accommodated the advanced diversity fairly well. She noted,

however, that they are still using primarily the U.S. experience as the default measurement; they need a more inclusive benchmarking technique to support a globalized business strategy. Their knowledge management systems and learning organization principles would be key in helping them create that perspective over time.

So, what could she tell the audience next week? The International Society of Management has invited her to participate in a panel discussion. The topic: What competencies do global managers and teams need? She began to list key requirements—for the organization and group as well as the knowledge, skills, and abilities that managers and individual team members need in order to succeed.

Key Competencies for the Organization and Group

First and foremost, she thought, the organization and group must establish the right conditions—a fertile ground—by crafting **a working culture that recognizes the importance of the human factor and values diversity**. It includes:

- **An expanded framework and an inclusive compass, for assessing problems and solutions.** What works in one part of the world may not in another; all participants and constituents need to be considered. This requires an ability to analyze the employee's working environment and staffing methods in accordance with multiple legal systems, culturally sensitive motivational dynamics, and diverse administrative systems.
- **Cost-effective and efficient bridging mechanisms.** In addition to technical support (such as language converters), a bicultural staff, contracted interpreters, cross-cultural training, and networking in the community all help people identify cultural differences and pathways for connecting.
- **Flexible system designs to address the variety of organizing structures, processes, and rewards.** Instead of single methods, managers build portfolios, such as cafeteria plans for compensation, and interlinking modules that can be changed relatively easily.
- **A learning environment**[43] **fueled by solid knowledge management practices.** Here, mistakes are converted into assets and "failure" is not a face-saving disaster. Managers are encouraged to understand not only what works but also why it does.
- **A multimedia, culturally sensitive communications network that addresses the low/high context continuum.** Through a range of technologies, the network combines verbal and nonverbal methods to exchange information.
- **Enhanced conflict/conformity management system.** It utilizes a range of direct and indirect methods, from informal facilitators to formal arbitrators, for identifying and resolving problems in culturally appropriate ways.

• **Evaluation tools and processes that permit monitoring team dynamics without micromanaging team development.** Tools that focus on results, spotlight exceptions, and track changes allow groups latitude to engineer their own efficiencies.

Key Competencies for the Individual Manager

Individual managers and team members need to develop, in addition to competence in the job area:

- knowledge of other nations' cultures, histories, values, and customs
- knowledge of change management philosophies and practices
- knowledge of group development and dynamics
- the ability to be comfortable working with the unknown
- an ability to think in non-ethnocentric ways, to avoid the not-invented-here phobia
- a multifocus mind-set that considers the macro and micro levels simultaneously
- creative thinking, especially the ability to find opportunities in differences
- an ability to learn and adapt quickly, with a focus on continued learning
- an ability to build cross-cultural relationships based on respect and trust, including excellent cross-cultural and virtual communication skills
- applied scientific skills (good observation skills, ability to detect assumptions, ability to ask pertinent questions, ability to avoid stereotyping, understanding of validity issues, and ability to suspend judgment)
- high emotional intelligence with excellent stress management skills and the ability to see difficulties as part of the experience and not become frustrated by them as deviations from an ideal plan
- self-awareness of one's own strengths/weaknesses and cultural biases

Jill shook her head. Expecting one person to have all these skills and abilities may not be realistic. Educational systems, professional and industry forums, and corporate training/development programs can provide only part of the knowledge. Life experiences, traveling, and independent reading—all coupled with reflective thinking, add other needed dimensions. In the end, all members of the group need to contribute their strengths, to help one another, and share in the multifaceted responsibilities. Managing global teams is a group effort.

She logged on to the computer. It's like landscaping, she mused, thinking again of the black walnut tree and surveying all the wonderful colors and shapes before her. She entered her title: "Global Gardening: Growing a Team." She wondered: Could I create a Zen garden in the far east corner?

NOTES

1. The concepts and events described are derived from the literature and actual cases; the organization itself is fictitious.

2. B. W. Tuckerman and M. Jensen, "Stages of Small Group Development Revisited," *Group & Organization Studies* 2 (1977): 419–27. They listed the stages of group development as: forming, storming, norming, performing, and adjourning.

3. A. Gross and S. Lepage, "Asia HR Update, 2001," *International Focus* (2001). (SHRM Global Forum, 1800 Duke St., Alexandria, VA 22314-3400.) They stated that in China the "government will continue to strongly favor incoming businesses which stress labor-intensive production and services, while existing foreign-invested ventures will be prodded to employ even more workers and prevented from firing the inefficient workers they may already employ" (p. 4).

4. D. A. Victor, *International Business Communication* (New York: HarperCollins, 1992). He wrote " . . . cultures can be assigned some point on a continuum that stretches from high value placed on the individual (and little concern with group identification) to low value placed on the individual (and great concern with group identification). In the first type of culture, people see themselves primarily as individuals and stress such traits as self-freedom and self-reliance. In individualist cultures, people usually identify themselves only weakly with the groups to which they belong. Their strongest loyalties are to themselves (and perhaps to their immediate family). In collectivistic cultures, people generally view themselves more as group members than as individuals. They derive their identity in large part from the groups to which they belong and consequently hold a great deal of loyalty to those groups" (p. 102).

5. G. Ferraro, *The Cultural Dimension of International Business,* 3d ed. (Upper Saddle River, NJ: Prentice Hall, 1998). Referencing Hofstede's 1980 study, *Culture's Consequences*, Ferraro explains that power distance is a term used to measure how individuals from different cultures relate to authority in the workplace. Hofstede found that in some cultures there is great social distance between those who hold power and those who are affected by the power (high power distance). In such societies, subordinates and superordinates adhere to a rigid hierarchy, status is often ascribed (that is, based on age or gender), and social relations are highly formal. By contrast, some cultures characterized by low power distance tend to play down status distinctions while emphasizing less formal forms of communication and interaction (pp. 105–6).

6. G. Hofstede, *Culture's Consequences: International Differences in Work-Related Values* (Beverly Hills, CA: Sage, 1984). He shows France with a Power Distance Index higher than the one for the U.S. and Sweden with a lower one than the U.S. (p. 77).

7. C. Bartlett and S. Ghoshal, *Transnational Management* (Boston: Irwin McGraw-Hill, 2000). They describe the interaction more fully: "The Swedish top management was often frustrated in its efforts to get Italian managers to arrive at a consensus among themselves in solving problems. The Italian managers, in turn, expected the senior management to settle problems such as transfer pricing between Italian product lines and the UK sales offices. According to one senior Italian manager, ' . . . the key in this complex international organization is to have active mechanisms in place to create—and force—the necessary integration.' However, the Swedish CEO preferred to let them solve their own problems: 'Force is a word that is rarely heard in the Electrolux culture' " (p. 211).

8. W. Bulkeley, "IBM Documents Give Rare Look at Sensitive Plans on Offshoring," *Wall Street Journal*, Eastern Edition, vol. 243, Issue 12, p. A1. Bulkeley reported an internal IBM memo listing a comparison of $56 per hour in the United States versus $12.50 per hour in China for programmers; the article said IBM was considering moving jobs offshore in 2006.

9. P. Babcock, "America's Newest Export: White-Collar Jobs," *HR Magazine* 49, no. 4 (2004): 50–57. Travis Jacobsen, an EDS spokesman, is the cited source for the information. See the "No Apologies" insert (p. 55) to the article.

10. F. Trompenaars and C. Hampden-Turner, *Riding the Waves of Culture: Understanding Diversity in Global Business,* 2d ed. (New York: McGraw Hill, 1998). They report "Achievement-oriented corporations in Western countries often send young, promising managers on challenging assignments to faraway countries without realizing that the local culture will not accept their youthfulness and/or gender however well they achieve" (p. 116).

11. M. Dana and B. Lerner, *Black Walnut Toxicity* (West Lafayette, IN: Purdue University Cooperative Extension Services); at www.hort.purdue/edu/ext/HO-193.pdf. They explain the toxicity and its impact on various other types of plants and report that the information was known in some form since ancient times.

12. D. Bennett-Alexander and L. Hartman, *Employment Law for Business,* 4th ed. (Boston: Irwin McGraw-Hill, 2004). The Civil Rights Act of 1991, essentially an amendment to the 1964 Title VII provisions, extends U.S. jurisdiction to employees of American firms working overseas. However, if the U.S. provisions violate the laws of the other country, those local laws may have priority. (Similarly, specific trade agreement provisions can, in effect, override coverage of U.S. policies overseas.)

13. V. Du Feu, V. Edmunds, E. Gillow, and M. Hopkins, eds., *Update 6: EU & International Employment Law* (Bristol, England: Jordans, December 2003). They explain that a regulation applies in its entirety in all member states. A directive, however, per the Treaty of Rome, ". . . shall be binding, as to the result to be achieved upon each Member State to which it is addressed but shall leave the national authorities the choice of form and methods" (p. 23). Directives have covered such issues as: equal pay, equal treatment, working time, data protection, parental leave, burden of proof in sex discrimination cases, and part-time work, among others.

14. F. Foulkes and G. Zhu, "Recruiting in China: The Battle Moves To College Campuses," *International Update,* Issue 1 (2000) (SHRM Global Forum, 1800 Duke St., Alexandria, VA 22314-3400). They report that Foreign Invested Enterprises contributed 75 percent of the $500,000 in scholarship money at Beijing University. D. M. Bostwick, "HR Management Practices in Post-Soviet Russia," *International Focus* (1998) (SHRM Global Forum, 1800 Duke St., Alexandria, VA 22314-3400). Bostwick reports that, in Russia, where the primary recruiting method is word of mouth, companies are also trying to establish relationships with the major universities in Moscow and St. Petersburg.

15. A. Gross and G. Koolwal, "Trends in Human Resource Practices in Japan," *International Focus* (1999) (SHRM Global Forum, 1800 Duke St., Alexandria, VA 22314-3400). They report that, in Japan, since cultivating the school-to-work link has been a long-held domestic strategy, foreign enterprises must often "rely on temporary staffing, mid-career hiring, overseas Japanese, and expatriates to fill their positions" (p. 12).

16. A. Gross and C. Tran, "Update on HR Issues in Asia, September 2003," *International Focus* (2003) (SHRM Global Forum, 1800 Duke St., Alexandria, VA 22314-3400). They report that "Due to their treatment in Japanese companies, many female workers are opting to work for foreign companies that do not discriminate (or at least discriminate less) against their female employees. In these foreign companies, Japanese women workers are more able to utilize their knowledge and skills" (p. 8). They also report that work hours in Japanese firms are longer than U.S. norms; evening obligations and extended work hours are more frequent (p. 5). They cite a survey by the Japanese Trade Union Confederation which found that men in their early thirties worked over three thousand hours a year, an average of fifty-eight hours/week (p. 11).

17. GMAC, NFTC, and SHRM, *Global Relocation Trends 2000 Survey Report* (October 2000) (SHRM Global Forum, 1800 Duke St., Alexandria, VA 22314-3400). The study, which represents predominantly U.S. companies, reports that, while the number of expatriate assignments is increasing, the amount of increase is lower than in previous years. Furthermore, organizations are redesigning the positions, shifting the objectives of the assignment—often to include training a local successor—and reducing the length of stay.

18. A. Gross and T. McDonald, "Recruiting and Human Resources in China," *International Focus* (1998) (SHRM Global Forum, 1800 Duke St., Alexandria, VA 22314-3400). They report, ". . . as fabrication of credentials is a serious problem in China, it is very important to check the credentials of all potential candidates thoroughly. To further complicate the situation, references from state-owned enterprises do not bear any resemblance to references from western companies. The communist system does not place emphasis on 'references,' individual critiques or evaluations, thus making the credential checking process very time consuming" (p. 4).

19. The European Union Data Protection Directive, which went into effect in October 1998, prohibits the transfer of personal data to a country outside the EU that does not ensure an adequate level of protection. Greengard (1999) and Hopkins and Lehmann (2001) reported that the United States and China did not meet the EU standards. S. Greengard, "Privacy: An Increasingly Public Matter," *Workforce* 78, no. 10 (October 1999): 120–22. M. Hopkins and V. Lehmann, *SHRM Global Audio-Conference*, 6-13-01.

20. Victor, *International Business Communication*. In low-context cultures, such as Germany or the United States, people rely heavily on verbal communication (spoken and written words) to exchange ideas. By contrast, in high-context cultures, such as Saudi Arabia or Japan, nonverbal communication is more significant. (Note that this different emphasis on verbal versus nonverbal communication may manifest itself in several ways, such as the perceived need for documentation, the credibility of written contracts, the role of silence, or the comfort level with virtual environments.)

21. Ibid., 145.

22. Ferraro, *Cultural Dimension*. "M-time cultures, which are best represented by the United States, Germany, and Switzerland, emphasize schedules, a precise reckoning of time, and promptness. They view time as a discrete commodity that can be saved, wasted, borrowed, or killed. In contrast, P-time cultures emphasize the completion of transactions and the involvement of people rather than a rigid adherence to the clock. Being 'on time' is of less importance to P-time people than it is to M-time people. When two people from a P-time culture are interacting, they are more likely to continue what

they are doing until they have finished rather than end it and move on to the next scheduled activity, as would be the case with two M-time people" (p. 94).

23. D. B. Marron and D. G. Steel, "Which Countries Protect Intellectual Property? The Case of Software Piracy," *Economic Inquiry* 38, no. 2 (2000): 159–97. They found that violations of intellectual property laws occurred more in countries that have a collectivist culture, perhaps due to the belief that ideas are "public goods" for everyone to share.

24. Based on an actual event; the parties prefer to protect their identities.

25. Ferraro, *Cultural Dimension*. Information is based on a scenario described on p. 142 and p. 171.

26. L. Beamer and I. Varner, *Intercultural Communication in the Global Workplace*, 2d ed. (Boston: McGraw-Hill Irwin, 2001), 236–37.

27. V. H. Vroom, *Work and Motivation* (New York: Wiley, 1964). The Expectancy model basically says that people will be motivated to work if they perceive the level of effort expended will lead to the level of desired performance which, in turn, will result in an outcome or reward that is valued. If any of those connections are not believed to exist, the motivation will not exist. More detailed discussion of Vroom's and related models can be found in A. Shani and J. Lau, *Behavior in Organizations: An Experiential Approach,* 8th ed. (Boston: McGraw-Hill Irwin, 2005).

28. C. Ambrose and C. Kulik, "Old Friends, New Faces: Motivation Research in the 1990s," *Journal of Management* 25, no. 3 (1999): 231–92. They define the Protestant Work Ethic as "the degree to which individuals place work at or near the center of their lives" (pp. 3–4). Ferraro, *Cultural Dimension*. Ferraro explains: "The protestant ethic holds that people do not work for themselves alone. A person's work . . . comes from God, and it is through their work that people demonstrate their worth to both God and themselves. This notion . . . that work is not only respectable but actually virtuous . . ." is not shared everywhere (p. 97). In other cultures, people work out of necessity, "not because they derive dignity or self-worth from the process" (p. 99).

29. C. Shepherd, "Local Is More Than Language," *ITTraining* (July 2002): 30–32. Also see N. Van Dam and E. Rogers, "E-Learning Cultures around the World," *E-learning* (July 2002): 28–33.

30. Ambrose and Kulik, "Old Friends," 231–92. They, in reviewing goal-setting research, conclude: "Goal-setting is especially effective when feedback is provided that permits the individual to track progress relative to the goal" (p. 247).

31. S. Schneider and J. Barsoux, *Managing across Cultures* (London: Prentice Hall, 1997).

32. N. Lindholm, "National Culture and Performance Management in MNC Subsidiaries," *International Studies of Management & Organization* 29, no. 4 (1999–2000): 45–66. (Information based on p. 59.)

33. K. Endo, "Satei (Personal Assessment) and Interworker Competition in Japanese Firms," *Industrial Relations, Berkeley* 33, no. 1 (1994): 70–82. (Available from Bell & Howell Information and Learning, 300 N. Zeeb Road, P.O. Box 1346, Ann Arbor, MI, 48106-1346). The *satei* "that determines the rate of promotion and level of monthly pay is carried out every April. A *kakaricho* (first foreman) assigns to each of his or her workers a score of A to F based mainly on his or her assessment of three factors: (a) performance in previous periods, (b) eagerness to perform the job and attitude as a member of a work group and team, and (c) potential ability to perform jobs more effectively. A score of A or B represents a favorable rating, while a score of

E or F represents an unfavorable one. The *kacho* (section manager) reviews the *kakaricho*'s assessment and makes his or her own assessment of the worker, and the *bucho* (department manager) adjusts the scores assigned by the *kakaricho* and *kacho* to determine the final score. The distribution of final scores assigned to workers in a single unit is specified in advance by management. For example, of level SS1 to SS4 workers in a single unit, 5 percent receive A, 10 percent receive B, 20 percent receive C, 57 percent receive D, 6 percent receive E, and 2 percent receive F, with D considered the standard score. The worker is not informed of the final score" (p. 3).

34. Gross and Tran, "Update on HR Issues." They report that "... while pay-for-age is still the guiding principle, some of Japan's largest companies are utilizing pay-for-performance and are abandoning pay-for-age" (p. 6).

35. H. Shibata, "The Transformation of the Wage and Performance Appraisal System in a Japanese Firm," *International Journal of Human Resource Management* 11, no. 2 (2000): 294–313. Shibata studied a prominent, large electronics manufacturing corporation in Japan, looking at wage scales in the 1980s and 1990s. The old wage system had a basic wage composed of a personal wage that was determined, in part, by performance appraisal; a job wage; and an age-linked wage. In the new system the age-linked wage was abolished, the personal and job wages were integrated, and the performance-based component played a greater role, especially at the upper levels of the structure. He explained: "The wages of new hires are still determined by age and academic degree in the new wage system. Also, the new personal wage in Zone I, II or III includes mandatory wage increases. Therefore, the new wage does partially reflect an employee's age and seniority. However, the new system has no specifically age-linked wage increases. Furthermore, Zone IV in the new personal wage table has no mandatory wage increases. Performance appraisals in the new wage system have become stricter and have greater influence on wage increases and promotions. Overall then, the new wage system is more performance based" (pp. 304–5).

36. J. S. Adams, "Inequity in Social Exchange," *Advances in Experimental and Social Psychology* 2: 267–300. Equity Theory basically proposes that people will compare their own input/output ratio to the input/output ratio of someone else, called a "comparison other." If the ratios are not equal, they will try to adjust in some manner. Ambrose and Kulik, "Old Friends," 231–92. They report that reducing inputs when the self-ratio is lower than the other-ratio is a common strategy.

37. A. Gross and D. Thadani, "Asian Trends in Human Resources: After the Crisis," *International Focus* (1999). (SHRM Global Forum, 1800 Duke St., Alexandria, VA 22314-3400). They explain that the tax laws in China often make housing subsidies and other benefits, such as stock options, more attractive than higher wages.

38. L. Copeland and L. Griggs, *Going International: How to Make Friends and Deal Effectively in the Global Marketplace* (New York: Random House, 1985). They explain: "Self-determination is a concept almost outside the comprehension of many peoples. ... In Moslem countries from Libya and Turkey to Indonesia, the will of Allah influences every detail of life and many feel it is irreligious to plan for the future. Although many Moslem executives do think in terms of strategy and plans, even they will regard their efforts in the context of what God wills" (p. 13).

39. Based on S. Michailova, "Contrasts in Culture: Russian and Western Perspectives on Organizational Change," *Academy of Management Executive* 14, no. 4 (2000): 99–112.

40. K. Lewin, "Group Decision and Social Change," in G. E. Swanson, T. M. Newcomb, and E. L. Hartley, eds., *Readings in Social Psychology* (New York: Holt, Rinehart, & Winston, 1952), 459–73. Levin articulated this basic three-stage process in early discussions about change management.

41. Bennett-Alexander and Hartman, *Employment Law for Business.* "Employment at will is still the basic law in many states. However, the employment-at-will doctrine several years ago began to erode. There have been several judicial exceptions to the rule created by courts. The result is that, even though an employer can terminate an employee for any legal reason, if the reason is one that is determined to fall within an exception to the at-will doctrine, the employee can assert a claim for wrongful termination or discharge, for which the employee can receive damages or reinstatement" (p. 12).

42. DuFeu et al., *EU & International Employment Law.* They note that European law leans toward protecting the employee; often employers must have "just cause" to terminate a worker. A. Gross, "Employment in Japan: The Struggle for Change," *International Update* 3 (SHRM Global Forum, 1800 Duke St., Alexandria, VA 22314-3400). Gross reports that Japan has "...fairly strict workplace laws that make it difficult to dismiss workers. Still, companies can change an employee's title to a lesser title, lower his or her salary, change a job assignment, rewrite a job description to encompass clerical or other less significant activities, and move personnel from normal office surroundings to unpleasant ones, as in a vacant or basement area. Most employees get the hint and quit. Others, however, have decided that suicide is the only honorable way out" (paragraph 11).

43. D. Garvin, "Building a Learning Organization," *Harvard Business Review* (July–August 1993): 78–91. He explains that a learning organization is proficient at applying new knowledge gained from scientific, systematic problem-solving; experimentation; debriefing its own experiences; and benchmarking the best practices of others.

13

Toward the Transnationalization
of Corporate Culture

KLAUS GÖTZ AND NADINE BLEHER

T here is broad agreement among researchers as well as executives that
country culture strongly influences business culture. By the same token,
there is substantial evidence that organizations operating across borders, that
is, transnationally, routinely encounter cultural barriers. This chapter considers how forces of globalization are shaping the culture of global enterprises
in the midst of divergent country cultures. It does this by exploring a number
of theories about the underlying premises of culture and how culture influences corporate communications and cooperation. It discusses creative approaches corporations are using to overcome barriers between cultures, and
how these approaches indicate the emergence of various transnational forms
of corporate culture. These forms point toward a new paradigm of how the
culture of global enterprises is being shaped. While global convergence toward
homogeneous management practices and values seems unlikely, there is good
reason to believe that companies can build transnational corporate cultures.
Companies operating cross-culturally, however, need to prepare their employees for the communication and cooperation challenges they will face in a
global business environment.

FORCES OF GLOBALIZATION ARE INFLUENCING
BUSINESS CULTURE

Globalization of Consumption Patterns

The computerization of print media and the distribution of information via the Internet have made international sales of media products more profitable to producers and more accessible and affordable to consumers. Reduced transaction costs through electronic data processing and distribution, expanded markets, and economies of scale have stimulated the big suppliers of media and information services to form multinational media companies. Increasing globalization and concentration of the market for media and information services have resulted in an ongoing standardization of media products as well as a media culture that is relatively independent of location and context.[1] This phenomenon is called the globalization of consumption patterns.

Numerous researchers agree that cultural differences cannot weather the dynamic forces of global consumption and lifestyle orientations. Kenichi Ohmae asserts that neither geopolitical borders nor sociocultural differences can act as barriers against global consumption preferences: "Even social borders are starting to give way to the information- and technology-driven processes of convergence."[2] "It is a new kind of social process, something we have never seen before, and it is leading to a new kind of social reality: a genuinely cross-border civilization, nurtured by exposure to common technologies and sources of information."[3]

More traditional media like television, video, and cinema play an important role in the diffusion of global consumption patterns, because they are easily accessible and evade national and language frontiers.[4] Sociologist Mike Featherstone describes the sociocultural effects of this development the following way: "We can be immediately united with distant others with whom we can form a 'psychological neighborhood' or 'personal community' through . . . the shared experience of the news we get from watching television. This means that the locality is no longer the prime reference of our experiences."[5]

From an Island to a Crossroad: Time/Space Compression

Transnational communication—such as e-mail and videoconferencing, high-speed trains and planes, global mass media, the increase in international travel and migration—enables the creation of transnational relationships and the ability to surmount cultural differences between societies. "There is," says Mlinar, "a rapid increase in access to other subjects. Thus, individuals enter into (inter)dependence with an ever increasing number of actors in broader environments."[6] This is especially true for business. Increasingly, sales, marketing, supply, production, and R&D have been conducted globally, making companies more dependent on transnational communication and information flows. In his paper on transborder data flows and national sovereignty, the renowned communication scientist and business consultant William Drake argues that these new means of communication have reduced the physical bonding of an organization and its members to the respective location. "The more organizations depend, ultimately, upon flows and networks, the less they are influenced by the social contexts associated with the places of their location."[7]

In sum, technological innovations have enabled an increasing number of individuals to choose, create, and cultivate transnational communities according to their personal interests, values, habits, and attitudes. Due to the rising quantity of people, information, and ideas in transnational flow, points out Mlinar, it has become more difficult to uphold exclusively local cultures, work patterns, and living habits. There is a transformation under way—which could be metaphorically designated as the transition from identity as an island to identity as a crossroad. It is increasingly unlikely that a territorial unit can continue to preserve its distinctiveness . . . while there is an increasing probability that distinctive identity may be formed as a unique crossroad in the flow of people, goods, and ideas."[8]

Globalization Challenges Our Notions of Corporate Culture

Two views on culture have predominated among social scientists. Among political scientists, there are those who adhere to **realist** theories. Their primary assumption is that the international political system is dominated by rationally acting and unitary states whose primary aim is to safeguard their national sovereignty and security.[9] Realists assume that in the steady pursuit of national security and sovereignty, states conduct cultural politics to ensure national unity and ideological power.[10] Supporters of **classic** anthropological theories confirm this view, in that they hold that cultures are territorially bound. According to the classic model, culture is "a flow of meaning in face-to-face relationships between people who do not move around much"[11]; thus, sociocultural relationships and interactions must be analyzed in a territorially defined framework.

Both models—the classic and realist views of culture—imply that nationally created and maintained cultural differences might function as barriers with respect to international interaction. Differing cultural contexts, it follows, considerably limit the capacity of individuals to communicate and cooperate. In light of these two views, cultural differences are likely to pose important obstacles for the management of cross-nationally operating companies. Says Fons Trompenaars, the well-known intercultural consultant, "Other cultures are strange, odd, even shocking. Mistakes and confusion are inevitable."[12]

By contrast, other views are emerging that argue for a more nuanced and dynamic view of culture as it affects the management of transnational firms. These include:

- **Management practices are converging globally.** As communication, financial, and technological barriers are reduced and local management practices are exposed to alternative management models, some believe national differences in business management will decline and cross-national business principles and practices will increasingly be accepted. In keeping with his global world order model, the anthropologist Arjun Appadurai sees a growing *denationalization of cultural identification* and a transnationalization of cultural identities.[13]

- **Transnational corporate identity and culture can be developed.** Given that culture is not territorially bound, transnational communication and intercultural experience arguably provide the foundation for building transnational corporate identity and culture. This view espouses a dynamic model, stressing that individuals identify with many groups of very different kinds at the same time—classified by gender, race, language, class, nationality, etc. "Each person," concludes Immanuel Wallerstein, "participates in many cultures."[14] Moreover, these multiple cultures are subject to constant change, because they are interpreted and constructed in daily interactions with their respective participants.[15]

- **Political variables determine cultural differences.** According to this view, national identities are deliberately constructed and redefined through the strategic interaction of leaders and interest groups—within and outside a country. It downplays the role of states in favor of transnational activities among nonstate actors.[16] Cultural politics is believed to serve national leaders, ensuring their interests.[17] Says Wallerstein: "The sense of identity . . . has been the outcome of conscious pressures of political forces occupying particular roles and seeking specific objectives within the development of the world-system. The 'peoples' of the modern world have not always been there. They have been created."[18] Consequently, political interaction among national elites and the degree of openness or closure of a country help explain differences in management practices.[19]

- **Loyalty is shifting to interest group affiliations.** Another view, termed "turbulence theory," premises the diminishing authority of the state. As globalization has reduced the options of governments over domestic and foreign policy, citizens have begun to question their civic duty toward state authorities and to redirect their loyalty. This change results in group identification and cultural association relating more to individual, subnational, and transnational interests than to socialization as a "national culture."[20] By the same token, the primary allegiance for managers is transferred more and more to the enterprise.

- **Individual differences may be outweighing national differences.** Finally, because the world is empowering individuals due to the increasing flow of people, ideas, and information, they have more choices in modes of conduct, attitudes, values, and careers. As a result, a wide variety of individuals with scarce skills—including management skills—may become part of a growing workforce with global demand. As such, their skills transcend national and cultural differences. This can readily be seen in the appointments of Carlos Ghosn and Howard Stringer to CEO positions at two very Japanese enterprises, Nissan and Sony. Ghosn has gone on to become CEO at Renault.

Although the five dynamic views of culture differ in their explanations of the socioeconomic transnationalization process, they all recognize that culture is the result of social interaction across networks and organizations extending beyond national boundaries. This interaction generates common standards for conduct and common systems of meaning, allowing individuals to identify with multiple groups and cultures. Within this framework, culture is subject to constant change in response to its environment instead of being static and territorially defined. As a result, says Ulf Hannerz, "We can contrast in gross terms those cultures which are territorially defined (in terms of nations, regions, or localities) with those which are carried as collective structures of meaning by networks more extended in space, transnational or even global."[21]

But Globalization Does Not Dictate Convergence in Management Practice

Numerous empirical studies, in particular within the field of human resource management, seem to contradict the hypothesis of global convergence in management practices. At the beginning of the 1990s a wide range of management tools as well as the leadership style of executives still seemed to be evaluated according to national standards of reference. In a study conducted in 1993, Smith and Bond found that different country measurements of appropriate leadership behavior could lead to almost opposite outcomes. Smith and Bond found, for instance, that the workers of some industrial assembly plants in the United States and the United Kingdom expected their superiors to manage personal problems of team members in a discreet and interpersonal manner, whereas workers of such plants located in Hong Kong and Japan considered it appropriate that all team members discuss the personal problems of each team member, while the latter was absent. The German multinational firm Otto Versand used a third approach by establishing special offices that assisted employees in coping with personal problems that could interfere with job efficiency.[22]

Other empirical studies conducted by Geert Hofstede[23] and Newman and Nollen[24] found that business performance depends on congruence between effective management practices and the respective national cultures. While Hofstede surveyed the financial performance of a sample of 176 work units of one large American company in eighteen European and Asian countries,

Newman and Nollen found that a participative leadership style results in higher output performance only when applied in countries with low power distance social relationships. Based on their findings, Newman and Nollen concluded, "Multinational enterprises need to adapt their management practices to the national cultures in which they operate in order to achieve high business performance."[25]

New managers in foreign countries must consider the degrees of trust and collaboration among colleagues when setting management style. An American executive newly arrived in Paris illustrates an example of intercultural barriers to communication and cooperation. In Lisa Hoecklin's book *Managing Cultural Differences*, the American executive describes the difficulties he encountered due to cultural differences between him and his French subordinates.[26] First, according to his view, he perceived a lack of trust at the workplace in France. Due to this lack of trust concerning work relationships, he had serious difficulties finding ways to motivate his subordinates. Neither praise nor criticism seemed to be received without suspicion or defensiveness from his French subordinates. From the American expatriate's perspective, this lack of trust between colleagues inhibited his French subordinates from collaborating on projects instead of implementing jobs individually. As a further cultural distinction, the American and French managers appeared to have different role perceptions of themselves. Whereas American managers seem to consider themselves skillful coordinators of resources and activities, it seems to the American executive that a French manager bases his authority on a superior degree of knowledge and competence. Decentralization in the United States and centralization in France, so concludes the American expatriate, are the logical consequences of these differences in role perceptions.

The German workplace is often characterized by growing employees through apprenticeships, developing broad consensus on many decisions, and supporting promotions more by internal networks than by outside university affiliation. Glouchevitch describes three outstanding features of the "German management model" which he perceives as uniquely German:

- The comprehensive apprenticeship system.
- The legally anchored and widely accepted framework of employee co-decision.
- The typical entrance and career advancement of management offspring.[27]

Glouchevitch depicts the German apprenticeship system as one aspect of the principle of social responsibility, which he perceives as a common value within German society. He asserts that the number of apprenticeships and financial resources that are invested in employee development are important criteria for societal evaluation of a German company. Glouchevitch also believes that this comprehensive apprenticeship system provides German companies with a comparative advantage vis-à-vis their worldwide competitors. This system produces skilled employees in the workshop and management floors and creates loyalty toward the employer, which in turn leads to high productivity and product quality. Additionally, the search for consensus to eliminate or prevent conflicts functions as a second component of German comparative advantage. Germany has a unique comprehensive incentive system to generate consensus, be it through "codecision," where employees are represented in the supervisory board of big companies, or in employee councils, which have considerable legal authority over working conditions in big and middle-sized German firms. Finally, Glouchevitch asserts that there is a considerable difference between Germany, the United States, the UK, and Japan when it comes to career advancement to middle and senior management. In Germany, highly qualified individuals do not attain management positions through university affiliations. Career advancement seems to be more reliant on building affiliations and networks within a company as the individual's career progresses.[28]

Box 13.1 ICI Developed a Successful Program to Reduce Barriers between Italian and British Employees

The British company Imperial Chemical Industries provides a good example of reducing the barriers to cross-cultural communication.[29] This case also illustrates how companies can gain a comparative advantage by tackling such problems through corporate learning. During the 1990s, Imperial Chemical Industries (ICI) started an initiative called Project Management in a Multi-Cultural Environment, to tackle communication problems encountered when British and Italian work units tried to collaborate. Guided by experts, British and Italian managers exchanged perceptions of the work attitudes and business culture of their respective colleagues. The British managers found their Italian counterparts excessively flexible, undisciplined, not very time-conscious, and averse to planning, but also considered them creative entrepreneurs. The Italians perceived their British colleagues as being obsessed with rules and procedures, inflexible, suspicious, slow and ponderous, but characterized them on the positive side as disciplined and good planners. Both groups then analyzed their ways of doing business and concluded that either way made perfect sense within their respective business environments. One Italian manager summarized, "Our Italian business environment requires us to struggle every day against turbulence, and therefore we need a flexible attitude. Operating according to the British methods and conventions can lead to a loss of opportunities. Worse, we would be dead in a few months."[30] From this workshop both the British and the Italians recognized the respective advantages of each other's management styles. Participants agreed to use the management style, or a mixture of styles, most appropriate to the nature of each joint project.

DIFFERING COUNTRY MANAGERS SHARE
SOME MANAGEMENT BEHAVIOR VALUES BUT
DIVERGE ON OTHERS

In research conducted in six Western nations and Japan, Itzhak Harpaz found that workers in each country, age group, and hierarchy group valued "interesting work" as their number one goal.[31] The results of an empirical study conducted by Bigoness and Blakely [32] provide less clear findings, but can also be referred to when researching value convergence. For their empirical research, Bigoness and Blakely had a total of 567 managers from twelve nations (with Japan as the only Asian representative) rank four groups of values describing the most desirable management behaviors. Managers from Japan attributed more importance to the first two value groups (clean, obedient, polite, responsible and cheerful, forgiving, helpful and loving) than managers from all other countries. Managers from the United States, the UK, and Japan attributed to the third value dimension (broadminded, capable and courageous) less importance than managers from the other countries. In sum, the results of the empirical study indicate convergence at large, with national differentiation in particular dimensions.

European Managers Have Created a "Common
Way of Being European" in Contrast to U.S.
and Japanese Counterparts

A comprehensive study by the European Round Table of Industrialists and the Groupe Ecole Supérieure de Commerce de Lyon found that, although differences in European management styles persist, the common history of Europe together with recent steps toward European integration have promoted a convergence of management practices within Europe. Interviews with 51 high-level managers from 40 large and internationally operating European, Japanese, and U.S. companies revealed common European management characteristics, in contrast to U.S. and Japanese counterparts. Major differences were noted about orientation toward people, internal negotiation, managing international diversity, and managing between extremes.[33] The first attribute of this common European management approach—orientation toward people—includes a common practice and legal obligation for social responsibility, high respect for individual fulfillment, and a high degree of individual freedom regarding task implementation.[34] The second feature of European management style—internal negotiation—demands that European managers explain and convince people and bargain with external and internal stakeholders.[35]

The third characteristic—managing international diversity—comprises respect for different management styles and market characteristics, frequently realized through decentralization of work units and integration through people rather than through structures.[36] The fourth feature of European management style—managing between extremes—describes the capacity of European managers to overcome tensions between individualism and teamwork, and short-term and long-term orientation as well as mutual loyalty between employee and firm (in-house training versus staff turnover). Although the authors do not expect a convergence of European management practices toward one homogeneous model, these characteristics demonstrate a common way of being European[37] in contrast to U.S. and Japanese managers.[38]

EXAMPLES OF EMERGING TRANSNATIONAL CORPORATE CULTURE

IKEA: Share the Values

To overcome barriers in cross-border communication and cooperation, companies have been increasing their efforts to create a strong transnational corporate mind set and culture. A good example is the case of the globally operating furnishing company IKEA.[39] Executive leaders of IKEA set clear guidelines in favor of the diffusion and reinforcement of IKEA's basic company values in business units worldwide. The objective is to motivate and guide Ikea through common values without having to rely on a central hierarchy. The management of IKEA hopes to involve the company's employees through consensus with the values of IKEA's founder: egalitarianism, simplicity, humbleness, hard work, and no waste. All organizational aspects from hiring procedures, employee formation, management guidelines, dress code, product design, and selling are in line with these basic values. For the selection of new staff, for instance, IKEA's human resource managers are instructed to find people who have similar values worldwide. As a follow-up measure, new employees are introduced to IKEA's corporate values in corporate development programs, including employee trips to the Swedish home of the company.

Elf Aquitaine: Unity through Professionalism

The French industrial conglomerate Elf Aquitaine overcomes intercultural communication barriers through a worldwide company culture primarily based on the technological superiority of all employees. Unity through professionalism as the strategy was formulated by the executive vice president of Elf Aquitaine Norway during the mid-1990s.[40] With the help of major programs in skill development and knowledge exchange, the management of Aquitaine has created a **community of skills** and group cohesion based on a common understanding of goals.

Hoffmann–La Roche: Strategic Planning Is Everybody's Business

Hoffmann-La Roche (HLR), a European pharmaceutical company, recently launched a corporate program to build a globally oriented mindset. Using an MBA-type curriculum, Hoffmann-La Roche has tried to blend management concepts and knowledge and to support high-potential managers in building their own transnational networks.[41] Another program to integrate managers worldwide is the broad involvement of many middle- and high-level managers in the company's strategic planning. This way Hoffmann-La Roche hopes to strengthen the identification of managers with the company as a "community of interests."[42] To facilitate companywide rotation of managers across borders, HLR installed a decentralized system of a free employment market with no barriers among divisions, countries, and functions. Managers are free to define recruitment policies within their units and yet also to apply for open positions within the company according to their preferences.[43]

Unilever: Strategy Is Corporate; Service Is Local

Multinational Unilever, whose product portfolio includes a wide array of consumer goods, is often considered the prototype of a truly transnational company because its managers worldwide share a common vision and understanding of the corporate strategy while at the same time respecting national markets and national consumer preferences. Elaborate recruitment policies, international job rotation, formal training programs, transnational project teams, and regular meetings built a common company culture in Unilever. All these tools were designed for the purpose of the so-called "Unileverization" of the company's employees.[44]

The move toward a common corporate culture began in the 1940s, when Unilever decided to hire local, in-country managers at its different country locations. Those managers felt an urgent need to build a common corporate culture as a means to improve cross-border cooperation and companywide unity. In the 1990s, Unilever opened an international management training college in the UK, where every year 300 to 400 managers from company sites all over the world are encouraged to think transnationally, share experiences, and build transnational networks. Similar to Hoffmann-La Roche, Unilever also resorts to job postings across companies, countries, and product lines, and conducts regular placements of managers in foreign subsidiaries. The transnationalization of the company also is reflected in the corporate structure that partly relies on centralized units like research, finance, and packaging, yet depends on the knowledge and competence of managers in decentralized units regarding local market product expertise. Additionally, product groups are divided into global fast food, international food, and national food groups. The directors responsible for a group of products work together in the form of an executive triad, with each responsible for profits in a specified group of countries. Unilever's high degree of transnationalization also shows in its senior management. The executive committee of Unilever comprises managers from seven different nations (July 2002).

The positive effects of a strong transnational company culture on the reduction of cross-cultural barriers are corroborated by some results of an empirical study conducted by Harrison, McKinnon, Wu, and Chow. The study found that although changing work teams contradicted the value system of their national culture, many Taiwanese employees adapted well to such teams because their employer promoted changing teams to create a company culture that facilitated project team operation.[45]

COMMON THREADS POINT TO A NEW PARADIGM

Management Practices Converge in EU Member Countries

Calori and Seidel explain the common components of a European management style based on the shared political history of the European peoples.[46] With the development of nation-states across Europe from the 1650s to the 1950s, Calori and Seidel observe increasing diversity in the cultural practices of European peoples. This diversity resulted from political actions taken by governments to unify the population ideologically.[47] Conversely, with the progressive integration of Western Europe through the formation of the European Common Market (now the European Union) in the 1950s, the authors observe an increasing convergence of management characteristics within the member countries. Calori provides the case of the small European countries the Netherlands, Belgium, and Luxembourg that corroborates the causal relationship between political action and convergence of cultural characteristics across countries. These countries opened much earlier to external influences than other European countries and, as a result, they now exhibit a blend of managerial practices.[48]

Chinese Managers Suffered Long Isolation

Considerable differences have been found in the views of Chinese and U.S. managers about effective management practices and motivational techniques. These differences have been attributed to the long-lasting, politically motivated isolation of Chinese society from Western influences during the postwar period until the late 1970s. Because of the political situation in China, most Chinese managers could not get involved in debates on new concepts of management theory, nor were they allowed to experiment with new management tools. The ensuing managerial style did not lend itself to globalization.[49]

Managers from Hong Kong and the United States Differ Strongly Only on Values Such as Social Hierarchy and Personal Virtue

The empirical study conducted by the Chinese Culture Connection[50] also supports the argument made by Wallerstein. Based on a framework of relevant Eastern values, the Chinese Culture Connection conducted a study aimed at finding potential differences in the values held by managers from Hong Kong and the United States. Significant differences in the managers' values were found for only one of the four tested value dimensions. This dimension comprised those values that reflect Confucian teachings like social hierarchy, protection of the status quo, and personal virtue. On three of the four tested value dimensions (integration, human-heartedness, and moral discipline), the study resulted in no measurable differences between the responses given by U.S. and Hong Kong managers. Ralston et al. explain this finding by the considerable exposure of Hong Kong to Western influences. As a British colony, so the authors argue, Hong Kong functioned within a similar legal and educational environment while at the same time still being influenced by Eastern cultural heritage.[51]

Common Interests Beat Culture

In her empirical research on national culture and the belief formation of managers, Lívia Markóczy finds that the strongest determinant of similarity among managers' beliefs was not the nationality of the respondents, but shared membership in a favored functional area within the organization.[52] Studying five organizations that operate in Hungary with substantial foreign participation, Markóczy observed that the managers of the functional area that had recently been promoted in organizational importance within the company, and therefore received a higher share of available resources, recognized their common interest of maintaining their privileged position and formed alliances to do so across nationalities. Markóczy found that managers from Holland, Belgium, the United States, the UK, Australia, and Hungary who worked in the promoted corporate unit developed similar beliefs about corporate goals, causal relationships, and strategies relevant to the success of their organizations. Markóczy ascribes this development of similar beliefs to the fact that the favored managers could realize improvement in their current situation and expect higher job security and chances to get promoted.[53] Although not as significant, Markóczy also finds a correlation between technical training as well as involvement in strategic decision-making and belief formation. She therefore concludes: Beliefs about what issues are strategically relevant and how these influence each other might be more affected by the existing strategic and political process in an organization or by the professional experience or training of managers than by their general national-cultural background.[54]

Individual Trumps Collective Identity

In their study on cultural differences concerning the values of U.S., Hong Kong, and Chinese managers, Ralston et al.[55] analyzed the relative contributions between groups (in comparison to within groups) for each of four value dimensions developed by the Chinese Culture Connection.[56] The authors of the study observed that individual differences between managers of the same national group accounted for a majority of the variance between country effects.[57] The results of the study have to be interpreted with caution because they could also indicate an increasing individualization of daily life experiences. Such individualization could be due to the fact, as suggested by the anthropologist Arjun Appadurai,[58] that the present world order is characterized by a constant flow of people, information, and ideas. We have not found any further empirical studies that corroborate or weaken the view that increasing individualization is occurring at the expense of group cultures.

MANAGEMENT LESSONS FOR TRANSNATIONAL ENTERPRISES

We conclude that a global convergence toward homogeneous management practices and values seems unlikely. Although there are indications that political and economic assimilation across countries is taking place in Europe, the results of present-day research corroborate the argument that considerable diversity will persist. Designers of organizational development programs for transnationally operating organizations should, therefore, create options for developing intercultural competence. Transnational organizations should implement educational programs to help employees overcome cultural differences in order to work together more efficiently.

The **creation of a transnational corporate identity and culture is possible**, as suggested by the cases of IKEA, Hoffmann-La Roche, Unilever, and other strongly globalized companies. The model IKEA chose for building its transnational corporate identity, however, has been criticized because it is so heavily oriented toward Swedish national culture. We agree that the simple transnationalization of a national culture across its borders might be accompanied by considerable losses to a company's creativity as well as its flexibility. The success of IKEA's strategy, that is, the one-directional transfer of the Swedish management model into other cultural environments, is rather surprising. The reasons for its success are not clear. Did the values IKEA chose for its transnational glue coincide accidentally with the values of a wide range of other national cultures? Or, are IKEA's values particularly susceptible to transnationalization and cultural convergence because they represent important values of our contemporary times and globalized world?

It is possible to make constructive use of cultural diversity. Diversity can considerably increase an organization's potential to perceive, interpret, and seize internal and environmental opportunities or prevent risks. Organizations that manage to use such potentials have better chances to perform well in an environment of global competition. Organizational development programs should, therefore, aim at creating a transnational corporate culture that institutionalizes methods and corporate values that favor the constructive use of cultural diversity. The methods employed by Unilever and Hoffmann-La Roche are illustrative: the rotation of employees across functions, departments, and countries; the installation of transnational project teams to tackle organizational challenges; an internal transnational employment market that encourages expatriation; and common educational programs for employees.

For us, **the dynamic concept of culture as social construct in constant change provides a better explanation of the present world order** than a rather static and territory-bound concept of culture. We found a few examples of empirical research that make use of political and economic factors to explain their findings; these studies corroborate the hypothesis of the political creation of culture. We support this argument. We recognize that culture has been and still is an important instrument in the struggle for economic and political power and survival between countries as well as within them. Politically and economically interested actors have been trying, with some success, to shape and change culture according to their interests. For the designers of organizational development programs, this carries a positive message: the above illustrated empirical examples that corroborate a dynamic model of culture also imply that corporate culture can be shaped and thereby be instrumental not only for the reduction of intercultural barriers to communication and cooperation, but also for the constructive use of intercultural diversity.

Although we found very few empirical analyses of interest-based group affiliation versus association according to nationality, the considerable weight of interests in the formation of groups and alliances has been strongly confirmed in many other areas of social science, particularly within the realm of economic theories on organization.[59] Organizational developers who support the argument for interest-based group affiliation should be aware that organization members have to have an interest in the values and practices of the corporate culture they are intended to identify with; to this end, a constructive incentive system must be established. Other variables, such as the degree of international experience and similar versus different educational backgrounds should also be considered.

We would like to make two final remarks concerning further empirical research on this subject. First, we conclude that past analyses might have neglected variables that could be of considerable relevance for the explanation of differences and similarities in management styles and values across nations. Researchers who base their empirical studies on a dynamic concept of culture ought to take more seriously the recent increase in cross-cultural experiences of organizations as well as the potential for organizational learning. For the analysis of differences and similarities in management styles, variables like **degree of international experience, similar versus different educational backgrounds, weak or strong corporate culture, similar or different business environments that implicate greater or less border-crossing activity,** and finally, **external changes that alter or have altered the environment of companies** could be of great relevance. Including such variables in statistical tests of theories could show that the explanatory power of national culture for determining managerial values, beliefs, and practices is itself a function of some of the above-mentioned variables. Second, we have observed that for the empirical analysis of values, attitudes, and management tools, empirical results might be easier to evaluate when interviews and questionnaires are based on the comparison of statements with respect to situational descriptions rather than on single-word concepts, which leave wide room for individual interpretation.

NOTES

1. David Morley and Kevin Robins, *Spaces of Identity: Global Media, Electronic Landscapes, and Cultural Boundaries* (London, New York: Routledge, 1995), 17.

2. Kenichi Ohmae, *The End of the Nation-State: The Rise of Regional Economies* (New York, London, Toronto, Sydney, Tokyo, Singapore: Free Press, 1995), 30.

3. Ibid., 38.

4. Stuart Hall, "The Local and the Global: Globalisation and Ethnicity," in Anthony King, *Culture, Globalization and the World-System: Contemporary Conditions for the Representation of Identity* (Binghamton, NY: Macmillan Education Ltd., 1991), 27.

5. Mike Featherstone, "Localism, Globalism, Cultural Identity," in Rob Wilson and Dissanayake Wimal, *Global—Local: Cultural Production & the Transnational Imaginary* (Durham, London: Duke University Press, 1996), 63.

6. Zdravko Mlinar, "Individuation and Globalization: The Transformation of Territorial Social Organization," in Zdravko Mlinar, *Globalization and Territorial Identities* (Brookfield, Hong Kong, Singapore, Sydney: Avebury, 1992), 15.

7. William J. Drake, "Territoriality and Intangibility: Transborder Data Flows and National Sovereignty," in Daarle Nordenstrend, and Herbert I. Schiller, *International Communication in the 1990s* (Norwood, NJ: Ablex Publishing, 1993), 286.

8. Mlinar, "Individuation," 2.

9. The classical works are by Hans J. Morgenthau, *Politics among Nations: The Struggle for Power and Peace* (New York: Knopf, 1950); Kenneth Neal Waltz, *Man, the State and War: A Theoretical Analysis* (New York: Columbia University Press, 1959); and Stanley Hoffmann, "Obstinate or Obsolete? The Fate of the Nation-State and the Case of Western Europe," in *Daedalus* 95 (1966): 892–908.

10. Jongsuk Chay, *Culture and International Relations* (New York; Westport, CT; London: Praeger, 1990), 267.

11. Ulf Hannerz, "Scenarios for Peripheral Cultures," in King, *Culture, Globalization,* 117.

12. Fons Trompenaars, *Handbuch Globales Managen: Wie man kulturelle Unterschiede im Geschäftsleben versteht, deutsch von Werner Grau* (Düsseldorf, Wien, New York, Moskau: Econ Verlag, 1993), 251.

13. Arjun Appadurai, "Disjuncture and Difference in the Global Cultural Economy," in Mike Featherstone, *Global Culture: Nationalism, Globalization and Modernity: A Theory* (Culture & Society special issue) (London, Newbury Park, New Delhi: Sage Publications, 1990), 295–310.

14. See Immanuel Wallerstein, *Geopolitics and Geoculture: Essays on the Changing World-System, Studies in Modern Capitalism* (Cambridge: Cambridge University Press, 1991), 158.

15. Michael Carrithers, *Why Humans have Cultures: Explaining Anthropology and Social Diversity* (Oxford, New York: Oxford University Press, 1992), 9.

16. Leslie Sklair, *Sociology of the Global System,* 2d ed. (London, New York, Toronto, Sydney, Tokyo, Singapore et al.: Simon & Schuster International Group, 1991), 6–10 and 31–37; Stephen Gill, *Gramsci, Historical Materialism and International Relations,* 1st ed. (Cambridge: Cambridge University Press, 1993), passim; or Susan Strange, "The Retreat of the State: The Diffusion of Power in the World Economy," *Cambridge Studies in International Relations* 49, Cambridge University Press (1996): passim.

17. Immanuel Wallerstein, *The Modern World System* (New York: Academic Press, 1974); Anthony D. Smith, "Towards a Global Culture?" in *Theory, Culture & Society* 7 no. 2 & 3 (1990): 71–93, and Benedict Anderson, *Imagined Communities: Reflections on the Origin and Spread of Nationalism* (London: Verso, 1983).

18. Wallerstein, *Geopolitics,* 141.

19. Ibid., 158.

20. R.B.A. Di Muccio and James N. Rosenau, "Turbulence and Sovereignty in World Politics: Explaining the Relocation of Legitimacy in the 1990s and Beyond," in Mlinar, *Globalization and Territorial Identities,* 60–76.

21. Ulf Hannerz, "Cosmopolitans and Locals in World Culture," in Featherstone, *Global Culture,* 239.

22. Philip Glouchevitch, *Juggernaut. The German Way of Business: Why It Is Transforming Europe—and the World* (1992; Spanish translation, Santiago de Chile: Andrés Bello, 1993), 31.

23. Geert Hofstede, *Culture's Consequences: International Differences in Work-Related Values* (Newbury Park, CA: Sage, 1980).

24. Karen L. Newman and Stanley D. Nollen, "Culture and Congruence: The Fit between Management Practices and National Culture," in *Journal of International Business Studies* 27, no. 4 (1996): 753–80.

25. Ibid., 754.

26. Lisa Hoecklin, *Managing Cultural Differences: Strategies for Competitive Advantage* (Wokingham, England: Addison-Wesley, 1995), 12–13.

27. Glouchevitch, *Juggernaut,* 135–37.

28. Ibid., 167.

29. Hoecklin, *Managing Cultural Differences,* 18–20.

30. Ibid., 20.

31. Itzhak Harpaz, "The Importance of Work Goals: An International Perspective," *Journal of International Business Studies* 21, no. 1 (1990): 75–93.

32. William J. Bigoness and Gerald L. Blakely, "A Cross-National Study of Managerial Values," in *Journal of International Business Studies* 27, no. 4 (1996).

33. Roland Calori, Jean-Paul Valla, and Philippe de Woot, "Common Characteristics: The Ingredients of European Management," in Roland Calori and Philippe de Woot, *A European Management Model: Beyond Diversity* (Hertfordshire: Prentice Hall International, 1994), 31.

34. Ibid., 32–36.

35. Ibid., 36–38.

36. Ibid., 38–44.

37. Philippe de Woot, "Towards a European model of management," in Calori and de Woot, *European Management Model*, 261.

38. Dominique Turcq, "Is There a U.S. Company Management Style in Europe?" in Calori and de Woot, *European Management Model*, 83–111; and Etsu Yoneyama, "Japanese Subsidiaries: Strengths and Weaknesses," in Calori and de Woot, *European Management Model*, 112–31.

39. Hoecklin, *Managing Cultural Differences*, 57–60.

40. Ibid., 63–64.

41. Tugrul Atamer, Pancho Nunes, and Michel Berthelier, "Integrating Diversity: Case Studies," in Calori and de Woot, *European Management Model*, 214.

42. Ibid., 219.

43. Ibid., 230.

44. Floris A. Maljers, "Inside Unilever: The Evolving Transnational Company," *Harvard Business Review,* no. 92506 (1992): 1–7.

45. Graeme L. Harrison, Jill L. McKinnon, Anne Wu, and Chee W. Chow, "Cultural Influences on Adaptation To Fluid Workgroups and Teams," in *Journal of International Business Studies* 31, no. 3 (2000): 498.

46. Roland Calori and Fred Seidel, "The Dynamics of Management Systems in Europe," in Calori and de Woot, *European Management Model*, 55–78.

47. Wallerstein, *Modern World System*; and Wallerstein, *Geopolitics.*

48. Roland Calori, "The Diversity of Management Systems," in Calori and de Woot, *European Management Model*, 21.

49. James P. Neelankavil, Anil Mathur, and Yong Zhang, "Determinants of Managerial Performance: A Cross-Cultural Comparison of the Perception of Middle-Level Managers in Four Countries," in *Journal of International Business Studies* 31, no. 1 (2000): 134.

50. Chinese Culture Connection, "Chinese Values and the Search for Culture-Free Dimension of Culture," in *Journal of Cross-Cultural Psychology* 18 (1987): 143–64.

51. David A. Ralston, David J. Gustafson, Priscilla M. Elsass, Fanny Cheung, and Robert H. Terpstra, "Eastern Values: A Comparison of Managers in the United States, Hong Kong, and the People's Republic of China," in *Journal of Applied Psychology* 77, no. 5 (1992): 664 and 669.

52. Lívia Markóczy, "National Culture and Strategic Change in Belief Formation," in *Journal of International Business Studies* 31, no. 3 (2000): 427–42.

53. Ibid., 437.

54. Ibid., 438.

55. Ralston et al., *Eastern Values*, 664–71.

56. Chinese Culture Connection, "Chinese Values."

57. Ralston et al., *Eastern Values*, 667–69.

58. Appadurai, "Disjuncture."

59. Mancur Olsen Jr., *The Logic of Collective Action* (Cambridge: Harvard University Press, 1971).

14

Ethics and Corporate Social Responsibility

J. DAVID MORRISSY

During the last two decades, phenomenal growth in the globalization of business and a corresponding increase in ethical conflicts faced by multinational firms such as Nestlé (infant food formula controversy), Lockheed (problem of bribery), Union Carbide (Bhopal tragedy), Mitsubishi (sexual harassment), Ford-Bridgestone/Firestone (tire crisis), Royal Dutch Shell (environmental controversy), Nike (sweatshop conditions in Southeast Asia), Enron, ImClone, Adelphia, Tyco, Qwest, Global Crossing, and WorldCom (accounting irregularities and fraud), Johnson & Johnson (falsification of data to cover lapses in the manufacture of Eprex), and McDonald's (exploitation of workers and human health) have spurred research interest in international business ethics.[1]

GLOBAL CAPITALISM ENTAILS MORAL IMPERATIVES

The number and magnitude of ethical lapses by multinational firms evoke a troubling question: is globalization infusing a Gresham's law of competitive amorality into world markets, whereby bad corporate practices threaten to drive out good corporate practices in a disastrous "race to the bottom"? Global managers must reevaluate their corporate ethical and social responsibilities and reassess the competencies they need to direct the global competitive "race to the top."

To grapple with the issue of responsible global capitalism (RGC), in 2002 John H. Dunning invited fourteen scholars of economic and social issues to participate in "exploratory ventures into relatively new territory," namely, "the moral imperatives of global capitalism."[2] He directed the group's efforts to discern a "set of ethical standards—both general and specific to RGC—to which all participants must adhere." The difficulty of this quest is underscored by the essays of two of Dunning's contributors, who write that Islamic and Buddhist views undercut the validity of the assumption of global capitalism. One, reflecting an Islamic perspective, acknowledges global capitalism as "a reality only in the sense of the global reach of Euro-American capitalism."[3] The other, a Buddhist, characterizes the money culture of capitalism as being contrary to his culture, which does not view income and wealth as the primary criterion of well-being.[4]

FOUR DIMENSIONS OF CORPORATE
SOCIAL RESPONSIBILITY

Corporations that enter into the global market, regardless of country culture or economic orientation, must act responsibly. Corporate social responsibility (CSR) has multiple facets that go beyond ethical standards; it must also focus on the rightness of corporate relations with respect to economic, legal, and discretionary responsibilities.[5]

- **Ethical responsibilities:** The firm's duty to abide by the society's core ethical values concerning right and wrong behavior.
- **Economic responsibilities:** The firm's duty to make a profit and generate wealth, to produce and distribute goods and services, and to provide employment and income for workers.
- **Legal responsibilities:** The firm's duty to obey the law.
- **Discretionary responsibilities:** The firm's duty to use its resources for social betterment in ways of its own choosing.

Challenge: Ethical Responsibilities

The root meaning of the Greek word "ethics" is custom, the way people behave that is taken as a standard or "a principle of right or good conduct" (*American Heritage Dictionary*). The ethical challenge is more daunting in a global environment in which corporations and their managers must operate in multiple cultures where ethical values are diverse and the informal observance of them is even more disparate. Maria Joseph Christie, S.J., describes culture as "a shared set of meanings and standards by which the members of society regulate their lives," and adds that "culture plays a significant role in the ethical reasoning and ethical attitudes of a person."[6] Therefore, global managers of corporations operating in different cultures around the world must adapt their corporate ethical guidelines to accommodate various cultures while maintaining consistency in the ethical values practiced by all parts of the corporation.

Challenge: Economic Responsibilities

Beyond ethical duties, corporations have responsibilities to the economies in which they operate, although the extent of those responsibilities has long been debated. Adam Smith relied on the "invisible hand of the marketplace" to fulfill those responsibilities. Nonetheless, he acknowledged that businessmen accept a further responsibility, up to a point: "Every individual endeavors to employ his capital . . . in the support of domestic industry; provided always that he can thereby obtain the ordinary, *or not a great deal less than the ordinary* profits of stock" (emphasis added).[7] Milton Friedman's more rigid doctrine asserts that "there is one and only one social responsibility of business—to use its resources and engage in activities designed to increase its profits" and that "acceptance by corporate officials of a social responsibility other than to make as much money for their stockholders as possible . . . is a fundamentally subversive doctrine."[8]

Peter Drucker countered that "Friedman's 'pure' position—to eschew all social responsibility—is not tenable. . . . Business and other institutions of our society . . . cannot be pure, however desirable that may be. Their own self-interest alone forces them to be concerned with society and community and to be predisposed to shoulder responsibility beyond their own main areas of task and responsibility."[9] Konosuke Matsushita, the eponymous founder of the Japanese global electronics company, agreed, writing in 1931 that "the mission of a manufacturer is to overcome poverty, to relieve society as a whole from the misery of poverty and bring it wealth . . . not simply to enrich the enterprise, but all society."[10] Professors Steven L. Wartick and Donna J. Wood expand the societal relationship of business and government into the international context: "Business organizations convert inputs to outputs to satisfy society's material needs and wants *within a context created by government activities.* Business-government relations, then, are a central focus of business and society analysis, whether in a single nation or internationally" (emphasis in original).[11]

Today the international dimension of economic responsibilities challenges global corporations because the numerous countries in which they operate are governed by differing economic regimes with varying compliance expectations. Achieving social responsibility is even more internally challenging for transnational corporations with globally dispersed autonomous units, each exercising specific functional decision-making for the corporation as a whole.

Growing intolerance for corporations that exploit the workforce or environment of poor countries in order to escape from the regulatory standards of their own industrialized home countries has fired up demonstrators against the World Trade Organization (WTO) in Seattle and at later WTO meeting sites. Organizers have focused pressure on such diverse niches in the marketplace as college bookstores—for selling sweatshirts and athletic shoes at prices 50 to 100 times the one or two dollars paid to workers in Asian sweatshops[12]—and

DeBeer's diamond exhibitions, where demonstrators have protested to protect the homeland game reserve of Kalahari tribesmen in Botswana.[13] Some activists have discovered that such exploitation overseas is in violation of U.S. laws. The perception of complicity in human rights violations has landed a number of U.S. firms with household names—Coca-Cola, DelMonte, Occidental Petroleum, ExxonMobil, ChevronTexaco, Citigroup, and Bank of America—as defendants in cases filed in U.S. courts under the Alien Tort Claims Act, an obscure 214-year-old statute once used to combat piracy.[14] Although some of the cases may seem frivolous, five of them are against firms operating in Colombia, where 90 percent of the murders of union leaders worldwide have taken place.

Challenge: Legal Responsibilities

In 2000 the Sicilian capital of Palermo was chosen to host a major UN conference on crime prevention because of the symbolism of that city's wresting cultural hegemony from the Mafia in the previous decade. UN efforts, however, have not fully curbed global lawlessness, neither in its member governments nor in organized crime syndicates. As a result, crime prevention remains a formidable challenge for managers in both domestic and international markets. In 2005, Jeffrey Garten estimated that illegal trade amounts to $1 trillion, about 10 percent of global trade, largely in narcotics smuggling ($900 billion), but also substantial amounts in illicit weapons sales ($10 billion), cross-country dumping of toxic wastes ($12 billion), smuggling women and children for sex exploitation ($7 billion), and pirated movies and stolen art ($6 billion).[15] Global crime is a tenacious adversary for individual countries. UN researcher Michael Johnson describes how this hazard increases the vulnerability of both governments and global corporations:

> Because the agents of cross-border corruption are capable of doing business almost everywhere, it is difficult to hold them accountable anywhere. . . . Even when domestic governments or international organizations decide to confront the problem, their finite resources and limited mandates may not be a match politically or economically for powerful interests, often working in secret . . . sustained by illegal trafficking in money, drugs, technology, arms, and human beings.[16]

Observing laws in various countries with different legal systems may lead to conflicting practices (bribery, money-laundering, interest payments, and subsurface mineral rights, among others). Where unethical practices are prevalent, globally as well as domestically, corporations encounter what Johnson characterizes as two types of "especially worrisome" countries that managers must learn to cope with and ultimately help transform.[17]

The first type comprises the "source" countries of cross-border corruption, which are home to the mafias, drug cartels, and other outlaw enterprises that peel off a small share of their take for host government leaders who provide legal and political protection at home and abroad. Former World Bank president James Wolfensohn described such corruption as a disease that soon infects legitimate domestic and international transactions of governments and business.[18] Prime candidates for bribery are the arms and technology industries and international construction and contracting firms, in which a relatively small "contribution" can win a multimillion-dollar contract.

The second type emanates from the "vulnerable" countries that are economically and politically weak, dependent on external markets and technology, and rife with domestic corruption. Worrisome countries diminish their potential for sustainable growth and threaten to infect traditional trade and investment flows. A study by Jakob Svensson finds a "strong relationship between income and corruption" and that "corrupt countries have significantly lower levels of human capital stock, proxied by years of schooling of the total population aged over 25 years."[19] Consulting firm A. T. Kearney also finds a negative correlation between government corruption and openness to external competition or globalization, reporting that "investors perceive public officials and politicians as less corrupt in more globalized countries such as Singapore, Finland, and Sweden but more underhanded in closed countries such as Indonesia and Nigeria."[20]

The CSR domain that pertains to corporate legal responsibilities requires managers to obey the laws that evolve from a country's governance—"organized activities primarily intended to structure society by defining and enforcing the 'rules of the game' that apply to everyone, and legitimizing certain exceptions to those rules."[21] However, global managers operate in many different countries and are challenged by the multiple legal systems that are grounded in different cultural traditions—some secular and some religious. Legal frameworks based on religious beliefs present a challenge to managers who try to reconcile the procedures of their corporate secular-based operations with practices based on religious tenets.

The tenets of Islam, for example, are the basis for *shari'ah* that defines legal procedures for the 1.3 billion people of Islamic faith. One tenet involves gender discrimination in ways that are troubling for global managers because it violates the UN Declaration of Human Rights and the equal employment opportunities laws of the home countries of many multinational companies. Not all Islamic nations impose gender discrimination as their official policy; Turkey has not done so since the founding of its secular government under Kemal Ataturk in 1926. Many nations do discriminate, but characterize their gender practices as preferential treatment of women.

Corporations face a difficult choice. On the one hand, if they advise their female employees to disregard local rules, their female employees' effectiveness may be sharply reduced or their physical safety put at risk. On the other hand, if managers reduce a female employee's tasks to suit local custom, she may successfully claim in court in her home country that her rights were violated.

Challenge: Discretionary Responsibilities

Economists R. E. Freeman and J. Liedka stake out a visionary position: "Corporations are places in which both individual human beings and human communities engage in caring activities that are aimed at mutual support and unparalleled human achievement."[22]

As a domain of CSR, discretionary, or philanthropic, responsibility is the duty to contribute to social betterment along the lines of the corporation's own choosing. Taken collectively, the needs, especially those of the developing countries, are limitless—corporate resources, however, are not. Therein lies the challenge. How, without jeopardizing their corporate competitiveness, are global managers to allocate a portion of their resources for social betterment, a goal that is the most expansive and arguably the least compelling of the CSR domains? Why? How much? To whom? And for what purpose?

Even with corporate earnings well beyond survival, that is, average rates of return, some economists, notably Friedman, believe those earnings belong to the stockholders and should not be subject to a manager's or a board's arbitrary disposition. Further, they assume that if the owners wish to be philanthropic, they could do so out of their own personal earnings. Some wealthy entrepreneurs have done just that, for example, Alfred Nobel, Henry Ford, and Bill Gates, who wanted to return something to society by, respectively, promoting world peace, sponsoring studies of public issues, and combating disease worldwide. Corporations are also donors; however, according to a 2005 PricewaterhouseCoopers study, their contributions are more focused on community and corporate benefits such as satisfying employee wishes (56%), networking (54%), and attracting clients (27%).[23] The question of how much is still a matter of discretion. There is no standard for calibrating the metrics of philanthropy because the unmet needs of the world community are boundless.

PARADIGM SHIFT—CSR HAS WORLDWIDE AND STRATEGIC IMPLICATIONS

Corporations are being forced to reassess whether their access abroad to low-wage workforces and unprotected environments is a bargain devoid of any CSR liabilities. Managers must be as ready to acknowledge corporate responsibility for potential risks in host countries as they would in their home countries. Failure to remedy problems early on has led to enormous accumulated damages and, in some cases, arraignment on criminal charges in host-country courts. India took Union Carbide to court after its plant in Bhopal blew up in 1984, although local officials were negligent in their inspections of safety measures such as scrubbers, a cooling system, and auxiliary containment tanks that had been left inoperable. As a result, hot toxic gases spewed over 25 square miles, killing 3,000 residents and seriously injuring another 40,000.[24]

In assessing the incident, Wartick wrote: "The impact of Union Carbide's Bhopal disaster was only worsened by the company's initial offer to compensate victims at the rate of $100 per death and $5 per injury, an apparently reasonable rate for the local culture, but an outrageously low rate in light of world public opinion."[25] Twenty years later, victims were still owed compensation, whereupon an outraged Indian court ordered in 2005 that payments be made without further delay.

As managers gain broader experience in globalized markets, they are wise to recognize that they must adhere to their host countries' values just as conscientiously as they would their own parent country's values. Creating jobs is an economic social responsibility of business, and deference to a country's employment policies is essential. When Hewlett-Packard (HP) abruptly decided to cut 1,240 jobs in France in 2005, it was pressured to change its decision with the admonition that companies "must respect the territory in which they operate and the people they work with." As a result, HP subsequently reconsidered its decision and reduced the number of workers to be terminated by 300.[26] In contrast, IBM cut a similar number of jobs that year with no fanfare because it had consulted with the government and the trade unions.

Firms, therefore, must now assess their corporate social responsibilities according to their *worldwide* dimensions in all of their domains—ethical, economic, legal, and discretionary. Managers of the 63,000 enterprises that control 821,000 subsidiaries in 145 WTO member countries are drawn into cross-border perspectives on social responsibilities that increasingly replace the stovepipe perspective that once characterized the distance between corporate parents and their affiliates in matters relating to host governance, culture, and human relations. Annual mergers and acquisitions collectively valued at between $2 trillion and $3 trillion, and particularly individual megadeals (175 in 2000) valued at more than $1 billion, add intensity to the fusion of corporate social responsibility.[27]

The size and world-class competencies of merged firms result in such complex configurations of large autonomous corporate components in many countries that it is difficult to designate any single one of them as the parent company. For example, transnational organizational formats are evolving with a virtual suite of executives whose core functional responsibilities are dispersed to countries endowed with an advantage in that expertise. The *Financial Times* reported that Sanofi-Aventis has adopted the following multicountry research model: "A typical drug development path at Sanofi would be to discover an idea in Italy, send it to Hungary for chemical work, then do preclinical development in the UK, before completing clinical work in the US."[28] Some companies structure their core functions permanently in multicountry settings. Table 14.1 depicts how three technology industries distribute their core functional responsibilities around the world in a permanent transnational format.

TABLE 14.1. Technology Companies with Globally Dispersed Core Function Responsibilities

Technology Company	Headquarters	Engineering	Marketing	Manufacturing
Logitech International	Switzerland	—	Silicon Valley	Taiwan
Trend Micro	Tokyo	Taiwan	Silicon Valley	—
WIPRO	Silicon Valley	India	Silicon Valley	—

Source: "Borders Are So 20th Century," *Business Week* (September 22, 2003): 68–73.

To the extent that acquisitions or alliances involve mature foreign firms, the diverse ethical and cultural orientations of the executives of the acquired subsidiaries may be in conflict with those of the acquiring corporation. As firms become transnational, acquisitions and affiliates may be so large that they operate as quasi-autonomous units setting worldwide standards for certain functions within the corporation's CSR. CSR practices relating to human rights or environmental protection that are considered acceptable in the acquisition or host country may be flagrantly unethical or even illegal in the acquiring corporation's country. The parent company's managers may not only lose some control of their acquisition's practices, but also risk being implicated in practices contrary to the corporation's principles of social responsibility.

Regional trade agreements are drawing separate national economies together into larger economic entities while still moving toward closer integration in their governance. Managers need to study the various modes of access to, and the levers of influence with, the negotiating teams to discern any changes in negotiating strategies and to track the progress being made by the teams. The EU is fifty years in the making and its approach to lobbying government is shifting from an indirect public affairs approach to one of direct appeals to the politicians in charge of the issues in Brussels.[29]

MANAGERIAL COMPETENCIES

The challenges that thwart a corporation's fulfilling its social responsibilities are made more complex by the scope of globalization. These challenges demand of managers a new set of competencies beyond those required for ethical leadership in one's home-country operations.

Ethical Responsibilities Call for Strong, Culturally-Sensitive Leadership

Managers must possess strong charismatic leadership to influence the ethical behavior of their employees around the world in order to counter the competing reality of the practical ethical lessons their employees learn on the job. Through direct exchanges with superiors, peers, and subordinates, employees soon learn to what extent an informal set of ethical standards exists in offices and on the plant floor. According to one study of four thousand employees, it is these standards that influence the employee's perceptions of how official ethical policies are observed, violations are sanctioned, and the actual level of ethical compliance is shaped. The study found that 10 percent of the employees reported that they follow their own value systems; another 10 percent acknowledged that they would exploit situations in contravention of ethical standards, provided the penalty would be less than the benefit, and the risk of being discovered is low. In the other two sets of 40 percent each, one set would always try to observe company policies; the other set would go along with the work group, skirting ethical compliance if that happened to be the group norm.[30] Therefore, as much as 90 percent of these employees' observance of corporate ethics is grounded in the perceived ethical charisma of corporate executives, and 10 percent is due to the power of sanctions.

A corporate manager's expectations regarding ethical compliance must always be available to the global workforce, typically through a corporate code of ethics. In addition, independent communication channels are needed to ensure employees of privacy in reporting violations. In 1994, H. Vernon-Wortzel estimated that 90 percent of the *Fortune* 500 companies and half of the smaller firms had codes for employee guidance on functional business areas.[31] Codes can vary in length; as a guide for managers, the U.S. Sentencing Commission outlines seven minimal requirements for establishing an organization's ethical compliance program (see Box 14.1).[32] The first three relate to developing standards, appointing responsible personnel, and delegating discretionary authority. The fourth states the need for communications through publications and training programs. The last three requirements deal with surveillance, enforcement, and sanctions to ensure compliance.

Since the 1990s, proactive managers of multinational corporations have been distributing business codes that include but go beyond ethical compliance codes to convey in writing to each and every worker and to every

---

Box 14.1 Minimum Requirements for Ethical Compliance Programs

1. Standards and procedures such as codes of ethics, reasonably capable of detecting and preventing misconduct
2. High-level personnel responsible for ethics compliance programs
3. No substantial discretionary authority given to individuals with a propensity for misconduct
4. Effective communication of standards and procedures via ethics training programs
5. Establishment of systems to monitor, audit, and report misconduct
6. Consistent enforcement of standards, codes, and punishments
7. Continuous improvement of the ethical compliance program

stakeholder group the corporation's commitment to social responsibility. Muel Kaptein, who has studied the codes of 200 of the largest multinationals from 17 countries, finds that only 105 firms from 17 countries could supply business codes for his intensive study and evaluation.[33] Kaptein states that "a business code is a policy document that defines the responsibilities of the corporation toward its stakeholders and/or the conduct the corporation expects of employees."[34] He notes that "most corporate codes, whether extensively or concisely, pay attention to consumers, investors, employees, society and the natural environment."[35] According to one study of CSR and the Internet, "The most successful firms describe their corporate social responsibility on the World Wide Web" in order to provide stakeholders worldwide with access to corporate CSR statements.[36] In decreasing order, the principles cited most frequently for dealing with stakeholders were transparency, honesty, fairness, empathy, stimulating stakeholders to raise concerns, accountability, and dialogue.[37]

With corporate ownership crisscrossing the globe, managers and particularly CEOs are forming a class of "executives without borders." They have acquired a special competence in managing at high levels their corporation's social responsibilities in multicultural settings. These borderless executives possess a "worldly mindset" that J. Gosling and H. Mintzberg describe as derived from "landing in different places . . . [they] join a plurality of world-views [in] a world made up of edges and boundaries like a patchwork."[38] Is this class of executives reaching out through employees, clients, and suppliers likely to reduce the differences in cultural values that underpin ethical orientations across borders? To some extent, the homogenization of cultural values is fueled by such business associations and catalyzed by the rapid spread of telecommunications media and mechanisms. However, cross-cultural sensitivity will remain a requisite management competency as long as cultures remain so diverse. Even if a corporation's global workforce was totally acculturated to its commercial environment, the ethical responsibilities of global managers would still extend to their dealings with local stakeholders who remain steeped in their own idiosyncratic value systems for decades to come.

In decades past, executives assigned to international posts returned to their home posts to find their career paths lagging behind their domestic cohorts. Today, assignments with executive decision-making experience overseas not only build up their international social capital, but also function as fulcrum points that leverage careers upward. Sir Howard Stringer, the Welsh-born CEO of U.S. Sony Corporation, was chosen by Sony's board to be chairman and CEO over Sony's native visionary, Ken Kutaragi.[39] Stringer's first steps in his mission to shake up the Japanese corporate icon were tempered by his understanding of Japanese culture. He had to limit his first cut to ten thousand employees, far less than he and Wall Street analysts thought adequate. Siemens's recently retired CEO, Heinrich von Peirer, agrees that his own transformation at Siemens began with his partial immersion overseas, particularly in America. It charted the route for future CEOs like current chairman Klaus Kleinfeld, who was chosen because of his U.S. and other international management experience. Von Peirer admits that his Americanization of Siemens stemmed from adopting management methods he learned from GE's CEO Jack Welch. However, von Peirer was culturally sensitive and avoided "neutron" Jack's penchant for job-cutting because it was antithetical to Germany's management and labor codetermination culture, in which 50 percent of a company's supervisory board is elected by workers.[40] He learned how to translate his highly nuanced German into the Wall Street analysts' simple declarative sentences under the brusque tutelage of an investment banker on road shows promoting the listing of Siemens on the New York Stock Exchange.

Beyond real-world exposure across the globe, managers need special intellectual cross-cultural competency that enables them to learn from academic studies and research that supplement the vivid lessons learned on the ground. A conceptual understanding of many cultures can be gained more efficiently through such studies than through travel. For instance, the theoretical insights gained through the study of different cultures by Geert Hofstede can help managers understand, or at least anticipate, idiosyncratic responses to ethical issues that arise in those cultures.[41] Hofstede measured the values of 116,000 IBM employees from fifty countries along four value dimensions (Power Distance, Individualism/Collectivism, Masculinity/Femininity, and Uncertainty Avoidance). The value responses (see Table 14.2) do not measure the ethical probity of the respondents or of their cultures, but rather suggest orientations that underlie responses to certain ethical issues. The following define Hofstede's value dimensions with examples of how each might lead to ethical conflicts.

Power Distance: This value measures the degree of acceptance of inequality in the dispersion of authority within organizations. A high score reflects a preference for hierarchical management-exercising authority through many strata of supervisors, each with limited discretionary authority. Obedience to superiors can be so ingrained that subordinates might be inclined to follow a superior's directives, even if they are perceived to be unethical. Low scorers prefer flatter organizational charts, seek less guidance, and regard authority as an intrusion from above.

Individualism/Collectivism: High scorers have a preference for self-reliance and relative emotional detachment from their organizations, particularly distant units, and may be regarded as mavericks ready to embark on solutions or initiatives that are inconsistent with corporate practices and policy guidance. Low scorers prefer to seek group consensus and value cooperation, loyalty, and seniority. Favoritism based on kinship or social relations is preferred to arm's-length dealings in business, which can lead to practices such as nepotism, anticompetitiveness, insider trading, and cronyism.

Masculinity/Femininity: High scores reflect an inclination toward aggressive, competitive values, and forceful pursuit of demanding targets with

TABLE 14.2. Scores on Four Value Dimensions

Country	Power Dist.	Individ/ Collect.	Masc./ Femin.	Uncert. Avoid.	Country	Power Dist.	Individ/ Collect.	Masc./ Femin.	Uncert. Avoid.
Argentina	49	46	56	86	Malaysia	104	26	50	36
Australia	36	90	61	51	Mexico	81	30	69	82
Austria	11	55	79	70	Netherlands	38	80	14	53
Belgium	65	75	54	94	Norway	31	69	8	50
Brazil	69	38	49	76	New Zealand	22	79	58	49
Canada	39	80	52	48	Pakistan	55	14	50	70
Chile	63	23	28	86	Panama	95	11	44	86
Colombia	67	13	64	80	Peru	64	16	42	87
Costa Rica	35	15	21	86	Philippines	94	32	64	44
Denmark	18	74	16	23	Portugal	63	27	31	104
Ecuador	78	8	63	67	S. Africa	49	65	63	49
Finland	33	63	26	59	Salvador	66	19	40	94
France	68	71	43	86	Singapore	74	20	48	8
Germany	35	67	66	65	Spain	57	51	42	86
Gr. Britain	35	89	66	35	Sweden	31	71	5	29
Greece	60	35	57	112	Switzerland	34	68	70	58
Guatemala	95	6	37	101	Taiwan	58	17	45	69
Hong Kong	68	25	56	29	Thailand	64	20	34	64
Indonesia	78	14	46	48	Turkey	66	37	45	85
India	77	48	56	40	Uruguay	61	36	38	100
Iran	58	41	43	59	U.S.	40	91	62	46
Ireland	28	70	68	35	Venezuela	81	12	73	76
Israel	13	54	47	81	Yugoslavia	76	27	21	88
Italy	50	76	70	75	Regions:				
Jamaica	45	39	68	13	E. Africa	64	27	41	52
Japan	54	46	95	92	W. Africa	77	20	46	54
S. Korea	60	18	39	85	Arab Countries	80	38	53	68

Source: Geert Hofstede, *Cultures and Organizations* (1997), collated from pp. 87, 99, 123, and 141.

little regard for relationships among the group apart from achieving the targets. Low scorers are concerned about nurturing the relationships of those engaged in a group effort, and are not related to gender discrimination within a culture.

Uncertainty Avoidance: High scores reflect an intolerance of uncertainty and a preference for rules, planning, and standard operations that are documented and explicit. The management style is formal, focusing on planning, implementing, and controlling, and less receptive to innovation or improvisation. Low scorers prefer taking risks to achieve high performance, finding detailed ethics regulations too constricting.

Hofstede's research results can offer managers a more dynamic understanding of a country's cultural responses to ethical issues by plotting two or more values for selected countries on the same graph. For example, if one plots scores for individualism/collectivism and uncertainty avoidance against each other, the result suggests the differences in the degree of receptivity that ethical compliance and business codes may receive. Hofstede explains that "whereas in strong uncertainty-avoidance individualist countries, rules will tend to be explicit and written. In strong uncertainty-avoidance collectivist countries, rules are often implicit and rooted in tradition."[42] This latter group "will tend to eliminate intergroup conflict by denying it and either trying to assimilate or repress minorities." However, collectivist countries with weak uncertainty avoidance "may contain different groups, with strong group identities, but are more likely to find a modus vivendi in which the groups tolerate and complement each other."[43]

Hofstede also concludes from that evidence that "collectivism is the rule in our world, and individualism is the exception,"[44] and further that "large power distance countries are likely to be more collectivist . . . in which people are dependent on in-groups . . . *usually* also dependent on power figures" (emphasis in original). This tendency can foster a strong sense of camaraderie within a corporation's affiliate overseas, but it should also be taken as a cautionary signal that in the broader context of host country governance cronyism may be prevalent.

Economic Responsibilities Require Enterprises to Respect Human, Governmental, and Environmental Resources

CSR's economic domain enjoins corporations to make a profit and, in doing so, to generate wealth by producing and distributing goods and services that create jobs and income for societies. The forces of globalization are driving corporations to unbundle the components of their value chains and disperse their links in developing countries that eagerly welcome their investments as a means of promoting their own emerging economies. As a result, corporations have similar economic responsibilities to these host countries as they do to their own home countries, that is, to respect their host countries' human, governmental, and environmental resources.

A basic competency that managers need in order to fulfill this responsibility is a deep conviction that their roles can be constructive and not derailed by corrupt governance intent on exploiting their human and physical resources. N. Bowie and P. Vaaler, two ethicists who support a global collegial approach to CSR, suggest that "linkages among national markets . . . will promote a consensus against many forms of discriminatory behavior and encourage competitive 'race to the top' standards . . . by most ethically rigorous MNCs."[45] Many managers, however, are concerned that, regardless of how lofty their corporate standards are, they must compete with corporations that are

TABLE 14.3. Differential Socioeconomic Traits of Workers in Growing and Lagging Economies

	Average Percent GDP Growth (1990–1998)	Percent Males Completing Fifth Grade	Percent of Population Earning Less than $1/day
Rapid Growth	8.1	97	7.5
Lagging Growth	3.6	64	34.1

Source: "Global Capitalism," *Business Week* (November 6, 2000): 78.

"ethically challenged" and, as a result, they can be drawn into a race not to the top but a race to the bottom that is mired in an economy of sweatshops and environmental pollution.

The Asian tigers have shown the world by their rising productivity and living standards that the race, if not to the top, is one of substantially raising the bottom. China's wages for textile workers rose from $50 a month in the mid-1980s to $250 a month by 2000 according to one eyewitness report.[46] Table 14.3 compares four rapidly developing countries (Chile, China, Malaysia, and South Korea) with four countries (Guatemala, India, Nigeria, and South Africa) that lag in development The negative correlation between levels of education and levels of earnings per day and GDP growth reveal, not surprisingly, the driving force of the race to the bottom for some countries. With education, workers' competency and productivity rises, making the countries' industries and workforces more competitive. And success induces sweatshop workers to migrate to higher-paying industries. The interindustry migration potential puts upward pressure on wages, forcing sweatshop owners to seek new sources of low wages in other countries in a proverbial race to the bottom.

Managers must understand the roles that national and international governments and nongovernmental organizations (NGOs) can play in helping reverse the competitive race to the bottom. The corporation that is alone in raising its standards finds itself vulnerable and noncompetitive. Competent managers working with local governments, regional government associations, UN agencies, NGOs, and other stakeholders can spur changes not only in labor conditions, but also in dealing with other CSR areas such as health and environmental hazards. Influencing government officials in host countries to raise the regulatory standards for wage and work conditions for all competing industries may reduce industry resistance. Host country officials, however, may balk, fearing that raising labor costs could trigger an exodus of companies going offshore in search of lower-wage countries.

Therefore, managers will need to urge host countries to work with each other to set common standards globally, or at least regionally. Managers will also need to be flexible and persistent in pursuing the support of like-minded NGOs and stakeholders to rid world markets of unacceptably harsh competitive wage and work conditions. Activist NGOs and concerned stakeholders, using global-intensive media scrutiny, have already aroused public antipathy in the marketplace against sweatshop producers of textiles, apparel, and footwear that could not be ignored. On a cooperative voluntary basis, corporations such as Levi Strauss, Nike, Salomon AG, Reebok International Ltd., Liz Claiborne, Gap Inc., Toys 'R' Us, and Mattel Inc. have responded by putting programs in place to monitor their contractor production sites for violations of worker rights.

NGOs can perform a dual function. First, they can work to convince host governments that the following internationally recognized worker rights should be locally enforced:

- The right of association
- The right to organize and bargain collectively
- Prohibition on the use of any form of forced or compulsory labor
- Minimum age for employment of children
- Acceptable conditions of work with respect to minimum wages, hours of work, and occupational safety and health[47]

Second, NGOs can pressure domestic retailers who attempt to circumvent worker rights by sourcing in countries that do not respect or enforce worker rights. For example, antilogging groups concerned about the impact of denuded forests on local native livelihoods, as well as on the global climate, have demonstrated at lumber outlets such as Lowe's and the Home Depot to win their support for monitoring logging operations overseas. Earthworks, a mine watchdog group, has demonstrated against the metal-mining companies that have built up vast mounds of cyanide-laced rock that resemble "the near equivalent of nuclear waste dumps that must be tended in perpetuity," with cleanup costs estimated at $54 billion for U.S. sites alone.[48] Seventy percent of gold is mined in developing countries "in ways that would never be tolerated in wealthier nations, such as dumping tons of waste into rivers, bays and oceans."[49] Earthworks picketed New York jewelers in a "No Dirty Gold" campaign. As a result, Tiffany's chairman committed his company to buy gold only from a mine that does not use cyanide.

Global managers need to be aware of the wider role that courts are now playing in countering practices that devastate physical and economic environments. The courts of developed and developing nations have charged corporations with the cost of cleaning up the environment decades after the damage was done. This happened to GE in 2005 for dumping polychlorinated biphenyl (PCB) into the Hudson River decades earlier. In cases where companies have gone bankrupt or have lacked sufficient funds to finance the cleanup, societal victims of pollution have sued directors of the polluting companies for compensation. Similarly, those who suffered losses due to Enron's and WorldCom's failures have won court cases against the directors of these companies by forcing them to pay $13 million and $18 million, respectively, out of their own funds to settle the claims against their companies."[50]

Legal Responsibilities Require Managers to Respect and Strengthen the Rule of Law

Managers must understand political governance in order to fulfill their corporate legal responsibility when a host country is incompetent or corrupt in administering the law. Global managers who have executive experience in several countries can help improve the legal environment by appraising the elements of the country's ethical infrastructure, namely:

• Political commitment
• Effective legal framework
• Accountability mechanisms
• Professional socialization mechanisms
• Public service conditions conducive to ethics
• Ethics-coordinating bodies
• Public involvement and scrutiny by active civil society

Beyond a solid ethical infrastructure, the Organisation for Economic Co-Operation and Development (OECD) warns that the "mission statements of an agency should communicate values in order to internalize them within the agency's professionals and communicate to the public the importance the agency places on the values."[51] Making the expected standards visible to the public is a prerequisite for building trust in public institutions as is issuing an ethics code, imposing criminal sanctions on active and passive corruption, requiring officials to report misconduct, and protecting whistle-blowers.

Managers can draw on OECD and UN efforts aimed at improving ethics-based management in the developing world in cosponsored international conferences and publications. One such effort is the 1997 United Nations Development Programme (UNDP) conference results published in *Corruption & Integrity Improvement Initiatives in Developing Countries*.[52] In some cases, managers participated in the efforts of multilateral organizations to extend the sphere of ethically committed countries. When the East European members of the OECD shifted from a communist system to a capitalist system and needed assistance in designing and implementing the elements of an ethics-based management infrastructure, the OECD undertook an outreach program called SIGMA—Support for Improvement in Governance and Management—to jump-start their ethics management infrastructure.[53] The program provided assistance in preparing civil service legislation, adopting independent audits and financial controls, drafting public procurement legislation, and initiating transparency mechanisms.

Managers' efforts to enhance the legal environment will enable their corporations to function more efficiently by reducing the heavy burden of corruption in the marketplace. Transparency International attests to the pervasiveness of corruption in the surveys it conducts and publishes in its annual Corruption Perceptions Index a ranking of each country from a high of 10 to a low of 1.[54] An A. T. Kearney study produced an Index of Globalization that reveals the costly impact of corruption. Developing countries that reduce corruption and nurture freedom achieve a higher degree of globalization and attract the lion's share of private-sector investment flowing to developing countries.[55]

Corporate managers must support the efforts of their governments and those of other nations to establish a global bulwark against individual country lapses and international crime syndicates. The U.S. experience in combating bribery suggests that changes in the laws of one country can be the basis for making unethical business practices illegal in other countries and can raise the level of ethical observance among all countries. This process was demonstrated by the U.S. enactment of the Foreign Corrupt Practices Act (FCPA) in 1977 that outlawed bribery as a crime at home and abroad. In February 1999, after two decades of urging by the United States, twenty-five OECD member governments along with Argentina, Brazil, Chile, Slovakia, and Bulgaria made bribery "punishable by effective, proportionate and dissuasive criminal penalties comparable to bribery of domestic officials."[56] The measure's intent was to target governments' greatest ethical concern, namely, the "supply side" of corruption, the area in which the private sector influences public officials who have discretionary decision-making authority.

State-owned enterprises in the developing world can also be a common source of corruption and therefore are increasingly targeted for privatization. Managers can provide advice to help governments in privatizing their public corporations to help ensure that the privatizations conform to WTO disciplines such as the Agreement on Government Procurement and Article XVII of the General Agreement on Tariffs and Trade (GATT) on State Trading Enterprises. Advice on the key features of such transactions can help governments meet the following criteria for privatizations:

- Competition to discipline costs and pricing
- Transparency to ensure fair treatment for all participants
- Independent judicial procedures to penalize those involved in criminal violations of the free-market system[57]

Discretionary Responsibilities Incorporate Socially Beneficial Goals into Business Objectives

A growing number of advocates for corporate philanthropy reject Milton Friedman's severe proscription on philanthropy and argue that corporate managers can actually increase their corporation's profits by creatively funding good causes. This school of CSR thinking is espoused by L. Lawrence Embley in his 1993 book *Doing Well While Doing Good.*[58] He argues that cause-related marketing offers an effective link between business enrichment and its obligation to nonprofit causes. Global managers who pursue this objective choose socially beneficial goals that are related to their corporations' business objectives. For example, American Express ran an advertising campaign that tied the use of its credit card to contributions to fund the restoration of Ellis Island and the Statue of Liberty. Embley notes that "product and services pitches now directly incorporate themes such as the environment, individuals with disabilities, illiteracy, education, and pure emotional sentiment."[59] Corporate assistance must be genuine to prevent such good works from being characterized as clever marketing in effect and hypocritical in intent. Embley warns that corporate advertisers who abuse this approach do not escape the scrutiny of watchdog groups like the Council of Economic Priorities. The Council reverses any benefits won falsely by publicly identifying such companies and unveiling their hypocrisy.[60]

CONCLUSION

If market capitalism is to thrive as a constructive force in the global economy, a common framework must evolve for the principles of corporate social responsibility with which all countries can comply despite their sharply diverse cultural underpinnings. The challenge of shaping such a global discipline falls initially to the main leaders of market capitalism, that is, the managers of transnational enterprises. Their performance will be judged according to the four dimensions of CSR: ethical, economic, legal, and discretionary. Their success will depend on appreciating the cultural heritage of each country and devising ways that adapt to the commercial traditions of each country while adhering to the global CSR framework. To ensure that global enterprises observe their CSR responsibilities, their managers must implement effective ethics compliance programs, complete with codes, monitors, and sanctions. To encourage all nations to comply with a global CSR framework, transnational managers need to adopt *an attitude and a strategic posture* that commits their corporations to work with their trade associations, host governments, and nongovernmental organizations to collectively raise CSR standards to improve the human, governmental, and environmental conditions of the world.

NOTES

1. Maria Joseph Christie, Ik-Whan Kwon, Philipp Stroebel, and Raymond Baumhart, "A Cross-Cultural Comparison of Ethical Attitudes of Business Managers: India, Korea, and the United States," *Journal of Business Ethics* 46 (2003): 263–87.

2. John Dunning, *Making Globalization Good* (Oxford: Oxford University Press, 2003), 8, 13.

3. Ibid., 198.

4. Ibid., 242.

5. Steven L. Wartick and Donna J. Wood, *International Business and Society* (Malden, MA: Blackwell Publishers, 2000), 75. See also A. B. Carrol, "The Four Faces of Corporate Citizenship," *Business and Society Review* (1999): 100–101, and "A Three-Dimensional Conceptual Model of Corporate Social Performance," *Academy of Management Review* 4 (1979): 497–505.

6. Christie et al., "Cross-Cultural Comparison," 264.

7. Adam Smith, *The Wealth of Nations* (New York: Modern Library, 1937), 421.

8. Milton Friedman, *Capitalism & Freedom* (Chicago: University of Chicago Press, 1962), 133.

9. Peter F. Drucker, *Management: Tasks, Responsibilities, Practices* (New York: Harper & Row, 1974), 349.

10. Tanri Abeng, "Business Ethics in the Islamic Context," in Georges Enderle, ed., *International Business Ethics: Challenges and Approaches* (Notre Dame, IN: University of Notre Dame Press, 1999), 239.

11. Wartick and Wood, *International Business*, 44.

12. "Global Capitalism: Can It Be Made to Work Better?" *Business Week* (November 6, 2000): 86.

13. "Protest of Botswana's Bushmen Kicks Up Dust," *Financial Times* (September 28, 2005): 6.

14. J. Forero, "Rights Groups Overseas Fight U.S. Concerns in U.S. Courts," *New York Times,* June 26, 2003, A3.

15. Jeffrey E. Garten, "The Pirates of Global Trade," *Business Week* (October 10, 2005): 130.

16. Michael Johnson, "Cross-Border Corruption: Points of Vulnerability and Challenges for Reform," *Corruption & Integrity Improvement Initiatives in Developing Countries* (New York: United Nations Development Programme and the OECD Development Center, 1998), 13–15.

17. Ibid., 16.

18. Ibid., 132.

19. Jakob Svensson, "Eight Questions about Corruption," *Journal of Economic Perspectives* (Summer 2005): 27.

20. A. T. Kearney, Inc., "Measuring Globalization," *Foreign Policy* (January–February, 2001): 61.

21. Wartick and Wood, *International Business*, 23.

22. R. E. Freeman and J. Liedka, "Corporate Social Responsibility: A Critical Approach," *Business Horizons* (July–August 1991): 93.

23. Hubert B. Herring, "Why Do Companies Give Money Away? Count the Reasons," *New York Times,* November 13, 2005, Section 3, 2.

24. Alfred A. Marcus, *Business & Society: Ethics, Government, and the World Economy* (Boston: Irwin, 1993), 631.

25. Wartick and Wood, *International Business*, 69.

26. *Sydney Morning Herald*, November 11, 2005.

27. Medard Gabel and Henry Bruner, *Global Inc.: An Atlas of the Multinational Corporation* (New York: New Press, 2003), 32.

28. A. Jack and M. Arnold, "Beyond the US: Sanofi-Aventis Finds Strength in a Multicultural Research Model," *Financial Times* (October 17, 2005): 8.

29. *Financial Times* (October 3, 2005): 8.

30. O. Ferrell, J. Fraedrich, and L. Ferrell, *Business Ethics: Ethical Decisionmaking and Cases,* 5th ed. (Boston: Houghton Mifflin, 2002), 156.

31. H. Vernon-Wortzel, *Business and Society: A Managerial Approach* (Boston: Irwin, 1994), 145.

32. Ferrell et al., *Business Ethics,* 179.

33. Muel Kaptein, "Business Codes of Multinational Firms: What Do They Say?" *Journal of Business Ethics* 50 (2004): 17.

34. Ibid., 13.

35. Ibid., 18.

36. J. Snider, R. Hill, and D. Martin, "Corporate Social Responsibility in the 21st Century: A View from the World's Most Successful Firms," *Journal of Business Ethics* (2003): 48, 184.

37. Kaptein, "Business Codes," 21.

38. J. Gosling and H. Mintzberg, "The Five Minds of a Manager," *Harvard Business Review* (November 2003): 58.

39. D. Pilling and M. Nakamoto, "Sony Chief Wields His Axe with Sensitivity," *Financial Times* (September 26, 2000): 23.

40. T. Stewart and L. O'Brien, "Transforming an Industrial Giant: An Interview with Heinrich von Pierer," *Harvard Business Review* (February 2005): 3.

41. Geert H. Hofstede, *Cultures and Organizations: Software of the Mind* (New York: McGraw-Hill, 1997), 128.

42. Ibid.

43. Ibid., 129.

44. Ibid., 54.

45. N. Bowie and P. Vaaler, "Universal Moral Standards," in Georges Enderle, ed., *International Business Ethics: Challenges and Approaches* (Notre Dame, IN: University of Notre Dame Press, 1999), 169–71.

46. Nicholas Kristof and S. WuDunn, "Two Cheers for Sweatshops," *New York Times Magazine* (September 24, 2000): 71.

47. U.S. Trade Representative, *2002 Annual Report,* 51.

48. J. Perlez and K. Johnson, "Behind Gold's Glitter: Torn Lands and Pointed Questions," *New York Times,* October 24, 2005, A1, A10, A11.

49. Ibid.

50. K. Eihenwald, "Ex-Directors of Enron to Chip in on Settlement," *New York Times,* January 8, 2005, B1.

51. J. Bertok, *Trust in Government: Ethics Measures in OECD Countries* (Paris: Organisation of Economic Co-Operation and Development, 2000), 18.

52. United Nations Development Programme, *Corruption & Integrity Improvement Initiatives in Developing Countries* (New York: United Nations Development Programme and the OECD Development Center, 1998).

53. Ibid., 27, 79.

54. Internet address: www.transparency.org/cpi/2005/2005.10.18.cpi.

55. A. T. Kearney, Inc., "Measuring Globalization," 56–64.

56. S. Rose-Ackerman, *Corruption and the Global Economy: Corruption & Integrity Improvement Initiatives in Developing Countries* (New York: United Nations Development Programme and the OECD Development Center, 1998), 27.

57. U.S. Trade Representative, *2003 Trade Policy Agenda*, 35.

58. L. Lawrence Embley, *Doing Well While Doing Good* (Englewood Cliffs, NJ: Prentice Hall, 1993).

59. Ibid., 66.

60. Ibid., 67.

Conclusions

An Emerging Global Management Paradigm

CLARENCE J. MANN

M anagers of enterprises with global agendas are caught in the middle between the forces and counterforces of globalization. This "squeeze play," delineated in the Overview, presents enterprises with opportunities and challenges. Due to the nature of the global environment, the two are inextricably linked. Opportunities arise as new markets open, technologies converge and disseminate, new suppliers and sources of capital and talent become accessible, and enterprises find it possible to add value to their products and services through networks of international alliances. These opportunities will multiply over the next three to four decades as global markets and the world economy expand more than tenfold to encompass $90 to $130 trillion in global commerce.

Enterprises face challenges as they try to seize these opportunities. The economic forces that largely are driving globalization run up against infrastructural and institutional constraints as well as political and cultural boundaries residing within and among the two hundred diverse countries that make up the highly fragmented nation-state system. Governments are focused on serving national interests, which often are at odds with the free play of forces at work in the global economy. While a wide variety of very significant international institutions exists to bridge these differences—such as the World Trade Organization (WTO), the International Monetary Fund (IMF), the World Bank Group's Multilateral Investment Guaranty Agency (MIGA), and a host of inter- and nongovernmental regulatory and coordinating organizations as well as bilateral and regional agreements and facilitating protocols and practices—they operate largely at the behest of the nation-state system.

In order to thrive in this emerging global environment, enterprises and their managers must deliberately embrace and constructively integrate both the forces and counterforces of globalization. Only through this embrace, akin to a bear hug, are managers likely to grasp and deal realistically with the opportunities they discern. This is the distinctive role of managers, for—taken together—these forces define the playing field of global business. But it is a role that requires a distinctive mindset and the willingness to act on it in the midst of the ambiguities and complexities of the global business environment. What has been learned about this mindset?

TEN TOUCHSTONES OF AN EMERGING MANAGEMENT PARADIGM

Managers of global enterprises need to adopt new perspectives on literally every business function. These perspectives are framed by a broader management paradigm or mindset through which events, information, and tasks are processed and understood. Many aspects of this emerging paradigm have been identified in the literature to date, but they need to be drawn together to appreciate their far-reaching impact on management thinking. Nor is this mindset simply ancillary or an "add-on" to existing management practices, for the forces at work in the global environment are interdependent and pervasive. Existing management techniques, concepts, and methods remain relevant in large part, but their application and the outcomes they serve need rethinking. Thus, traditional market analysis must adapt to the impact of cultural nuances on consumer tastes, purchasing habits, and promotional techniques. These are lessons Wal-Mart has had to learn, sometimes the hard way, as it expands into such diverse markets as Argentina, Indonesia, Brazil, and Germany.

In other cases, however, the shift in thinking entails **new management modes**. This is true for marketing managers, who now must be concerned as much about a firm's upstream capabilities as the marketing and sales side. The shift, as Dell's customized business model readily exemplifies across the world, is from "make and sell" to "sense and respond." Marketing management is now joined intimately with supply chain management. They are but two sides of the same coin. Moreover, firms who have tailored their management practices to a country-specific environment may need, like Nissan and Renault, to build an elaborate collaborative process that bridges their cultural and operational differences—thereby enabling them to carry out a common alliance strategy.

Drawing insights from the various chapters, the emerging management paradigm can be seen through a sketch of ten prominent features. The features discussed here are by no means exhaustive, but simply indicate how managers must think differently about their tasks in order to function effectively in the global environment.

1. Global Perspective

Opportunities do not arise in a vacuum. They are the product of insight and capabilities that others don't possess. Opportunities bring challenges, which may stymie an enterprise from cost-effectively implementing its business model. Challenges arise in the form of institutional limitations, bottlenecks, or cultural practices in the marketplace or larger environment. In the highly diverse global economy, moreover, challenges for firms often include the absence of appropriate institutions and accepted practices that would enable or minimize the risks to a firm's operations. Ironically, opportunities may arise precisely because an institutional weakness or void creates a need that businesses can fill, just as Federal Express and UPS supplement state postal services with more rapid and reliable international delivery.

Given the dichotomy between opportunities and challenges, a global perspective provides managers with a decisive advantage. By monitoring market and industry trends across the world in terms of their firms' capabilities, managers can glean clues of how their industry and markets are changing and can determine which opportunities make sense. This is in large part the message of chapters 1, 8, 9, and 10, which advocate a holistic understanding of how enterprises come to terms with their larger environment and how they capture and employ knowledge strategically. Piecemeal or superficial analyses, often the product of checklists, tend to blind managers to underlying insights of how markets are evolving and societies are changing.

For this reason, too, managers of accounting and finance functions need to broaden their perspectives beyond the numbers and appreciate how the interplay of national tax and accounting systems and practices around the world is creating a more transparent and potentially more accountable business environment (chapters 9 and 10). Similarly, while the transnationalization of corporate culture is becoming a real possibility (chapter 13), it needs to be supported by an emerging "class of executives without borders" who possess a "worldly mindset" (chapter 14). Given enduring aspects of country cultures and differences in regulatory regimes, firms with global agendas are by no means converging toward a uniform approach, but they are recognizing that corporate strategy needs to incorporate social benefits and respect social values from a wide variety of corporate venues.

2. Four-Tiered Industry Environment

At every step of operations, managers need to navigate their way through four environments: global, regional, national, and local. These tiers represent a complex layering of policies, regulations, allied interests, distribution channels, consumer standards and preferences, and sales & services, ranging from the most global to the most local aspects of a firm's operations. While trade barriers have fallen steeply across the world, most cross-border activity is in fact regional rather than global. The European Union and the North American Trade Association demonstrate this fact. But even this regional dominance is shattered by such national giants as the United States, Japan, and the emerging markets of China and India (chapter 5).

Moreover, no industries are either fully global or entirely local. Highly global industries like oil may be subject to the "law of one price," but even then supply is largely in the hands of OPEC member state governments while consumption depends heavily on a wide variety of local and national tax policies and subsidies. Predominantly local industries like medical and restaurant services, by contrast, must reckon with international price fluctuations and the availability of inputs, including the labor force. An accurate understanding of any industry, especially during the next three decades or so, requires an appreciation of which aspects of an industry are influenced primarily by global, regional, national, or local conditions. This is particularly critical to the marketing and supply chain functions that run the length of the value chain. Managers will need to track all four dimensions carefully and how they interact with each other economically, politically, and culturally.

3. Competing by Reinventing the Industry

In the decades following World War II, it was perhaps accurate to define competition in terms of firms within industries. The pace of technological change and convergence, however, has transformed this dynamic—from beating the competition to reinventing the industry (chapter 1). The obvious examples are as legendary and diverse as McDonald's, Sony, Starbucks, Wal-Mart, Apple, Microsoft, Netscape, and Google.

The global diffusion of technology has broadened and complicated this picture even more as centers of excellence arise from once-marginal economies around the world. In light of recent legislation strengthening patent protection for knowledge-based products, for instance, India is becoming a powerhouse in the software and very likely the telecommunications, pharmaceutical, and medical fields. Microsoft and Nokia as well as General Motors all have research facilities there. In manufacturing, China is becoming dominant in appliances and consumer electronics. The growing purchasing power of emerging countries with major populations, moreover, offers new market and product development opportunities. Alcatel, for example, consolidated its extensive telecommunications interests in China into one of six global Alcatel research and innovation centers, thereby establishing China as a major pillar of its world R&D and sourcing network. Equally intriguing, given the advances in information technology and communications, today's villages are rapidly becoming both viable production centers and attractive markets (chapter 2). Firms building business models to address these needs are generating global industries of the future.

4. Three-Dimensional Integrative Strategy

In the complex global environment, strategy is not simply concerned with achieving objectives, but with enabling the enterprise to thrive holistically as an organization. Three defining characteristics of the global environment—**unremitting innovation** through technological advances; the political, cultural, and institutional **diversity among countries**; and **intensifying competition** worldwide—require enterprises to integrate the technological, organizational, and transactional dimensions of strategy. On an ongoing basis, as discussed in chapter 1, firms need to balance productivity with innovation, geographical dispersion of assets with coordinated decision-making, and the development of core competencies with the support of reliable value networks. A change in the value trade-off for any one of these three dimensions affects the other two. An appropriate balance among them—which varies for each enterprise—in turn enables firms to achieve productive performance; access to markets, resources, and factors of production; and the ability to focus in depth on sustaining competitive advantage. Due to the fragmented nature of the legal environment, however, the emphasis on innovation necessarily skews this balance in favor of partnering firms and countries that respect and protect intellectual property (chapters 5 and 6).

Well-formulated strategy acts as a lodestar, providing firms with both foresight and a point for rallying widely dispersed and culturally diverse managers around a common vision. For this reason, strategic thinking permeates the value chain and every chapter in this book, being as essential for human resource selection and development (chapters 4 and 12) as for marketing, supply chain and knowledge management (chapters 2, 3, and 8). It is a key quality for leadership at every level of the organization. Seen as a continuing process for assessing an enterprise's value proposition and rethinking its direction, strategy guides enterprise growth and renewal in a complex environment.

5. Continuously Evolving Future of the Enterprise

Because the process of globalization is decades long and will vary by industry, each firm will need to pace itself in terms of the forces driving globalization. This implies an evolving vision, value proposition, and the core competencies that accompany them (chapter 1). The one predictable component of these aspects is continuing change. Major successes like Microsoft and Intel repeatedly have improved, extended, and shifted their value propositions over the years as changes in technology and competition indicated.

As these changes occur, they may upend cherished values and traditions. Siemens, for example, was forced to accept that Chinese engineers at its R&D center outside Beijing could design and produce a cellphone more cost-effectively, and in keeping with Siemens standards and the Chinese market, than could Siemens engineers in Stuttgart. Firms' evolving futures, therefore, are likely not only to reshape their value propositions, but to re-configure the scope and location of their operations, their supply chains, and their workforce around the world.

6. Multilevel Dispersed Functions

The geographical fragmentation of the world among two-hundred-odd countries, each with its own regulatory regime, institutions, and cultural heritage, presents insuperable obstacles to firms that seek to reduce their business models to a global "one size fits all." So, despite the temptation to streamline operations globally, most cross-border activity remains regional, for logistically and culturally a firm's region tends to offer the most familiar and accessible market. Even within their regions, firms must respond to the de-mands of national governments and to local cultures and distribution systems.

To effectively compete, therefore, managers need to think simultaneously in terms of a four-tiered industry environment and configure their operations accordingly. This entails multilevel business functions and decision-making that are centralized at some levels and decentralized and geographically dis-persed at other levels (chapter 1). At the global level, for instance, emphasis may be placed on strategy, investor relations, finance, and corporate culture, while supply chains and production may be aggregated more around regions and marketing and sales focused more at the national and local levels. But the configuration of activities and functions will vary from industry to industry and firm to firm. Many major brands and logos, such as "Coca-Cola," are promoted globally, leaving other aspects of the value chains (e.g., bottling plants) to be sited nationally or even locally. Likewise, supply chains for scarce resources or highly specialized components may be structured and coordi-nated globally, while supplier relationships are managed locally. However functions are configured, they require good channels of communication and carefully defined coordination throughout the organization.

7. Collaborative Ethos

Paradoxically, intensifying competition in the global economy calls on firms to pursue more collaborative management practices. This is required both internally among affiliates and their employees and externally with suppliers and even competitors. Internally, the collaborative ethos is driven by the recognition that competitive advantage today depends largely on recruiting well-qualified knowledge workers, engaging them well in productive and in-novative work, enhancing their skills, and retaining them for the long term. For this reason enterprises also need systems in place that reward collabora-tion among their affiliates. This ethos is personified by consensus-building leaders such as Carlos Ghosn (chapter 11), who brought Nissan back from the edge of bankruptcy and shaped a valuable alliance with Renault. It is also critically needed in the daily activities of global teams—often interfacing on-line—whose members from diverse cultures, work ethics, and learning styles pool their differences to achieve innovative outcomes (chapter 12). In this context, "managing global teams is a team effort." This is why facilitation plays such a vital role.

Also important for external relations, firms and their leaders need to be open to collaboration as they build value networks up- and downstream. The number of alliances has mushroomed into the hundreds of thousands during the last decade, a sure sign that partnering has become a way of life. Alliances require managers to shift their thinking and style from hierarchical to hori-zontal or **relationship management**. Above all, relationships are built on trust. Trust among partners is not mere wish, but based on mutually beneficial objectives, clear channels of communication, ongoing accountability, and ap-propriate operating standards and systems that link the partnering organiza-tions. Healthy trust recognizes that alliances have boundaries, for partners are independent firms with their own goals, operating parameters and intellectual property. Indeed, in some respects they may be competitors, or potentially so. Certain aspects of partnering firms, therefore, are likely to be off limits. And because alliances are costly, especially in management resources, they should be measured and periodically assessed against a cost/benefit metric suitable to (and possibly different for) each partner. Relationship management has a style and rationale of its own.

8. Open Systems Thinking

Systems thinking is a cornerstone for management in the global environ-ment. It is both a mental discipline for seeing the whole and a mode of analysis, as discussed in chapter 1, that enables managers to track relation-ships and see patterns of change rather than static "snapshots." It teaches, in effect, that the environment is a dynamic interplay of economic, political, and cultural forces, and that all actions and behavior have consequences, some of which are unforeseen, too complex, or too remote to be adequately assessed when decisions are taken. It requires, as Peter Senge argues, a systems lan-guage to replace our linear vocabulary in order to visualize and build feedback processes into decision-making. For these several reasons, strategy-making must be understood as a cyclical process with periodic reevaluations (chapter 1), supply chains need to be managed as integrated logistical systems (chapter 3), human resource development must be integrated with strategy (chapter 4), legal requirements must be understood within a matrix of in-teractive legal systems (chapter 6), countries must be analyzed and monitored as evolving social systems (chapter 7), knowledge management needs to encompass learning and continuous improvement (chapter 8), the impact of accounting and financial systems on enterprises and their affiliates must be assessed interactively (chapters 9 and 10), team management is a group effort (chapter 12), and ethically responsible behavior must be structured into the enterprise through corporate codes and ethical compliance programs (chapter 14).

9. Legitimizing Diversity

Competition today is driven by innovation. This means that the most critical resource for enterprises is talented and skilled people. Intellectual capital has replaced financial capital as the scarce resource. Diversity not only is a constant fact of life, therefore, it is the future of every enterprise with a global agenda. While diversity is often considered largely in racial or ethnic terms, in fact it needs to be grasped much more broadly and to encompass cultural values, lifestyles, work ethics, thought patterns, and individual preferences and idiosyncrasies. Diversity is being shaped in addition by state policies and practices as well as by the communications and information media that roam the airwaves and cyberspace. This is particularly true as people everywhere are looking increasingly for interesting work, are shifting personal loyalties to interest groups, and, as a result, are becoming less attached to national cultures (chapter 13). The resulting complexity, as chapter 12 sums up, is "diversity management squared."

As a consequence of growing workforce diversity and the time/space compression in global travel and communication, it is necessary to think of culture in dynamic rather than static terms (chapter 13). This has two implications for management. First, for diversity to benefit the global enterprise, it needs to be legitimized and channeled into fruitful activities. Fundamentally, this requires open-minded managers, who encourage the cross-cultural flow and dissemination of differing viewpoints and ideas, supported by an accepting corporate culture and facilitated by readily accessible information and communication systems. Such open-mindedness is embedded through human development practices that rotate personnel through the enterprise (chapter 4), through an IT infrastructure that increases the absorptive capacity and institutional memory of the enterprise (chapter 8), through leadership that facilitates the sharing and integration of knowledge across the enterprise (chapter 11), and through the formation and management of globally diverse teams that encourage creative problem-solving (chapter 12). In open-minded corporate cultures, diversity becomes the driver of innovation—for product development, market penetration, and strategic direction. Second, and equally important, transnational enterprises can generate common organizational cultures without suppressing or denying cultural diversity within their workforces. A number of firms, such as IKEA, Elf Acquitaine, Hoffmann-La Roche, and Unilever, appear to be successful at doing this (chapter 13).

10. Responsible Market Capitalism

Seen from the perspective of the political and cultural realms of society, markets arguably have no soul. For markets allocate capital, jobs, and other resources based on efficiencies, foreseeable profits, and sales of goods to those with purchasing power. When they operate efficiently, they are the most powerful engines of growth. Those who prosper have generally gauged markets correctly, but not necessarily many of the needs of communities and societies where their businesses operate. The trouble is that markets are not always efficient, the market "playing field" is not always level, and vast differences exist in purchasing power—leaving many consumers relatively untouched by the benefits of global capitalism. Moreover, important aspects of culture, such as family values and community traditions, are left out of the market equation and may be threatened by market competition. The many reasons for these deficiencies and the threats they entail are covered in the Overview and chapters 6, 7, 9, 10, and 14.

As a result, if market capitalism is to survive as the dominant economic system driving globalization, its major economic players must become its moral champions. This means that enterprises with a stake in the success of global market capitalism must operate from a mindset that is respectful of, responds to, and takes responsibility for all levels of the global environment. This includes not only "playing by the rules" of a free and fair market system, but also advocating for and complementing those rules as appropriate to ensure that the system functions equitably for societies as a whole. As discussed in chapter 14, this mindset can be defined from four perspectives—ethical, economic, legal, and discretionary. Of course, the number one mandate of any enterprise is to employ sound and resourceful management. But beyond that, enterprises and their managers should incorporate socially beneficial values from their country environments into their products, services, and operations to the extent this is economically feasible. Doing this is both a mindset and an imperative.

COMPETENCIES FOR DEPLOYING
THE EMERGING PARADIGM

To make a difference for the enterprise, the emerging paradigm must be deployed through management competencies. This includes having a relevant working knowledge of the subject area. Such knowledge is specific largely to each business function, but must be grasped within the full environmental and organizational context of each enterprise. The chapters indicate to a large extent the nature of this knowledge in their discussions of the challenges that globalization poses to a particular business activity. Due to the multifaceted nature of global and country environments, this knowledge encompasses aspects of all the social sciences as well as of technologies that affect business functions. Some business functions, such as knowledge management, marketing, and accounting and finance, are being transformed by information technologies.

Management competencies themselves provide the skills, methods, systems, disciplines, and practices that managers need in order to take advantage of the opportunities and insights they identify in the global environment. In a real sense, these competencies are simply extensions and applications of the mindset and management modes just discussed. For this reason, each chapter concludes by identifying a number of competencies pertinent to the challenges and the shift in thinking required for that particular business function or topic. Thus, because global leaders within an enterprise must shift their self-image from positional authority to consensus-building, logically they must adopt the skills of facilitators (chapter 11). Similarly, because global team members need to develop a multifocus mindset in order to work effectively with cultural diversity, they need to develop the techniques of conflict management (chapter 12). And because intensifying competition requires strategists to think constantly about enhancing their firm's value proposition, they must develop an aptitude for assessing and managing risk (chapter 1) and for using true costs to evaluate all components of the value chain (chapter 3).

While the competencies covered in this book are intended to be exercised by managers and work groups within an enterprise, they also need to be embedded to a large extent in the policies, systems, and culture of the organization if they are to be effective. In effect, individual competencies need to become organizational competencies as well. Thus, strategy-making cannot become a process of enterprise renewal without an organization-wide process for periodically visioning, collecting data, assessing new initiatives, setting priorities, and allocating resources. The process needs to integrate all the major line and staff functions of the enterprise. Further, few of the areas covered in this book could be managed effectively without a well-tailored information system that enables managers to scan the external environment, generate institutional memory that is easily accessed, track the flow of value chain activities, and monitor accounting and financial data. Finally, the policies, systems, and culture of the enterprise serve to set standards of performance, enable and reinforce good practices, and encourage managers to build their individual skills. This is why human resource development (chapter 4), sound governance (chapter 9), qualities of global leadership (chapter 11), the transnationalization of corporate culture (chapter 13), and ethical compliance programs (chapter 14) are so strategically important to firms. Individual and organizational competencies, therefore, go hand-in-hand.

ABOUT THE EDITORS AND CONTRIBUTORS

Glenda J. Barrett is Professor and Director of Human Resource Management Programs at University of Maryland University College Graduate School of Management & Technology. Areas of specialization include: employee relations, human resource development, contingent workforce issues, organizational communication, and change management. Over twenty years of managerial and consulting experience include serving as Program Manager at Boeing and Customer Relations Director at ACT.

Nadine Bleher graduated in political science from the Free University of Berlin after spending an academic year at Stanford University. During this time Bleher completed two research projects in association with Professor Klaus Götz for the Daimler-Benz Corporation, which were published in 1999 and 2000; subsequently, she was in charge of a project to coordinate the international expansion of a company based in Spain.

William G. Frenkel is Adjunct Assistant Professor at University of Maryland University College Graduate School of Management & Technology. Being principal attorney with the Law Offices of William Frenkel in New York City, he has practiced U.S. and international law for over sixteen years with LeBoeuf Lamb and Skadden Arps in New York, Frankfurt am Main, and Moscow and as Associate General Counsel to Metromedia International Group in New York, Moscow, and Vienna. Areas of specialization and publication include: cross-border investment, commercial, technology, and intellectual property transactions, privatization, mergers and acquisitions, international private equity investments, and IT, Internet, and e-commerce law.

Klaus Götz is Professor and Director of the Center for Human Resource Management at University of Koblenz-Landau, Germany. He is also visiting professor at universities in Klagenfurt, Innsbruck, Graz, Zurich, and Murmansk, and honorary professor at the University of Bremen. From 1982 to 2002, Götz managed corporate human resource development and education programs, including at DaimlerChrylser. Areas of interest include: leadership, on-the-job training, management models, trust-building in organizations, and human resource strategy.

Vinod K. Jain is a member of the faculty and Senior Director, Professional Programs, at the Robert H. Smith School of Business, University of Maryland. Teaching and research interests include: strategy, international management, performance measurement and management, and knowledge management. Prior to returning to academia in 1989, Jain worked in industry for some twenty years with major corporations, including Macmillan Publishers, Molins, and Coca-Cola.

Saad Laraqui is Associate Professor and Program Director at University of Maryland University College Graduate School of Management & Technology, where he teaches international business, finance, and economics. Laraqui is Director of Economic Affairs of the American Moroccan Institute (AMI). Research interests include: foreign direct investment, economic integration, and global economics, with regional interest in the Middle East and North Africa.

Joe Manickavasagam is Adjunct Associate Professor at University of Maryland University College Graduate School of Management & Technology. He served the World Bank for almost twenty years as a senior staff in operations and staff functions in Washington, DC, and overseas. He has held management positions at Exxon (Esso) and Sime Darby Group of Companies in East Asia. Dr. Manickvasagam's expertise includes international management, institutional development/capacity building and human resources management.

Clarence J. Mann is Professor and Associate Chair, Global MBA, Executive MBA, and Master of International Management Programs at University of Maryland University College Graduate School of Management & Technology. He also is Director of UMUC's Institute for Global Management. Areas of specialization and publication include: strategic planning and international business transactions, technology transfer and technology ventures, and international and European Union law. Over twenty years of professional experience in law practice, including as general counsel, Sears Roebuck's International Operations. He was also CEO, A.T. International.

J. David Morrissy is Adjunct Professor at University of Maryland University College Graduate School of Management & Technology and at the University of Virginia. He served as Economics Professor at Al-Hikma University, in Baghdad, Republic of Iraq, and lecturer-in-residence at Wyzsza Skola Biznesu in Nowy Sacz, Poland. Areas of specialization include: international trade policy and negotiations, globalization, and business ethics. Major professional experience includes: Deputy Special Counsel to the U.S. Trade Representative in the Executive Office of the President and as management training consultant to multinational corporations.

Frank R. Power is Adjunct Associate Professor at University of Maryland University College Graduate School of Management & Technology. Areas of specialization include: international business, strategic management, marketing, supply chain management, and energy technology. Over forty years of managerial and consulting experience include Assistant Postmaster General, Vice President of Sea-Land Corporation, Vice President of Aminoil Inc., and Director of Planning for R. J. Reynolds Industries. Power has also taught at George Washington University, Manhattan College, and Sophia University (Tokyo). Power is both an attorney and a licensed professional engineer.

Alfred S. Raider is Professor at University of Maryland University College Graduate School of Management & Technology, specializing in advertising and public relations. Areas of teaching include: international marketing, direct marketing, electronic marketing, and marketing management. He operated Raider Advertising and planned and executed advertising campaigns for a variety of clients including General Motors' Oldsmobile Division, Toyota, Fiat, and the Carrier Corporation. As an attorney, Raider worked on marketing practices and export promotion programs for the U.S. Congress.

Linda L. Smith is Professor at University of Maryland University College Graduate School of Management & Technology. Areas of specialization include: cross-cultural communications, leadership, organizational culture, and knowledge management. Smith has over twenty years of professional management and leadership experience, including work with the Ford Foundation and the National Institutes of Health.

INDEX

Branded entertainment, 77
Bribery, 329
Bridging function of ideology, 187–88
Bristol-Myers Squibb, 49
British Petroleum (BP), 63–64, 109
Business culture. *See* Corporate culture
Business intelligence tools, 206
Business model, 38
Business operations, minimizing legal
    risks to: disputes between local parties
    and governments, 152–53;
    extraterritorial reach and conflicts of
    law, 153–56; foreign investment,
    156–58; government regulation, 151;
    intellectual property and e-commerce,
    150–51; overview of, 149
Business practices and cultural issues,
    22–23
Business process outsourcing, 217
Business strategy and human resources
    development, 113
Buzz marketing, 77

Canon, 49
Capital: flows of, 248–49; free movement
    of, 8–9; human, 20, 111–13;
    intellectual, 111–13. *See also* Capital
    markets
Capitalism, 313–14. *See also* Market
    capitalism
Capital markets: commodities,
    derivatives, and, 243; debt markets
    and, 241–42; equity markets and,
    240–41; Islamic law and, 243;
    overview of, 239; trade finance
    and, 242
Capturing knowledge, 199
Chile, 222
China: awakening of, 220–21;
    counterfeiting and, 150; credentials
    and references in, 291 n.18; foreign
    direct investment and, 235;
    management competencies and,
    140–41; management style in, 305–6;
    Microsoft Corporation in, 166–67;
    mobile phones and, 75–76; paradigm
    shift and, 139–40; trade and, 7,
    138–39
Cisco, 86, 113, 140
Citibank, 15, 73, 80
Civil litigation, 152
Civil Rights Act of 1991, 290 n.12

Classic theories of culture, 297
Clutter, advertising, 77
Codes of ethics, 321–22
Collaborative ethos, 339–40
Commodities trading, 249–51
Common interest and corporate
    culture, 306
Common Market of the South
    (MERCOSUR), 132–33
Communication: cross-cultural, 301;
    human resources development
    managers and, 116; time/space
    compression and, 296–97; verbal
    versus nonverbal, 291 n.20
Community of Practice (CoP), 114–16,
    206, 211
Competencies. *See* Management
    competencies
Competition: continuous innovation and,
    107–8; cultural differences and,
    251–52; as intensifying, 51–52, 203;
    multipoint, 203; by reinventing
    industry, 337; technology and, 136–37
Competitive advantage, building, 40–43
Complexity of global trade, 123–25
Conflict, perceptions of, 282–83
Conflicts of laws, 147, 153–56
Consciousness, global, 14–16
Constraints: country-specific, 188–90;
    underlying, 39–40
Consumption patterns, 296
Continuous improvement, 201
Coordination of assets, 49
Core competence, 38–39, 51
Corning, 36
Corporate counsel. *See* Legal
    environment
Corporate culture: challenges to notions
    of, 297–99; consumption patterns and,
    296; country culture and, 295;
    disseminating, 109; Elf Aquitaine and,
    303; global leadership and, 271–73;
    Hoffmann-La Roche and, 304; IKEA
    and, 303; management competencies,
    307–9; paradigm shift in, 305–7; time/
    space compression and, 296–97;
    transnationalizing, 258; Unilever and,
    304–5
Corporate governance, 194, 221–22,
    226–27
Corporate process triangle (CPT), 170,
    174–75, 188